P9-DMG-548

Teach Yourself VISUALLY™ COMPLETE

Excel® 2013

by Paul McFedries

V̈isual™
A Wiley Brand

LONGWOOD PUBLIC LIBRARY

Teach Yourself VISUALLY™ Complete Excel® 2013

Published by
John Wiley & Sons, Inc.
10475 Crosspoint Boulevard
Indianapolis, IN 46256

www.wiley.com

Published simultaneously in Canada

Copyright © 2013 by John Wiley & Sons, Inc., Indianapolis, Indiana

No part of this publication may be reproduced, stored in a retrieval system or transmitted in any form or by any means, electronic, mechanical, photocopying, recording, scanning or otherwise, except as permitted under Sections 107 or 108 of the 1976 United States Copyright Act, without either the prior written permission of the Publisher, or authorization through payment of the appropriate per-copy fee to the Copyright Clearance Center, 222 Rosewood Drive, Danvers, MA 01923, (978) 750-8400, fax (978) 646-8600. Requests to the Publisher for permission should be addressed to the Permissions Department, John Wiley & Sons, Inc., 111 River Street, Hoboken, NJ 07030, 201-748-6011, fax 201-748-6008, or online at www.wiley.com/go/permissions.

Wiley publishes in a variety of print and electronic formats and by print-on-demand. Some material included with standard print versions of this book may not be included in e-books or in print-on-demand. If this book refers to media such as a CD or DVD that is not included in the version you purchased, you may download this material at http://booksupport.wiley.com. For more information about Wiley products, visit www.wiley.com.

Library of Congress Control Number: 2013936427

ISBN: 978-1-118-65374-6

Manufactured in the United States of America

10 9 8 7 6 5 4 3 2 1

Trademark Acknowledgments

Wiley, the Wiley logo, Visual, the Visual logo, Teach Yourself VISUALLY, Read Less - Learn More and related trade dress are trademarks or registered trademarks of John Wiley & Sons, Inc. and/or its affiliates. Excel is a registered trademark of Microsoft Corporation. All other trademarks are the property of their respective owners. John Wiley & Sons, Inc. is not associated with any product or vendor mentioned in this book.

LIMIT OF LIABILITY/DISCLAIMER OF WARRANTY: THE PUBLISHER AND THE AUTHOR MAKE NO REPRESENTATIONS OR WARRANTIES WITH RESPECT TO THE ACCURACY OR COMPLETENESS OF THE CONTENTS OF THIS WORK AND SPECIFICALLY DISCLAIM ALL WARRANTIES, INCLUDING WITHOUT LIMITATION WARRANTIES OF FITNESS FOR A PARTICULAR PURPOSE. NO WARRANTY MAY BE CREATED OR EXTENDED BY SALES OR PROMOTIONAL MATERIALS. THE ADVICE AND STRATEGIES CONTAINED HEREIN MAY NOT BE SUITABLE FOR EVERY SITUATION. THIS WORK IS SOLD WITH THE UNDERSTANDING THAT THE PUBLISHER IS NOT ENGAGED IN RENDERING LEGAL, ACCOUNTING, OR OTHER PROFESSIONAL SERVICES. IF PROFESSIONAL ASSISTANCE IS REQUIRED, THE SERVICES OF A COMPETENT PROFESSIONAL PERSON SHOULD BE SOUGHT. NEITHER THE PUBLISHER NOR THE AUTHOR SHALL BE LIABLE FOR DAMAGES ARISING HEREFROM. THE FACT THAT AN ORGANIZATION OR WEBSITE IS REFERRED TO IN THIS WORK AS A CITATION AND/OR A POTENTIAL SOURCE OF FURTHER INFORMATION DOES NOT MEAN THAT THE AUTHOR OR THE PUBLISHER ENDORSES THE INFORMATION THE ORGANIZATION OR WEBSITE MAY PROVIDE OR RECOMMENDATIONS IT MAY MAKE. FURTHER, READERS SHOULD BE AWARE THAT INTERNET WEBSITES LISTED IN THIS WORK MAY HAVE CHANGED OR DISAPPEARED BETWEEN WHEN THIS WORK WAS WRITTEN AND WHEN IT IS READ.

FOR PURPOSES OF ILLUSTRATING THE CONCEPTS AND TECHNIQUES DESCRIBED IN THIS BOOK, THE AUTHOR HAS CREATED VARIOUS NAMES, COMPANY NAMES, MAILING, E-MAIL AND INTERNET ADDRESSES, PHONE AND FAX NUMBERS AND SIMILAR INFORMATION, ALL OF WHICH ARE FICTITIOUS. ANY RESEMBLANCE OF THESE FICTITIOUS NAMES, ADDRESSES, PHONE AND FAX NUMBERS AND SIMILAR INFORMATION TO ANY ACTUAL PERSON, COMPANY AND/OR ORGANIZATION IS UNINTENTIONAL AND PURELY COINCIDENTAL.

Contact Us

For general information on our other products and services please contact our Customer Care Department within the U.S. at 877-762-2974, outside the U.S. at 317-572-3993 or fax 317-572-4002.

For technical support please visit www.wiley.com/techsupport.

Sales | Contact Wiley at (877) 762-2974 or fax (317) 572-4002.

Credits

Acquisitions Editor
Aaron Black

Project Editor
Amanda Gambill

Technical Editor
Namir Shammas

Senior Copy Editor
Kim Heusel

Editorial Director
Robyn Siesky

Business Manager
Amy Knies

Senior Marketing Manager
Sandy Smith

**Vice President and Executive
Group Publisher**
Richard Swadley

**Vice President and Executive
Publisher**
Barry Pruett

Project Coordinator
Patrick Redmond

Graphics and Production Specialists
Ronda David-Burroughs
Jennifer Mayberry
Christin Swinford

Quality Control Technician
Lindsay Amones

Proofreading and Indexing
Debbye Butler
BIM Indexing & Proofreading Services

About the Author

Paul McFedries has been writing computer books since 1991. He is the author of more than 80 titles, including *Teach Yourself VISUALLY Windows 8*, *Windows 8 Visual Quick Tips*, *The Facebook Guide for People Over 50*, *iPhone 5 Portable Genius*, and *iPad 4th Generation and iPad mini Portable Genius,* all available from Wiley.

Paul's books have sold more than 4 million copies worldwide. He is also the proprietor of Word Spy (www.wordspy.com), a website that tracks new words and phrases as they enter the English language. Paul invites you to visit his personal website at www.mcfedries.com. You can also follow him on Twitter @paulmcf and @wordspy.

Author's Acknowledgments

It goes without saying that writers focus on text and I certainly enjoyed focusing on the text that you will read in this book. However, this book is more than just the usual collection of words and phrases designed to educate and stimulate the mind. A quick thumb through the pages will show you that it also includes copious screenshots, meticulous layouts, and sharp fonts. All of this is made possible by Wiley's immensely talented group of designers and layout artists.

They are all listed in the Credits section on the previous page, and I thank them for creating another gem. Of course, what you read in this book must also be accurate, logically presented, and free of errors. Ensuring all of this was an excellent group of editors that I got to work with directly, including project editor Amanda Gambill, copy editor Kim Heusel, and technical editor Namir Shammas. Thanks to all of you for your exceptional competence and hard work. Thanks, as well, to Wiley acquisitions editor Aaron Black for asking me to write this book.

How to Use This Book

Who This Book Is For

This book is for the reader who has never used this particular technology or software application. It is also for readers who want to expand their knowledge.

The Conventions in This Book

1 Steps

This book uses a step-by-step format to guide you easily through each task. **Numbered steps** are actions you must do; **bulleted steps** clarify a point, step, or optional feature; and **indented steps** give you the result.

2 Notes

Notes give additional information — special conditions that may occur during an operation, a situation that you want to avoid, or a cross-reference to a related area of the book.

3 Icons and Buttons

Icons and buttons show you exactly what you need to click to perform a step.

4 Tips

Tips offer additional information, including warnings and shortcuts.

5 Bold

Bold type shows command names or options that you must click or text or numbers you must type.

6 Italics

Italic type introduces and defines a new term.

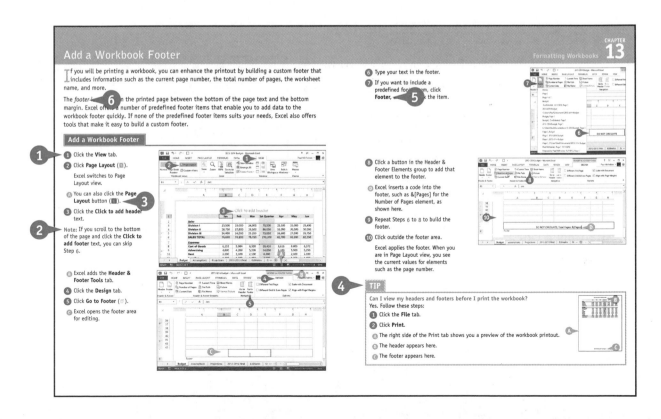

Table of Contents

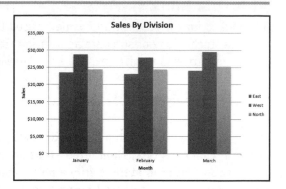

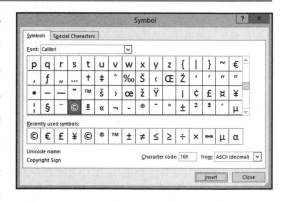

Chapter 3 — Working with Ranges

Chapter 4 — Working with Range Names

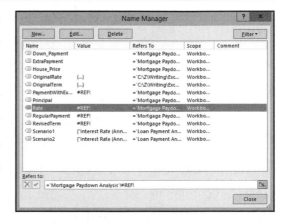

Table of Contents

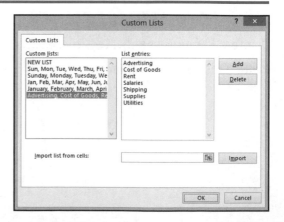

Chapter 7   Making Excel More Efficient

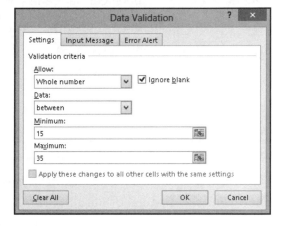

Table of Contents

Chapter 8   Building Formulas and Functions

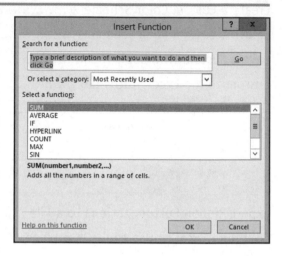

Chapter 9   Getting More Out of Formulas

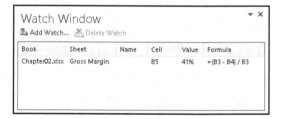

Chapter 10 — Manipulating Worksheets

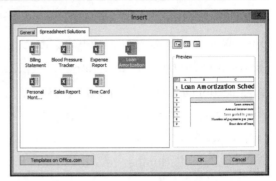

Chapter 11 — Dealing with Workbooks

Table of Contents

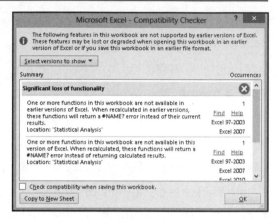

Chapter 14   Printing Workbooks

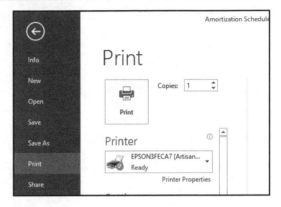

Chapter 15   Working with Tables

Table of Contents

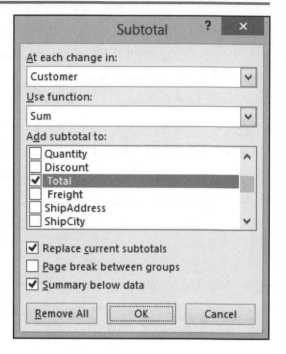

Chapter 18   Visualizing Data with Charts

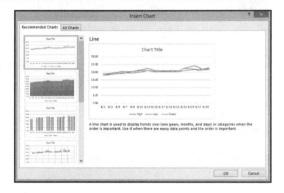

Table of Contents

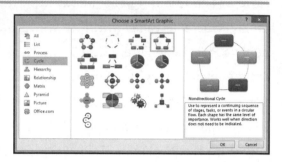

Chapter 21   Querying Data Sources

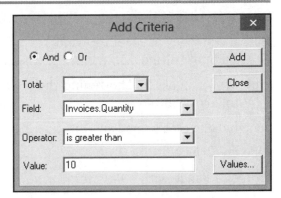

Chapter 22   Collaborating with Others

Table of Contents

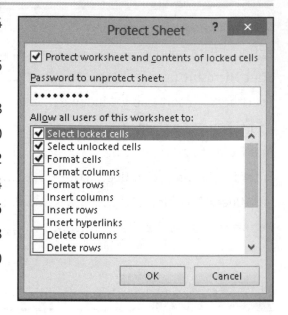

Chapter 25 | Learning VBA Basics

CHAPTER 1

Working with Excel

You use Microsoft Excel to create *spreadsheets*, which are documents that enable you to manipulate numbers and formulas to create powerful mathematical, financial, and statistical models quickly. In this chapter, you learn about Excel, take a tour of the program's features, and learn how to customize some aspects of the program.

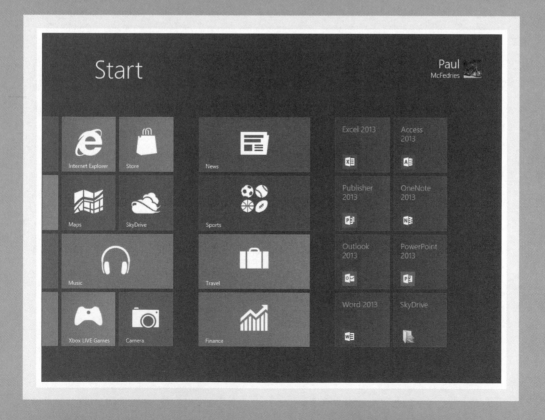

Get to Know Excel

Working with Excel involves two basic tasks: building a spreadsheet and then manipulating the data on the spreadsheet. Building a spreadsheet involves adding data such as numbers and text, creating formulas that run calculations, and adding functions that perform specific tasks. Manipulating spreadsheet data involves calculating totals, adding data series, organizing data into tables, and visualizing data with charts.

This section just gives you an overview of these tasks. You learn about each task in greater detail as you work through the book.

Build a Spreadsheet

Add Data

You can insert numbers, text, and other characters into any cell in the spreadsheet. Click the cell that you want to work with and then type your data in the formula bar. This is the large text box above the column letters. Your typing appears in the cell that you selected. When you are done, press **Enter**. To edit existing cell data, click the cell and then edit the text in the formula bar.

1	Expense Budget Calculation			
2				
3		January	February	March
4	Advertising	4,600	4,200	5,200
5	Rent	2,100	2,100	2,100
6	Supplies	1,300	1,200	1,400
7	Salaries	16,000	16,000	16,500
8	Utilities	500	600	600

Add a Formula

A *formula* is a collection of numbers, cell addresses, and mathematical operators that performs a calculation. In Excel, you input a formula in a cell by typing an equal sign (=), and then the formula text. For example, the formula =B1-B2 subtracts the value in cell B2 from the value in cell B1.

1	Expense Budget Calculation			
2				
3		January	February	March
4	Advertising	4,600	4,200	5,200
5	Rent	2,100	2,100	2,100
6	Supplies	1,300	1,200	1,400
7	Salaries	16,000	16,000	16,500
8	Utilities	500	600	600
9	2012 TOTAL	24,500	24,100	25,800

Add a Function

A *function* is a predefined formula that performs a specific task. For example, the AVERAGE function calculates the average of a list of numbers, and the PMT function calculates a loan or mortgage payment. You can use functions on their own, preceded by =, or as part of a larger formula. Click the **Insert Function** button (*fx*) to see a list of the available functions.

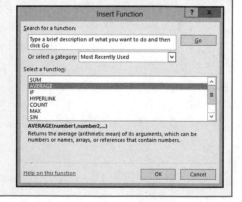

Manipulate Data

Calculate Totals Quickly

If you just need a quick sum of a list of numbers, click a cell below the numbers, and then click the **Sum** button (Σ), which is available in the Home tab of the Excel Ribbon. You can also select the cells that you want to sum, and their total appears in the status bar.

	A	B	C	D
1	Sales By Division			
2		January	February	March
3	East	$23,500	$23,000	$24,000
4	West	$28,750	$27,900	$29,500
5	North	$24,400	$24,300	$25,250
6		=SUM(B3:B5)		

Fill a Series

Excel enables you to save time by completing a series of values automatically. For example, if you need to input the numbers 1 to 100 in consecutive cells, you can type just the first few numbers, select the cells, and then click and drag the lower-right corner to fill in the rest of the numbers. With Excel, you can also fill in dates, as well as the names for weekdays and months.

	A
1	January 1, 2013
2	January 2, 2013
3	January 3, 2013
4	January 4, 2013
5	January 5, 2013
6	January 6, 2013
7	January 7, 2013
8	January 8, 2013
9	January 9, 2013
10	January 10, 2013

Manage Tables

The row-and-column format of a spreadsheet makes Excel suitable for simple databases called *tables*. Each column becomes a field in the table, and each row is a record. You can sort the records, filter the records to show only certain values, and add subtotals.

	Account Name	Account Number	Invoice Number	Invoice Amount	Due Date
3					
4	Door Stoppers Ltd.	01-0045	117328	$58.50	2/2/2013
5	Door Stoppers Ltd.	01-0045	117319	$78.85	1/16/2013
6	Door Stoppers Ltd.	01-0045	117324	$101.01	1/26/2013
7	Door Stoppers Ltd.	01-0045	117333	$1,685.74	2/11/2013
8	Chimera Illusions	02-0200	117334	$303.65	2/12/2013
9	Chimera Illusions	02-0200	117350	$456.21	3/15/2013
10	Chimera Illusions	02-0200	117345	$588.88	3/6/2013
11	Chimera Illusions	02-0200	117318	$3,005.14	1/14/2013
12	Renaud & Son	07-0025	117331	$565.77	2/8/2013

Add a Chart

A *chart* is a graphic representation of spreadsheet data. As the data in the spreadsheet changes, the chart also changes to reflect the new numbers. Excel offers a wide variety of charts, including bar charts, line charts, and pie charts.

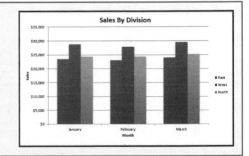

Start Excel

Before you can perform tasks such as adding data and building formulas, you must first start Excel. This brings the Excel window onto the Windows desktop, and you can then begin using the program. How you start Excel depends on which version of Windows you are using. In this section, you learn how to start Excel 2013 in Windows 8 and in Windows 7.

This task and the rest of the book assume that you have already installed Excel 2013 on your computer.

Start Excel

Start Excel in Windows 8

1 In the Windows 8 Start screen, click **Excel 2013**.

The Microsoft Excel window appears on the desktop.

Note: Click **Blank workbook** to open a new Excel file.

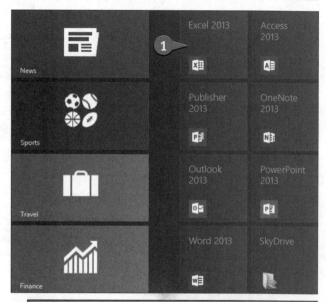

Start Excel in Windows 7

1 Click **Start**.

The Start menu appears.

2 Click **All Programs**.

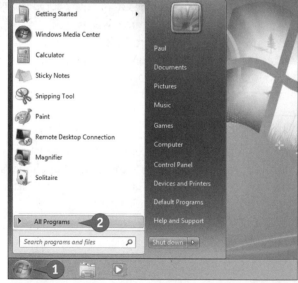

The All Programs menu appears.

3 Click **Microsoft Office 2013**.

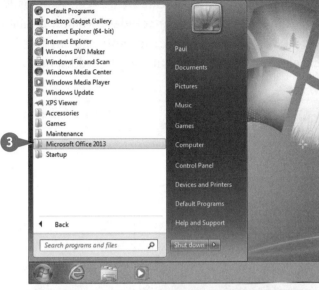

The Microsoft Office menu appears.

4 Click **Excel 2013**.

The Microsoft Excel window appears on the desktop.

Note: Click **Blank workbook** to open a new Excel file.

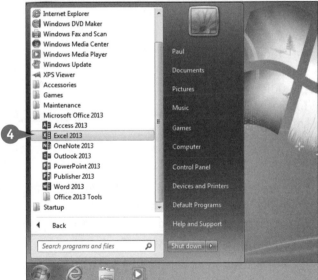

TIP

Are there faster methods I can use to start Excel?

Yes. After you have used Excel a few times in Windows 7, it should appear on the main Start menu in the list of your most-used programs. If so, you can click that icon to start the program. You can also add the Excel icon to the Start menu by following Steps **1** to **3** in the "Start Excel in Windows 7" subsection, right-clicking the **Excel 2013** icon, and then clicking **Pin to Start Menu**. If you are using Windows 8, you can right-click the **Excel 2013** tile and then click **Pin to Taskbar** to add the Excel icon to the desktop taskbar.

Tour the Excel Window

To get up to speed quickly with Excel, it helps to understand the various elements of the Excel window. These include standard window elements such as the title bar, window controls, and status bar; Office-specific elements such as the Ribbon, Quick Access Toolbar, and File tab; and Excel-specific elements such as the worksheet.

Ⓐ Title Bar

The title bar displays the name of the current workbook.

Ⓑ Quick Access Toolbar

This area gives you one-click access to commands that you use often. To learn how to customize this toolbar, see the section "Customize the Quick Access Toolbar" later in this chapter.

Ⓒ Ribbon

This area gives you access to all the Excel commands, options, and features. To learn how to use this element, see the following section, "Work with the Excel Ribbon."

Ⓓ Workbook Window Controls

You use these controls to minimize, maximize, restore, and close the current workbook window.

Ⓔ File Tab

Click this tab to access file-related commands, such as Save and Open.

Ⓕ Worksheet

This area displays the current worksheet, and it is where you will do most of your Excel work.

Ⓖ Status Bar

This area displays messages about the current status of Excel, the results of certain operations, and other information.

Work with the Excel Ribbon

You use the Ribbon element to access all the features, commands, and options in Excel. The Ribbon is organized into various tabs, such as File, Home, and Insert, and each tab contains a collection of controls that are related in some way. For example, the File tab contains controls related to working with files, such as opening, saving, and printing them. Similarly, the Insert tab contains controls related to inserting objects into a worksheet. Each tab usually includes buttons, lists, and check boxes.

There is no menu bar in Excel, so you do not use pull-down menus to access commands.

Work with the Excel Ribbon

1 Click the tab that contains the Excel feature you want to work with.

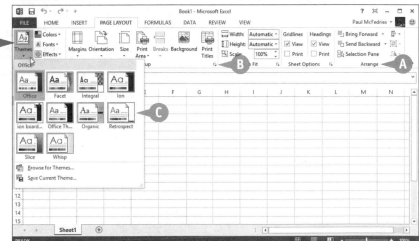

Excel displays the controls in the tab.

A Each tab is organized into groups of related controls, and the group names appear here.

B In many groups, you can click the **Dialog box launcher** button (⌐) to display a dialog box that contains group settings.

2 Click the control for the feature.

C If the control displays a list of options, click the option you want.

Excel runs the command or sets the option.

Work with the Excel Galleries

In the Excel Ribbon, a *gallery* is a collection of preset options that you can apply to the selected object in the worksheet. To get the most out of galleries, you need to know how they work.

Although some galleries are available all the time, in most cases you must select an object — such as a range of cells or a clip art image — before you work with a gallery.

Work with the Excel Galleries

Work with a Gallery List

1 If necessary, click the object to which you want to apply an option from the gallery.

2 Click the tab that contains the gallery you want to use.

3 Click the gallery's **More** arrow ( ).

A You can also scroll through the gallery by clicking the **Down** ( ) and **Up** ( ) arrows.

Excel displays a list of the gallery's contents.

4 Move the mouse pointer ( ) over a gallery option.

B Excel displays a preview of the effect.

5 Click the gallery option you want to use.

Excel applies the gallery option to the selected object.

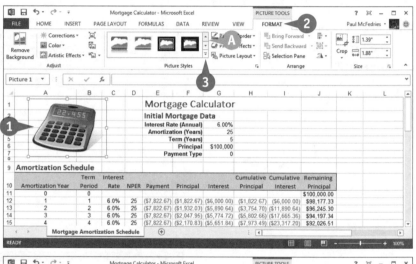

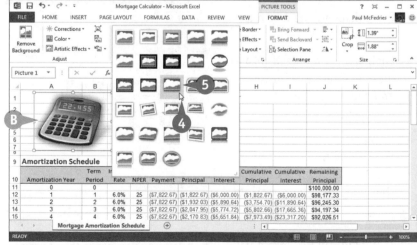

Work with a Drop-Down Gallery

1 If necessary, click the object to which you want to apply an option from the gallery.

2 Click the tab that contains the gallery you want to use.

3 Click the gallery's drop-down arrow ().

Excel displays a list of the gallery's contents.

4 If the gallery contains one or more subgalleries, click the one you want to use.

Excel displays the subgallery's contents.

C If a gallery has commands that you can run, those commands appear at the bottom of the gallery menu.

5 Move the mouse pointer () over a gallery option.

D Excel displays a preview of the effect.

6 Click the gallery option you want to use.

Excel applies the gallery option to the selected object.

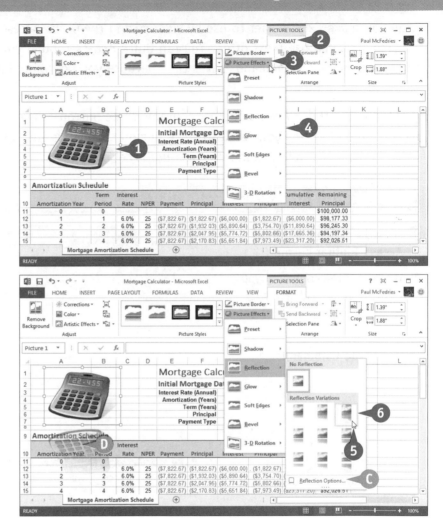

TIP

If I find the gallery preview feature distracting, can I turn it off?

Yes. The Live Preview feature is often handy because it shows you exactly what will happen when you click a gallery option. However, as you move the mouse pointer () through the gallery, the previews can be distracting. To turn off Live Preview, click the **File** tab, click **Options**, click the **General** tab, and then click the selected **Enable Live Preview** check box () so it is cleared (). Click **OK**.

Customize the Quick Access Toolbar

You can make Excel easier to use by customizing the Quick Access Toolbar to include the Excel commands you use most often. You run Quick Access Toolbar commands with a single click, so adding your favorite commands saves time because you no longer have to search for and click a command in the Ribbon.

By default, the Quick Access Toolbar contains three buttons: Save, Undo, and Redo. However, with just a couple of clicks, you can also add common commands such as New and Open to the Quick Access Toolbar, as well as hundreds of other Excel commands.

Customize the Quick Access Toolbar

① Click the **Customize Quick Access Toolbar** button (▼).

Ⓐ If you see the command you want, click it, and skip the rest of the steps in this section.

② Click **More Commands**.

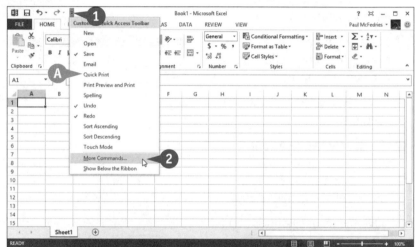

The Excel Options dialog box appears.

Ⓑ Excel automatically displays the Quick Access Toolbar tab.

③ Click the **Choose commands from:** drop-down arrow (▼).

④ Click the command category you want to use.

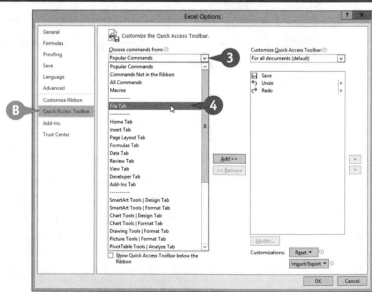

5 Click the command you want to add.

6 Click **Add**.

C Excel adds the command.

D If you want to remove a command, click it, and then click **Remove**.

7 Click **OK**.

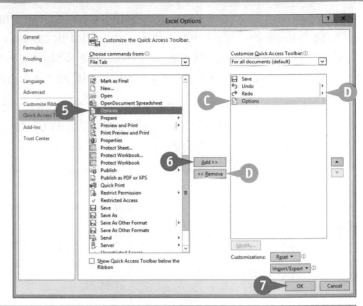

E Excel adds a button for the command to the Quick Access Toolbar.

Note: Another way to remove a command is to right-click it, and then click **Remove from Quick Access Toolbar**.

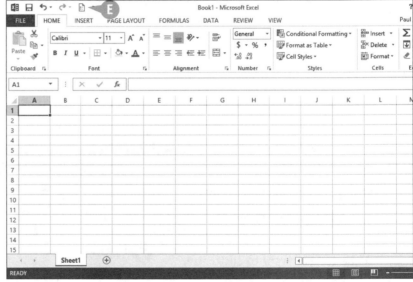

TIPS

Can I create space on the Quick Access Toolbar for more buttons?

Yes. You can increase the space for the Quick Access Toolbar by moving it below the Ribbon. This gives the toolbar the full width of the Excel window, so you can add more buttons. Click the **Customize Quick Access Toolbar** button (▼), and then click **Show Below the Ribbon**.

Is there a faster way to add buttons to the Quick Access Toolbar?

Yes. If the command you want to add appears on the Ribbon, you can add a button for the command from the Ribbon. Click the Ribbon tab that contains the command, right-click the command, and then click **Add to Quick Access Toolbar**. Excel inserts a button for the command on the Quick Access Toolbar.

Customize the Ribbon

You can improve your Excel productivity by customizing the Ribbon with extra commands that you use frequently. The Ribbon is a handy tool because it enables you to run Excel commands with just a few clicks of the mouse. However, the Ribbon does not include every Excel command. If there is a command you use frequently, you should add it to the Ribbon for easy access.

To add a new command to the Ribbon, you must first create a new tab or a new group within an existing tab, and then add the command to the new tab or group.

Customize the Ribbon

Display the Customize Ribbon Tab

1 Right-click any part of the Ribbon.

2 Click **Customize the Ribbon**.

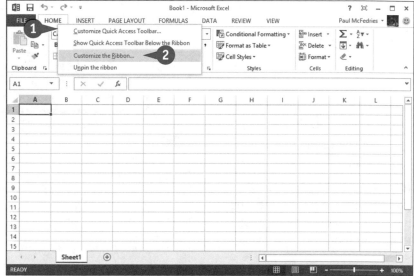

Add a New Tab or Group

The Excel Options dialog box appears.

Ⓐ Excel automatically displays the Customize Ribbon tab.

1 Click the tab you want to customize.

Ⓑ You can also click **New Tab** to create a custom tab.

2 Click **New Group**.

Ⓒ Excel adds the group.

3 Click **Rename**.

4 Type a name for the group.

5 Click **OK**.

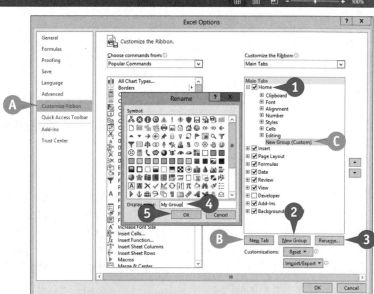

14

Add a Command

1. Click the **Choose commands from:** drop-down arrow (∨).

2. Click the command category you want to use.

3. Click the command you want to add.

4. Click the custom group or tab you want to use.

5. Click **Add**.

Ⓓ Excel adds the command.

Ⓔ If you want to remove a custom command, click it, and then click **Remove**.

6. Click **OK**.

Ⓕ Excel adds the new group and command to the Ribbon.

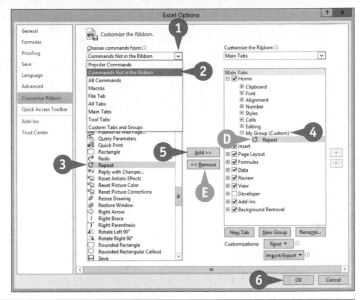

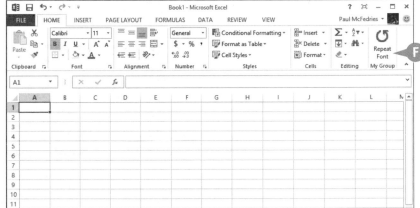

TIPS

Can I customize the tabs that appear when I select an Excel object?

Yes. To customize these *tool tabs*, right-click any part of the Ribbon, and then click Customize the Ribbon. The Excel Options dialog box appears with the Customize Ribbon tab displayed. Click the **Customize the Ribbon** drop-down arrow (∨), and then click **Tool Tabs**. Click the tab you want, and then follow the steps in this section to customize it.

How do I restore the Ribbon to its default configuration?

Right-click any part of the Ribbon and then click **Customize the Ribbon** to display the Excel Options dialog box with the Customize Ribbon tab displayed. To restore a tab, click the tab, click **Reset**, and then click **Restore only selected Ribbon tab**. To remove all customizations, click **Reset,** and then click **Restore all customizations**.

Change the View

You can adjust Excel to suit what you are currently working on by changing the view to match your current task. The view determines how Excel displays your workbook.

Excel offers three views: Normal, which is useful for building and editing worksheets; Page Layout, which displays worksheets as printed pages; and Page Break Preview, which displays the page breaks as blue lines, as described in the first Tip in this section.

Change the View

Switch to Page Layout View

1 Click the **View** tab.

2 Click **Page Layout**.

Ⓐ You can also click the **Page Layout** button (▦).

Ⓑ Excel switches to Page Layout view.

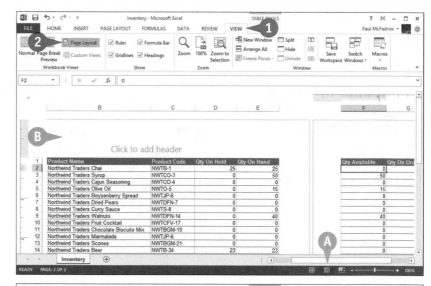

Switch to Page Break Preview

1 Click the **View** tab.

2 Click **Page Break Preview**.

Ⓒ You can also click the **Page Break Preview** button (▥).

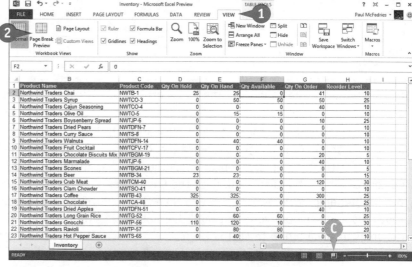

D Excel switches to Page Break Preview.

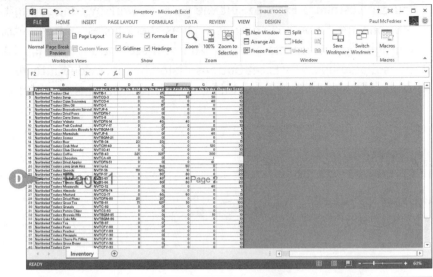

Switch to Normal View

1 Click the **View** tab.

2 Click **Normal**.

E You can also click the **Normal** button (⊞).

Excel switches to Normal view.

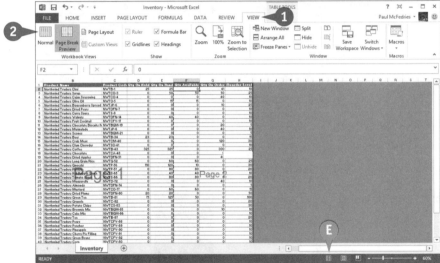

TIPS

What does Page Break Preview do?

A *page break* is a position within a worksheet where a new page begins when you print. When you switch to Page Break Preview, Excel displays page breaks as blue lines. If a page break occurs in a bad position, use the mouse pointer (▷) to click and drag the page break to a new position.

Can I change the view to make my workbook take up the entire screen?

Yes. You can switch the workbook to Full Screen mode by clicking the **Full Screen Mode** icon (▣) in the upper-right corner of the window. Full Screen mode removes many window features, including the Ribbon, Quick Access Toolbar, and the formula and status bars. To exit Full Screen mode, click the horizontal strip at the top of the screen, and then click the **Full Screen Mode** icon (▣).

Configure Excel Options

You can customize Excel to suit the way you work by configuring the Excel options. These options are dialog box controls such as check boxes, option buttons, and lists that enable you to configure many aspects of Excel. To use these options, you must know how to display the Excel Options dialog box. The Excel Options dialog box is divided into several tabs, such as General, Formulas, Save, and Customize Ribbon. Each tab contains a collection of related options.

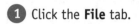

Configure Excel Options

1 Click the **File** tab.

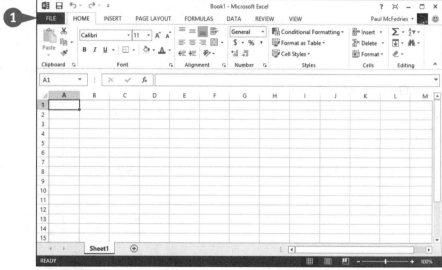

2 Click **Options**.

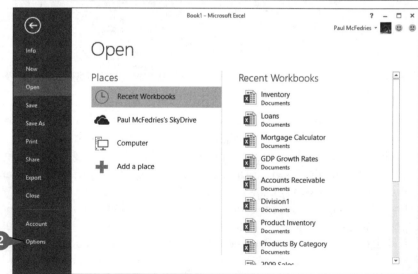

The Excel Options dialog box appears.

③ Click a tab on the left side of the dialog box to choose the configuration category you want to work with.

Ⓐ The controls that appear on the right side of the dialog box change according to the tab you select.

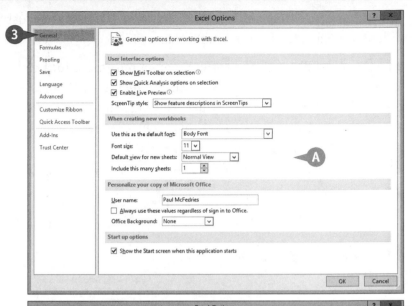

④ Use the controls on the right side of the dialog box to configure the options you want to change.

⑤ Click **OK**.

Excel puts the new options into effect.

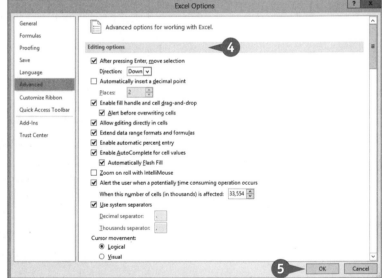

TIPS

Are there faster methods I can use to open the Excel Options dialog box?

Yes. Some features of the Excel interface offer shortcut methods that get you to the Excel Options dialog box faster. For example, right-click the Ribbon and then click **Customize Ribbon** to open the Excel Options dialog box with the Customize Ribbon tab displayed. From the keyboard, you can open the Excel Options dialog box by pressing `Alt`+`F`, and then pressing `T`.

How do I know what each option does?

Excel offers pop-up descriptions of some — but, unfortunately, not all — of the options. If you see a small *i* with a circle around it to the right of the option name, it means pop-up help is available for that option. Hover the mouse pointer (⇖) over the option. After a second or two, Excel displays a pop-up description of the option.

Add Excel to the Windows Taskbar

I f you use Excel regularly, you can start the program with just a single mouse click by adding an icon for Excel to the Windows taskbar.

When you install Excel, the setup program pins a tile for Excel to the Windows 8 Start screen. This is helpful only if you use the Start screen regularly. If you use the desktop more often, you might prefer pinning Excel to the taskbar. The following instructions assume that you are running Excel in Windows 8, but you can also set this up in Windows 7.

Add Excel to the Windows Taskbar

① With Excel running, right-click the Excel icon in the taskbar.

② Click **Pin this program to taskbar.**

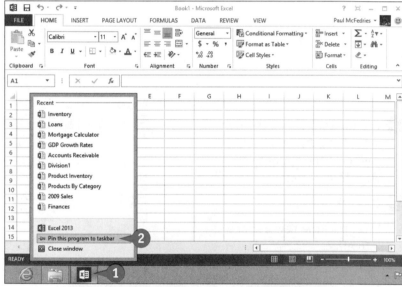

Ⓐ After you quit Excel, the icon remains on the taskbar, and you can now launch Excel by clicking the icon.

Quit Excel

When you finish your work with Excel, you should shut down the program. This reduces clutter on the desktop and taskbar, and conserves memory and other system resources. When you quit Excel, the program checks your open workbooks to see if any of them have unsaved changes. If Excel detects a workbook that has unsaved changes, it prompts you to save the file. This is a very important step because it prevents you from losing work, so be sure to save your changes when Excel prompts you.

Quit Excel

① Right-click the Excel icon in the taskbar.

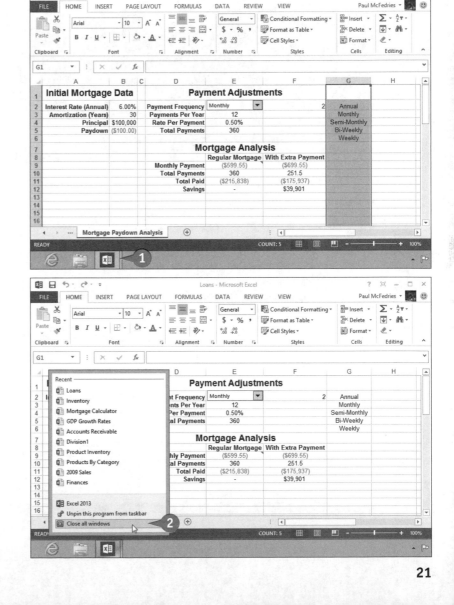

② Click **Close all windows**.

Note: If you have only one Excel workbook open, click **Close window** instead.

Note: If you have any open documents with unsaved changes, Excel prompts you to save those changes.

CHAPTER 2

Inputting and Editing Data

Are you ready to start building a spreadsheet? To create a spreadsheet in Excel, you must know how to type data into the worksheet cells, and how to edit that data to fix typos, adjust information, and remove data you no longer need.

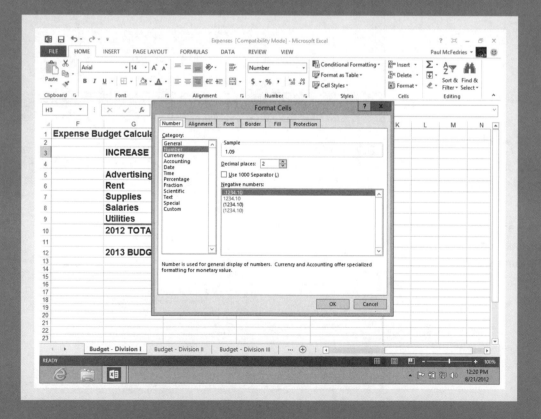

Learn the Layout of a Worksheet

In Excel, a spreadsheet file is called a *workbook*, and each workbook consists of one or more *worksheets*. These worksheets are where you type your data and formulas, so you need to know the layout of a typical worksheet.

In particular, you need to know that worksheets are laid out in rows and columns, that a cell is the intersection of a row and column that has its own unique address, and that a range is a collection of cells. You also need to be familiar with worksheet tabs and the Excel mouse pointer.

A Cell

A *cell* is a box in which you type your spreadsheet data.

B Column

A *column* is a vertical line of cells with a unique letter that identifies it.

C Row

A *row* is a horizontal line of cells with a unique number that identifies it.

D Cell Address

Each cell has its own *address* determined by the letter and number of the intersecting column and row. Column C and row 10's address is C10.

E Range

A *range* is two or more cells indicated by the addresses of the top-left and bottom-right cells. The range between column H, row 11 and column J, row 14 is H11:J14.

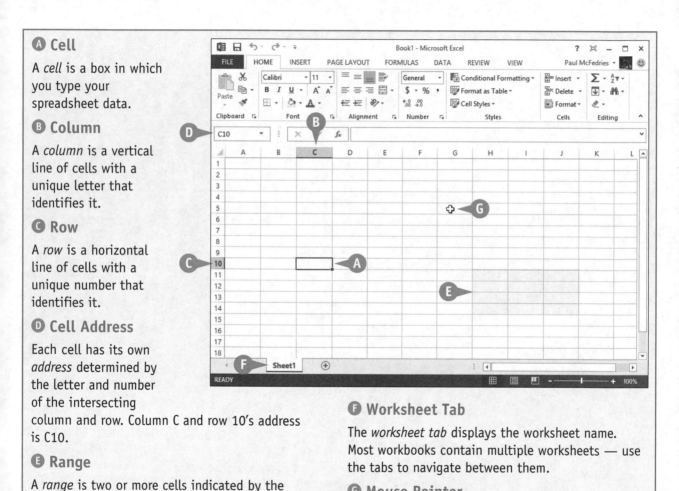

F Worksheet Tab

The *worksheet tab* displays the worksheet name. Most workbooks contain multiple worksheets — use the tabs to navigate between them.

G Mouse Pointer

Use the Excel mouse pointer (⊕) to select cells.

Understanding the Types of Data You Can Use

You might think that Excel would accept only numeric input, but it is actually much more flexible than that. Therefore, to build a spreadsheet in Excel, it helps to understand the different types of data that Excel accepts. There are three main types of data that you can type in a cell: Text, numbers, and dates and times. Excel places no restrictions on where, how, or how often you can input these types of data on a worksheet.

Text

Text entries can include any combination of letters, symbols, and numbers. You use text most often to describe the contents of worksheets. This is very important because even a small spreadsheet can become a confusing jumble without some kind of guidelines. Most text entries are usually labels, such as *Sales* or *Territory*, that make a worksheet easier to read. However, text entries can also be text or number combinations for items such as phone numbers and account codes.

4	Door Stoppers Ltd.	01-0045
5	Door Stoppers Ltd.	01-0045
6	Door Stoppers Ltd.	01-0045
7	Door Stoppers Ltd.	01-0045
8	Chimera Illusions	02-0200
9	Chimera Illusions	02-0200
10	Chimera Illusions	02-0200
11	Chimera Illusions	02-0200
12	Renaud & Son	07-0025
13	Renaud & Son	07-0025
14	Renaud & Son	07-0025
15	Rooter Office Solvents	07-4441
16	Reston Solicitor Offices	07-4441
17	Lone Wolf Software	07-4441
18	Emily's Sports Palace	08-2255
19	Emily's Sports Palace	08-2255

Accounts Receivable Data

Numbers

Numbers are the most common type of Excel data. The numbers you type in a cell can be dollar values, weights, interest rates, temperatures, or any other numerical quantity. In most cases, you just type the number that you want to appear in the cell. However, you can also precede a number with a dollar sign ($) or other currency symbol to indicate a monetary value, or follow a number with a percent sign (%) to indicate a percentage value.

GDP, annual growth rate (Sour

Country	2006	2005	2004
Austria	2.5%	1.3%	1.7%
Belgium	2.6%	0.5%	2.5%
Canada	1.7%	1.9%	2.1%
China	10.1%	9.7%	9.4%
Denmark	2.8%	2.8%	1.9%
Finland	5.1%	2.6%	3.4%
France	1.4%	1.1%	1.9%
Germany	2.9%	1.0%	1.3%
Greece	3.9%	3.3%	4.4%
Hungary	4.1%	4.3%	5.0%
Iceland	0.9%	5.5%	6.7%
Ireland	3.0%	3.2%	2.4%
Italy	1.5%	-0.6%	0.2%
Japan	2.2%	1.9%	2.7%
Netherlands	2.7%	1.3%	1.6%

Dates and Times

Many spreadsheets include dated information, such as invoices and sales. You can type the full date (August 23, 2013), or use a forward slash (8/23/2013) or hyphen (8-23-2013) as a date separator. The order in which you type the date values depends on your regional settings. For example, in the United States the format is month/day/year. For time values, you use a colon (:) as a time separator, followed by either a.m. or p.m. — for example, 9:15 a.m.

	Current Date	20-Mar-13
Due Date	**Date Paid**	**Days Overdue**
2/2/2013		
1/16/2013	1/16/2013	
1/26/2013		
2/11/2013		37
2/12/2013	2/16/2013	
3/15/2013		5
3/6/2013	3/6/2013	
1/14/2013		65
2/8/2013		40
4/9/2013		
2/13/2013		35
2/15/2013	3/2/2013	
3/30/2013	4/14/2013	
1/29/2013	1/24/2013	

Type Text in a Cell

The first step when building a spreadsheet is to type the text data that defines the spreadsheet's labels or headings. Most labels appear in the cell to the right of or above the data. Most headings appear at the top of a column or to the left of a row.

You can use text for more than labels and headings. You can also type text as data, such as a database of book titles. You can write notes that explain sections of the worksheet, and add reminders for yourself or others about missing data, or other to-do items.

Type Text in a Cell

1 Click the cell in which you want to type the text.

Ⓐ Excel marks the current cell by surrounding it with a thick border.

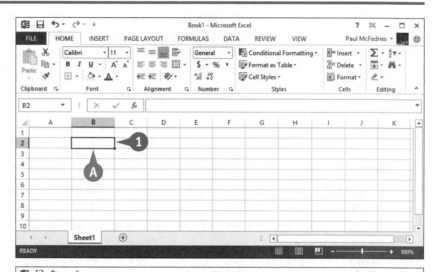

2 Start typing your text.

Ⓑ Excel opens the cell for editing and displays the text as you type.

Ⓒ Your typing also appears in the formula bar.

Note: Rather than typing the text directly into the cell, you can also type the text into the formula bar.

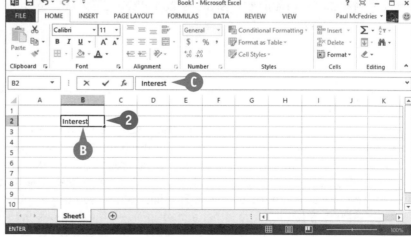

③ When your text entry is complete, press **Enter**.

Ⓓ If you do not want Excel to move the selection, click **Enter** (✓) or press **Ctrl**+ **Enter** instead.

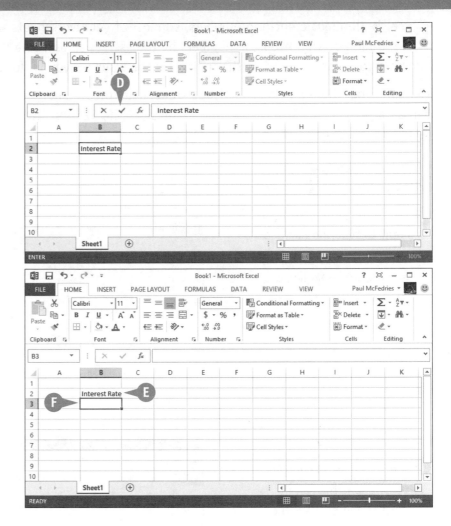

Ⓔ Excel closes the cell for editing.

Ⓕ If you pressed **Enter**, Excel moves the selection to the cell below.

TIPS

When I press Enter, the selection moves to the next cell down. Can I make the selection move to the right instead?

Yes. When you finish adding data to a cell, press ▶. This tells Excel to close the current cell for editing and move the selection to the next cell on the right. If you prefer to move left instead, press ◀; if you prefer to move up, press ▲.

When I start typing text into a cell, why does Excel sometimes display the text from another cell?

This is called AutoComplete. If the letters you type at the start of a cell match the contents of another in the worksheet, Excel fills in the full text from the other cell under the assumption that you are repeating the text in the new cell. If you want to use the text, click **Enter** (✓) or press **Enter**; otherwise, just keep typing.

Type a Number in a Cell

Excel is all about crunching numbers, so most of your worksheets will include numeric values. Although you will often use numbers by themselves as part of a database or table, many of the numbers you type are used as the inputs for the formulas you build, as described in Chapter 6.

You can type whole numbers (5, 1,024), decimals (0.25, 3.14), negative numbers (-10, -6.2), percentages (6%, 25.9%), or currency values ($0.25, $24.99). However, you need to know how to input these numeric values.

Type a Number into a Cell

1 Click the cell in which you want to type the number.

A Excel surrounds the cell with a thick, green border.

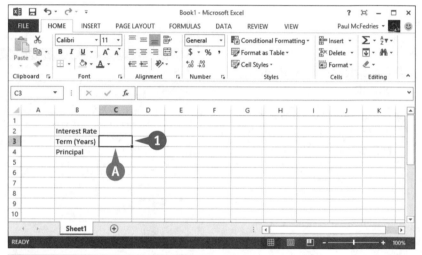

2 Start typing the number.

B Excel opens the cell for editing and displays the number as you type.

C Your typing also appears in the formula bar.

Note: Rather than typing the number directly into the cell, you can type it into the formula bar.

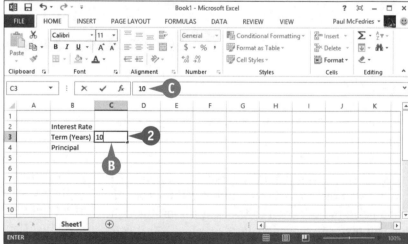

3 When your number is complete, press **Enter**.

D If you do not want Excel to move the selection, click **Enter** (✓) or press **Ctrl** + **Enter** instead.

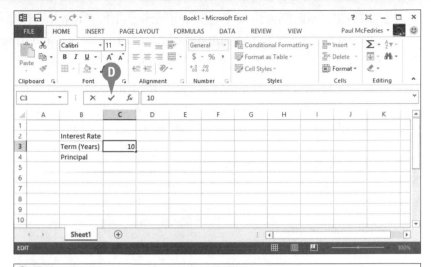

E Excel closes the cell for editing.

F To input a percentage value, type the number followed by a percent sign (%).

G To input a currency value, type the dollar sign ($) followed by the number.

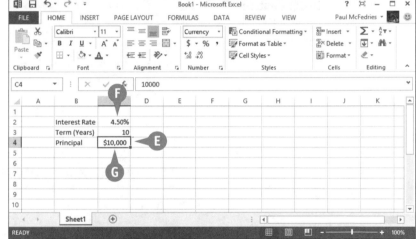

TIPS

Can I use symbols (such as a comma, decimal point, or minus sign) when I type a numeric value?
Yes. If your numeric value is in the thousands, you can include the thousands separator (,). If you type **10,000**, Excel displays the value as 10,000. If your numeric value includes decimals, you can include the decimal point (.) when you type the value. If your numeric value is negative, precede the value with a minus sign (−).

Is there a quicker way to repeat a number rather than retyping it?
Yes. Excel offers a few methods for doing this. The easiest method is to select the cell directly below the value you want to repeat and then press **Ctrl** + **'**. Excel adds the value to the cell. For another method, see the section "Fill a Range with the Same Data" in Chapter 3.

Type a Date or Time in a Cell

Many Excel worksheets use dates and times either as part of the sheet data or for use in calculations, such as the number of days an invoice is overdue. For these and similar uses, you need to know how to input date and time values into a cell.

The date format you use depends on your location. In the United States, you can use the month/day/year format (8/23/2013). The time format also depends on your location, but the general format is hour:minute:second, followed by a.m. or p.m., such as 3:15:30 p.m.

Type a Date or Time in a Cell

Type a Date

1. Click the cell in which you want to type the date.

   A Excel marks the current cell by surrounding it with a thick, green border.

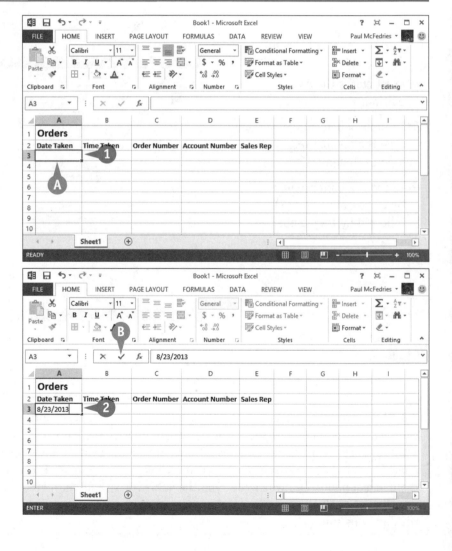

2. Type the date.

Note: See the following Tip to learn which date formats your version of Excel accepts.

3. When your date is complete, press **Enter**.

   B If you do not want Excel to move the selection, click **Enter** (✓) or press **Ctrl** + **Enter**.

   Excel closes the cell for editing.

Type a Time

1. Click the cell in which you want to type the time.

C Excel marks the current cell by surrounding it with a thick, green border.

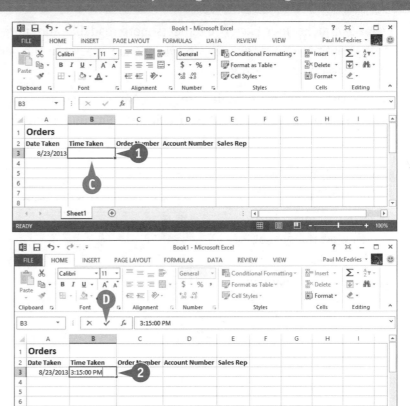

2. Type the time.

Note: See the following Tip to learn which time formats your version of Excel accepts.

3. When your time is complete, press Enter.

D If you do not want Excel to move the selection, click **Enter** (✓) or press Ctrl + Enter.

Excel closes the cell for editing.

TIP

How can I tell which date and time formats my version of Excel accepts?

1. Click the **Home** tab.

2. Click the **Dialog box launcher** button (🖫) in the **Number** group.

3. Click the **Number** tab.

4. Click **Date**.

5. Click the **Locale (location)** drop-down arrow (⌄), and then click your location.

6. Examine the **Type** list to see the available date formats.

7. Click **Time**.

8. Examine the **Type** list to see the available time formats.

9. Click **Cancel**.

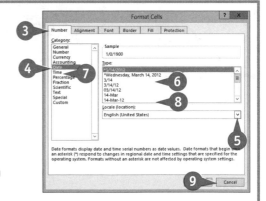

Insert a Symbol

You can make your Excel worksheets more readable and more useful by inserting special symbols that enhance your text. These symbols are special in the sense that they are not available via your keyboard's standard keys.

These special symbols include foreign characters such as ö and é, mathematical symbols such as ° and ∞, financial symbols such as ¢ and ¥, commercial symbols such as © and ®, and many more.

Insert a Symbol

1. Click the cell in which you want the symbol to appear.

2. Type the text that you want to appear before the symbol, if any.

3. Click the **Insert** tab.

4. Click **Symbols**.

5. Click **Symbol**.

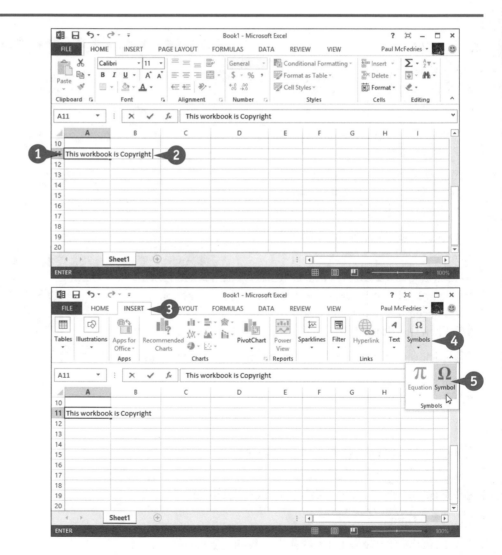

The Symbol dialog box appears.

⑥ Click the **Symbols** tab.

⑦ Click the symbol you want to insert.

Note: Many other symbols are available in the Webdings and Wingdings fonts. To see these symbols, click the **Font** drop-down arrow (⌄), and then click either **Webdings** or **Wingdings**.

⑧ Click **Insert**.

ⓐ Excel inserts the symbol.

⑨ Repeat Steps 7 and 8 to insert any other symbols you require.

⑩ Click **Close**.

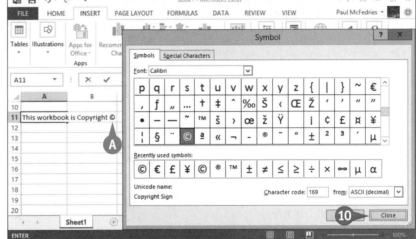

TIP

Are there keyboard shortcuts available for symbols I use frequently?
Yes, in many cases. In the Symbol dialog box, click the drop-down arrow (⌄) in the **from** list, and then select **ASCII (decimal)**. Click the symbol you want to insert and then examine the number in the Character code text box. This number tells you that you can input the symbol via the keyboard by holding down `Alt`, pressing `0`, and then typing the number. For example, you can input the © symbol by pressing `Alt`+`0` `1` `6` `9`. Be sure to type all numbers on the keyboard's numeric keypad.

Edit Cell Data

The data that you type in a worksheet cell is not set in stone after you press Enter or click **Enter** (✓). Whether you input text, numbers, dates, or times, if the data you type into a cell changes or is incorrect, you can edit the data to update or fix the information. You can edit cell data either directly in the cell or by using the formula bar.

Edit Cell Data

1 Click the cell in which you want to edit the text.

2 Press F2.

You can also double-click the cell you want to edit.

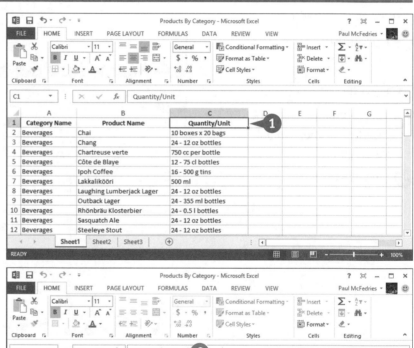

A Excel opens the cell for editing and moves the cursor to the end of the existing data.

B Excel displays Edit in the status bar.

C You can also click inside the formula bar and edit the cell data there.

3 Make your changes to the cell data.

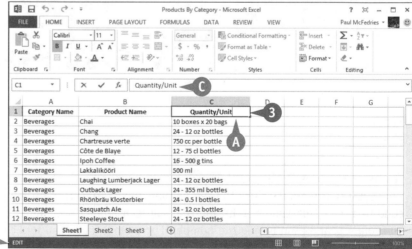

④ When you finish editing the data, press Enter.

Ⓓ If you do not want Excel to move the selection, click **Enter** (✓) or press Ctrl + Enter.

Ⓔ Excel closes the cell for editing.

Ⓕ If you pressed Enter, Excel moves the selection to the cell below.

TIPS

Is there a faster way to open a cell for editing?

Yes. Move the mouse pointer (⊕) over the cell you want to edit, center it over the character where you want to start editing, and double-click. Excel opens the cell for editing and positions the cursor at the spot where you double-clicked.

I made a mistake when I edited a cell. Do I have to fix the text manually?

Most likely not. If the cell edit was the last action you performed in Excel, press Ctrl + Z or click the **Undo** button (↺) in the Quick Launch toolbar. If you have performed other actions in the meantime, click the **Undo** drop-down arrow (☑), and then click the edit in the list that appears. Doing this, however, also undoes the other actions you performed after the edit.

Delete Data from a Cell

If your worksheet has a cell that contains data you no longer need, you can delete that data. This helps to reduce worksheet clutter, ensures that your worksheet does not contain erroneous or unnecessary data, and makes your worksheet easier to read.

If you want to delete data from multiple cells, you must first select those cells; see the section "Select a Range" in Chapter 3. To delete cells and not just the data, see the section "Delete a Range" in Chapter 3.

Delete Data from a Cell

Delete Cell Data

1 Select the cell that contains the data you want to delete.

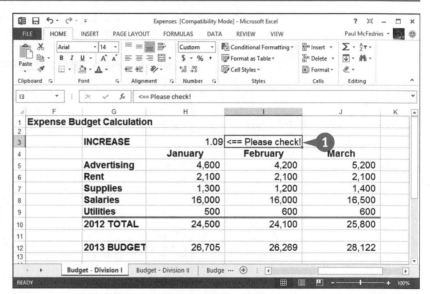

2 Click the **Home** tab.

3 Click **Clear** ( ).

4 Click **Clear Contents**.

Note: You can also delete cell data by pressing Delete.

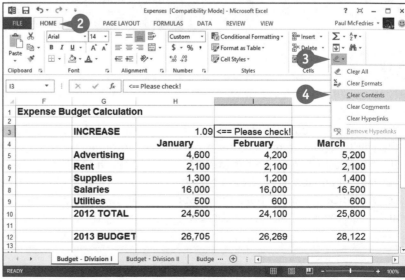

Ⓐ Excel removes the cell data.

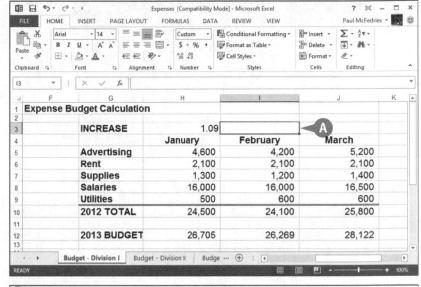

Undo Cell Data Deletion

1 Click the **Undo** drop-down arrow (▾).

2 Click **Clear**.

Note: If the data deletion was the most recent action you performed, you can undo it by pressing Ctrl + Z or by clicking **Undo** (↺).

Ⓑ Excel restores the data to the cell.

TIPS

When I delete cell data, Excel keeps the cell formatting intact. Is it possible to delete the data and the formatting?
Yes. Excel offers a command that deletes everything from a cell. First, select the cell with the data and formatting that you want to delete. Click **Home**, click **Clear** (✎), and then click **Clear All**. Excel removes both the data and the formatting from the selected cell.

Is it possible to delete just a cell's formatting?
Yes. Excel offers a command that deletes just the cell formatting while leaving the cell data intact. Select the cell with the formatting that you want to delete. Click **Home**, click **Clear** (✎), and then click **Clear Formats**. Excel removes just the formatting from the selected cell.

CHAPTER 3

Working with Ranges

In Excel, a *range* is a collection of two or more cells that you work with as a group rather than separately. This enables you to fill the range with values, move or copy the range, sort the range data, and insert and delete ranges. You learn these and other range techniques in this chapter.

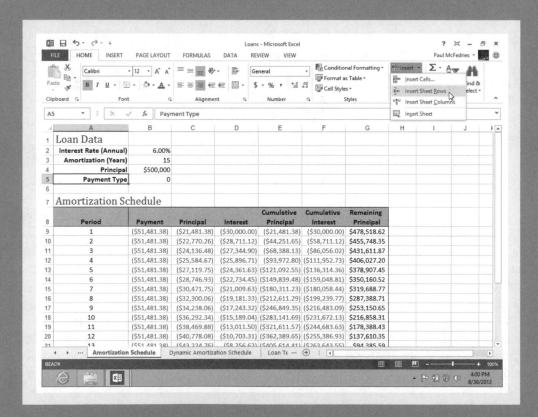

Select a Range

To work with a range in Excel, you must first select the cells that you want to include in the range. After you select the range, you can fill it with data, move it to another part of the worksheet, format the cells, and perform the other range-related tasks that you learn about in this chapter.

You can select a range as a rectangular group of cells, as a collection of individual cells, or as an entire row or column.

Select a Range

Select a Rectangular Range

1 Position the mouse pointer (⊕) over the first cell you want to include in the range.

2 Click and drag the mouse pointer (⊕) over the cells you want to include in the range.

Ⓐ Excel selects the cells.

3 Release the mouse button.

Select a Range of Individual Cells

1 Click in the first cell that you want to include in the range.

2 Hold down Ctrl and click in each of the other cells that you want to include in the range.

Ⓑ Each time you click in a cell, Excel adds it to the range.

3 Release Ctrl.

Select an Entire Row

1 Position the mouse pointer (⊕) over the header of the row you want to select and the pointer becomes the row selector (→).

2 Click the row header.

C Excel selects the entire row.

To select multiple rows, click and drag across the row headers or hold down **Ctrl** and click each row header.

Select an Entire Column

1 Position the mouse pointer (⊕) over the header of the column you want to select and the pointer becomes the column selector (↓).

2 Click the column header.

D Excel selects the entire column.

To select multiple columns, click and drag across the column headers, or hold down **Ctrl** and click each column header.

TIPS

Are there keyboard techniques I can use to select a range?

Yes. To select a rectangular range, navigate to the first cell you want to include, hold down **Shift**, and then press ← or ↓ to extend the selection. To select a row, navigate to any cell within it and press **Shift**+**Spacebar**. To select a column, navigate to any cell within it and press **Ctrl**+**Spacebar**.

Is there an easy way to select every cell in the worksheet?

Yes. Either press **Ctrl**+**A**, or click the **Select All** button (◢) in the upper-left corner of the worksheet (**A**).

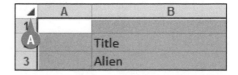

Fill a Range with the Same Data

If you need to fill a range with the same data, you can save time by getting Excel to fill the range for you. The AutoFill feature makes it easy to fill a vertical or horizontal range with the same value, but you can also fill any selected range. This method is much faster than typing the same data in each cell.

See the previous section, "Select a Range," to learn how to select a range of cells.

Fill a Range with the Same Data

Fill a Vertical or Horizontal Range

1 In the first cell of the range you want to work with, type the data you want to fill.

2 Position the mouse pointer (⊕) over the bottom-right corner of the cell and it becomes the pointer fill (+).

3 Click and drag the pointer fill (+) down to fill a vertical range or across to fill a horizontal range.

4 Release the mouse button.

Ⓐ Excel fills the range with the initial cell value.

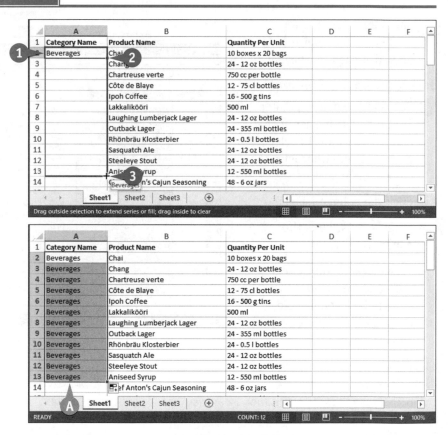

Fill a Selected Range

1 Select the range you want to fill.

2 Type the text, number, or other data.

3 Press Ctrl + Enter.

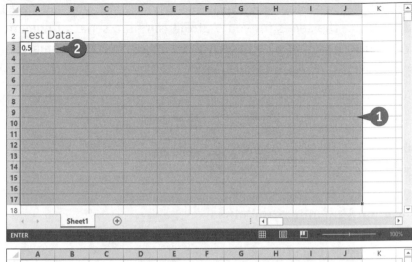

B Excel fills the range with the value you typed.

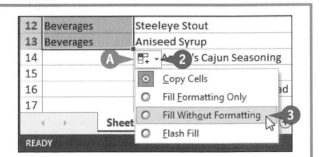

TIP

How do I fill a vertical or horizontal range without also copying the formatting of the original cell?
Follow these steps:

1 Perform Steps 1 to 4 to fill the data.

A Excel displays the AutoFill Options smart tag (⊞).

2 Click the **AutoFill Options** drop-down arrow (⌄).

3 Click **Fill Without Formatting**.

Excel removes the original cell's formatting from the copied cells.

Fill a Range with a Series of Values

If you need to fill a range with a series of values, you can save time by using the AutoFill feature to create the series for you. AutoFill can fill a series of numeric values such as 5, 10, 15, 20, and so on; a series of date values such as January 1, 2013, January 2, 2013, and so on; or a series of alphanumeric values such as Chapter 1, Chapter 2, Chapter 3, and so on.

You can also create your own series with a custom step value, which determines the numeric difference between each item in the series.

Fill a Range with a Series of Values

AutoFill a Series of Numeric, Date, or Alphanumeric Values

1. Click in the first cell and type the first value in the series.

2. Click in an adjacent cell and type the second value in the series.

3. Select the two cells.

4. Position the mouse pointer (⊕) over the bottom-right corner of the second cell. The pointer (⊕) becomes the pointer fill (**+**).

5. Click and drag the pointer fill (**+**) down to fill a vertical range or across to fill a horizontal range.

   Ⓐ As you drag through each cell, Excel displays the series value that it will add to the cell.

6. Release the mouse button.

   Ⓑ Excel fills the range with a series that continues the pattern of the initial two cell values.

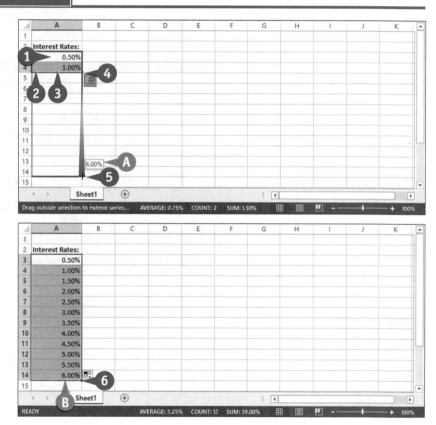

Fill a Custom Series of Values

1. Click in the first cell and type the first value in the series.

2. Select the range you want to fill, including the initial value.

3. Click the **Home** tab.

4. Click **Fill** (⬇).

5. Click **Series**.

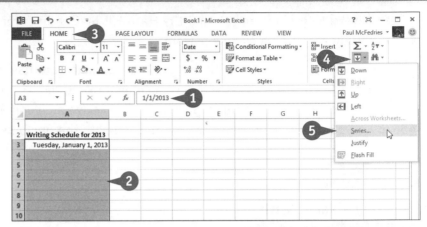

The Series dialog box appears.

6. In the Type group, select the type of series you want to fill. The empty radio button (○) is filled (◉).

7. If you selected Date in Step **6**, select an option in the Date unit group. The empty radio button (○) is filled (◉).

8. In the Step value text box, type the value you want to use.

9. Click **OK**.

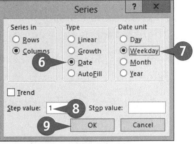

C Excel fills the range with the series you created.

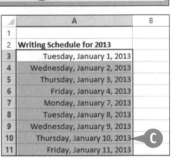

Can I create my own AutoFill series?

Yes. You can create a *custom list*, which is a series of text values. When you add the first value in your custom list, you can then use AutoFill to fill a range with the rest of the series. Follow these steps:

1. Click the **File** tab.

2. Click **Options**.

   The Excel Options dialog box appears.

3. Click **Advanced**.

4. Scroll down to the General section, and then click **Edit Custom Lists**.

   The Custom Lists dialog box appears.

5. Click **NEW LIST**.

6. In the List entries box, type each item in your list, and press Enter after each item.

7. Click **Add**.

8. Click **OK** to return to the Excel Options dialog box.

9. Click **OK**.

Flash Fill a Range

You can save time and effort by using the Flash Fill feature in Excel to fill a range of data automatically based on a sample pattern.

There are many ways to use Flash Fill, but the most common are flash filling a range with extracted or formatted data. For example, if you have a column of full names, you might want to extract the first names and create a new column. Similarly, if you have a column of phone numbers formatted as 1234567890, you might want a new column that formats the numbers as (123) 456-7890.

Flash Fill a Range

Flash Filling a Range with Extracted Data

1 Make sure the column of original data has a heading.

2 Type a heading for the column of extracted data.

3 Type the first value you want in the new column.

4 Begin typing the second value.

A Excel recognizes the pattern and displays suggestions for the rest of the column.

5 Press Enter.

B Excel flash fills the column with the extracted data.

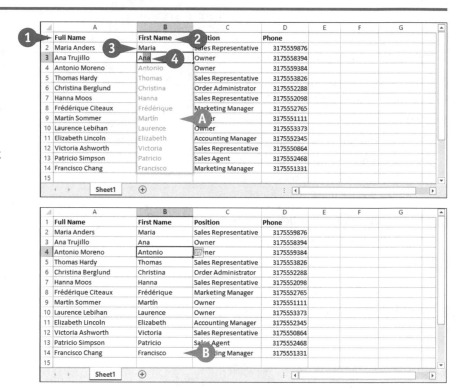

46

Flash Filling a Range with Formatted Data

1 Make sure the column of original data has a heading.

2 Type a heading for the new column of formatted data.

3 Type the first value you want in the new column.

4 Begin typing the second value.

C Excel recognizes the pattern and displays suggestions for the rest of the column.

5 Press **Enter**.

D Excel flash fills the column with the formatted data.

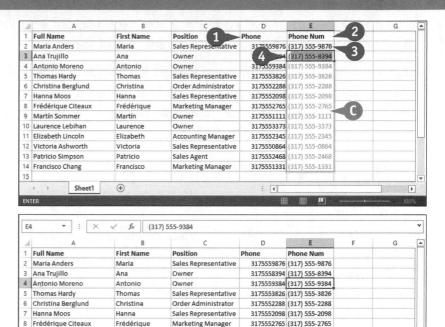

TIPS

Why do I not see the automatic Flash Fill suggestions when I type the sample data?
To see the Flash Fill suggestions, you must have headings at the top of both the original column and the filled data column. The flash fill column must also be adjacent to the original column, and the sample entries you make in the fill column must occur one after the other. Also, the suggestions usually only work with text data, not numeric data.

Can I still use Flash Fill even though I do not see the automatic suggestions?
Yes, you can still invoke Flash Fill on any range by running the Ribbon command. In the fill range, type the first value, and then select that value and the rest of the fill range. Click the **Data** tab, and then click **Flash Fill** (📇). Excel flash fills the selected range.

Move or Copy a Range

If your worksheet is not set up the way you want, you can restructure or reorganize the worksheet by moving an existing range to a different part of the sheet.

You can also make a copy of a range, which is a useful technique if you require a duplicate of the range elsewhere, or if you require a range that is similar to an existing range. In the latter case, after you copy the range, you can then edit the copied version of the data as needed.

Move or Copy a Range

Move a Range

1. Select the range you want to move.

2. Position the mouse pointer (⊕) over any outside border of the range. The pointer (⊕) becomes the range border pointer (⇱).

3. Click and drag the range to the new location. The range border pointer (⇱) becomes the mouse pointer (⇱).

A. Excel displays an outline of the range.

B. Excel displays the address of the new location.

4. Release the mouse button.

C. Excel moves the range to the new location.

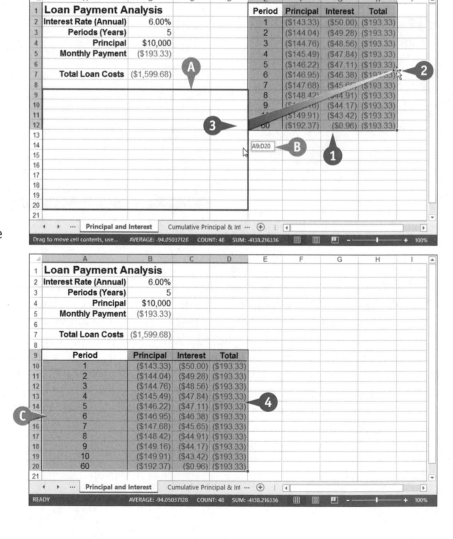

48

Copy a Range

1 Select the range you want to copy.

2 Press and hold **Ctrl**.

3 Position the mouse pointer (✥) over any outside border of the range. The pointer (✥) becomes the copy pointer (⇖).

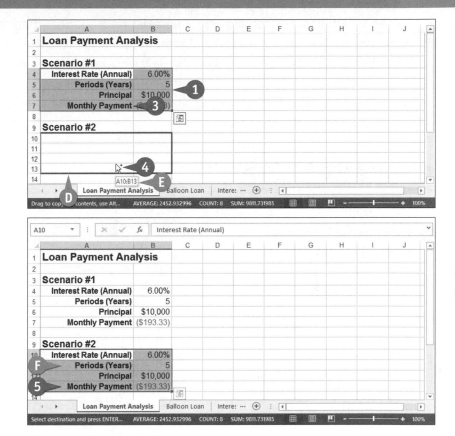

4 Click and drag the range to the location where you want the copy to appear.

D Excel displays an outline of the range.

E Excel displays the address of the new location.

5 Release the mouse button.

6 Release **Ctrl**.

F Excel creates a copy of the range in the new location.

TIPS

Can I move or copy a range to another worksheet?

Yes. Click and drag the range as described in this section. Remember to hold down **Ctrl** to copy the range. Press and hold **Alt**, and then drag the mouse pointer (⇖) over the tab of the sheet you want to use as the destination. Excel displays the worksheet. Release **Alt**, and then drop the range on the worksheet.

Can I move or copy a range to another workbook?

Yes. If you can see the other workbook on-screen, click and drag the range as described in this section, and then drop it on the other workbook. Hold down **Ctrl** to copy the range, or select the range, and click the **Home** tab, click **Cut** (✂) to move the range or **Copy** (🗐) to copy it. In the other workbook, select the cell where you want the range, click **Home**, and then click **Paste** (📋).

Insert a Row or Column

You can insert a row or column into your existing worksheet data to accommodate more information. The easiest way to add more information to a worksheet is to add it to the right or at the bottom of your existing data. However, you will often find that the new information you need to add fits naturally within the existing data. In such cases, you first need to insert a new row or column in your worksheet at the place where you want the new data to appear, and then add the new information in the blank row or column.

Insert a Row or Column

Insert a Row

1. Click any cell in the row below where you want to insert the new row.

2. Click the **Home** tab.

3. Click the **Insert** drop-down arrow ($\vee$).

4. Click **Insert Sheet Rows**.

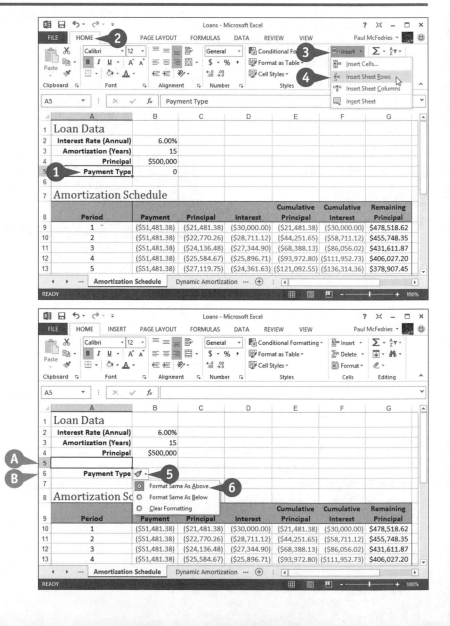

A Excel inserts the new row.

Note: You can also right-click the header of an existing row, and then click **Insert**.

B The rows below the new row shift down.

5. Click the **Insert Options** smart tag (✐).

6. Select a formatting option for the new row. The empty radio button (○) is filled (⦿).

Insert a Column

1. Click any cell in the row to the right of where you want to insert the new column.

2. Click the **Home** tab.

3. Click the **Insert** drop-down arrow (⌄).

4. Click **Insert Sheet Columns**.

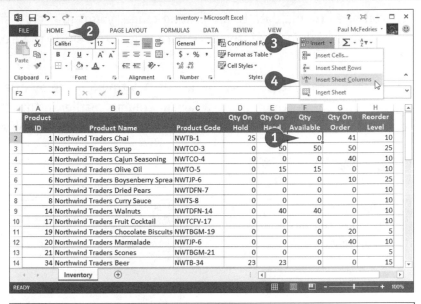

C. Excel inserts the new column.

Note: You can also right-click the header of an existing column, and then click **Insert**.

D. The columns to the right of the new column shift to the right.

5. Click the **Insert Options** smart tag (❖).

6. Select a formatting option for the new column. The empty radio button (○) is filled (◉).

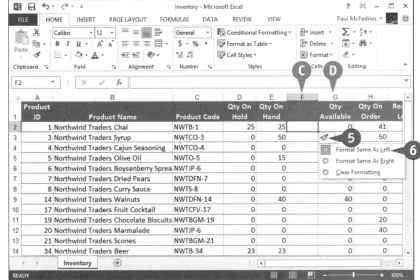

TIP

Can I insert more than one row or column at a time?

Yes. You can insert as many new rows or columns as you need. First, select the same number of rows or columns that you want to insert. (See the section "Select a Range" earlier in this chapter to learn how to select rows and columns.) For example, if you want to insert four rows, select four existing rows. For rows, be sure to select existing rows below where you want the new rows inserted and then follow Steps 2 to 4 in the "Insert a Row" subsection. For columns, be sure to select existing columns to the right of where you want to insert the new columns and then follow Steps 2 to 4 in the "Insert a Column" subsection.

Insert a Cell or Range

If you need to add data to an existing range, you can insert a single cell or a range of cells within that range. When you insert a cell or range, Excel shifts the existing data to accommodate the new cells.

Although you can create room for new data within a range by inserting an entire row or column, as explained in the section "Insert a Row or Column" earlier in this chapter, this causes problems for some types of worksheet layouts. You can work around such problems by inserting just a cell or range.

Insert a Cell or Range

1 Select the cell or range where you want the inserted cell or range to appear.

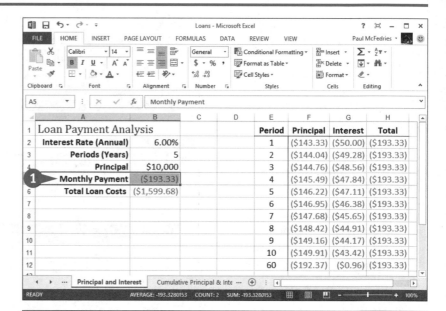

2 Click the **Home** tab.

3 Click the **Insert** drop-down arrow (▼).

4 Click **Insert Cells**.

Note: You can also press Ctrl + Shift + =.

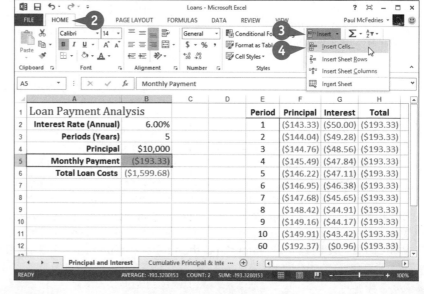

The Insert dialog box appears.

⑤ Select the option that corresponds to how you want Excel to shift the existing cells. The empty radio button (○) is filled (◉).

Note: In most cases, if you select a horizontal range, you should click the **Shift cells down** option; if you select a vertical range, you should click the **Shift cells right** option.

⑥ Click **OK**.

Ⓐ Excel inserts the cell or range.

Ⓑ The existing data shifts down, as in this example, or to the right.

⑦ Click the **Insert Options** smart tag (⬦).

⑧ Select a formatting option for the new row. The empty radio button (○) is filled (◉).

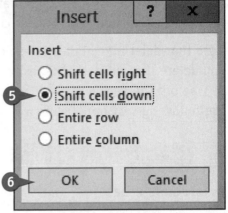

	A	B	C	D	E	F	G	H
1	Loan Payment Analysis				Period	Principal	Interest	Total
2	Interest Rate (Annual)	6.00%			1	($143.33)	($50.00)	($193.33)
3	Periods (Years)	5			2	($144.04)	($49.28)	($193.33)
4	Principal	$10,000			3	($144.76)	($48.56)	($193.33)
5					4	($145.49)	($47.84)	($193.33)
6	Monthly Payment	($193.33)			5	($146.22)	($47.11)	($193.33)
7	Total Loan Costs	($1,599.68)			6	($146.95)	($46.38)	($193.33)
8					7	($147.68)	($45.65)	($193.33)
9					8	($148.42)	($44.91)	($193.33)
10					9	($149.16)	($44.17)	($193.33)
11					10	($149.91)	($43.42)	($193.33)
12					60	($192.37)	($0.96)	($193.33)

Format Same As Above
Format Same As Below
Clear Formatting

Principal and Interest   Cumulative Principal & Inte ···   ⊕

READY

100%

TIPS

Under what circumstances would I insert a cell or range instead of inserting an entire row or column?
In most cases, it is better to insert a cell or range when you have other data to the left, right, above, or below the existing range. If you have data to the left or right of the existing range, inserting an entire row would create a gap in the other data.

How do I know which cells to select to get my inserted cell or range in the correct position?
The easiest way to do this is to select the existing cell or range that is where you want the new cell or range to appear. If you want the new range to be A5:B5, as shown in this section's example, select the existing A5:B5 range. When you insert the new range, Excel shifts the existing cells (down in this case) to accommodate it.

Delete Data from a Range

If your worksheet has a range that contains data you no longer need, you can delete that data. This helps to reduce worksheet clutter and makes your worksheet easier to read.

Note that deleting cell data does not adjust the structure of your worksheet in any way. That is, after you delete the cell data, the rest of your worksheet data remains intact and in the same place that it was before the data deletion. If you want to delete cells and not just the data within the cells, see the following section, "Delete a Range."

Delete Data from a Range

Delete Range Data

1 Select the range that contains the data you want to delete.

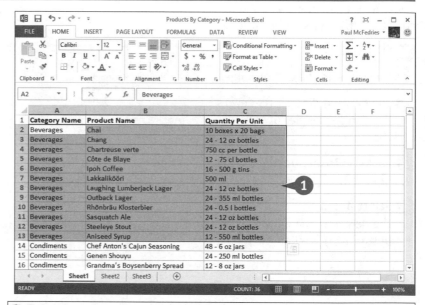

2 Click the **Home** tab.

3 Click **Clear** (✐).

4 Click **Clear Contents**.

Ⓐ If you want to delete the range data and its formatting, click **Clear All** instead.

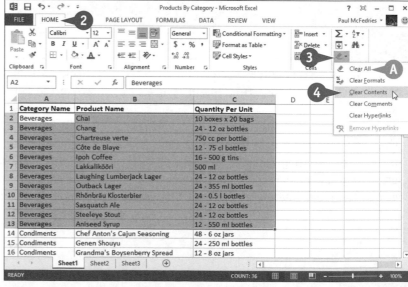

Ⓑ Excel removes the range data.

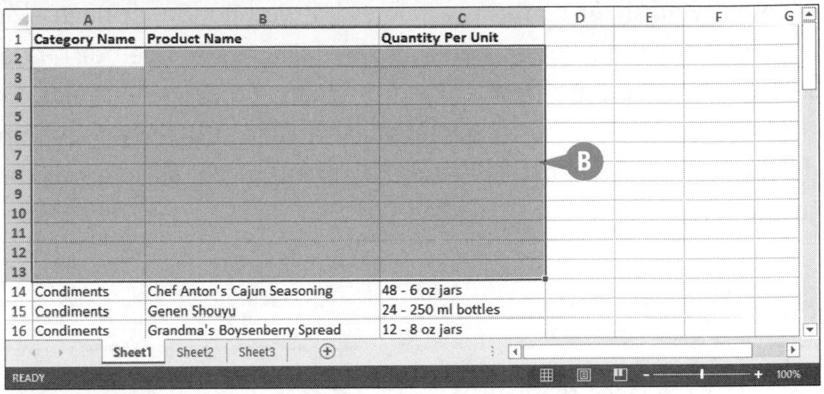

Undo Range Data Deletion

1. Click the **Undo** drop-down arrow (▾).
2. Click **Clear**.

Note: If the data deletion was the most recent action you performed, you can undo it by pressing Ctrl+Z or by clicking **Undo** (↶).

Ⓒ Excel restores the data to the range.

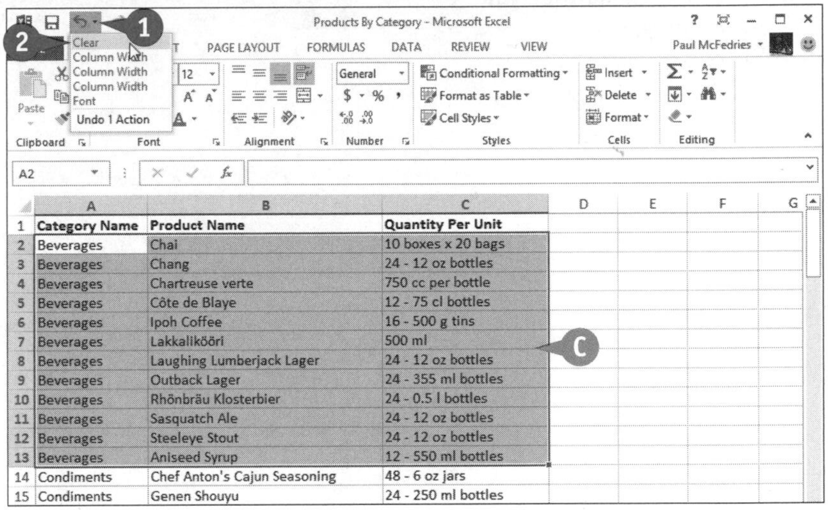

TIPS

Are there faster ways to delete the data from a range?

Yes. Probably the fastest method is to select the range and then press Delete. You can also select the range, right-click any part of the range, and then click **Clear Contents**.

Is it possible to delete a cell's numeric formatting?

Yes. Select the range with the formatting that you want to remove, click **Home**, click **Clear** (◆), and then click **Clear Formats**. Excel removes all the formatting from the selected range. If you prefer to delete only the numeric formatting, click **Home**, click the **Number Format** drop-down arrow (▾), and then click **General**.

Delete a Range

If your worksheet contains a range that you no longer need, you can delete that range. Note that this is not the same as deleting the data within a cell or range, as described in the previous section, "Delete Data from a Range." When you delete a range, Excel deletes not just the data within the range, but also the range cells. Excel then shifts the remaining worksheet data to replace the deleted range. Excel displays a dialog box that enables you to choose whether the data shifts up or to the left.

Delete a Range

1 Select the range that you want to delete.

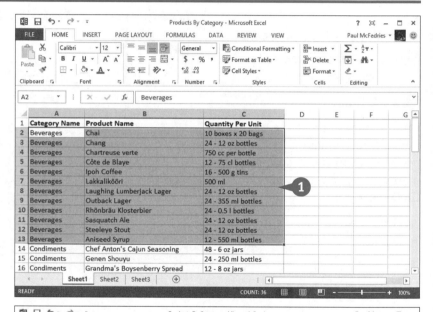

2 Click the **Home** tab.

3 Click the **Delete** drop-down arrow (⌄).

4 Click **Delete Cells**.

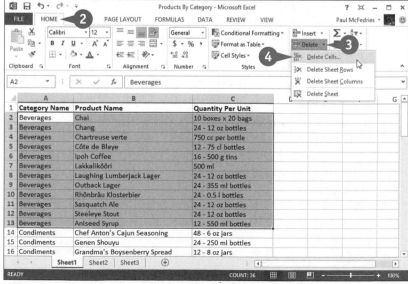

The Delete dialog box appears.

⑤ Select the option that corresponds to how you want Excel to shift the remaining cells after it deletes the range. The empty radio button (○) is filled (◉).

Note: In most cases, if you have data below the selected range, you should click the **Shift cells up** option; if you have data to the right of the selected range, you should click the **Shift cells left** option.

⑥ Click **OK**.

Ⓐ Excel deletes the range and shifts the remaining data.

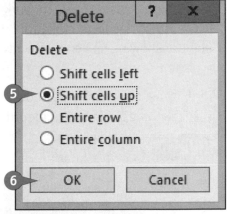

TIPS

Are there faster ways to delete a range?
Yes. Probably the fastest method is to select the range and then press Ctrl + - . You can also select the range, right-click any part of the range, and then click **Delete**. Both methods display the Delete dialog box.

How do I delete a row or column?
To delete a row, select any cell in the row, click the **Home** tab, click the **Delete** drop-down arrow (⌄), and then click **Delete Sheet Rows**. To delete a column, select any cell in the column, click the **Home** tab, click the **Delete** drop-down arrow (⌄), and then click **Delete Sheet Columns**. Note, too, that you can delete multiple rows or columns by selecting at least one cell in each row or column.

Hide a Row or Column

If you do not need to see or work with a row or column temporarily, you can make your worksheet easier to read and to navigate by hiding the row or column. Hiding a row or column is also useful if you are showing someone a worksheet that contains private or sensitive data that you do not want the person to see.

Hiding a row or column does not affect other parts of your worksheet. In particular, formulas that use or rely on data in the hidden rows and columns still display the same results.

Hide a Row or Column

Hide a Row

1. Click in any cell in the row you want to hide.

2. Click the **Home** tab.

3. Click **Format**.

4. Click **Hide & Unhide**.

5. Click **Hide Rows**.

Note: You can also hide a row by pressing Ctrl + 9.

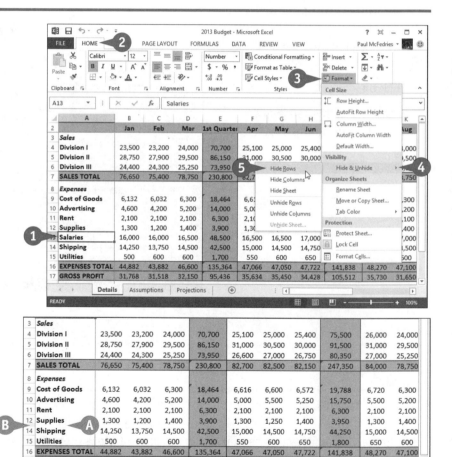

A. Excel removes the row from the worksheet display.

B. Excel displays a double-line heading border between the surrounding rows to indicate that a hidden row lies between them.

Another way to hide a row is to move the mouse pointer (⟱) over the bottom edge of the row heading. The mouse pointer (⟱) becomes the row resize pointer (✛). Click and drag the edge up until the height displays 0.

Hide a Column

1 Click in any cell in the column you want to hide.

2 Click the **Home** tab.

3 Click **Format**.

4 Click **Hide & Unhide**.

5 Click **Hide Columns**.

Note: You can also hide a column by pressing **Ctrl**+**0**.

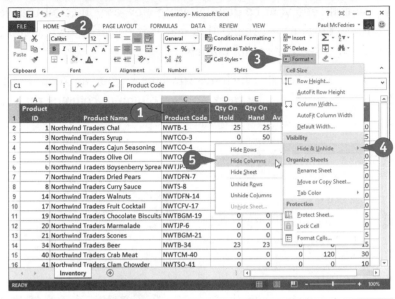

C Excel removes the column from the worksheet display.

D Excel displays a slightly thicker heading border between the surrounding columns to indicate that a hidden column lies between them.

Another way to hide a column is to move the mouse pointer (⊕) over the right edge of the column heading. The mouse pointer (⊕) becomes the column resize (✛). Click and drag the edge left until the width displays 0.

TIP

How do I display a hidden row or column?

To display a hidden row, select the rows above and below it, click **Home**, click **Format**, click **Hide & Unhide**, and then click **Unhide Rows**. Alternatively, move the mouse pointer (⊕) between the headings of the selected rows. The mouse pointer (⊕) becomes the row resize pointer (✛). Double-click, and then, to unhide row 1, right-click the top edge of the row 2 header. Click **Unhide**.

To display a hidden column, select the columns to the left and right of it, click **Home**, click **Format**, click **Hide & Unhide**, and then click **Unhide Columns**. Alternatively, move the mouse pointer (⊕) between the headings of the selected columns. The mouse pointer (⊕) becomes the column resize pointer (✛). Double-click, and then, to unhide column A, right-click the left edge of the column B header. Click **Unhide**.

Freeze a Row or Column

You can keep your column labels in view as you scroll the worksheet by freezing the row or rows that contain the labels. This makes it easier to review and add data to the worksheet because you can always see the column labels.

If your worksheet also includes row labels, you can keep those labels in view as you horizontally scroll the worksheet by freezing the column or columns that contain the labels.

Freeze Rows or Columns

Freeze Rows

1. Scroll the worksheet so that the row(s) you want to freeze is visible.

2. Select the cell in column A that is one row below the last row you want to freeze.

   For example, if you want to freeze row 1, select cell A2.

3. Click the **View** tab.

4. Click **Freeze Panes**.

5. Click **Freeze Panes**.

   Excel freezes the rows.

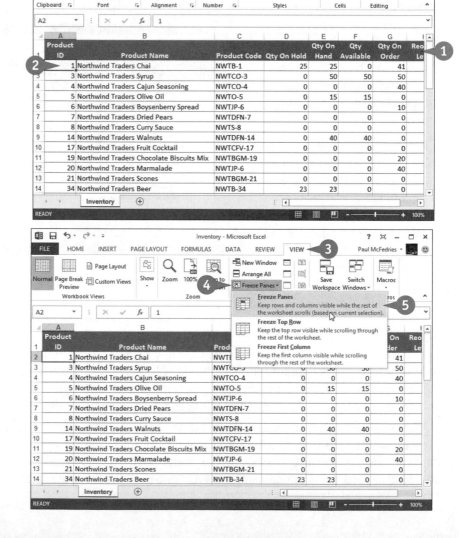

Freeze Columns

1. Scroll the worksheet so that the column(s) you want to freeze is visible.

2. Select the cell in row 1 that is one row to the right of the last column you want to freeze.

   For example, if you want to freeze column A, select cell B1.

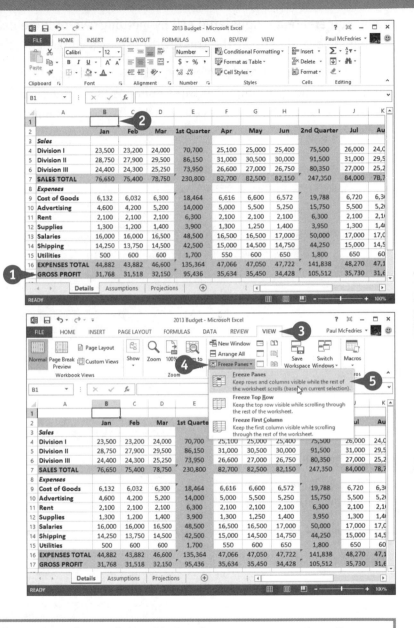

3. Click the **View** tab.

4. Click **Freeze Panes**.

5. Click **Freeze Panes**.

   Excel freezes the columns.

TIPS

Are there easier methods I can use to freeze just the top row or first column?
Yes. To freeze just the top row, click **View**, click **Freeze Panes**, and then click **Freeze Top Row**. To freeze just the first column, click **View**, click **Freeze Panes**, and then click **Freeze First Column**. Note that in both cases you do not need to select a cell in advance.

How do I unfreeze a row or column?
If you no longer require a row or column to be frozen, you can unfreeze it by clicking **View**, clicking **Freeze Panes**, and then clicking **Unfreeze Panes**.

Merge Two or More Cells

You can create a single large cell by merging two or more cells. For example, it is common to merge several cells in the top row to use as a worksheet title.

Another common reason for merging cells is to create a label that applies to multiple columns of data. For example, if you have three columns labeled *January*, *February*, and *March*, you could select the three cells in the row above these labels, merge them, and then use the merged cell to add the label *First Quarter*.

Merge Two or More Cells

1 Select the cells that you want to merge.

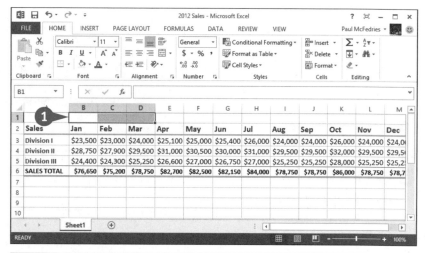

2 Click the **Home** tab.

3 Click the **Merge & Center** drop-down arrow (⌄).

4 Click **Merge Cells**.

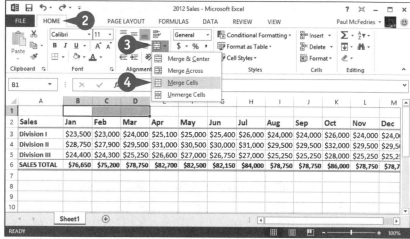

Ⓐ Excel merges the selected cells into a single cell.

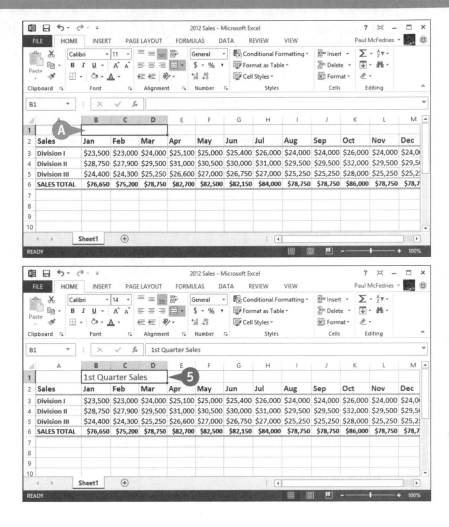

5 Type your text in the merged cell.

TIP

How do I center text across multiple columns?
This is a useful technique for your worksheet titles or headings. You can center a title across the entire worksheet, or you can center a heading across the columns to which it refers. Follow Steps 1 to 3 and then click **Merge & Center**. Excel creates the merged cell and formats the cell with the Center alignment option. Any text you type into the merged cell appears centered within the cell.

Transpose a Row or Column

You can use the Transpose command in Excel to turn a row of data into a column of data, or a column of data into a row of data.

The Transpose command is useful when you type data into a row (or column) or receive a worksheet from another person that has data in a row (or column), and you decide the data would be better presented as a column (or row). You can also transpose rows and columns together in a single command, which is handy when you need to restructure a worksheet.

Transpose Rows and Columns

1 Select the range that includes the data you want to transpose.

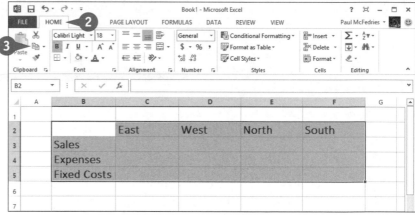

2 Click the **Home** tab.

3 Click **Copy** (📋).

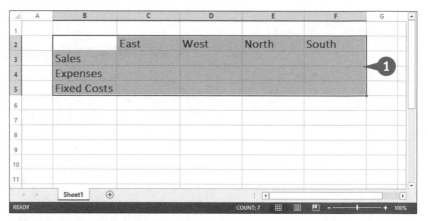

4 Click where you want the transposed range to appear.

5 Click the **Paste** drop-down arrow (⌄).

6 Click **Transpose** (▥).

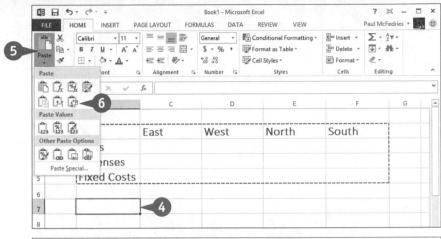

A Excel transposes the data, and then pastes it to the worksheet.

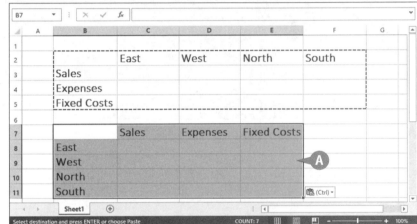

TIPS

How do I know which cells to select?
The range you select before copying depends on what you want to transpose. If you want to transpose a single horizontal or vertical range of cells, then select just that range. If you want to transpose a horizontal range of cells and a vertical range of cells at the same time, select the range that includes all the cells, as shown in this section's example.

Can I transpose range values as well as range labels?
Yes. The Transpose command works with text, numbers, dates, formulas, and any other data you can add to a cell. If you have a rectangular region of data that includes row labels, column labels, and cell values within each row and column, you can select the entire range and transpose it.

CHAPTER 4

Working with Range Names

You can make it easier to navigate Excel worksheets and build Excel formulas by applying names to your ranges. This chapter explains range names and shows you how to define, edit, and use range names.

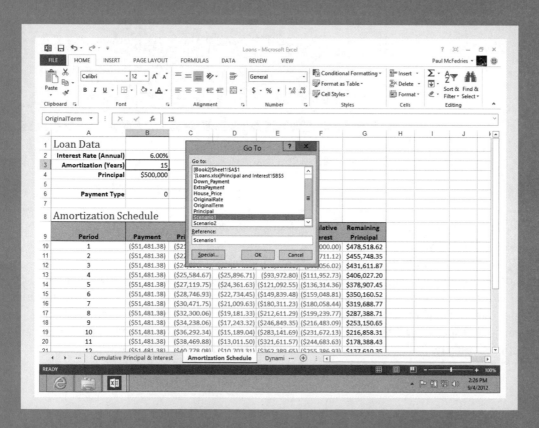

Understanding the Benefits of Range Names

A *range name* is a text label that you apply to a single cell or to a range of cells. Once you define a name for a range, you can use that name in place of the range coordinates, which has several benefits. These benefits include making your worksheets more intuitive and making your work more accurate. In addition, a range name is easier to remember than range coordinates, it does not change when you move the underlying range, and it makes it easier to navigate your worksheets.

More Intuitive

Range names are more intuitive than range coordinates, particularly in formulas. For example, if you see the range B2:B10 in a formula, the only way to know what the range refers to is to

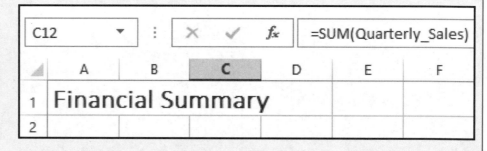

look at the data. However, if you see the name Quarterly_Sales in the formula, then you already know to what the range refers.

More Accurate

Range names are more accurate than range coordinates. Consider the range address A1:B3, which consists of four pieces of information: the column (A) and row (1) of the cell in the upper-left corner of the range, and the column (B) and row (3) of the

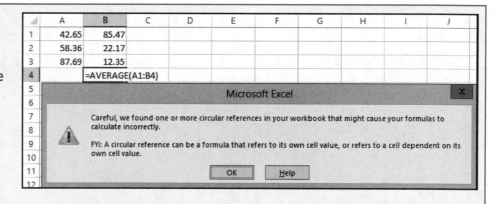

cell in the lower-right corner. If you get even one of these values wrong, it can cause errors throughout a spreadsheet. By contrast, with a range name you need only reference the actual name.

Easier to Remember

Range names are easier to remember than range coordinates. For example, if you want to use a particular range in a formula, but that range is not currently visible, to get the coordinates

◢	A	B	C	D	E
1	*Project Financial Overview*				
2	Project Expenses	=Sum(Project_Expenses)			
3	Project Revenues				
4					

you must scroll until you can see the range and then determine the range's coordinates. However, if you have already assigned the range an intuitive name such as Project_Expenses, you can add that name directly without having to view the range.

Names Do Not Change

Range names do not change when you adjust the position of a range, as they do with range coordinates. For example, if you move the range A1:B5 to the right by five columns, the range coordinates change to F1:G5. If you have a formula that references

=SUM(Project_Expenses)

	F	G	H	I	J	K
	Project Financial Overview					
	Project Expenses	$46,295				
	Project Revenues	$52,234				

that range, Excel updates the formula with the new range coordinates, which could confuse someone examining the worksheet. By contrast, a range name does not change when you move the range.

Easier Navigation

Range names make it easier to navigate a worksheet. For example, Excel has a Go To command that enables you to choose a range name, and Excel takes you directly to the range. You can also use the Name box to select a range name and navigate to that range. You can also use Go To and the Name box to specify range coordinates, but working with range coordinates is much more difficult.

Define a Range Name

Before you can use a range name, either in a formula or to navigate a worksheet, you must first define the range name. You can define as many names as you need, and you can even define multiple names for the same range.

You can create range names manually, or you can get Excel to create the names for you automatically based on the existing text labels in a worksheet. To do this, see the following section, "Use Worksheet Text to Define a Range Name."

Define a Range Name

1 Select the range you want to name.

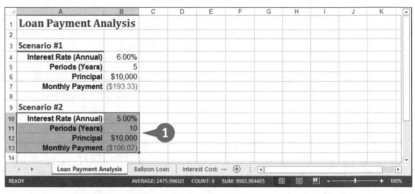

2 Click the **Formulas** tab.

3 Click **Define Name**.

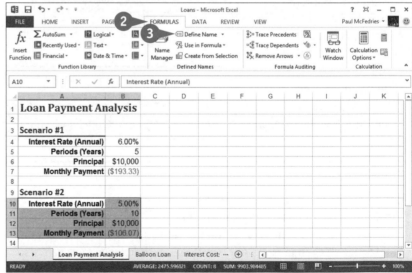

The New Name dialog box appears.

④ Type the name you want to use in the **Name** text box.

Note: The first character of the name must be a letter or an underscore (_). The name cannot include spaces or cell references, and it cannot be any longer than 255 characters.

Note: You can only use a particular range name once in a workbook.

⑤ Click **OK**.

Excel assigns the name to the range.

Ⓐ The new name appears in the Name box whenever you select the range.

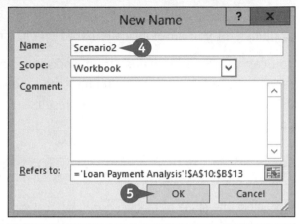

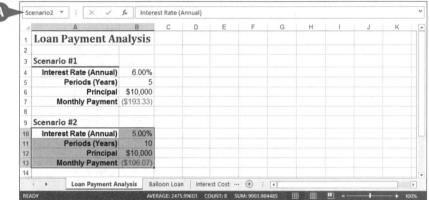

TIP

Is there an easier way to define a range name?

Yes. You can follow these steps to bypass the New Name dialog box:

① Select the range you want to name.

② Click inside the **Name** box.

③ Type the name you want to use.

④ Press Enter.

Excel assigns the name to the range.

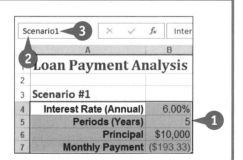

Use Worksheet Text to Define a Range Name

If you have several ranges to name, you can speed up the process by getting Excel to create the names for you automatically based on each range's text labels.

You can create range names from worksheet text when the labels are in the top or bottom row of the range, or the left or right column of the range. For example, if you have a column named Company, using the technique in this section results in that column's data being assigned the range name Company.

Use Worksheet Text to Define a Range Name

1 Select the range or ranges you want to name.

A Be sure to include the text labels you want to use for the range names.

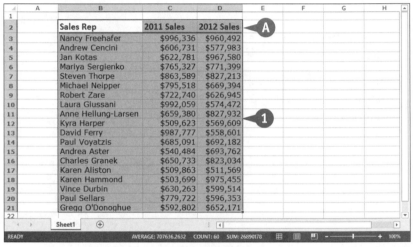

2 Click the **Formulas** tab.

3 Click **Create from Selection**.

The Create Names from Selection dialog box appears.

④ Select the setting or settings that correspond to where the text labels are located in the selected range. The empty check box (□) is filled (☑).

If Excel has activated a check box that does not apply to your data, click it. The selected check box (☑) is cleared (□).

⑤ Click **OK**.

Excel assigns the text labels as range names.

Ⓑ When you select one of the ranges, the range name assigned by Excel appears in the Name box.

Note: If the label text contains any illegal characters, such as a space, Excel replaces each of those characters with an underscore (_).

TIPS

Is there a faster way to run the Create from Selection command?
Yes. Excel offers a keyboard shortcut for the command. Select the range(s) with which you want to work, and then press Ctrl + Shift + F3. Excel displays the Create Names from Selection dialog box. Follow Steps 4 and 5 to create the range names.

Can I automatically assign a name to the data in a table with labels in the top row and left column?
Yes. To assign a name to the data range, type a label in the top-left corner of the table. When you run the Create from Selection command on the entire table, Excel assigns the top-left label to the data range, as shown here.

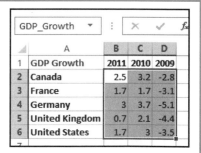

Navigate a Workbook Using Range Names

One of the big advantages of defining range names is that they make it easier to navigate a workbook. You can choose a range name from a list and Excel automatically selects the associated range. This works even if the named range exists in a different worksheet of the same workbook.

Excel offers two methods for navigating a workbook using range names: the Name box and the Go To command.

Navigate a Workbook Using Range Names

Using the Name Box

1 Open the workbook that contains the range with which you want to work.

2 Click the **Name** box drop-down arrow (⌄).

3 Click the name of the range you want to select.

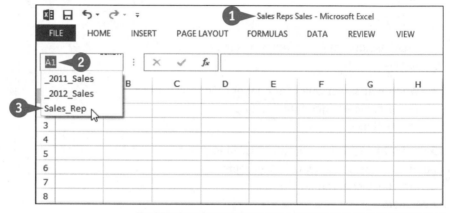

A Excel selects the range.

Using the Go To Command

1. Open the workbook that contains the range with which you want to work.

2. Click the **Home** tab.

3. Click **Find & Select** (▲).

4. Click **Go To**.

Note: You can also select the Go To command by pressing Ctrl + G.

The Go To dialog box appears.

5. Click the name of the range you want to select.

6. Click **OK**.

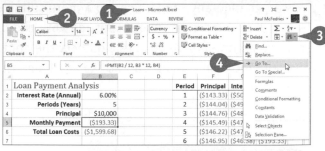

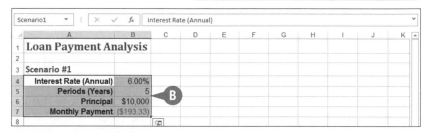

Ⓑ Excel selects the range.

TIP

Can I navigate to a named range in a different workbook?

Yes, but it is not easy:

1. Follow Steps 1 to 4 in the "Using the Go To Command" subsection.

2. In the **Reference** text box, type: **'[workbook] worksheet'!name**.

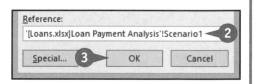

Replace *workbook* with the filename of the workbook; replace *worksheet* with the name of the worksheet that contains the range; replace *name* with the range name.

3. Click **OK**.

Change a Range Name

You can change any range name to a more suitable or accurate name. Changing a range name is useful if you are no longer satisfied with the original name you applied to a range or if the existing name no longer accurately reflects the contents of the range. You might also want to change a range name if you do not like the name that Excel generated automatically from the worksheet labels.

If you want to change the range coordinates associated with a range name, see the second Tip.

Change a Range Name

1 Open the workbook that contains the range name you want to change.

2 Click the **Formulas** tab.

3 Click **Name Manager**.

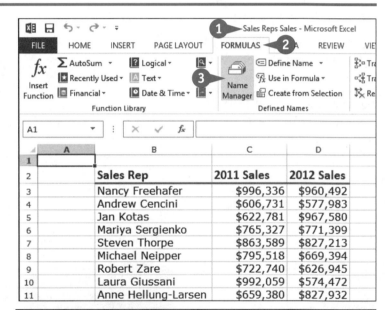

The Name Manager dialog box appears.

4 Click the name you want to change.

5 Click **Edit**.

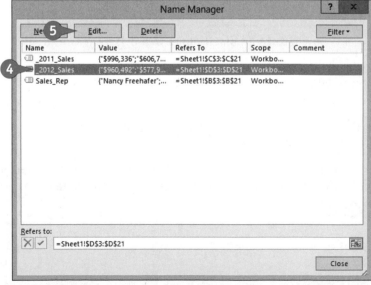

The Edit Name dialog box appears.

6 Use the **Name** text box to edit the name.

7 Click **OK**.

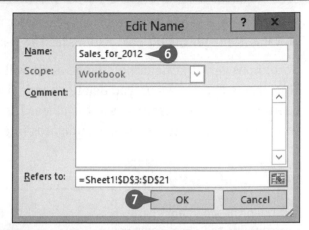

A The new name appears in the Name Manager dialog box.

8 Repeat Steps 4 to 7 to rename other ranges as needed.

9 Click **Close**.

Excel closes the dialog box and returns you to the worksheet.

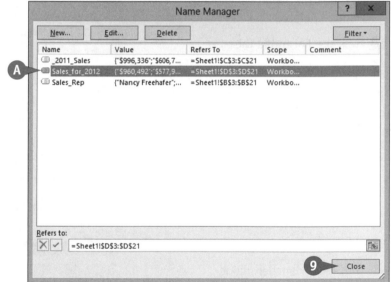

TIPS

Is there a faster method I can use to open the Name Manager dialog box?
Yes. Excel offers a shortcut key that enables you to bypass Steps 2 and 3. Open the workbook that contains the range name you want to change, and then press Ctrl+F3. Excel opens the Name Manager dialog box.

Can I assign a name to a different range?
Yes, you can modify the name of an existing workbook to refer to a new range. Follow Steps 1 to 5 to open the Edit Name dialog box. Click inside the **Refers to** reference box, click and drag the mouse pointer (⊕) on the worksheet to select the new range, and then press Enter. Click **Close**.

Delete a Range Name

If you have a range name that you no longer need, you should delete it. This reduces clutter in the Name Manager dialog box, and makes the Name box easier to navigate.

Note, however, that deleting a range name will generate an error in any formula that uses the name. This occurs because when you delete a range name, Excel does not convert the name to its range coordinates in formulas that use the name. Therefore, before deleting a range name, you should convert that name to its range coordinates in every formula that uses the name.

Delete a Range Name

1 Open the workbook that contains the range name you want to delete.

2 Click the **Formulas** tab.

3 Click **Name Manager**.

Note: You can also open the Name Manager dialog box by pressing Ctrl + F3.

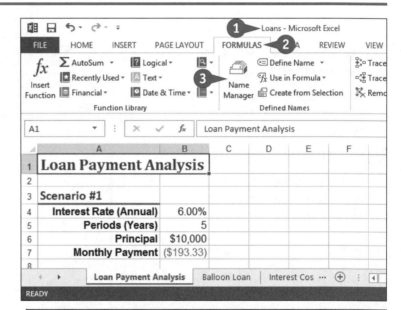

The Name Manager dialog box appears.

4 Click the name you want to delete.

5 Click **Delete**.

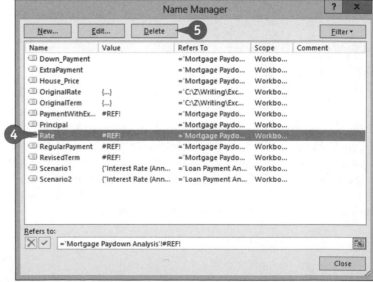

Excel asks you to confirm the deletion.

⑥ Click **OK**.

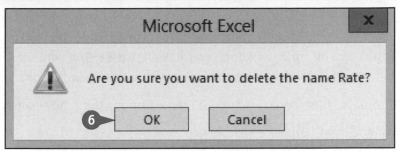

Ⓐ Excel deletes the range name.

⑦ Repeat Steps 4 to 6 to delete other range names as needed.

⑧ Click **Close**.

Excel closes the dialog box and returns you to the worksheet.

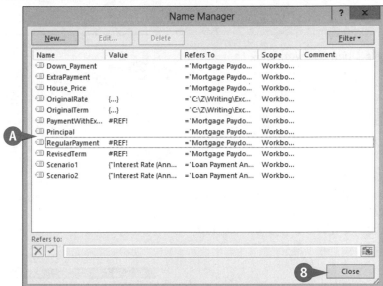

TIP

Is there a faster way to delete multiple range names?
Yes. You can delete two or more range names at once. First, follow Steps 1 to 3 to display the Name Manager dialog box, and then select the range names you want to delete. To select consecutive names, click the first one you want to delete, hold down Shift, and then click the last one you want to delete. To select non-consecutive names, hold down Ctrl, and then click each name you want to delete. When you have selected the names you want to remove, click **Delete**, and then click **OK** when Excel asks you to confirm the deletion. Click **Close** to return to the worksheet.

Paste a List of Range Names

To make your workbook easier to use, particularly for other people who are not familiar with the names you have defined, you can paste a list of the workbook's range names to a worksheet. This is also useful for a workbook you have not used in a while. Examining the list of range names can help you familiarize yourself once again with the workbook's contents.

The pasted list contains two columns: One for the range names and one for the range coordinates associated with each name.

Paste a List of Range Names

1. Open the workbook that contains the range names you want to paste.

2. Select the cell where you want the pasted list to appear.

Note: Excel will overwrite existing data, so select a location where there is no existing cell data or where it is okay to delete the existing cell data.

3. Click the **Formulas** tab.

4. Click **Use in Formula**.

5. Click **Paste Names**.

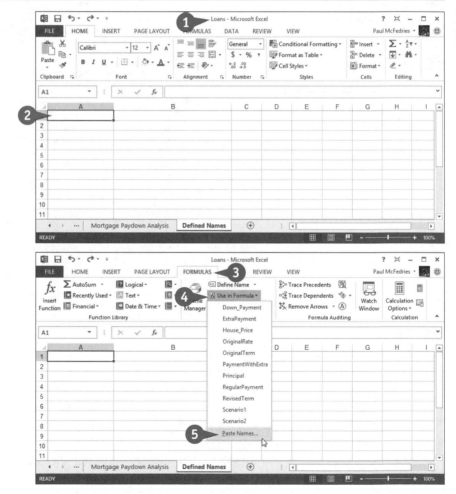

The Paste Name dialog box appears.

6 Click **Paste List**.

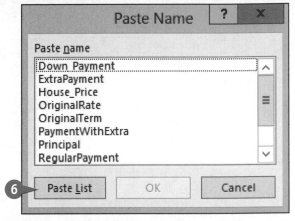

Excel closes the Paste Name dialog box.

A Excel pastes the list of range names to the worksheet.

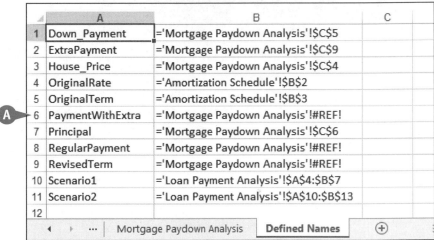

TIP

Is there a faster method I can use to paste a list of range names?
Yes — Excel offers a handy keyboard shortcut you can use. Open the workbook that contains the range names you want to paste, and then select the cell where you want the pasted list to appear. Press F3 to open the Paste Name dialog box, and then click **Paste List**.

CHAPTER 5

Formatting Excel Ranges

Microsoft Excel 2013 offers many commands and options for formatting ranges, including the font, text color, text alignment, background color, number format, column width, row height, and more.

Change the Font or Font Size

When you work in an Excel worksheet, you can add visual appeal to a cell or range by changing the font. In this section and throughout this book, the term *font* is synonymous with *typeface*, and both terms refer to the overall look of each character.

You can also make labels and other text stand out from the rest of the worksheet by changing the font size. The font size is measured in *points*, where there are roughly 72 points in an inch.

Change the Font or Font Size

Change the Font

1 Select the range you want to format.

2 Click the **Home** tab.

3 Click the drop-down arrow (⌄) in the **Font** list.

Ⓐ When you use the mouse pointer (⇡) to point to a typeface, Excel temporarily changes the selected text to that typeface.

4 Click the typeface you want to apply.

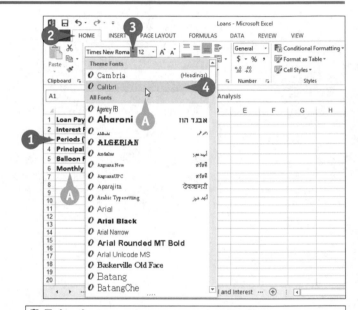

Ⓑ Excel applies the font to the text in the selected range.

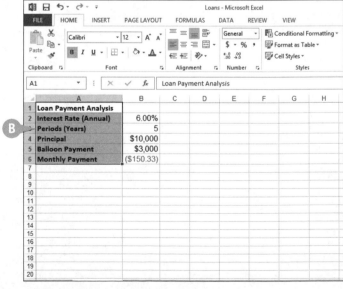

Change the Font Size

① Select the range you want to format.

② Click the **Home** tab.

③ Click the drop-down arrow (⌄) in the **Font Size** list.

Ⓒ When you use the mouse pointer (⇗) to point to a font size, Excel temporarily changes the selected text to that size.

④ Click the size you want to apply.

Ⓓ You can also type the size you want in the Size text box.

Ⓔ Excel applies the font size to the text in the selected range.

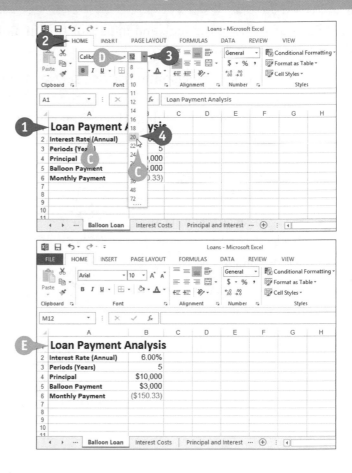

TIPS

In the Theme Fonts section of the Font list, what do the designations Body and Headings mean?
When you create a workbook, Excel automatically applies a document theme to the workbook, and that theme includes predefined fonts. The theme's default font is referred to as Body, and it is the font used for regular worksheet text. Each theme also defines a Headings font, which Excel uses for cells formatted with a heading or title style.

Can I change the default font and font size?
Yes. Click the **File** tab and then click **Options** to open the Excel Options dialog box. Click the **General** tab, click the **Use this as the default font** drop-down arrow (⌄), and then click the typeface you want to use as the default. Click the **Font size** drop-down arrow (⌄), and then click the size you prefer to use as the default. Click **OK**.

Apply Font Effects

You can improve the look and impact of text in an Excel worksheet by applying font effects to a cell or to a range.

Font effects include common formatting such as **bold**, which is often used to make labels stand out from regular text; *italic*, which is often used to add emphasis to text; and underline, which is often used for worksheet titles and headings. You can also apply special effects such as ~~strikethrough~~, superscripts (for example, x^2+y^2), and subscripts (for example, H_2O).

Apply Font Effects

1 Select the range you want to format.

2 Click the **Home** tab.

3 To format the text as bold, click the **Bold** button (**B**).

A Excel applies the bold effect to the selected range.

4 To format the text as italic, click the **Italic** button (*I*).

5 To format the text as underline, click the **Underline** button (**U**).

B Excel applies the effects to the selected range.

6 Click the **Font** dialog box launcher (⌐).

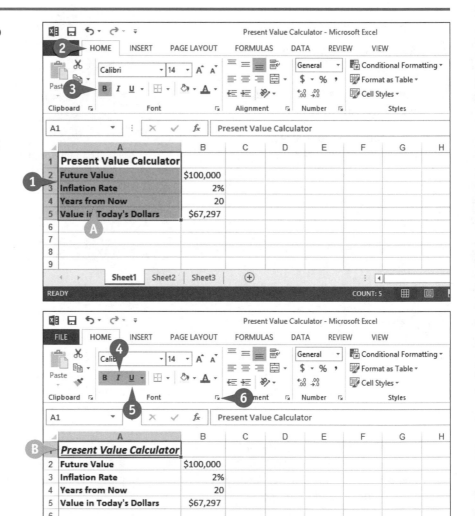

The Format Cells dialog box appears with the Font tab displayed.

7 To format the text as strikethrough, click the empty **Strikethrough** check box (□), and it is filled (☑).

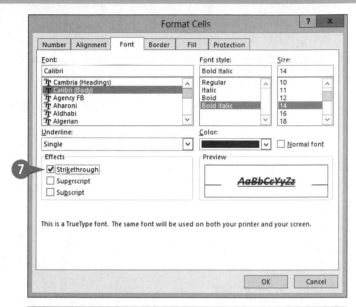

8 To format the text as a superscript, click the empty **Superscript** check box (□), and it is filled (☑).

C To format the text as a subscript, click the empty **Subscript** check box (□), and it is filled (☑).

9 Click **OK**.

Excel applies the font effects.

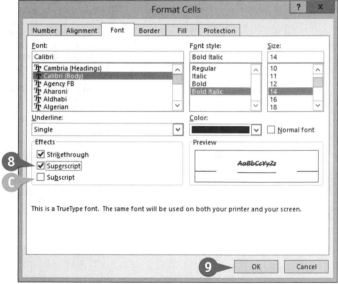

Are there any font-related keyboard shortcuts I can use?
Yes. Excel supports the following font shortcuts:

Press	To
Ctrl + B	Toggle the selected range as bold
Ctrl + I	Toggle the selected range as italic
Ctrl + U	Toggle the selected range as underline

Press	To
Ctrl + 5	Toggle the selected range as strikethrough
Ctrl + 1	Display the Format Cells dialog box

Change the Font Color

When you work in an Excel worksheet, you can add visual interest by changing the font color. Most worksheets are meant to convey specific information, but that does not mean the sheet has to be plain. By adding a bit of color to your text, you make your worksheets more appealing. Color can also make a worksheet easier to read by differentiating titles, headings, and labels from regular text.

You can change the font color by applying a color from the workbook's theme, from the Excel palette of standard colors, or from a custom color that you create.

Change the Font Color

Select a Theme or Standard Color

1 Select the range you want to format.

2 Click the **Home** tab.

3 Click the drop-down arrow (⌄) in the **Font Color** list (▲).

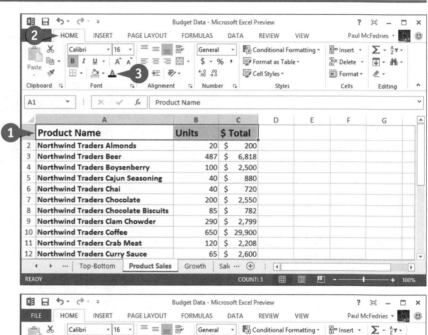

4 Click a theme color.

Ⓐ Alternatively, click one of the Excel standard colors.

Ⓑ Excel applies the color to the selected range.

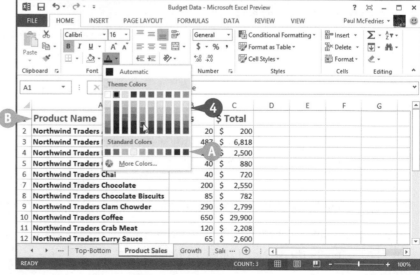

Select a Custom Color

1 Select the range you want to format.

2 Click the **Home** tab.

3 Click the drop-down arrow (☐) in the **Font Color** list (▲).

4 Click **More Colors**.

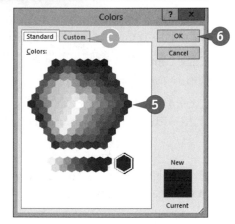

The Colors dialog box appears.

5 Click the color you want to use.

ⓒ You can also click the **Custom** tab, and then either click the color you want or type the values for the Red, Green, and Blue components of the color.

6 Click **OK**.

Excel applies the color to the selected range.

TIP

How can I make the best use of fonts in my documents?

- Do not use many different typefaces in a single document. Stick to one, or at most two, typefaces to avoid the ransom note look.
- Avoid overly decorative typefaces because they are often difficult to read.
- Use bold only for document titles, subtitles, and headings.
- Use italics only to emphasize words and phrases, or for the titles of books and magazines.
- Use larger type sizes only for document titles, subtitles, and, possibly, the headings.
- If you change the text color, be sure to leave enough contrast between the text and the background. In general, dark text on a light background is the easiest to read.

Align Text Within a Cell

You can make your worksheets easier to read by aligning text and numbers within each cell. By default, Excel aligns numbers with the right side of the cell, and it aligns text with the left side of the cell. You can also align numbers or text with the center of each cell.

Excel also allows you to align your data vertically within each cell. By default, Excel aligns all data with the bottom of each cell, but you can also align text with the top or middle.

Align Text Within a Cell

Align Text Horizontally

1 Select the range you want to format.

2 Click the **Home** tab.

3 In the Alignment group, click the horizontal alignment option you want to use:

Click **Align Text Left** (≡) to align data with the left side of each cell.

Click **Center** (≡) to align data with the center of each cell.

Click **Align Text Right** (≡) to align data with the right side of each cell.

Excel aligns the data horizontally within each selected cell.

Ⓐ In this example, the data in the cells is centered.

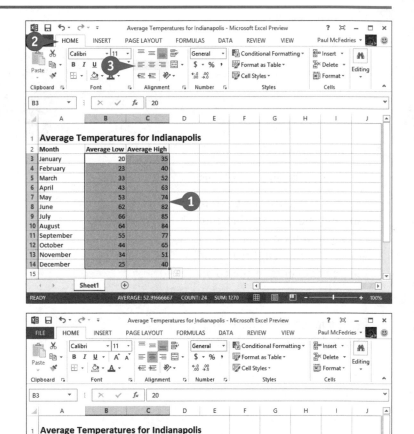

Align Text Vertically

1. Select the range you want to format.

2. Click the **Home** tab.

3. In the Alignment group, click the vertical alignment option you want to use:

   Click **Top Align** (≡) to align data with the top of each cell.

   Click **Middle Align** (≡) to align data with the middle of each cell.

   Click **Bottom Align** (≡) to align data with the bottom of each cell.

   Excel aligns the data vertically within each selected cell.

B. In this example, the text is aligned with the middle of the cell.

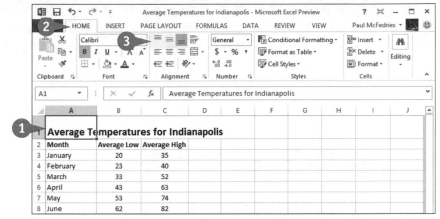

TIPS

How do I align text with both the left and right sides of the cell?

This is called *justified* text. It is useful if you have a lot of text in one or more cells. Select the range, click the **Home** tab, and then click the dialog box launcher (⌷) in the Alignment group. The Format Cells dialog box appears with the Alignment tab displayed. In the **Horizontal** list, click the drop-down arrow (⌄), and then click **Justify**. Click **OK**.

How do I indent cell text?

Select the range you want to indent, click the **Home** tab, and then click the Alignment group's dialog box launcher (⌷). In the Alignment tab, click the **Horizontal** list drop-down arrow (⌄), and then click **Left (Indent)**. Use the **Indent** text box to type the indent (in characters), and then click **OK**. You can also click the **Increase** (⇥) or **Decrease** (⇤) **Indent** buttons in the Home tab's Alignment group.

Center Text Across Multiple Columns

You can make a worksheet more visually appealing and easier to read by centering text across multiple columns. This feature is most useful when you have text in a cell that you use as a label or title for a range. Centering the text across the range makes it easier to see that the label or title applies to the entire range.

Center Text Across Multiple Columns

1 Select a range that consists of the text with which you want to work and the cells across which you want to center the text.

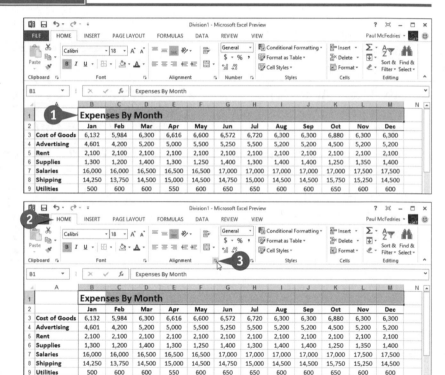

2 Click the **Home** tab.

3 In the **Alignment** group, click the dialog box launcher (⌐).

Excel opens the Format Cells dialog box with the Alignment tab displayed.

④ Click the **Horizontal** drop-down arrow (⌄), and then click **Center Across Selection**.

⑤ Click **OK**.

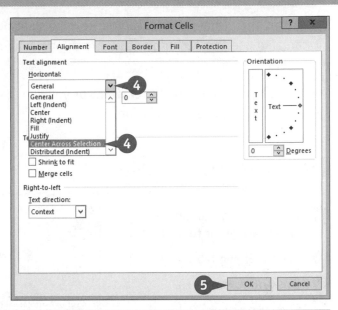

Ⓐ Excel centers the text across the selected cells.

	A	B	C	D	E	F	G	H	I	J	K	L	M
1						Expenses By Month							
2		Jan	Feb	Mar	Apr	May	Jun	Jul	Aug	Sep	Oct	Nov	Dec
3	Cost of Goods	6,132	5,984	6,300	6,616	6,600	6,572	6,720	6,300	6,300	6,880	6,300	6,300
4	Advertising	4,601	4,200	5,200	5,000	5,500	5,250	5,500	5,200	5,200	4,500	5,200	5,200
5	Rent	2,100	2,100	2,100	2,100	2,100	2,100	2,100	2,100	2,100	2,100	2,100	2,100
6	Supplies	1,300	1,200	1,400	1,300	1,250	1,400	1,300	1,400	1,400	1,250	1,350	1,400
7	Salaries	16,000	16,000	16,500	16,500	16,500	17,000	17,000	17,000	17,000	17,000	17,500	17,500
8	Shipping	14,250	13,750	14,500	15,000	14,500	14,750	15,000	14,500	14,500	15,750	15,250	14,500
9	Utilities	500	600	600	550	600	650	650	600	600	650	600	600

TIP

Is there an easier way to center text across multiple columns?
Yes, although this technique also merges the selected cells into a single cell. (See Chapter 3 to learn more about merging cells.) Follow these steps:

① Repeat Steps 1 and 2.

② In the Alignment group, click the **Merge & Center** button (▤).

Excel merges the selected cells into a single cell and centers the text within that cell.

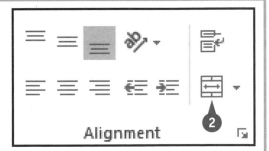

Alignment

Rotate Text Within a Cell

You can add visual interest to your text by slanting the text upward or downward in the cell. You can also use this technique to make a long column heading take up less horizontal space on the worksheet.

You can choose a predefined rotation, or you can make cell text angle upward or downward by specifying the degrees of rotation.

Rotate Text Within a Cell

1 Select the range containing the text you want to angle.

2 Click the **Home** tab.

3 Click **Orientation** (⤜).

Ⓐ If you want to use a predefined orientation, click one of the menu items, and skip the rest of the steps.

4 Click **Format Cell Alignment**.

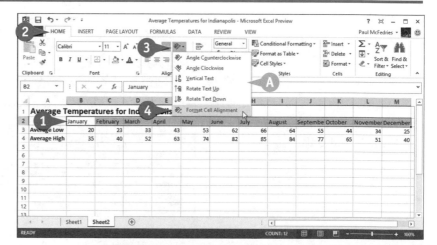

The Format Cells dialog box appears with the Alignment tab displayed.

5 Click an orientation marker.

Ⓑ You can also use the Degrees spin box to type or click a degree of rotation. (See the Tip at the end of this section.)

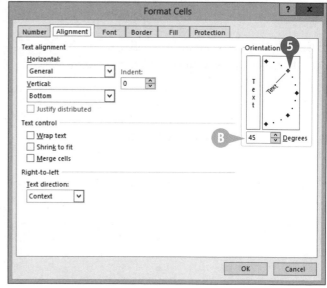

C You can click the vertical text area to display your text vertically instead of horizontally in the cell.

6 Click **OK**.

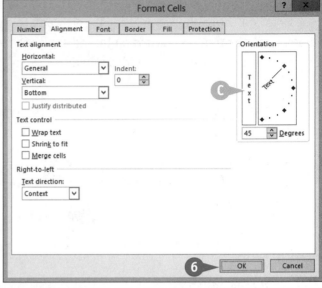

D Excel rotates the cell text.

E The row height automatically increases to contain the slanted text.

F You can reduce the column width to free up space and make your cells more presentable.

TIP

How does the Degrees spin box work?

If you use the Degrees spin box to set the text orientation, you can set the orientation to a positive number, such as 25, and Excel angles the text in an upward direction. If you set the text orientation to a negative number, such as –40, Excel angles the text in a downward direction.

You can specify values in the range from 90 degrees (which is the same as clicking the Rotate Text Up command in the Orientation menu) to –90 degrees (which is the same as clicking the Rotate Text Down command).

Add a Background Color to a Range

You can make a range stand out from the rest of the worksheet by applying a background color to the range. Note, however, that if you want to apply a background color to a range based on the values in that range — for example, red for negative values and green for positive — it is easier to apply a conditional format, as described in the section "Apply a Conditional Format to a Range" later in this chapter.

You can change the background color by applying a color from the workbook's theme, from the Excel palette of standard colors, or from a custom color that you create.

Add a Background Color to a Range

Select a Theme or Standard Color

1. Select the range you want to format.

2. Click the **Home** tab.

3. Click the drop-down arrow (⌄) in the **Fill Color** list (🎨).

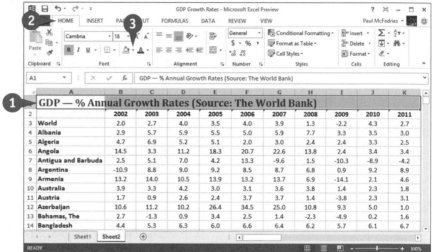

4. Click a theme color.

Ⓐ Alternatively, click one of the standard Excel colors.

Ⓑ Excel applies the color to the selected range.

Ⓒ To remove the background color from the range, click **No Fill**.

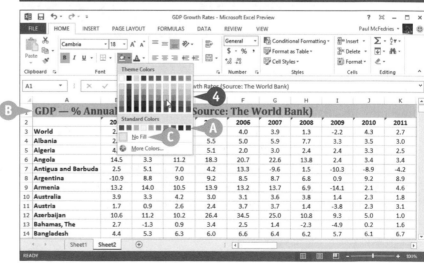

Select a Custom Color

1. Select the range you want to format.

2. Click the **Home** tab.

3. Click the drop-down arrow (⌄) in the **Fill Color** list (🅰).

4. Click **More Colors**.

   The Colors dialog box appears.

5. Click the color you want to use.

   Ⓓ You can also click the **Custom** tab, and then either click the color you want or type the values for the Red, Green, and Blue components of the color.

6. Click **OK**.

   Excel applies the color to the selected range.

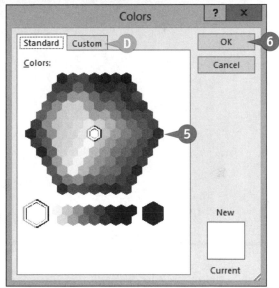

TIPS

Are there pitfalls to watch out for when applying background colors?

Yes. The biggest pitfall is applying a color that clashes with the range text. For example, if the default text is black and you apply a dark background color, the text will be very difficult to read. Always use either a light background color with dark-colored text, or vice versa.

Can I apply a background that fades from one color to another?

Yes. This is called a *gradient* effect. Select the range, click the **Home** tab, and then click the Font group's dialog box launcher (⌐). Click the **Fill** tab, and then click **Fill Effects**. In the Fill Effects dialog box, use the **Color 1** and **Color 2** drop-down arrows (⌄) to choose your colors. Click an option in the **Shading styles** section; the empty radio button (○) changes to a full radio button (⦿). Click **OK**.

Apply a Number Format

You can make your worksheet easier to read by applying a number format to your data. For example, if your worksheet includes monetary data, you can apply the Currency format to display each value with a dollar sign and two decimal places.

Excel offers 10 number formats, most of which apply to numeric data. However, you can also apply the Date format to date data, the Time format to time data, and the Text format to text data.

Apply a Number Format

1. Select the range you want to format.

2. Click the **Home** tab.

3. Click the **Number Format** drop-down arrow ([⌄]).

4. Click the number format you want to use.

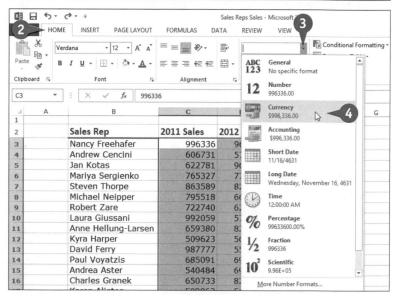

Ⓐ Excel applies the number format to the selected range.

Ⓑ For monetary values, you can click **Accounting Number Format** ($).

Ⓒ For percentages, you can click **Percent Style** (%).

Ⓓ For large numbers, you can click **Comma Style** (').

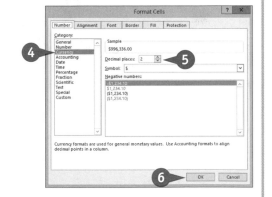

	A	B	C	D	E	F	G
1							
2		Sales Rep	2011 Sales	2012 Sales			
3		Nancy Freehafer	$996,336.00	$960,492.00			
4		Andrew Cencini	$606,731.00	$577,983.00			
5		Jan Kotas	$622,781.00	$967,580.00			
6		Mariya Sergienko	$765,327.00	$771,399.00			
7		Steven Thorpe	$863,589.00	$827,213.00			
8		Michael Neipper	$795,518.00	$669,394.00			
9		Robert Zare	$722,740.00	$626,945.00			
10		Laura Giussani	$992,059.00	$574,472.00			
11		Anne Hellung-Larsen	$659,380.00	$827,932.00			
12		Kyra Harper	$509,623.00	$569,609.00			
13		David Ferry	$987,777.00	$558,601.00			
14		Paul Voyatzis	$685,091.00	$692,182.00			
15		Andrea Aster	$540,484.00	$693,762.00			
16		Charles Granek	$650,733.00	$823,034.00			
17		Karen Aliston	$509,863.00	$511,569.00			
18		Karen Hammond	$503,699.00	$975,455.00			
19		Vince Durbin	$630,263.00	$599,514.00			
20		Paul Sellars	$779,722.00	$596,353.00			
21		Gregg O'Donoghue	$592,802.00	$652,171.00			

TIP

Can I have more control over the number formats?
Yes. Follow these steps to use the Format Cells dialog box:

1 Select the range you want to format.

2 Click the **Home** tab.

3 Click the **Number** group's dialog box launcher (⌟).

The Format Cells dialog box appears with the Number tab displayed.

4 In the **Category** list, click the format you want.

5 Use the displayed controls (these vary depending on what you chose in Step 4) to customize the number format.

6 Click **OK** and the format is applied.

Change the Number of Decimal Places Displayed

You can make your numeric values easier to read and interpret by adjusting the number of decimal places that Excel displays. For example, you might want to ensure that all dollar-and-cent values show two decimal places, while dollar-only values show no decimal places. Similarly, you can adjust the display of percentage values to suit your audience by showing more decimals (greater accuracy but more difficult to read) or fewer decimals (less accuracy but easier to read).

You can either decrease or increase the number of decimal places that Excel displays.

Change the Number of Decimal Places Displayed

Decrease the Number of Decimal Places

1. Select the range you want to format.

2. Click the **Home** tab.

3. Click the **Decrease Decimal** button ($\overset{.00}{\to .0}$).

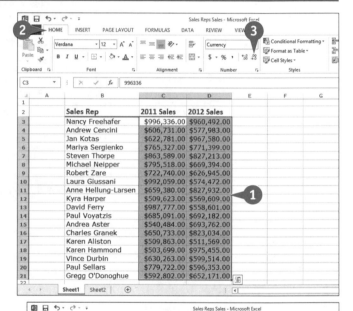

Ⓐ Excel decreases the number of decimal places by one.

4. Repeat Step 3 until you get the number of decimal places you want.

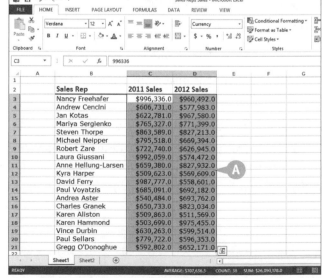

Increase the Number of Decimal Places

1. Select the range you want to format.

2. Click the **Home** tab.

3. Click the **Increase Decimal** button ($\begin{smallmatrix}\leftarrow 0 \\ .00\end{smallmatrix}$).

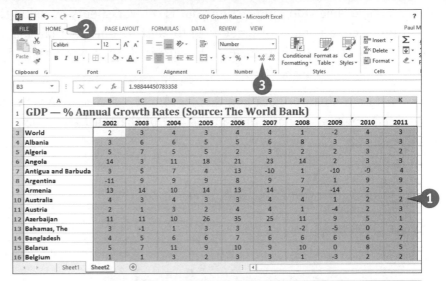

B. Excel increases the number of decimal places by one.

4. Repeat Step 3 until you get the number of decimal places you want.

TIP

My range contains values with different decimal places. What happens when I change the number of decimal places?

In this situation, Excel uses the value that has the most displayed decimal places as the basis for formatting all the values. For example, if the selected range has values that display no, one, two, or four decimal places, Excel uses the value with four decimals as the basis. If you click **Decrease Decimal** ($\begin{smallmatrix}.0 \\ \rightarrow .0\end{smallmatrix}$), Excel displays every value with three decimal places; if you click **Increase Decimal** ($\begin{smallmatrix}\leftarrow 0 \\ .00\end{smallmatrix}$), Excel displays every value with five decimal places.

Apply an AutoFormat to a Range

You can save time when formatting your Excel worksheets by using the AutoFormat feature. This feature offers a number of predefined formatting options that you can apply to a range all at once. The formatting options include the number format, font, cell alignment, borders, patterns, row height, and column width.

AutoFormats are ideal for data in a tabular format, particularly when you have headings in the top row and left column, numeric data in the rest of the cells, and a bottom row that shows the totals for each column.

Apply an AutoFormat to a Range

1 Select the range you want to format.

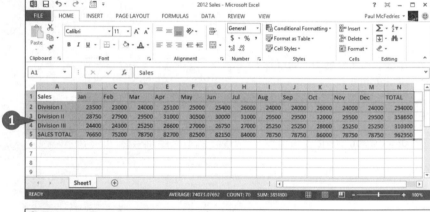

2 Click **AutoFormat** (⬚).

Note: See Chapter 1 to learn how to add a button to the Quick Access Toolbar. In this case, you must add the QuickFormat button.

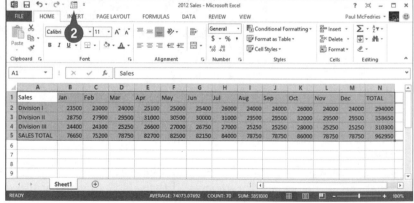

The AutoFormat dialog box appears.

③ Click the AutoFormat you want to use.

④ Click **OK**.

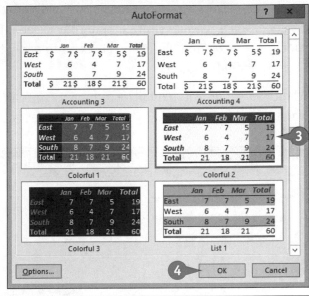

Ⓐ Excel applies the AutoFormat to the selected range.

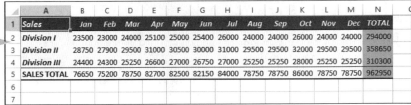

TIPS

Can I apply an AutoFormat without using some of its formatting?

Yes. You can control all six formats that are part of each AutoFormat: Number, Font, Alignment, Border, Patterns, and Width/Height. Follow Steps **1** to **3** to choose the AutoFormat you want. Click **Options** to expand the dialog box and display the Formats. Click the filled check boxes (☑) for each option you do not want to apply and the check boxes are cleared (☐). Click **OK**.

How do I remove an AutoFormat?

If you do not like (or need) the AutoFormat you applied to the cells, you can revert them to a plain, unformatted state. Select the range, and then click **AutoFormat** (🖼) to display the AutoFormat dialog box. At the bottom of the format list, click **None**, and then click **OK**. Excel removes the AutoFormat from the selected range.

Apply a Conditional Format to a Range

You can make a worksheet easier to analyze by applying a conditional format to a range. A *conditional format* is formatting that Excel applies only to cells that meet the condition you specify. For example, you can tell Excel to apply the formatting only if a cell's value is greater than some specified amount.

When you set up your conditional format, you can specify the font, border, and background pattern, which helps to ensure that the cells that meet your criteria stand out from the other cells in the range.

Apply a Conditional Format to a Range

1 Select the range with which you want to work.

2 Click the **Home** tab.

3 Click **Conditional Formatting**.

4 Click **Highlight Cells Rules**.

5 Click the operator you want to use for your condition.

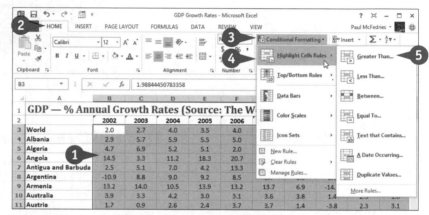

An operator dialog box appears, such as the Greater Than dialog box shown here.

6 Type the value you want to use for your condition.

Ⓐ You can also click the **Collapse Dialog** button (🔳), and then click a worksheet cell.

Depending on the operator, you may need to specify two values.

7 Click the **with** drop-down arrow (🔽), and then click the formatting you want to use.

Ⓑ To create your own format, click **Custom Format**.

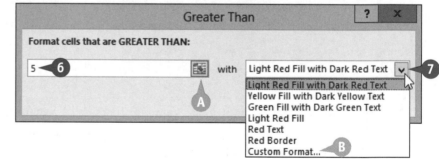

8 Click **OK**.

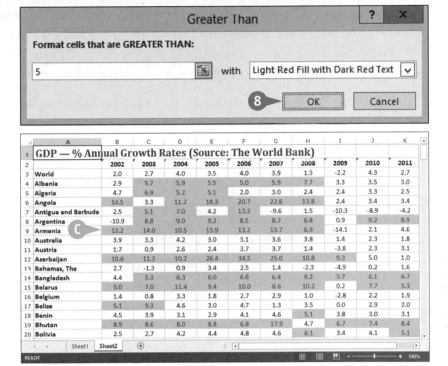

Greater Than

Format cells that are GREATER THAN:

5 with Light Red Fill with Dark Red Text

8 ⟶ OK   Cancel

C Excel applies the formatting to cells that meet your condition.

	A	B	C	D	E	F	G	H	I	J	K
1	GDP — % Annual Growth Rates (Source: The World Bank)										
2		2002	2003	2004	2005	2006	2007	2008	2009	2010	2011
3	World	2.0	2.7	4.0	3.5	4.0	3.9	1.3	-2.2	4.3	2.7
4	Albania	2.9	5.7	5.9	5.5	5.0	5.9	7.7	3.3	3.5	3.0
5	Algeria	4.7	6.9	5.2	5.1	2.0	3.0	2.4	2.4	3.3	2.5
6	Angola	14.5	3.3	11.2	18.3	20.7	22.6	13.8	2.4	3.4	3.4
7	Antigua and Barbuda	2.5	5.1	7.0	4.2	13.3	-9.6	1.5	-10.3	-8.9	-4.2
8	Argentina	-10.9	8.8	9.0	9.2	8.5	8.7	6.8	0.9	9.2	8.9
9	Armenia	13.2	14.0	10.5	13.9	13.2	13.7	6.9	-14.1	2.1	4.6
10	Australia	3.9	3.3	4.2	3.0	3.1	3.6	3.8	1.4	2.3	1.8
11	Austria	1.7	0.9	2.6	2.4	3.7	3.7	1.4	-3.8	2.3	3.1
12	Azerbaijan	10.6	11.2	10.2	26.4	34.5	25.0	10.8	9.3	5.0	1.0
13	Bahamas, The	2.7	-1.3	0.9	3.4	2.5	1.4	-2.3	-4.9	0.2	1.6
14	Bangladesh	4.4	5.3	6.3	6.0	6.6	6.4	6.2	5.7	6.1	6.7
15	Belarus	5.0	7.0	11.4	9.4	10.0	8.6	10.2	0.2	7.7	5.3
16	Belgium	1.4	0.8	3.3	1.8	2.7	2.9	1.0	-2.8	2.2	1.9
17	Belize	5.1	9.3	4.6	3.0	4.7	1.3	3.5	0.0	2.9	2.0
18	Benin	4.5	3.9	3.1	2.9	4.1	4.6	5.1	3.8	3.0	3.1
19	Bhutan	8.9	8.6	8.0	8.8	6.8	17.9	4.7	6.7	7.4	8.4
20	Bolivia	2.5	2.7	4.2	4.4	4.8	4.6	6.1	3.4	4.1	5.1

Sheet1 Sheet2 ⊕

READY

TIPS

Can I set up more than one condition for a single range?

Yes. Excel enables you to specify multiple conditional formats. For example, you could set up one condition for cells that are greater than one value, and a separate condition for cells that are less than another. You can apply unique formats to each condition. Follow Steps 1 to 8 to configure the new condition.

How do I remove a conditional format from a range?

You can delete it. Follow Steps 1 to 3 to select the range and display the Conditional Formatting menu, and then click **Manage Rules**. Excel displays the Conditional Formatting Rules Manager dialog box. Click the **Show formatting rules for** drop-down arrow (⌄), and then click **This Worksheet**. Click the conditional format you want to remove, and then click **Delete Rule**. Click **OK** to return to the worksheet.

Apply a Style to a Range

You can reduce the time it takes to format your worksheets by applying the predefined Excel styles to your ranges. Excel comes with more than 20 predefined styles for different worksheet elements such as headings, numbers, calculations, and special range types such as explanatory text, worksheet notes, and warnings. Excel also offers two dozen styles associated with the current document theme.

Each style includes the number format, cell alignment, font typeface and size, border, and fill color.

Apply a Style to a Range

1 Select the range you want to format.

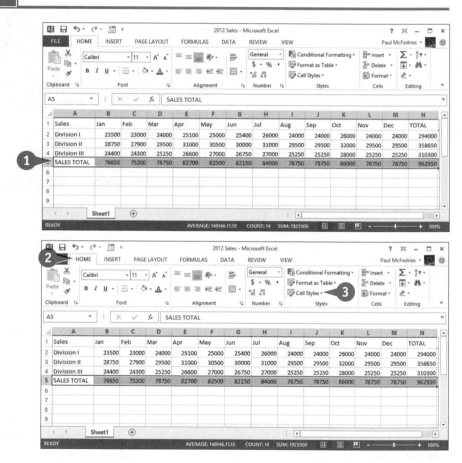

2 Click the **Home** tab.

3 Click **Cell Styles**.

Excel displays the Cell Styles gallery.

④ Click the style you want to apply.

Note: If the style is not exactly the way you want, you can right-click the style, click **Modify**, and then click **Format** to customize the style.

Ⓐ Excel applies the style to the range.

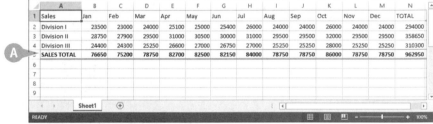

TIPS

Are there styles I can use to format tabular data?

Yes. Excel comes with a gallery of table styles that offer formatting options that highlight the first row, apply different formats to alternating rows, and so on. Select the range that includes your data, click the **Home** tab, and then click **Format as Table**. In the gallery that appears, click the table format you want to apply.

Can I create my own style?

Yes. This is useful if you find yourself applying the same set of formatting options repeatedly. Follow Steps 1 to 4, apply your formatting to a cell or range, and then select that cell or range. Click **Home**, click **Cell Styles**, and then click **New Cell Style**. In the Style dialog box, type a name for your style, and then click **OK**.

Change the Column Width

You can make your worksheets neater and more readable by adjusting the column widths to suit the data contained in each column.

For example, if you have a large number or a long line of text in a cell, Excel may display only part of the cell value. To avoid this, you can increase the width of the column. Similarly, if a column only contains a few characters in each cell, you can decrease the width to fit more columns on the screen.

Change the Column Width

1 Click in any cell in the column you want to resize.

2 Click the **Home** tab.

3 Click **Format**.

4 Click **Column Width**.

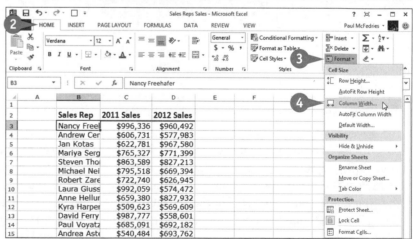

The Column Width dialog box appears.

5 In the Column width text box, type the width you want to use.

6 Click **OK**.

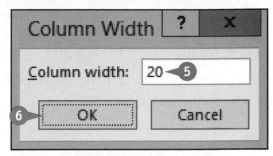

A Excel adjusts the column width.

B You can also move the mouse pointer (⊕) over the right edge of the column heading. The mouse pointer (⊕) changes to column resize (↔). Click and drag the edge to set the width.

	A	B	C	D	E
1					
2		Sales Rep	2011 Sales	2012 Sales	
3		Nancy Freehafer	$996,336	$960,492	
4		Andrew Cencini	$606,731	$577,983	
5		Jan Kotas	$622,781	$967,580	
6		Mariya Sergienko	$765,327	$771,399	
7		Steven Thorpe	$863,589	$827,213	
8		Michael Neipper	$795,518	$669,394	
9		Robert Zare	$722,740	$626,945	
10		Laura Giussani	$992,059	$574,472	
11		Anne Hellung-Larsen	$659,380	$827,932	
12		Kyra Harper	$509,623	$569,609	
13		David Ferry	$987,777	$558,601	
14		Paul Voyatzis	$685,091	$692,182	
15		Andrea Aster	$540,484	$693,762	
16		Charles Granek	$650,733	$823,034	
17		Karen Aliston	$509,863	$511,569	
18		Karen Hammond	$503,699	$975,455	
19		Vince Durbin	$630,263	$599,514	
20		Paul Sellars	$779,722	$596,353	
21		Gregg O'Donoghue	$592,802	$652,171	

Sheet1 Sheet2 ⊕

TIPS

Is there an easier way to adjust the column width to fit the contents of a column?

Yes. You can use the Excel AutoFit feature, which automatically adjusts the column width to fit the widest item in a column. Click any cell in the column, click **Home**, click **Format**, and then click **AutoFit Column Width**. Alternatively, move the mouse pointer (⊕) over the right edge of the column heading. After the mouse pointer (⊕) changes to column resize (↔), double-click.

Is there a way to change all of the column widths at once?

Yes. Click Select All (◢) to select the entire worksheet, and then follow the steps in this section to set the width you prefer.

Change the Row Height

You can make your worksheet more visually appealing by increasing the row heights to create more space. This is particularly useful in worksheets that are crowded with text. Changing the row height is also useful if the current height is too small and cuts off the cell text at the bottom.

If you want to change the row height to display multiline text within a cell, you must also turn on text wrapping within the cell. See the section "Wrap Text Within a Cell."

Change the Row Height

1 Select a range that includes at least one cell in every row you want to resize.

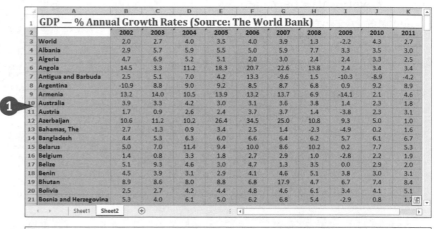

2 Click the **Home** tab.

3 Click **Format**.

4 Click **Row Height**.

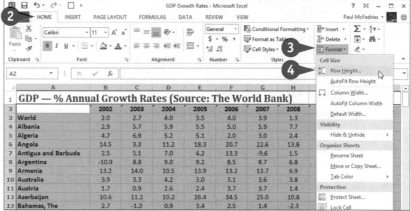

The Row Height dialog box appears.

5 In the Row Height text box, type the height you want to use.

6 Click **OK**.

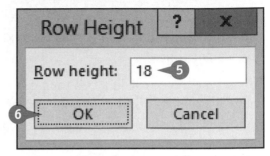

A Excel adjusts the row heights.

B You can also move the mouse pointer (⊕) over the bottom edge of a row heading. The mouse pointer (⊕) changes to row resize (✛). Click and drag the bottom edge to set the height.

A	B	C	D	E	F	G	H	I	J	K
1 GDP — % Annual Growth Rates (Source: The World Bank)										
2	2002	2003	2004	2005	2006	2007	2008	2009	2010	2011
3 World	2.0	2.7	4.0	3.5	4.0	3.9	1.3	-2.2	4.3	2.7
4 Albania	2.9	5.7	5.9	5.5	5.0	5.9	7.7	3.3	3.5	3.0
5 Algeria	4.7	6.9	5.2	5.1	2.0	3.0	2.4	2.4	3.3	2.5
6 Angola	14.5	3.3	11.2	18.3	20.7	22.6	13.8	2.4	3.4	3.4
7 Antigua and Barbuda	2.5	5.1	7.0	4.2	13.3	-9.6	1.5	-10.3	-8.9	-4.2
8 Argentina	-10.9	8.8	9.0	9.2	8.5	8.7	6.8	0.9	9.2	8.9
9 Armenia	13.2	14.0	10.5	13.9	13.2	13.7	6.9	-14.1	2.1	4.6
10 Australia	3.9	3.3	4.2	3.0	3.1	3.6	3.8	1.4	2.3	1.8
11 Austria	1.7	0.9	2.6	2.4	3.7	3.7	1.4	-3.8	2.3	3.1

TIPS

Is there an easier way to adjust the row height to fit the contents?
Yes. You can use the Excel AutoFit feature, which automatically adjusts the row height to fit the tallest item in a row. Click in any cell in the row, click **Home**, click **Format**, and then click **AutoFit Row Height**. Alternatively, move the mouse pointer (⊕) over the bottom edge of the row heading. After the mouse pointer (⊕) changes to row resize (✛), double-click.

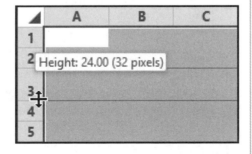

Is there a way to change all row heights at once?
Yes. Click Select All (◢) to select the entire worksheet. Then, either set the height manually (see the steps in this section), or move the mouse pointer (⊕) over the bottom edge of any row heading. The mouse pointer (⊕) changes to row resize (✛). Click and drag the edge to set the height of all rows.

Wrap Text Within a Cell

You can make a long text entry in a cell more readable by formatting the cell to wrap the text. *Wrapping* cell text means that the text is displayed on multiple lines within the cell instead of just a single line.

If you type more text in a cell than can fit horizontally, Excel either displays the text over the next cell if it is empty or displays only part of the text if the next cell contains data. To prevent Excel from showing only truncated cell data, you can format the cell to wrap text within the cell.

Wrap Text Within a Cell

1 Select the cell that you want to format.

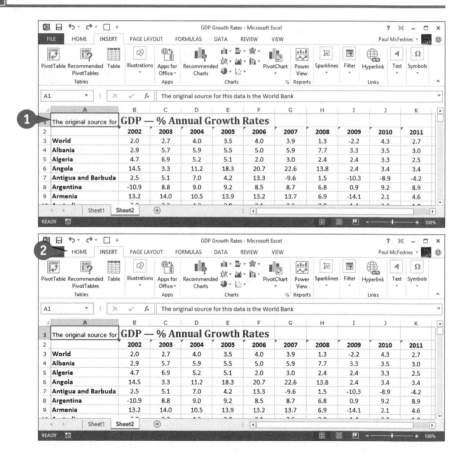

2 Click the **Home** tab.

3 Click **Wrap Text** ( ).

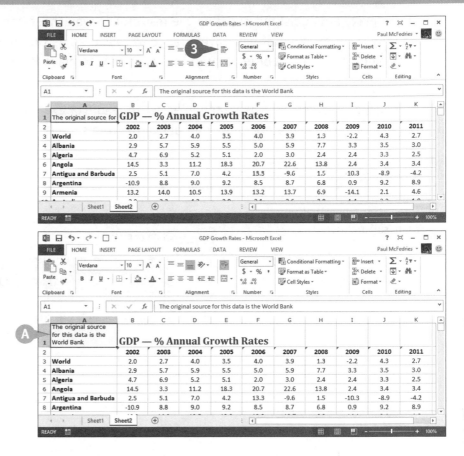

Excel turns on text wrapping for the selected cell.

A If the cell has more text than can fit horizontally, Excel wraps the text onto multiple lines and increases the row height to compensate.

TIP

My text is only slightly bigger than the cell. Can I view all of it without turning on text wrapping?

Yes, you can try several things. For example, you can widen the column until you see all your text; see the section "Change the Column Width" earlier in this chapter.

Alternatively, you can try reducing the cell font size. One way to do this is to choose a smaller value in the **Font Size** list of the Home tab's Font group. However, an easier way is to click the Alignment group's dialog box launcher ( ) to open the Format Cells dialog box with the Alignment tab displayed. Click the empty **Shrink to fit** check box ( ) and it is filled ( ). Click **OK**.

Add Borders to a Range

You can make a range stand out from the rest of your worksheet data by adding a border around the range. For example, if you have a range of cells used as the input values for one or more formulas, you could add a border around the input cells to make it clear that the cells in that range are related to each other.

You can also use borders to make a range easier to read. For example, if your range has totals on the bottom row, you can add a double border above the totals.

Add Borders to a Range

1 Select the range that you want to format.

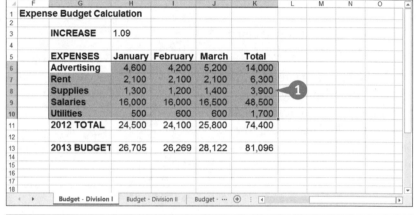

2 Click the **Home** tab.

3 Click the **Borders** drop-down arrow (🔽).

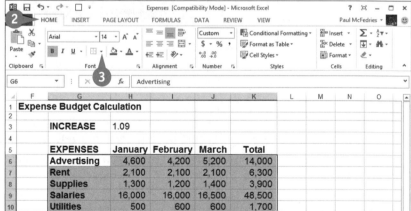

④ Click the type of border you want to use.

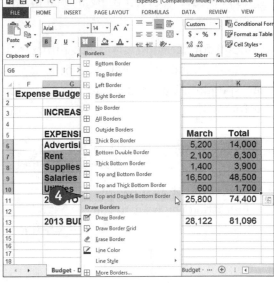

Ⓐ Excel applies the border to the range.

TIPS

How can I make borders stand out from the worksheet gridlines?

Click the **Borders drop-down arrow** (⌄), click **Line Style**, and then click a thicker border style. You can also click **Line Color,** and then click a color that is not a shade of gray, or you can turn off the gridlines. Click the **View** tab, and then in the Show group, click the selected **Gridlines** check box (☑), and it is cleared (☐).

Can I create a custom border?

Yes. Click the **Borders drop-down arrow** (⌄), and then click **Draw Border.** Use the **Line Style** and **Line Color** lists to configure your border. Click a cell edge to add a border to it. Click and drag a range to add a border around that range. To create a grid where the border surrounds every cell, click the **Draw Border Grid** command.

Copy Formatting from One Cell to Another

You can save yourself a great deal of time by copying existing formatting to other areas of a worksheet.

Although formatting cells is not difficult, it can be time-consuming to apply the font, color, alignment, number format, and other options. After you spend time formatting text or data, rather than spending time repeating the steps for other data, you can use the Format Painter tool to copy the formatting with a couple of mouse clicks.

Copy Formatting from One Cell to Another

① Select the cell that has the formatting you want to copy.

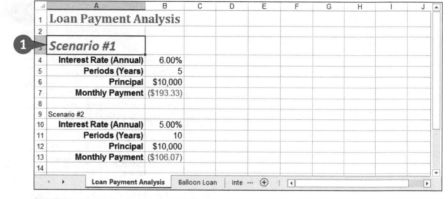

② Click the **Home** tab.

③ Click **Format Painter** (✸).

The mouse pointer (⊕) changes to the Format Painter (⊕▲).

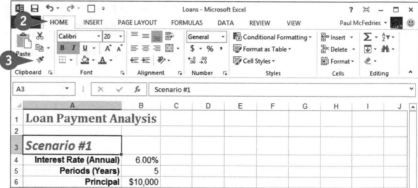

4 Click the cell to which you want to copy the formatting.

Note: If you want to apply the formatting to multiple cells, click and drag the Format Painter (⟟) over the cells.

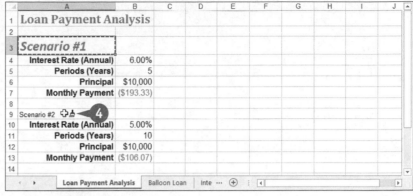

A Excel copies the formatting to the cell.

TIP

Is there an easy way to copy formatting to multiple cells or ranges?

Yes. If the cells are together, you can click and drag over the cells to apply the copied formatting. If the cells or ranges are not together, Excel offers a shortcut that means you do not have to select the Format Painter multiple times to copy formatting to multiple ranges.

Click the cell that contains the formatting you want to copy, click the **Home** tab, and then double-click **Format Painter** (✦). Click each cell to which you want to copy the formatting, or click and drag over each range that you want to format. When you are done, click **Format Painter** (✦) to cancel the Format Painter command.

CHAPTER 6

Maximizing Excel Customization

This chapter enables you to take control of Excel formatting through customization. You will learn how to build custom numeric formats; data and time formats; fill lists; cell styles; table styles; workbook colors, fonts, and themes; headers and footers; and more.

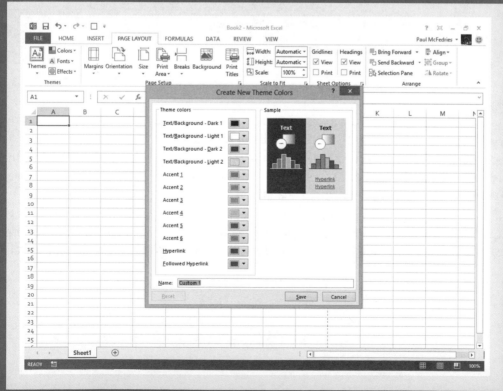

Create Custom Numeric Formats

You can create a custom cell format that displays information just how you want it. The formatting syntax and symbols are explained in the tip at the end of this section. Every Excel numeric format, whether built in or customized, has the following syntax:

positive;negative;zero;text

The four parts, separated by semicolons, determine how various numbers are presented. The first part defines how a positive number is displayed, the second part defines how a negative number is displayed, the third part defines how zero is displayed, and the fourth part defines how text is displayed.

Create Custom Numeric Formats

1. Select the range you want to format.

2. Click the **Home** tab.

3. In the **Number** group, click the dialog box launcher icon (⌐).

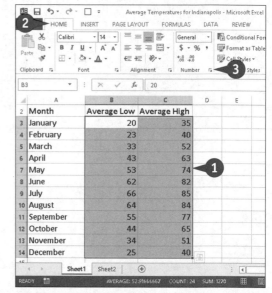

The Format Cells dialog box appears with the Number tab selected.

Ⓐ If you want to base your custom format on an existing format, click the category, and then click the format.

4. Click **Custom**.

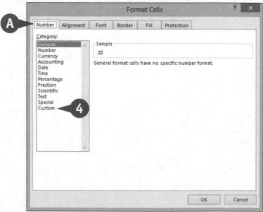

⑤ Type the symbols and text that define your custom format.

⑥ Click **OK**.

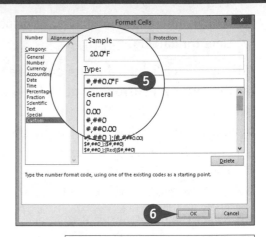

Ⓑ Excel applies the custom format.

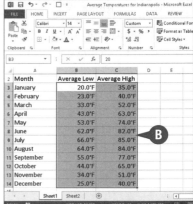

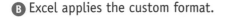

TIP

What symbols can I use to create custom numeric formats?

- **#.** Holds a place for a digit and displays the digit exactly as typed. If a number is not typed, Excel displays nothing.

- **0.** Holds a place for a digit and displays the digit exactly as typed. If a number is not typed, Excel displays 0.

- **?.** Holds a place for a digit and displays the digit exactly as typed. If a number is not typed, Excel displays a space.

- **. (period).** Sets the location of the decimal point.

- **, (comma).** Sets the location of the thousands separator. Excel marks only the location of the first thousand.

- **/ (forward slash).** Sets the location of the fraction separator.

- **%.** Multiplies the number by 100 (for display only) and adds the percent (%) character.

Create Custom Date and Time Formats

You can enhance your worksheet display of dates and times by creating your own custom date and time formatting.

Although Excel's built-in date and time formats are fine for most applications, you might need to create your own custom formats. For example, you might want to display just the day of the week (for example, Friday). To do this, you can create custom date and time formats. You can do so either by editing an existing format or by creating your own format. The formatting syntax and symbols are explained in the tip at the end of this section.

Create Custom Date and Time Formats

1 Select the range you want to format.

2 Click the **Home** tab.

3 In the **Number** group, click the dialog box launcher (⌐↓).

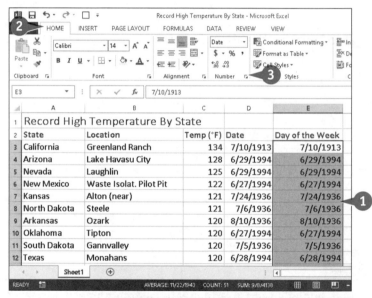

The Format Cells dialog box appears with the Number tab selected.

Ⓐ If you want to base your custom format on an existing format, click either the Date or Time category, and then click the format.

4 Click **Custom**.

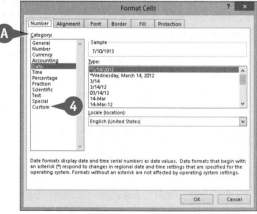

5 Type the symbols and text that define your custom format.

6 Click **OK**.

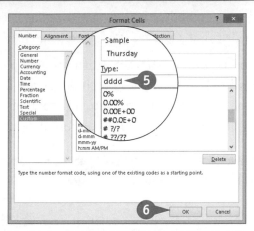

B Excel applies the custom format.

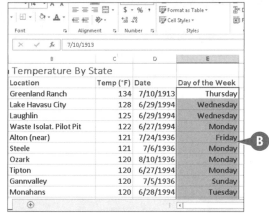

TIP

What symbols can I use to create custom date and time formats?

- **d.** Day number w/o zero (1-31).
- **dd.** Day number w/zero (01-31).
- **ddd.** Three-letter day abbreviation (Mon).
- **dddd.** Full day name (Monday).
- **m.** Month number w/o zero (1-12).
- **mm.** Month number w/zero (01-12).
- **mmm.** Three-letter month abbreviation (Aug).
- **mmmm.** Full month name (August).
- **yy.** Two-digit year (00-99).
- **yyyy.** Full year (1900-2078).

- **h.** Hour w/o zero (0-24).
- **hh.** Hour w/zero (00-24).
- **m.** Minute w/o zero (0-59).
- **mm.** Minute w/zero (00-59).
- **s.** Second w/o zero (0-59).
- **ss.** Second w/zero (00-59).
- **AM/PM, am/pm, A/P.** Time using a 12-hour clock.

Set the Default Width for All Columns

If you regularly widen or narrow your Excel columns, you can configure Excel with a new default width that matches your preferred size.

If you require a different width for a column, Excel gives you a couple of ways to proceed, as you learn in Chapter 5. These techniques are not time consuming for a column or two, but if you find yourself constantly inserting new columns and adjusting the width each time, then you should configure Excel to use your preferred column width as the default for the worksheet.

Set the Default Width for All Columns

1 Click the **Home** tab.

2 Click **Format**.

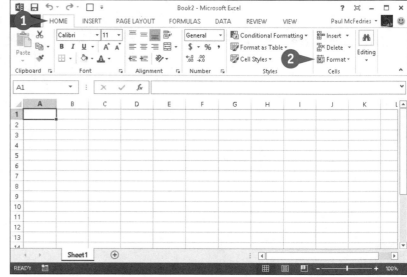

3 Click Default Width.

The Standard Width dialog box appears.

④ Type the column width you want to use.

⑤ Click **OK**.

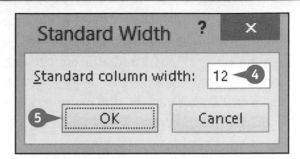

Ⓐ Excel formats all the columns with the new width.

Note: Each time you insert a new column in the current worksheet, Excel formats it with the new default width.

TIPS

Can I set the default width for an entire workbook or for Excel as a whole?

No. When you set the new default column width, Excel applies it to the current worksheet only. If you have other worksheets in the workbook, or if you add new worksheets, Excel does not use the new default column width in those other sheets. If you want to apply a default column width to multiple worksheets, hold down Ctrl and click the tab of each worksheet before following the steps in this section.

Can I return the default to its original value?

Yes. The original default column width in new Excel workbooks is 8.38 characters. To return to using this original value as the default column width, follow the steps in this section and, in Step 4, type **8.38**.

Create a Custom Fill List

As you learn in Chapter 3, you can type two values on a worksheet, select them, and then use the fill handle to create a series of values based on those two values. Using the fill handle to create a series is useful and efficient because it means you do not have to type all the series values manually. However, Excel can only create these automatic series from certain types of cell values: numbers, dates, times, or alphanumeric values that end with numbers. For other series that you use regularly, you can create a custom fill list.

Create a Custom Fill List

1 Click the **File** tab (not shown).

2 Click **Options**.

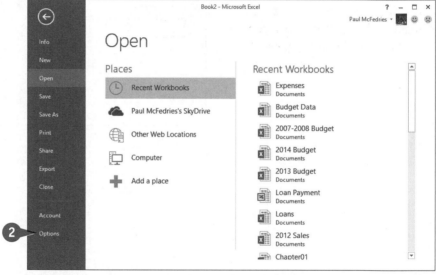

The Excel Options dialog box appears.

3 Click **Advanced**.

4 In the General section, click **Edit Custom Lists**.

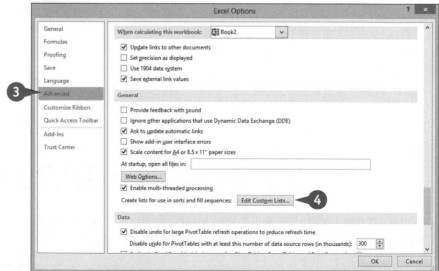

The Custom Lists dialog box appears.

5 Click **NEW LIST**.

6 Type an entry for the custom list.

7 Press Enter.

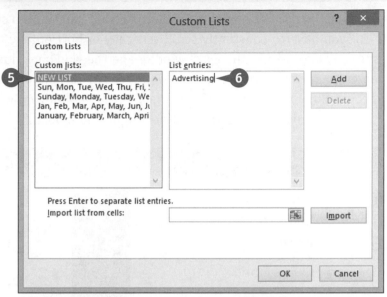

8 Repeat Steps 6 and 7 to define all the list entries.

9 Click **Add**.

A Excel adds the list.

10 Click **OK**.

Excel returns you to the Excel Options dialog box.

11 Click **OK** (not shown).

You can now use the custom fill list.

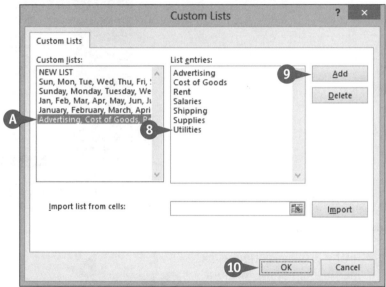

TIPS

Is there an easier way to create a custom fill list?

Yes. You can type the custom fill list values in advance on a worksheet. Once you have done that, select the range that contains the custom list entries, and then follow Steps 1 to 4 to open the Custom Lists dialog box. Click the **Import** button to add the list, and then click **OK**.

How do I delete a custom fill list?

Follow Steps 1 to 4 to open the Custom Lists dialog box. Click the list you no longer need, click the **Delete** button, and then click **OK** when Excel asks you to confirm the deletion. Click **OK** in the Custom Lists dialog box when you are done.

Maximize Work Space by Turning Off Window Elements

As your worksheet model grows beyond what can fit on a single screen, it can become frustrating if you have to constantly scroll vertically or horizontally to see other parts of the worksheet model. If maximizing the Excel window and the workbook does not solve the problem, then you can get more space to display the worksheet by turning off certain elements of the Excel window. Specifically, you can turn off the formula bar, the horizontal and vertical scroll bars, and the row and column headers. See also the section "Unpin the Ribbon."

Maximize Work Space by Turning Off Window Elements

1 Click the **File** tab (not shown).

2 Click **Options**.

The Excel Options dialog box appears.

3 Click **Advanced**.

4 In the Display section, click the selected **Show formula bar** check box (☑) and it is cleared (☐).

5 Click the selected **Show horizontal scroll bar check box** (☑) and it is cleared (☐).

6 Click the selected **Show vertical scroll bar** check box (☑) and it is cleared (☐).

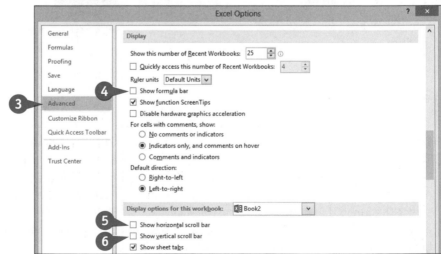

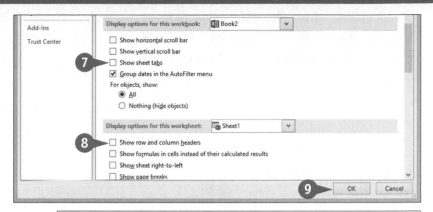

7 Click the selected **Show sheet tabs** check box (☑) and it is cleared (☐).

8 Click the selected **Show row and column headers** check box (☑) and it is cleared (☐).

9 Click **OK**.

Excel hides the window elements.

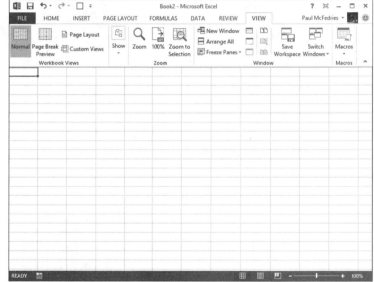

TIPS

Is there an easier way to hide the formula bar?
Yes. Click the **View** tab, and then click the **Show** button if you do not see the Show section. Click the selected **Formula Bar** and **Headings** check boxes (☑) and they are cleared (☐). You can also hide everything except the formula bar by clicking **Full Screen Mode** (⌐) in the title bar.

Can I toggle the status bar on and off?
No, Excel does not offer an option for toggling the status bar off and on. However, you can do this through the Visual Basic Editor window, which you display by pressing **Alt**+**F11**. In the Microsoft Visual Basic window, click **View**, and then click **Immediate Window**. (You can also press **Ctrl**+**G**.) In the Immediate window, type **Application. DisplayStatusBar=False**, and then press **Enter**.

Create a Custom Cell Style

Excel comes with several dozen predefined cell styles, many of which vary with the document theme. However, Excel also has many cell styles that are independent of the current theme, including styles for sheet titles and headings, and styles that identify totals, calculations, and output cells.

If none of the predefined cell styles is right for your needs, you can use the Format Cells dialog box to apply your own formatting. If you want to reuse this formatting in other workbooks, you should save the formatting options as a custom cell style.

Create a Custom Cell Style

1 Click the **Home** tab.

2 Click **Cell Styles**.

Ⓐ The Cell Styles gallery appears.

3 Click **New Cell Style**.

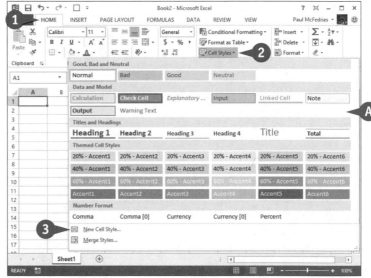

The Style dialog box appears.

4 Type a name for the style.

5 Click **Format**.

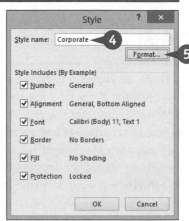

The Format Cells dialog box appears.

6 Use the tabs to select the formatting options you want in your cell style.

7 Click **OK**.

8 Click **OK** in the Style dialog box (not shown).

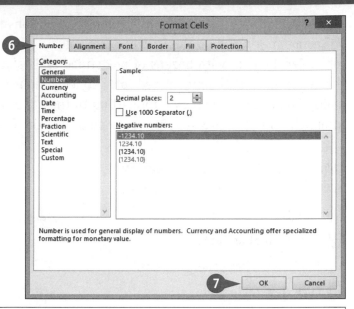

9 Click Cell Styles.

B Your cell style appears in the Custom section of the Cell Styles gallery.

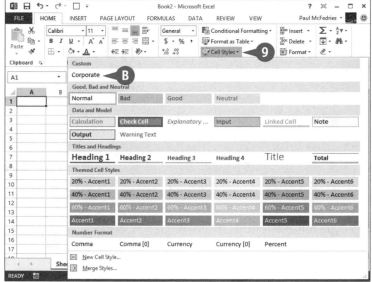

TIPS

Is there a quicker way to create a custom cell style?

After you format a cell using the options you want in your custom cell style, you can use that cell to create your custom style. Select the cell, follow Steps 1 to 3 to open the Style dialog box, name the new cell style, and then click **OK**.

How do I delete a custom cell style?

If you no longer need a custom cell style, you should delete it to reduce clutter in the Cell Styles gallery. Click the **Home** tab and then click **Cell Styles** to open the Cell Styles gallery. Right-click the custom cell style and then click **Delete**. Excel removes the custom cell style and clears the style's formatting from any cell to which you applied the style.

Build a Custom Table Style

A table style is a combination of formatting options that Excel applies to 13 different table elements, including the first and last column, the header row, the total row, and the entire table. Excel comes with dozens of predefined table styles, all of which vary with the document theme. If none of the predefined table styles is right for your needs, you can use the Format Cells dialog box to apply your own formatting to the various table elements. If you want to reuse this formatting in other workbooks, you should save the formatting options as a custom table style.

Build a Custom Table Style

1. Click the **Home** tab.

2. Click **Format as Table**.

Ⓐ The Table Styles gallery appears.

3. Click **New Table Style**.

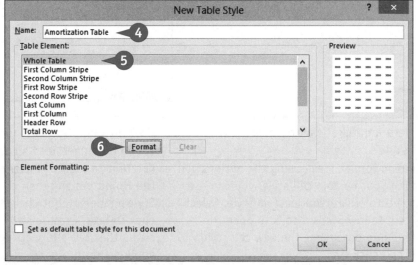

The New Table Style dialog box appears.

4. Type a name for the style.

5. Click the table element you want to format.

6. Click **Format**.

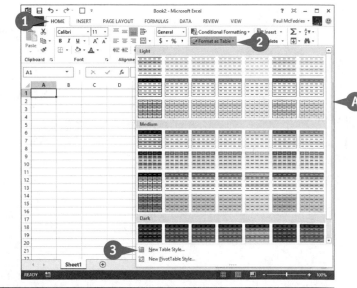

The Format Cells dialog box appears.

7 Use the tabs to select the formatting options you want in your cell style.

Note: Depending on the table element you are working with, some of the formatting options may be disabled.

8 Click **OK**.

9 Repeat Steps **5** to **8** to set the formatting for the other table elements, as needed.

10 Click **OK** in the New Table Style dialog box (not shown).

11 Click Format as Table.

B Your table style appears in the Custom section of the Table Styles gallery.

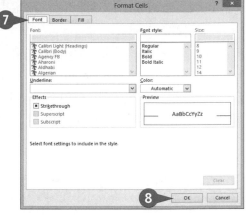

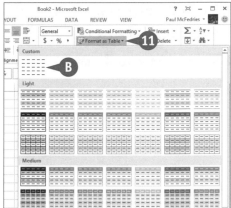

TIPS

Is there an easier way to apply the custom table style to my tables?
Yes. You can set the custom style as the default. When creating a new custom table style, follow Steps **1** to **9**, and then click the empty **Set as default table style for this document** check box (☐) and it is filled (☑). For an existing custom table style, click the **Home** tab, click **Format as Table**, right-click the custom style, and then click **Set As Default**.

How do I delete a custom table style?
Click the **Home** tab and then click **Format as Table** to open the Table Styles gallery. Right-click the custom table style, click **Delete**, and then click **OK**. Excel deletes the custom table style. Tables formatted with the style revert to the default table style.

Create a Custom Color Scheme

You can gain more control over the look of your workbooks by creating your own custom color scheme.

Each Excel theme comes with more than 20 built-in color schemes that make it easy to apply colors to your worksheets. However, if no scheme offers the exact colors you want, you can create your own scheme. Each scheme consists of 12 color elements that control the colors of text, backgrounds, chart data markers, and hyperlinks. See the Tip at the end of this section for a description of each element.

Create a Custom Color Scheme

1 Click the **Page Layout** tab.

2 Click **Theme Colors** (🔲).

3 Click **Customize Colors**.

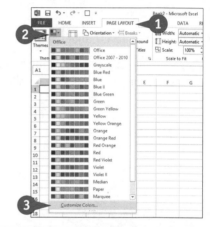

The Create New Theme Colors dialog box appears.

4 For each theme color, click the drop-down arrow (🔽), and then click the color you want for that element.

Ⓐ The Sample area shows what your custom color scheme looks like.

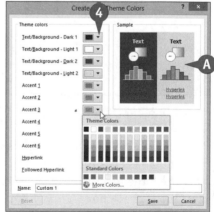

134

⑤ Type a name for your custom
color scheme.

⑥ Click **Save**.

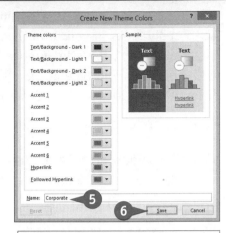

⑦ Click Theme Colors (📇).

Ⓑ Your custom color scheme
appears in the Custom section
of the Theme Colors gallery.

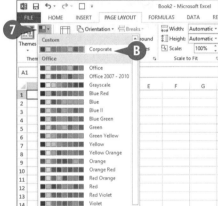

TIP

What do the various theme color elements represent?
Each scheme consists of 12 color elements, including the following:

- Text/Background - Dark 1: The dark text color that Excel applies when you choose a light
  background color.

- Text/Background - Light 1: The light text color that Excel applies when you choose a dark
  background color.

- Text/Background - Dark 2: The dark background color that Excel applies when you choose a light
  text color.

- Text/Background - Light 2: The light background color that Excel applies when you choose a dark
  text color.

- There are also six elements — Accent 1 through Accent 6 — that Excel uses as colors for chart data
  markers, as well as two colors for hyperlinks (followed and unfollowed).

Create a Custom Font Scheme

Each Excel theme comes with more than two dozen built-in font schemes that make it easy to apply fonts to your worksheets. Each font scheme defines two fonts: a larger font, called the *heading font*, for title and heading text; and a smaller font, called the *body font*, for regular worksheet text. The typeface is often the same for both types of text, but some schemes use two different typefaces, such as Cambria for titles and headings and Calibri for body text.

However, if no font scheme offers the exact typefaces you want, you can create your own scheme.

Create a Custom Font Scheme

1 Click the **Page Layout** tab.

2 Click **Theme Fonts** (A).

3 Click **Customize Fonts**.

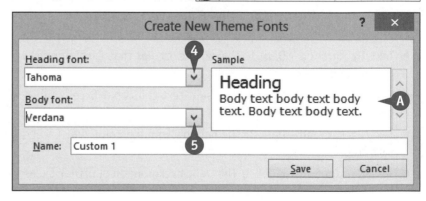

The Create New Theme Fonts dialog box appears.

4 Click the **Heading font** drop-down arrow (⌄), and then click the typeface you want to use for titles and headings.

5 Click the **Body font** drop-down arrow (⌄), and then click the typeface you want to use for regular text.

Ⓐ The Sample area shows what your custom font scheme looks like.

136

6 Type a name for your custom font scheme.

7 Click **Save**.

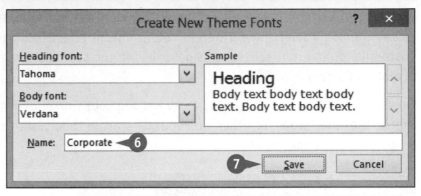

8 Click **Theme Fonts** (A).

B Your custom font scheme appears in the Custom section of the Theme Fonts gallery.

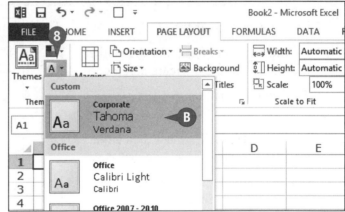

TIPS

Is there an easier way to create a custom font theme?
Yes. If an existing font scheme is close to what you want, you can use that font scheme as your starting point. In the Page Layout tab, click **Theme Fonts** (A), and then click the font scheme you want to use. Click **Theme Fonts** (A) again, and then click **Customize Fonts**. The font scheme you selected appears in the Create New Theme Fonts dialog box.

How do I remove a custom font theme?
If you no longer use a custom font scheme, you should delete it to reduce clutter in the Theme Fonts gallery and to make it easier to navigate your custom schemes. Click the **Page Layout** tab, and then click **Theme Fonts** (A). Right-click the custom font scheme you no longer need, click **Delete**, and then click **Yes** when Excel asks you to confirm the deletion.

Save a Custom Workbook Theme

If none of Excel's predefined workbook themes offers the formatting you require, you can modify any theme by selecting a different color, font, or effects scheme. You can even create your own custom color and font schemes, as described in the sections "Create a Custom Color Scheme" and "Create a Custom Font Scheme."

However, if you go to the trouble of formatting your workbook just right, it is time consuming to repeat the same steps for other workbooks. To avoid this, you can save your theme customizations as a new workbook theme.

Save a Custom Workbook Theme

1 Click the **Page Layout** tab.

2 Click **Theme Colors** (■), and then either click a color scheme or create a new one.

Note: For more information, see the section, "Create a Custom Color Scheme."

3 Click **Theme Fonts** (A), and then either click a font scheme or create a new one.

Note: For more information, see the section "Create a Custom Font Scheme."

4 Click **Theme Effects** (●), and then click the effect scheme you want to use.

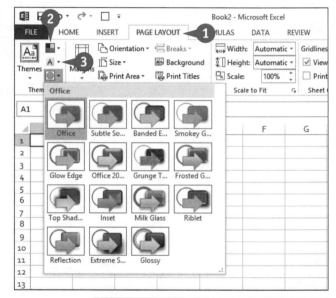

5 Click **Themes**.

6 Click **Save Current Theme**.

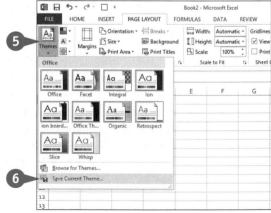

The Save Current Theme dialog box appears.

7 Type a name for your custom theme file.

8 Click **Save**.

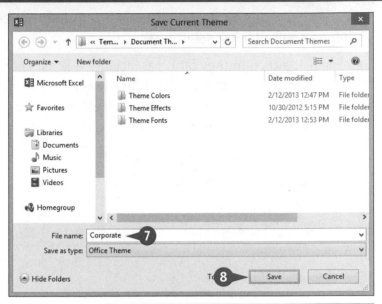

9 Click **Themes**.

A Your custom theme appears in the Custom section of the Themes gallery.

TIPS

Is there an easier way to create a custom workbook theme?
If an existing document theme is close to what you want, you can save some time by using that theme as your starting point. In the **Page Layout** tab, click the **Themes** button, and then click the theme you want to use. Follow Steps **2** to **7** to modify the theme and then save the custom theme file.

How do I delete a custom workbook theme?
If you no longer use a custom workbook theme, you should delete it to reduce clutter in the Themes gallery and to make it easier to navigate your custom themes. Click the **Page Layout** tab, and then click the **Themes** button. Right-click the custom theme you no longer need, click **Delete**, and then click **Yes** when Excel asks you to confirm the deletion.

Customize the Excel Status Bar

You can make the status bar more useful and easier to read by customizing it to show the information you most want to see.

For example, although the status bar includes a Scroll Lock indicator to tell you when Scroll Lock is on, it does not display the Caps Lock and Num Lock indicators by default, which are arguably more important. Similarly, you might prefer to see different numeric calculations, such as maximum and minimum values in the selection, or you might prefer to hide the Zoom slider if you never use it.

Customize the Excel Status Bar

1 Right-click the status bar.

A Excel displays the Customize Status Bar menu.

B A check mark (✓) indicates that the status bar currently displays the item.

C The values shown in the right side of the menu tell you the current value of each item.

2 Click a displayed item to hide it.

3 Click a hidden item to display it.

D Excel removes the item you want to hide from the status bar.

E Excel adds the item that you want to see on the status bar.

4 Repeat Steps 2 and 3 to continue customizing the status bar.

Unpin the Ribbon

The Ribbon takes up a lot of space in the Excel window that could otherwise be used to display worksheet data. Also, the Ribbon changes as you select different elements within a worksheet, such as an image, a table, or a chart, which can be distracting.

To get more space to work and to simplify the Excel interface, you can unpin the Ribbon so that it shows just the tabs. You can still work with the Ribbon by clicking the tabs, but once you have selected a command or option, Excel minimizes the Ribbon once again.

Unpin the Ribbon

1 Click **Unpin the ribbon** (^).

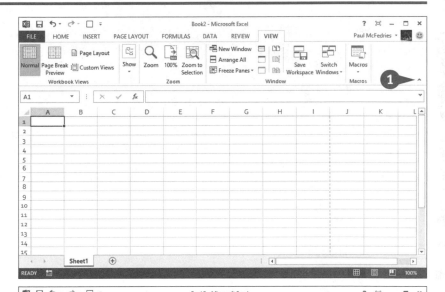

A Excel displays only the Ribbon tabs.

2 To restore the Ribbon, click a tab, and then click **Pin the ribbon** (✦).

Note: To toggle the Ribbon between unpinned and pinned, press Ctrl + F1, or right-click the Ribbon, and then click **Unpin the ribbon**.

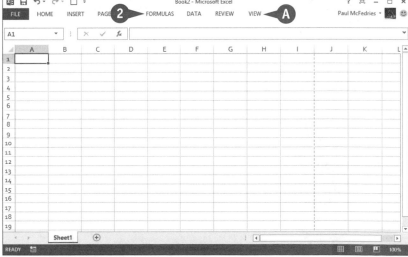

CHAPTER 7

Making Excel More Efficient

If you find yourself spending a major part of your day working with Excel, you can make those chores go faster — and so make your overall work life more productive — by making Excel as efficient as possible.

Export Ribbon Customizations to a File

Customizing the Ribbon or the Quick Access Toolbar is not difficult, but it can be time consuming, particularly if you want to make a substantial number of changes. If you use Excel on another computer, you will likely want to have the same customizations on the other computer so that you are dealing with a consistent interface no matter where you do your spreadsheet work. To make this easier, you can export your customizations to a file. You can then import that file on the other computer, and Excel automatically applies the customizations for you.

Export Ribbon Customizations to a File

1 Right-click any part of the Ribbon.

2 Click **Customize the Ribbon**.

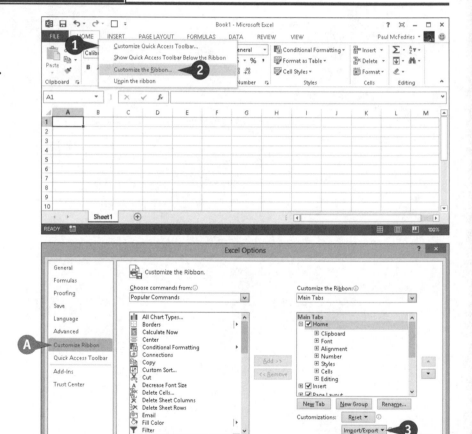

The Excel Options dialog box appears.

A Excel automatically displays the **Customize Ribbon** tab.

3 Click **Import/Export**.

4 Click **Export all customizations**.

The File Save dialog box appears.

5 Choose a location for the customization file.

6 Type a name for the file.

7 Click **Save**.

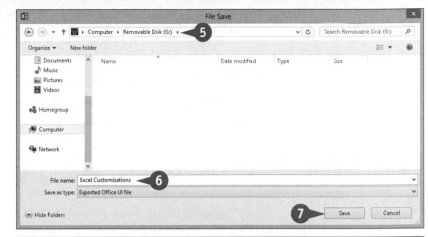

Excel saves the customizations to the file.

8 Click **Quick Access Toolbar**.

9 Repeat Steps 3 to 7 to export the Quick Access Toolbar customizations to a file.

10 Click **OK**.

You can now import the customizations to your other computer, as explained in the following Tip.

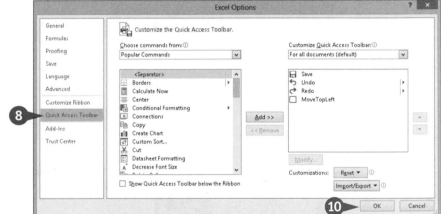

TIP

How do I apply the Ribbon and Quick Access Toolbar customizations on another computer running Excel?

You need to import the customization file that you exported when you followed the steps in this section. Note, however, that importing a customization file replaces any existing customizations that you have created.

On the computer you are customizing, right-click any part of the Ribbon and then click **Customize the Ribbon** to open the Excel Options dialog box with the **Customize Ribbon** tab displayed. Click **Import/ Export** and then click **Import customization file**. In the File Open dialog box, locate and then click the customization file, and then click **Open**. When Excel asks you to confirm that all of your existing customizations will be replaced, click **Yes**. Click the **Quick Access Toolbar** tab and then repeat these steps to import the Quick Access Toolbar customization file.

Configure Excel to Use the Mouse Wheel for Zooming

Zooming a worksheet is a useful technique. For example, you might want to zoom out of a large worksheet to get a sense of the overall structure of the worksheet data. Similarly, zooming in on a section of a worksheet enables you to focus on just that section.

You normally zoom by using either the controls in the View tab's Zoom group, or the status bar's Zoom slider. These techniques are fine if you only zoom occasionally. However, if you use the zoom feature frequently, it is a good idea to configure Excel to zoom using the mouse wheel.

Configure Excel to Use the Mouse Wheel for Zooming

1 Click the **File** tab.

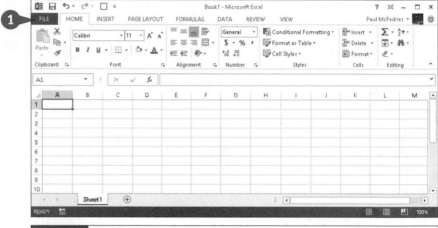

2 Click **Options**.

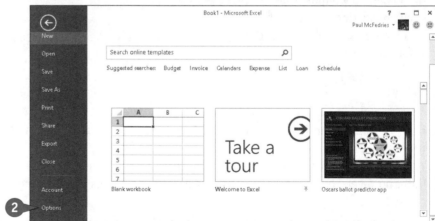

The Excel Options dialog box appears.

3 Click the **Advanced** tab.

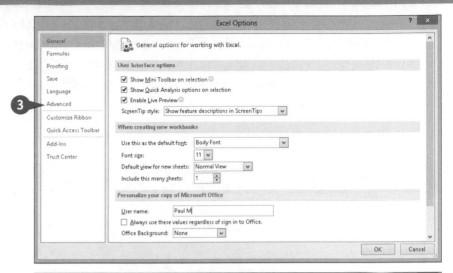

4 Click the empty **Zoom on roll with IntelliMouse** check box (☐) and it is filled (☑).

Note: Although the option name specifies the Microsoft IntelliMouse, this option works with any mouse that comes with a standard scroll wheel.

5 Click **OK**.

You can now zoom in and out of your Excel spreadsheets by turning the mouse wheel.

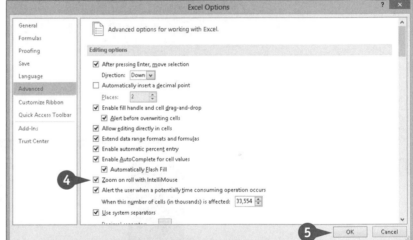

TIPS

How does zooming work with the mouse wheel?
When you select the **Zoom on roll with IntelliMouse** check box (☑), rolling the mouse wheel forward causes Excel to zoom in on the worksheet by 15 percent with each scroll. Rolling the mouse wheel backward causes Excel to zoom out of the worksheet by 15 percent with each scroll.

Can I still use the mouse wheel to scroll the worksheet?
Yes. When you deactivate the **Zoom on roll with IntelliMouse** check box (☐), rolling the mouse wheel causes Excel to scroll the worksheet (roll back to scroll down or forward to scroll up). You can use this technique even if you activate the **Zoom on roll with IntelliMouse** check box (☑) — just hold down the Ctrl key and roll the mouse wheel to scroll the worksheet.

Move in a Different Direction When You Press Enter

I n some situations, you might need to type a large amount of data in a row, either from left to right or right to left, or in a column from top to bottom. Although you can use the arrow keys to force the selection to move in the direction you want, the [Enter] key is larger than the arrow keys and, thus, faster to use and less prone to error. You can configure Excel to move the selection in the direction you prefer when you press [Enter].

Move in a Different Direction When You Press Enter

1 Click the **File** tab.

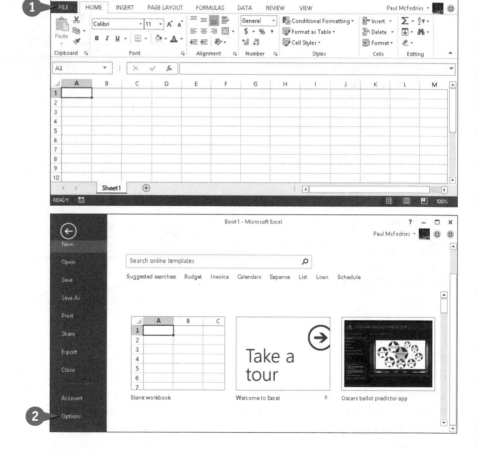

2 Click **Options**.

The Excel Options dialog box appears.

③ Click the **Advanced** tab.

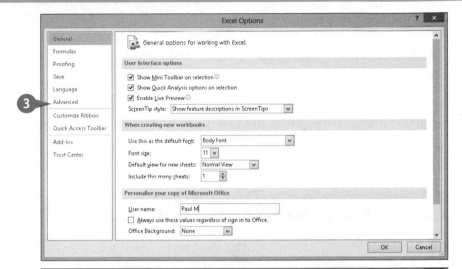

④ Make sure the **After pressing Enter, move selection** check box is selected (☑).

⑤ Click the **Direction** drop-down arrow (☑), and then click the direction that you want Excel to move the selection after you press Enter.

⑥ Click **OK**.

Excel now moves the selection in the direction you specified when you press Enter to confirm a cell entry.

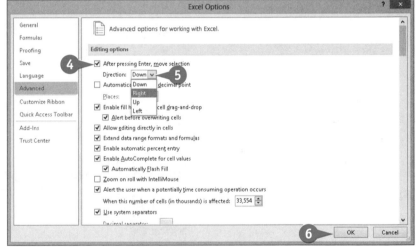

TIP

Is there another method I can use to force Excel to move the selection in a different direction?
If you have only a few data items to type, modifying Excel's options to specify the direction after pressing Enter might seem like overkill. However, you can force Excel to move the selection in the direction of the next cell entry by using the arrow keys. For example, suppose you are typing data in a row from left to right. When you finish editing a cell, press ➡ to move the selection to the next cell on the right. Similarly, you can press ⬅ to move the selection to the left, or you can press ⬆ to move the selection up.

Automatically Insert a Decimal Point

M any Excel data entry tasks require typing a list of values that use the same number of decimal places. The most common example is a list of currency amounts, which always have two decimal places. However, in a long list of values, the extra step required to type the decimal point slows you down.

To speed up this kind of data entry, configure Excel to add the decimal point automatically. For example, if you tell Excel to add two decimal places automatically, then when you type a number such as 123456, Excel enters the value into the cell as 1234.56.

Automatically Insert a Decimal Point

1 Click the **File** tab.

2 Click **Options**.

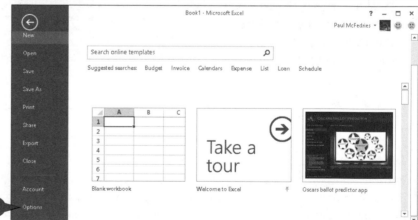

The Excel Options dialog box appears.

3 Click the **Advanced** tab.

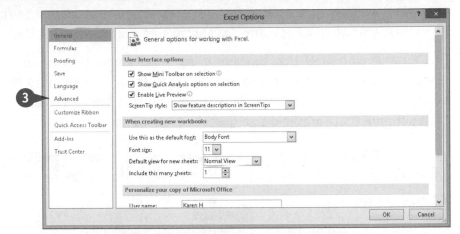

4 Click the empty **Automatically insert a decimal point** check box (□) and it is filled ☑).

5 Use the **Places** spin box to specify the number of decimal places you want Excel to add automatically.

6 Click **OK**.

Excel now inserts automatically the number of decimal places you specified when you type a numeric value into a cell.

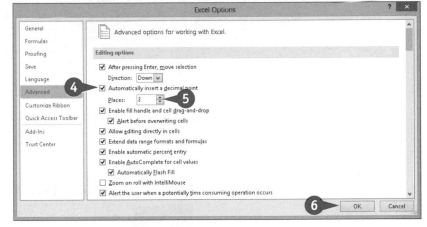

Note: Excel displays FIXED DECIMAL in the status bar to remind you that it will automatically insert the decimal point.

TIPS

Why does Excel still drop zeroes at the end of my entries?

Even in Fixed Decimal mode, Excel drops trailing zeroes from cell entries. For example, if you choose 2 in the Places spin box, and then type 12340 in a cell, Excel displays the entry as 123.4. If you always want two decimal places — that is, 123.40 — then you must format the cells using a two-decimal numeric format, such as Number or Currency.

How can I get Excel to always display more than two decimal places?

If you choose a number other than 2 in the Places spin box and you always want Excel to display that number of decimal places, you must format the cells with a custom numeric format, as described in Chapter 6. For example, the format 0.000 always displays three decimal places.

Configure When Excel Warns You about Long Operations

To avoid wasting time waiting for a long workbook recalculation to finish, you can configure Excel to warn you when an operation might take an excessively long time.

In a massive worksheet that contains many linked formulas or one or more large data tables, the number of operations required to recalculate the sheet can run into the millions. If that number exceeds 33,554,000 operations, Excel warns you that the recalculation might take some time. You can configure that threshold to a lower or higher number.

Configure When Excel Warns You about Long Operations

1 Click the **File** tab.

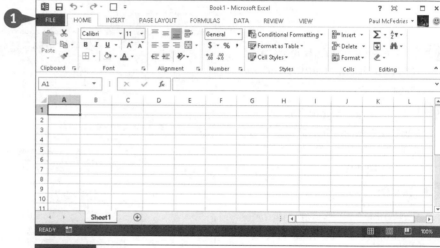

2 Click **Options**.

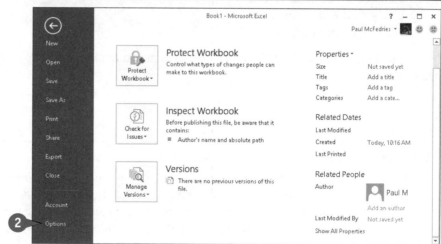

The Excel Options dialog box appears.

③ Click the **Advanced** tab.

④ Make sure that the **Alert the user when a potentially time consuming operation occurs** check box is selected (☑).

⑤ Use the **When this number of cells (in thousands) is affected** spin box to specify the threshold at which Excel displays the long operation warning.

Note: The number in the spin box appears in thousands. For example, if you type 1,000 in the spin box, then the threshold is one million cells.

⑥ Click **OK**.

Excel now warns you about time-consuming operations when the number of cells affected will be equal to or greater than the number you specified.

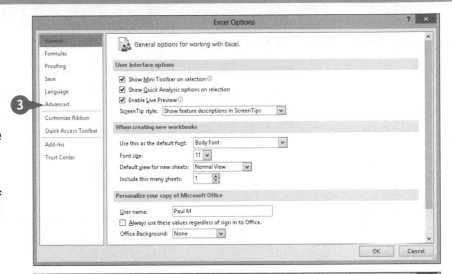

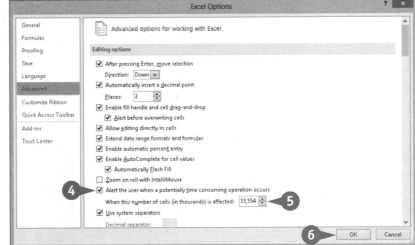

TIPS

What is the lowest threshold I can use?
Although you can type a value as small as 1 in the spin box, low values are not recommended because they generate excessive warnings. Unless you have a very slow computer, do not go under 10 million operations (10,000 in the spin box). Note, as well, that the maximum value you can specify is 999,999,999.

Do I really need Excel to warn me about long calculations?
If you have a fast computer with a lot of memory, Excel should be able to handle almost all real-world calculations relatively quickly, so you do not need it to warn you. In that case, deactivate the warning by following Steps **1** to **3**, and then clicking the selected **Alert the user when a potentially time consuming operation occurs** check box ☑); it is cleared (☐).

Make a Workbook Faster by Saving It as Binary

If you have a large or complex Excel workbook, you can make it open and save faster by converting it to the Excel binary file format.

If you have a worksheet that is very large — for example, several thousand rows or more, or several hundred columns or more — or is very complex, then the standard Excel file format may take a while to open and save. To improve the performance of such files, you can convert them to the Excel Binary Workbook file format, which uses special code that Excel can read and write much faster.

Make a Workbook Faster by Saving It as Binary

① Open the workbook you want to convert.

② Click the **File** tab.

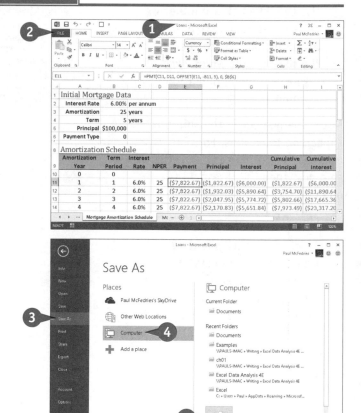

③ Click **Save As**.

④ Click **Computer**.

⑤ Click **Browse**.

The Save As dialog box appears.

6 Select a location for the new workbook.

7 Type a name for the new workbook.

Note: Because the new workbook will have a different file extension (.xlsb), you do not need to change the filename if you do not want to.

8 Click the **Save as type** drop-down arrow (⌄).

9 Click **Excel Binary Workbook.**

10 Click **Save**.

Excel saves the new file using the Excel Binary Workbook file format.

TIPS

Can I use a binary workbook with older versions of Excel?

No. The Excel Binary Workbook file format is compatible with Excel 2013, 2010, and 2007. If you want to improve file performance while maintaining compatibility with earlier versions of Excel, save your workbook using the Excel 97-2003 Workbook file format. This binary format is compatible with Excel 97 and all later versions.

Can I use the binary format if my workbook contains macros?

No. If you plan to use macros (covered in Chapter 25) use the Excel Macro-Enabled Workbook file format. Other than improved performance when opening and saving a file, there is no difference between the Excel Binary Workbook and the Excel Macro-Enabled Workbook file formats. Both support the same features, create files of approximately the same size, and perform the same once they are loaded into Excel.

Open a New Window for a Workbook

When building a spreadsheet, you often have to refer to existing sheet data. For example, when you construct a formula, you may need to refer to specific cells. In a large spreadsheet that does not fit the screen, the data you need to reference might not be visible, requiring you to scroll through the sheet. A better solution is to create a second window for the workbook, and then arrange both windows side-by-side (vertically or horizontally). This enables you to display what you are working on in one window and what you need to reference in the other.

Open a New Window for a Workbook

Create a New Workbook Window

1. Open the workbook you want to work with.

2. Click the **View** tab.

3. Click **New Window** (⊞).

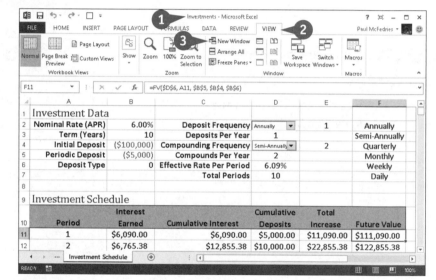

Arrange the Workbook's Windows

Ⓐ Excel creates a second window for the workbook and appends :2 to the name of the new window.

Ⓑ Excel also appends :1 to the name of the original window.

4. Click the **View** tab.

5. Click **Arrange All** (▥).

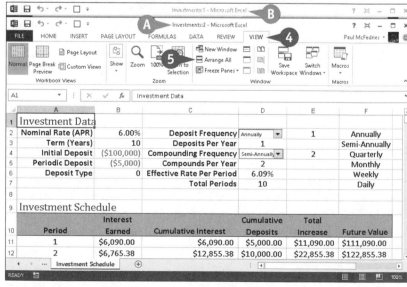

The Arrange Windows dialog box appears.

⑥ Click the empty **Horizontal** radio button (○) and it is filled (◉).

Ⓒ If your worksheet has just a few columns, you can click the empty **Vertical** radio button (○) and it is filled (◉).

⑦ Click the empty **Windows of active workbook** check box (□) and it is filled (☑).

⑧ Click **OK**.

Excel arranges the workbook's windows.

⑨ When you are done with the second window, click **Close** (×) to return to using just the original workbook window.

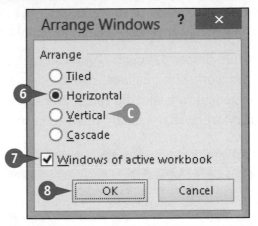

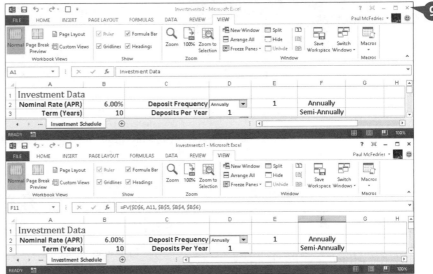

TIPS

Is there an easier way to monitor, say, the first few rows in my worksheet?

If you are using the new window to monitor either the first few rows or columns in the workbook, then you might find it easier to split the worksheet into panes instead of creating a new window. To learn how to split a worksheet into two panes, see Chapter 10.

Is there an easier way to monitor a single cell's value?

If you are using the new window to monitor a particular cell value in another part of the workbook, Excel offers another method for doing this: the Watch Window. You use this window to monitor the current value of one or more cells. To learn how to use this window, see Chapter 9.

Allow Only Certain Values in a Cell

You may find that some worksheet cells can only take a particular range of values. For example, a mortgage amortization term cell should probably take whole number values between 15 and 35.

To ensure proper data entry, you can set up *data validation* criteria that specify the allowed value(s). You can work with numbers, dates, times, or even text length, and set up criteria between two values, equal to a specific value, and so on. You can also tell the user what to type by adding an input message that appears when the user selects the cell.

Allow Only Certain Values in a Cell

1 Click the cell you want to restrict.

2 Click the **Data** tab.

3 Click **Data Validation** ( ).

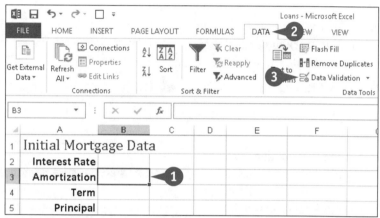

The Data Validation dialog box appears.

4 Click **Settings**.

5 Click the **Allow** drop-down arrow ( ), and then click the type of data you want to allow in the cell.

6 Click the **Data** drop-down arrow ( ), and then click the operator you want to use to define the allowable data.

7 Specify the validation criteria, such as the Maximum and Minimum values, as shown here.

Note: The criteria you see depend on the operator you chose in Step 6.

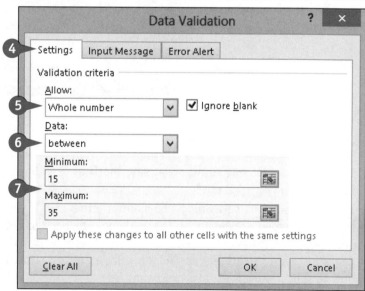

8 Click the **Input Message** tab.

9 Make sure the **Show input message when cell is selected** check box is activated (☑).

10 Type a message title.

11 Type the message you want to display.

12 Click **OK**.

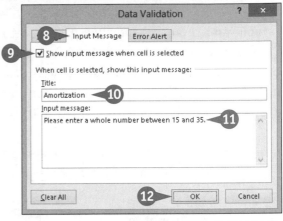

Ⓐ When the cell is selected, the input message appears.

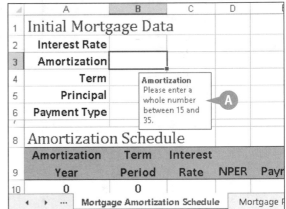

TIPS

Can I display a warning message when the user tries to type invalid data?

Yes. You can also configure an error message that displays when the user types data outside of the specified range. Follow Steps 1 to 3 to open the Data Validation dialog box, and then click the **Error Alert** tab. Make sure the **Show error alert after invalid data is entered** check box is selected (☑), and then specify the **Style**, **Title**, and **Error message**.

How do I delete data validation from a cell?

If you no longer need to use data validation on a cell, you should clear the settings. Follow Steps 1 to 3 to display the Data Validation dialog box, and then click the **Clear All** button. Excel removes all the validation criteria, as well as the input message and the error alert. Click **OK**.

Apply Text or Formatting to Multiple Worksheets

To apply text and formatting to a second worksheet, you can complete a worksheet, copy the range you want to apply, and then paste it into the other sheet. For a large number of sheets, however, Excel offers a much faster method. You can collect all the worksheets into a *group* where Excel treats the collection of sheets as a single worksheet. This means that any data you type into one sheet is included automatically in the same spot on every other sheet in the group. Similarly, any formatting applied to one sheet is also applied to the entire group.

Apply Text or Formatting to Multiple Worksheets

1 Click the tab of the first worksheet you want to include in the group.

2 Press and hold Ctrl.

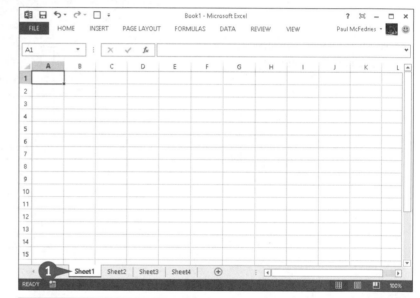

3 Click the tab of the next worksheet you want to include in the group.

Ⓐ Excel displays [Group] in the title bar to remind you that your worksheets are currently grouped.

Note: If you select a tab accidentally, click the tab again to remove the worksheet from the group.

4 Repeat Step 3 for each worksheet you want to include in the group.

5 Release the Ctrl key.

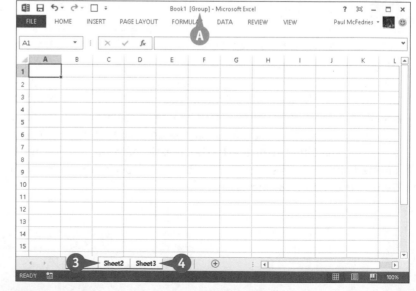

6 Add the text and other data you want to display on the grouped worksheets.

7 Apply the formatting that you want to use on the grouped worksheets.

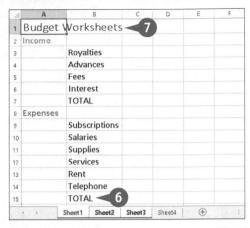

8 Click the tab of a worksheet in the group.

Ⓑ The data and formatting you added to the original worksheet also appear in the other worksheets in the group.

TIPS

Is there a quick way to select a large number of worksheet tabs?
Yes. If you have a workbook with many worksheets and you want to include most (or all) of them in your group, do not click each worksheet tab individually. Instead, right-click any tab, and then click **Select All Sheets**. Alternatively, click the first tab you want to include in the group, hold down **Shift**, and then click the last tab you want to include.

How do I remove a worksheet from a group?
To exclude a worksheet from the group, hold down **Ctrl** and click the worksheet's tab. To collapse the entire group, either click any tab that is not part of the group, or right-click a grouped tab, and then click **Ungroup Sheets**.

Use Dialog Box Controls to Input Data

The easiest way to enhance data entry speed and accuracy is to add dialog box controls — also called form controls — to your worksheet. These controls include check boxes and lists, which you are familiar with from dialog boxes.

Using form controls reduces the amount of typing required by the user typing data. For example, rather than typing Yes or No in a cell, you can activate or deactivate a check box instead. Similarly, rather than memorizing a cell's possible inputs, you can provide a list of the allowable values.

Use Dialog Box Controls to Input Data

Add a Control to a Worksheet

1 Click the **Developer** tab.

Note: See the first Tip to learn how to display the Developer tab.

2 Click **Insert**.

3 Click the control you want to add.

Ⓐ Be sure you choose a control from the Form Controls section of the Insert Controls gallery.

4 Click and drag on the worksheet at the spot where you want the control to appear.

The Excel mouse pointer (⊕) changes to pointer fill (+).

Ⓑ As you drag, Excel displays the border of the control.

5 When the control is the size and shape you want, release the mouse.

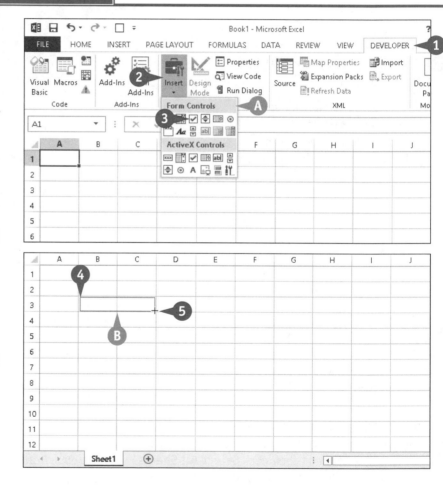

Ⓒ Excel adds the control to the worksheet.

⑥ If the control comes with a text label, right- or double-click it.

⑦ Click **Edit Text**.

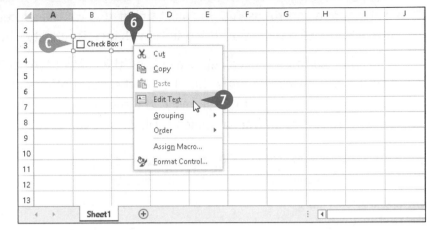

Excel opens the label text for editing.

⑧ Type a name for the control.

⑨ Click outside the control.

Excel removes the selection handles from the control.

Note: Hold down Ctrl and click the control to select it later.

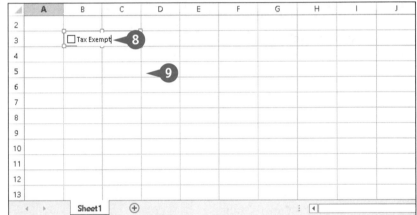

TIPS

How do I add the Developer tab to the Ribbon?
To use the worksheet form controls, you must customize the Excel Ribbon to display the Developer tab. Right-click any part of the Ribbon and then click **Customize the Ribbon**. The Excel Options dialog box appears with the **Customize Ribbon** tab displayed. In the **Customize the Ribbon** list box, click the empty **Developer** check box (☐) and it is filled (☑). Click **OK**.

Does Excel offer any methods for more precise placement of the form controls?
Yes, there are several. When you drag the control on the worksheet, you can make the control's border snap to the worksheet's cells by pressing the Alt key as you drag. If you want the control to be a perfect square, press Shift as you drag. If you want to center the control on the spot where you start dragging, press Ctrl as you drag.

continued ►

To make a form control useful, you must link it to a worksheet cell. When the user changes the state or value of the control, the resulting change is reflected in the linked cell.

The value you see in the linked cell depends on the control type control. A check box inserts the value TRUE when checked, and FALSE when unchecked. Option buttons return a number based on the selected option: the first option returns 1, the second option returns 2, and so on. Scroll bars and spin boxes return a value from a range of values that you specify.

Use Dialog Box Controls to Input Data (continued)

Link a Control to a Worksheet Cell

1 Right-click the control.

2 Click **Format Control**.

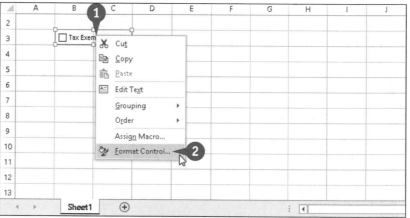

The Format Control dialog box appears with the **Control** tab displayed.

3 Click inside the **Cell link** box.

4 Click the cell you want to use to store the control's value.

A Excel inserts the cell address in the Cell link box.

5 Click **OK**.

When the user changes the value of the control, the new value appears in the linked cell.

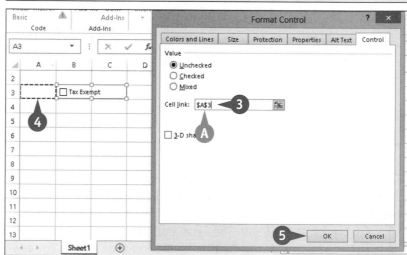

Populate a List Control with Values

1. Add the list items to the worksheet.

2. Right-click the list box or combo box control.

3. Click **Format Control**.

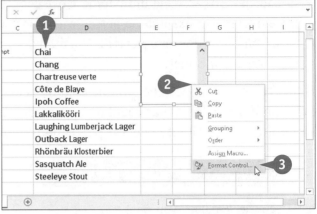

The Format Object dialog box appears.

4. Click inside the **Input range** box.

5. Select the list values.

Ⓑ Excel inserts the range address.

6. Click **OK**.

Ⓒ The values from the worksheet range appear as items in the list control.

TIPS

How do I specify the range of values for a scroll bar or spin box?

Right-click the control, and then click **Format Control**. In the **Control** tab of the Format Control dialog box, use the **Minimum value** and **Maximum value** spin boxes to specify the range. Use the **Incremental change** spin box to specify how much the control value changes when the user clicks a scroll or spin arrow. Click **OK**.

How do I get the selected list item in a worksheet cell?

When you click an item in a list control, the item's position in the list appears in the linked worksheet cell. To get the actual item, you need to add the following formula to a cell:

= INDEX(*input_range*, *cell_link*)

Replace *input_range* with the address of the range that holds the list values, and replace *cell_link* with the address of the control's linked cell.

Check for Accessibility Problems

Spreadsheets that seem ordinary to most people can pose special challenges to people with disabilities. For example, a person with a visual impairment might have trouble seeing images, charts, and other nontext elements. Similarly, a person with physical disabilities might have trouble navigating a worksheet.

If you have a workbook that will be used by people with disabilities, you should check for accessibility problems that could make it harder for them to read and navigate the document. You can use the Accessibility Checker task pane to look for these and other accessibility problems.

Check for Accessibility Problems

1 Open the workbook you want to check.

2 Click the **File** tab.

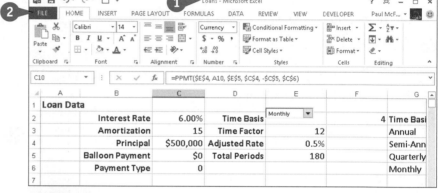

3 Click **Info**.

4 Click **Check for Issues**.

5 Click **Check Accessibility**.

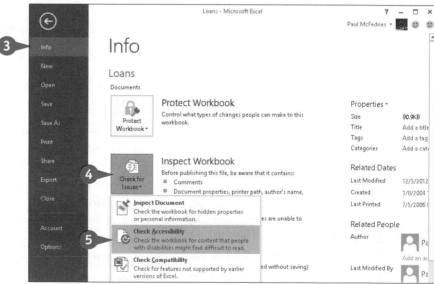

Ⓐ Excel displays the Accessibility Checker task pane.

⑥ Click an item in the **Inspection Results** section.

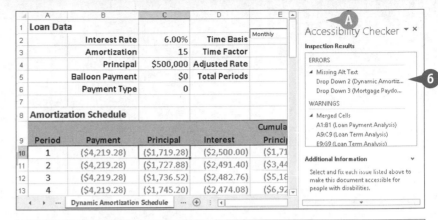

Ⓑ Excel uses the **Additional Information** section to tell you why you should fix the problem and the steps required to fix it.

TIP

How can I build worksheets to make them more accessible to people with disabilities?

Here are a few pointers to make a worksheet more accessible:

- Make extensive use of text headings to annotate the worksheet and make it easier to understand the structure of the sheet. In particular, every row and column should have a unique heading.

- Do not overuse white space such as blank rows and columns. White space usually helps make a worksheet look less cluttered, but a sheet that has little or no white space is much easier for people with disabilities to navigate. Use Excel formatting, such as row heights and column widths, to create space within the worksheet.

- Use named ranges whenever possible, as named ranges are relatively easy to navigate using the Go To command in Excel.

CHAPTER 8

Building Formulas and Functions

Are you ready to start creating powerful and useful worksheets by building your own formulas? This chapter explains formulas, shows you how to build them, and shows you how to incorporate the versatile worksheet functions in Excel into your formulas.

Understanding Excel Formulas

Although you can use Excel to create simple databases to store text, numbers, dates, and other data, the spreadsheets you create are also designed to analyze data and make calculations. Therefore, to get the most out of Excel, you need to understand formulas so that you can use them to analyze and perform calculations on your worksheet data.

To build accurate and useful formulas, you need to know the components of a formula, including operators and operands. You also need to understand arithmetic and comparison formulas and you need to understand the importance of precedence when building a formula.

Formulas

A *formula* is a set of symbols and values that perform some kind of calculation and produce a result. All Excel formulas have the same general structure: an equal sign (=) followed by one or more operands and operators. The equal sign tells Excel to interpret everything that follows in the cell as a formula. For example, if you type **=5+8** into a cell, Excel interprets the 5+8 text as a formula, and displays the result (13) in the cell.

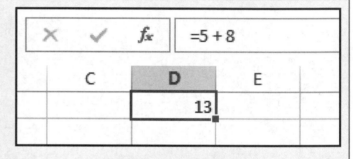

Operands

Every Excel formula includes one or more *operands*, which are the data that Excel uses in the calculation. The simplest type of operand is a constant value, which is usually a number. However, most Excel formulas include references to worksheet data, which can be a cell address (such as A1), a range address (such as B1:B5), or a range name. Finally, you can also use any of the built-in Excel functions as an operand.

Operators

In an Excel formula that contains two or more operands, each operand is separated by an *operator*, which is a symbol that combines the operands in some way, usually mathematically. Example operators include the plus sign (+) and the multiplication sign (*). For example, the formula =B1+B2 adds the values in cells B1 and B2.

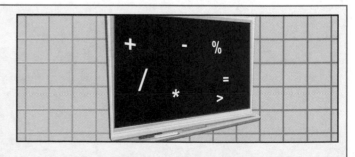

Arithmetic Formulas

An arithmetic formula combines numeric operands — numeric constants, functions that return numeric results, and fields or items that contain numeric values — with mathematical operators to perform a calculation. Because Excel worksheets primarily deal with numeric data, arithmetic formulas are by far the most common formulas used in worksheet calculations.

The table lists the seven arithmetic operators for arithmetic formulas:

Operator	Name	Example	Result
+	Addition	=10 + 5	15
–	Subtraction	=10 – 5	5
–	Negation	=–10	–10
*	Multiplication	=10 * 5	50
/	Division	=10 / 5	2
%	Percentage	=10%	0.1
^	Exponentiation	=10 ^ 5	100000

Comparison Formulas

A comparison formula combines numeric operands — numeric constants, functions that return numeric results, and fields or items that contain numeric values — with special operators to compare one operand with another. A comparison formula always returns a logical result. If the comparison is true, the formula returns the value 1, which is equivalent to the logical value TRUE. If the comparison is false, the formula returns the value 0, which is equivalent to the logical value FALSE.

The table lists the six operators for comparison formulas:

Operator	Name	Example	Result
=	Equal to	=10 = 5	0
<	Less than	=10 < 5	0
< =	Less than or equal to	=10 < = 5	0
>	Greater than	=10 > 5	1
> =	Greater than or equal to	=10 > = 5	1
< >	Not equal to	=10 < > 5	1

Operator Precedence

Most formulas include multiple operands and operators. A single formula can produce multiple answers. The order in which Excel performs the calculations is crucial. Consider the formula =3 + 5 ^ 2. If you calculate from left to right, you get 64 (3 + 5 = 8, and 8 ^ 2 = 64). However, if you perform the exponentiation first and the addition second, the result is 28 (5 ^ 2 = 25, and 3 + 25 = 28). Excel evaluates a formula according to the formula operators, as shown in the table:

Operator	Operation	Precedence
( )	Parentheses	1st
–	Negation	2nd
%	Percentage	3rd
^	Exponentiation	4th
* and /	Multiplication and division	5th
+ and –	Addition and subtraction	6th
= < < = > > = < >	Comparison	7th

Build a Formula

You can add a formula to a worksheet cell using a technique similar to adding data to a cell. To ensure that Excel treats the text as a formula, be sure to begin with an equal sign (=), and then type your operands and operators.

When you add a formula to a cell, Excel displays the formula result in the cell, not the actual formula. For example, if you add the formula =C3+C4 to a cell, that cell displays the sum of the values in cells C3 and C4. To see the formula, click the cell and examine the Formula bar.

Build a Formula

1 Click in the cell in which you want to build the formula.

2 Type =.

A Your typing also appears in the Formula bar.

Note: You can also type the formula into the Formula bar.

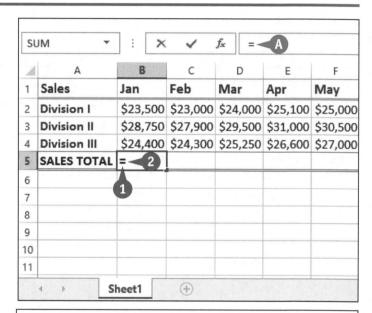

3 Type or click an operand. For example, to reference a cell in your formula, click in the cell.

B Excel inserts the address of the clicked cell into the formula.

4 Type an operator.

5 Repeat Steps 3 and 4 to add other operands and operators to your formula.

6 Click Enter (✓) or press **Enter**.

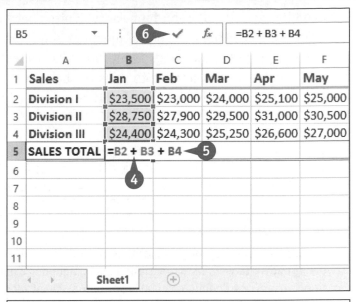

C Excel displays the formula result in the cell.

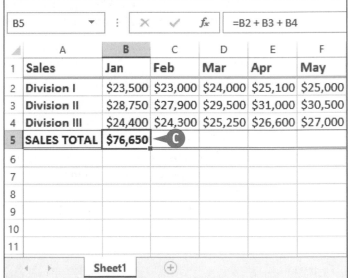

TIP

How do I make changes to a formula if Excel displays only its result?
While Excel only displays the formula result in the cell, it still keeps track of the original formula. To display the formula again, you have two choices: Click the cell and then edit the formula using the Formula bar, or double-click the cell to display the original formula in the cell and then edit the formula. In both cases, click **Enter** (✓) or press **Enter** when you finish editing the formula.

Understanding Excel Functions

To build powerful and useful formulas, you often need to include one or more Excel functions as operands. To get the most out of functions and to help you build formulas quickly and easily, you need to understand a few things about functions. For example, you need to understand the advantages of using functions and you need to know the basic structure of every function. To get a sense of what is available and how you might use functions, you need to review the Excel function types.

Functions

A *function* is a predefined formula that performs a specific task. For example, the SUM function calculates the total of a list of numbers, and the PMT (payment) function calculates a loan or mortgage payment. You can use functions on their own, preceded by =, or as part of a larger formula.

Function Advantages

Functions take you beyond basic arithmetic and comparison formulas by offering two main advantages. First, functions make simple but cumbersome formulas easier to use. For example, calculating a loan payment requires a complex formula, but the Excel PMT function makes this easy. Second, functions enable you to include complex mathematical expressions in your worksheets.

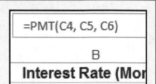

Function Structure

Every worksheet function has the same basic structure: NAME(Argument1, Argument2, ...). The NAME part identifies the function. In worksheet formulas and custom PivotTable formulas, the function name always appears in uppercase letters: PMT, SUM, AVERAGE, and so on. The items that appear within the parentheses are the functions' *arguments*. The arguments are the inputs that functions use to perform calculations. For example, the function SUM(B2, B3, B4) adds the values in cells B2, B3, and B4.

Common Mathematical Functions

Function	Description
MOD(number,divisor)	Returns the remainder of a number after dividing by the divisor
PI( )	Returns the value Pi
PRODUCT(number1,number2,...)	Multiplies the specified numbers
RAND( )	Returns a random number between 0 and 1
RANDBETWEEN(number1,number2)	Returns a random number between the two numbers
ROUND(number,digits)	Rounds the number to a specified number of digits
SQRT(number)	Returns the positive square root of the number
SUM(number1,number2,...)	Adds the arguments

Common Statistical Functions

Function	Description
AVERAGE(number1,number2,...)	Returns the average of the arguments
COUNT(number1,number2,...)	Counts the numbers in the argument list
MAX(number1,number2,...)	Returns the maximum value of the arguments
MEDIAN(number1,number2,...)	Returns the median value of the arguments
MIN(number1,number2,...)	Returns the minimum value of the arguments
MODE(number1,number2,...)	Returns the most common value of the arguments
STDEV(number1,number2,...)	Returns the standard deviation based on a sample
STDEVP(number1,number2,...)	Returns the standard deviation based on an entire population

Financial Functions

Most Excel financial functions use the following arguments:

Argument	Description
rate	The fixed rate of interest over the term of the loan or investment
nper	The number of payments or deposit periods over the term of the loan or investment
pmt	The periodic payment or deposit
pv	The present value of the loan (the principal) or the initial deposit in an investment
fv	The future value of the loan or investment
type	The type of payment or deposit: 0 (the default) for end-of-period payments or deposits; 1 for beginning-of-period payments or deposits

The following table lists some common financial functions:

Function	Description
FV(rate,nper,pmt,pv,type)	Returns the future value of an investment or loan
IPMT(rate,per,nper,pv,fv,type)	Returns the interest payment for a specified period of a loan
NPER(rate,pmt,pv,fv,type)	Returns the number of periods for an investment or loan
PMT(rate,nper,pv,fv,type)	Returns the periodic payment for a loan or investment
PPMT(rate,per,nper,pv,fv,type)	Returns the principal payment for a specified period of a loan
PV(rate,nper,pmt,fv,type)	Returns the present value of an investment
RATE(nper,pmt,pv,fv,type,guess)	Returns the periodic interest rate for a loan or investment

Add a Function to a Formula

To get the benefit of an Excel function, you must use it within a formula. You can use a function as the only operand in the formula, or you can include the function as part of a larger formula. The Insert Function feature makes it easy to choose the function you need and add the appropriate arguments. This dialog box enables you to display functions by category, and then choose the function you want from a list. You then see the Function Arguments dialog box that enables you to easily see and fill in the arguments used by the function.

Add a Function to a Formula

1 Click in the cell in which you want to build the formula.

2 Type **=**.

3 Type any operands and operators you need before adding the function.

4 Click the **Insert Function** button (*f*x).

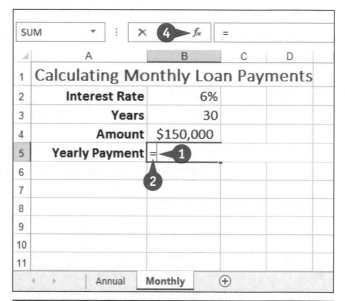

The Insert Function dialog box appears.

5 Click the drop-down arrow (⌄), and then click the category that contains the function you want to use.

6 Click the function.

7 Click **OK**.

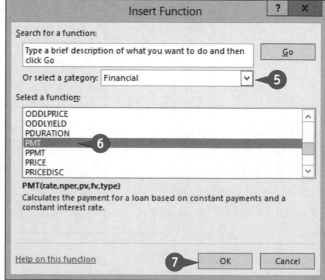

The Function Arguments dialog box appears.

8 Click inside an argument box.

9 Click the cell that contains the argument value.

You can also type the argument value.

10 Repeat Steps **8** and **9** to fill as many arguments as you need.

Ⓐ The function result appears here.

11 Click **OK**.

Ⓑ Excel adds the function to the formula.

Ⓒ Excel displays the formula result.

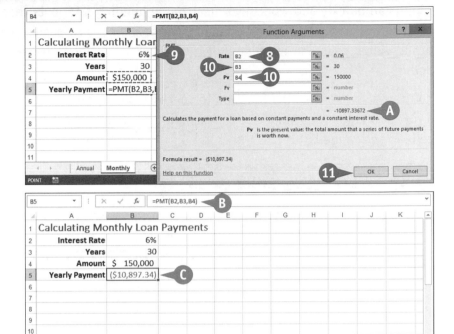

Note: In this example, the result appears in the parentheses to indicate a negative value. In loan calculations, money that you pay out is always a negative amount.

Note: If your formula requires any other operands and operators, press **F2**, and then type what you need to complete your formula.

TIPS

Do I have to specify a value for every function argument?

Not necessarily. Some function arguments are required to obtain a result, but others are optional. In the PMT function, for example, the rate, nper, and pv arguments are required, but the fv and type arguments are optional. When the Function Arguments dialog box displays a result for the function, you know you have typed all the required arguments.

How do I calculate a monthly financial result if I only have yearly values?

This is a common problem. To solve it, you must convert the rate and term to monthly values. Divide the annual interest rate by 12, and then multiply the term by 12. For example, if the annual rate is in cell B2, the term in years is in B3, and the loan amount is in B4, then the function PMT(B2/12, B3*12, B4) calculates the monthly payment.

Add a Row or Column of Numbers

You can quickly add worksheet numbers by building a formula that uses the Excel SUM function. When you use the SUM function in a formula, you can specify as the function's arguments a series of individual cells. For example, SUM(A1, B2, C3) calculates the total of the values in cells A1, B2, and C3.

You can also use the SUM function to specify a single argument, which is a range reference to either a row or a column of numbers. For example, SUM(C3:C21) calculates the total of the values in all the cells in the range C3 to C21.

Add a Row or Column of Numbers

1 Click in the cell where you want the sum to appear.

2 Type **=sum(**.

A When you begin a function, Excel displays a banner that shows you the function's arguments.

Note: In the function banner, bold arguments are required, and arguments that appear in square brackets are optional.

3 Use the Excel mouse pointer (⇨) to click and drag the row or column of numbers that you want to add.

B Excel adds a reference for the range to the formula.

④ Type **)**.

⑤ Click **Enter** (✓) or press
    Enter.

C22	⑤	✓ *fx*	=sum(C3:C21)					
	A	B	C	D	E	F	G	H
1								
2		**Sales Rep**	**2011 Sales**	**2012 Sales**				
3		Nancy Freehafer	$996,336	$960,492				
4		Andrew Cencini	$606,731	$577,983				
5		Jan Kotas	$622,781	$967,580				
6		Mariya Sergienko	$765,327	$771,399				
7		Steven Thorpe	$863,589	$827,213				
8		Michael Neipper	$795,518	$669,394				
9		Robert Zare	$722,740	$626,945				
10		Laura Giussani	$992,059	$574,472				
11		Anne Hellung-Larsen	$659,380	$827,932				
12		Kyra Harper	$509,623	$569,609				
13		David Ferry	$987,777	$558,601				
14		Paul Voyatzis	$685,091	$692,182				
15		Andrea Aster	$540,484	$693,762				
16		Charles Granek	$650,733	$823,034				
17		Karen Aliston	$509,863	$511,569				
18		Karen Hammond	$503,699	$975,455				
19		Vince Durbin	$630,263	$599,514				
20		Paul Sellars	$779,722	$596,353				
21		Gregg O'Donoghue	$592,802	$652,171				
22		**TOTAL**	=sum(C3:C21) ◀ ④					
23								

Sheet1 Sheet2 ⊕

C Excel displays the formula.

D Excel displays the sum in the cell.

C22		✕ ✓ *fx*	=SUM(C3:C21) **C**					
	A	B	C	D	E	F	G	H
1								
2		**Sales Rep**	**2011 Sales**	**2012 Sales**				
3		Nancy Freehafer	$996,336	$960,492				
4		Andrew Cencini	$606,731	$577,983				
5		Jan Kotas	$622,781	$967,580				
6		Mariya Sergienko	$765,327	$771,399				
7		Steven Thorpe	$863,589	$827,213				
8		Michael Neipper	$795,518	$669,394				
9		Robert Zare	$722,740	$626,945				
10		Laura Giussani	$992,059	$574,472				
11		Anne Hellung-Larsen	$659,380	$827,932				
12		Kyra Harper	$509,623	$569,609				
13		David Ferry	$987,777	$558,601				
14		Paul Voyatzis	$685,091	$692,182				
15		Andrea Aster	$540,484	$693,762				
16		Charles Granek	$650,733	$823,034				
17		Karen Aliston	$509,863	$511,569				
18		Karen Hammond	$503,699	$975,455				
19		Vince Durbin	$630,263	$599,514				
20		Paul Sellars	$779,722	$596,353				
21		Gregg O'Donoghue	$592,802	$652,171				
22		**TOTAL**	$13,414,518 ◀ **D**					
23								

Sheet1 Sheet2 ⊕

READY

TIPS

Can I use the SUM function to total rows and columns at the same time?
Yes. The SUM function works not only with simple row and column ranges, but also with any rectangular range. After you type **=sum(**, use the mouse pointer (⊕) to click and drag the entire range that you want to sum.

Can I use the SUM function to total only certain values in a row or column?
Yes. The SUM function can accept multiple arguments, so you can enter as many cells or ranges as you need. After you type **=sum(**, hold down **Ctrl** and either click each cell that you want to include in the total, or use the mouse pointer (⊕) to click and drag each range that you want to sum.

Build an AutoSum Formula

You can reduce the time it takes to build a worksheet as well as reduce the possibility of errors by using the Excel AutoSum feature. This tool adds a SUM function formula to a cell and automatically adds the function arguments based on the structure of the worksheet data. For example, if there is a column of numbers above the cell where you want the SUM function to appear, AutoSum automatically includes that column of numbers as the SUM function argument.

Build an AutoSum Formula

1 Click in the cell where you want the sum to appear.

Note: For AutoSum to work, the cell you select should be below or to the right of the range you want to sum.

2 Click the **Home** tab.

3 Click the **Sum** button (Σ).

A If you want to use a function other than SUM, click the **Sum** drop-down arrow (⌄), and then click the operation you want to use: Average, Count Numbers, Max, or Min.

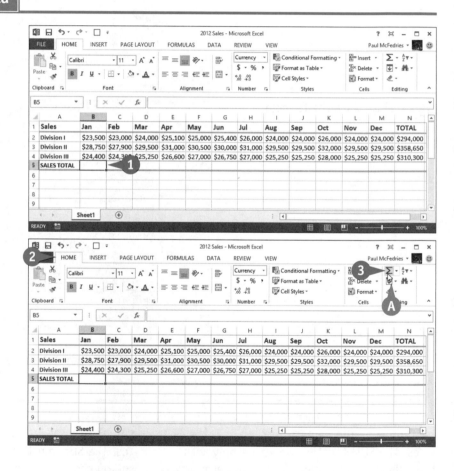

B Excel adds a SUM function formula to the cell.

Note: You can also press Alt + = instead of clicking the **Sum** button (Σ).

C Excel guesses that the range above (or to the left of) the cell is the one you want to add.

If Excel guessed wrong, you can select the correct range manually.

④ Click **Enter** (✓) or press Enter.

D Excel displays the formula.

E Excel displays the sum in the cell.

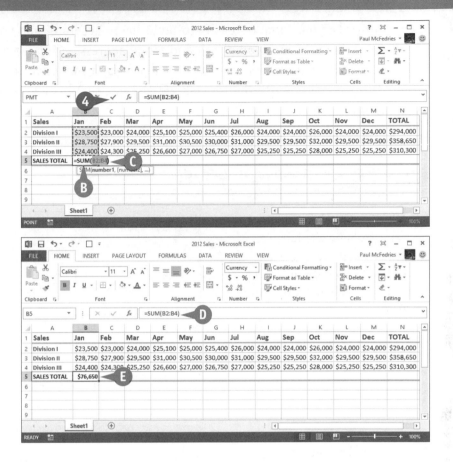

TIPS

Can I see the sum of a range without adding an AutoSum formula?

Yes. When you select any range, Excel adds the range's numeric values and displays the result in the middle of the status bar — for example, SUM: 76,650. By default, Excel also displays the Average and Count. If you want to see a different calculation, right-click the result in the status bar, and then click the operation you want to use: Numerical Count, Maximum, or Minimum.

Is there a faster way to add an AutoSum formula?

Yes. If you know the range you want to sum, and it is either a vertical column with a blank cell below it or a horizontal row with a blank cell to its right, select the range (including the blank cell). Then, click the **Sum** button (Σ) or press Alt + = . Excel populates the blank cell with a SUM formula that totals the selected range.

Add a Range Name to a Formula

You can make your formulas easier to build, more accurate, and easier to read by using range names as operands instead of cell and range addresses. For example, the formula =SUM(B2:B10) is difficult to decipher on its own, particularly if you cannot see the range B2:B10 to examine its values. However, if you use the formula =SUM(Expenses) instead, it becomes immediately obvious what the formula is meant to do.

See Chapter 4 to learn how to define names for ranges in Excel.

Add a Range Name to a Formula

1 Click in the cell in which you want to build the formula, type =, and then type any operands and operators you need before adding the range name.

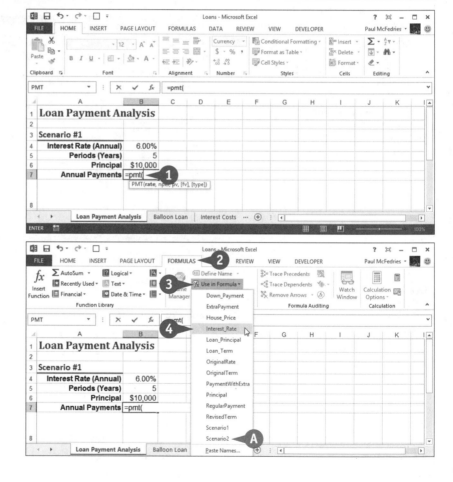

2 Click the **Formulas** tab.

3 Click **Use in Formula**.

A Excel displays a list of the range names in the current workbook.

4 Click the range name you want to use.

B Excel inserts the range name into the formula.

5 Type any operands and operators you need to complete your formula.

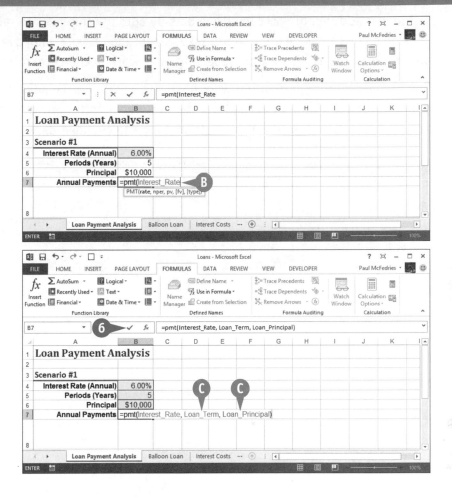

C If you need to insert other range names into your formula, repeat Steps 2 to 5 for each name.

6 Click **Enter** (✓) or press Enter .

Excel calculates the formula result.

TIPS

If I create a range name after I build my formula, can I convert the range reference to the range name?

Yes. Click the **Formulas** tab, click the **Define Name** drop-down arrow ( ), and then click **Apply Names** to open the Apply Names dialog box. In the Apply names list, click the range name you want, and then click **OK**. Excel replaces the associated range references with the range name in each formula within the worksheet.

Do I have to use the list of range names to insert range names into my formula?

No. As you build your formula, type the range name, or click the cell or select the range that has the defined name. Excel adds the name to your formula instead of the range address. To work from a list of defined range names, click an empty area of the worksheet, click **Formulas**, click **Use in Formula**, click **Paste Names**, and then click **Paste List**.

Reference Another Worksheet Range in a Formula

You can add flexibility to your formulas by adding references to ranges that reside in other worksheets. This enables you to take advantage of work you have done in other worksheets, so you do not have to waste time repeating your work in the current worksheet.

Referencing a range in another worksheet also gives you the advantage of having automatically updated information. For example, if the data in the other worksheet range changes, Excel automatically updates your formula to include the changed data.

Reference Another Worksheet Range in a Formula

1 Click in the cell in which you want to build the formula, type **=**, and then type any operands and operators you need before adding the range reference.

	A	J	K	L	M	N	O	P	Q	R	S
1		Jul	Aug	Sep	3rd Quarter	Oct	Nov	Dec	4th Quarter	TOTAL	
2	Sales										
3	Division I	26,000	24,000	24,000	74,000	26,000	24,000	24,000	74,000	294,000	
4	Division II	31,000	29,500	29,500	90,000	32,000	29,500	29,500	91,000	358,550	
5	Division III	27,000	25,250	25,250	77,500	28,000	25,250	25,250	78,500	310,000	
6	SALES TOTAL	84,000	78,750	78,750	241,500	86,000	78,750	78,750	243,500	962,550	
7	Expenses										
8	Cost of Goods	6,720	6,300	6,300	19,320	6,880	6,300	6,300	19,480	77,004	
9	Advertising	5,500	5,200	5,200	15,900	4,500	5,200	5,200	14,900	60,550	
10	Rent	2,100	2,100	2,100	6,300	2,100	2,100	2,100	6,300	25,200	
11	Supplies	1,300	1,400	1,400	4,100	1,250	1,350	1,400	4,000	15,950	
12	Salaries	17,000	17,000	17,000	51,000	17,000	17,500	17,500	52,000	201,500	
13	Shipping	15,000	14,500	14,500	44,000	15,750	15,250	14,500	45,500	176,250	
14	Utilities	650	600	600	1,850	650	600	600	1,850	7,200	
15	EXPENSES TOTAL	48,270	47,100	47,100	142,470	48,130	48,300	47,600	144,030	563,654	
16	GROSS PROFIT	35,730	31,650	31,650	99,030	37,870	30,450	31,150	99,470	398,896	
17								Difference from Last Year's Profit:	=R16 -		
18											

Budget | Assumptions | Projections | 2012-2013 Final | Es ⋯ ⊕ | ◀

2 Press **Ctrl** + **Page down** until the worksheet you want to use appears.

	A	B	C	D	E	F	G	H	I	J
1		Jan	Feb	Mar	1st Quarter	Apr	May	Jun	2nd Quarter	Jul
2	Sales									
3	Division I	21,620	21,160	22,080	64,860	23,092	23,000	23,368	69,460	23,920
4	Division II	26,450	25,576	27,140	79,166	28,520	28,060	27,600	84,180	28,520
5	Division III	22,448	22,080	23,230	67,758	24,472	24,840	24,610	73,922	24,840
6	SALES TOTAL	70,518	68,816	72,450	211,784	76,084	75,900	75,578	227,562	77,280
7	Expenses									
8	Cost of Goods	5,924	5,781	6,086	17,790	6,391	6,376	6,349	19,115	6,492
9	Advertising	4,830	4,410	5,460	14,700	5,250	5,775	5,513	16,538	5,775
10	Rent	2,205	2,205	2,205	6,615	2,205	2,205	2,205	6,615	2,205
11	Supplies	1,365	1,260	1,470	4,095	1,365	1,313	1,470	4,148	1,365
12	Salaries	16,800	16,800	17,325	50,925	17,325	17,325	17,850	52,500	17,850
13	Shipping	14,963	14,438	15,225	44,625	15,750	15,225	15,488	46,463	15,750
14	Utilities	525	630	630	1,785	578	630	683	1,890	683
15	EXPENSES TOTAL	46,611	45,523	48,401	140,535	48,864	48,848	49,556	147,268	50,119
16	GROSS PROFIT	23,907	23,293	24,049	71,249	27,220	27,052	26,022	80,294	27,161
17										
18										

Budget | Assumptions | Projections | 2012-2013 Final | ◀

③ Select the range you want to use.

④ Press Ctrl + Page up until you return to the original worksheet.

	Jul	Aug	Sep	3rd Quarter	Oct	Nov	Dec	4th Quarter	TOTAL
1	Jul	Aug	Sep	3rd Quarter	Oct	Nov	Dec	4th Quarter	TOTAL
3	23,920	22,080	22,080	68,080	23,920	22,080	22,080	68,080	270,480
4	28,520	27,140	27,140	82,800	29,440	27,140	27,140	83,720	329,866
5	24,840	23,230	23,230	71,300	25,760	23,230	23,230	72,220	285,200
6	77,280	72,450	72,450	222,180	79,120	72,450	72,450	224,020	885,546
8	6,492	6,086	6,086	18,663	6,646	6,086	6,086	18,818	74,386
9	5,775	5,460	5,460	16,695	4,725	5,460	5,460	15,645	63,578
10	2,205	2,205	2,205	6,615	2,205	2,205	2,205	6,615	26,460
11	1,365	1,470	1,470	4,305	1,313	1,418	1,470	4,200	16,748
12	17,850	17,850	17,850	53,550	17,850	18,375	18,375	54,600	211,575
13	15,750	15,225	15,225	46,200	16,538	16,013	15,225	47,775	185,063
14	683	630	630	1,943	683	630	630	1,943	7,560
15	50,119	48,926	48,926	147,971	49,959	50,186	49,451	149,595	585,368
16	27,161	23,524	23,524	74,209	29,161	22,264	22,999	74,425	300,178

Budget | ...ons | Projections | 2012-2013 Final

Ⓐ A reference to the range on the other worksheet appears in your formula.

⑤ Type any operands and operators you need to complete your formula.

⑥ Click **Enter** (✓) or press **Enter**.

Excel calculates the formula result.

fx =R16 - '2012-2013 Final'!R16

	Jul	Aug	Sep	3rd Quarter	Oct	Nov	Dec	4th Quarter	TOTAL
n I	26,000	24,000	24,000	74,000	26,000	24,000	24,000	74,000	294,000
n II	31,000	29,500	29,500	90,000	32,000	29,500	29,500	91,000	358,550
n III	27,000	25,250	25,250	77,500	28,000	25,250	25,250	78,500	310,000
TOTAL	84,000	78,750	78,750	241,500	86,000	78,750	78,750	243,500	962,550
f Goods	6,720	6,300	6,300	19,320	6,880	6,300	6,300	19,480	77,004
tising	5,500	5,200	5,200	15,900	4,500	5,200	5,200	14,900	60,550
	2,100	2,100	2,100	6,300	2,100	2,100	2,100	6,300	25,200
es	1,300	1,400	1,400	4,100	1,250	1,350	1,400	4,000	15,950
s	17,000	17,000	17,000	51,000	17,000	17,500	17,500	52,000	201,500
ng	15,000	14,500	14,500	44,000	15,750	15,250	14,500	45,500	176,250
s	650	600	600	1,850	650	600	600	1,850	7,200
SES TOTAL	48,270	47,100	47,100	142,470	48,130	48,300	47,600	144,030	563,654
PROFIT	35,730	31,650	31,650	99,030	37,870	30,450	31,150	99,470	398,896

Difference from Last Year's Profit: =R16 - '2012-2013 Final'!R16

Budget | Assumptions | Projections | 2012-2013 Final | Estimate: ...

TIPS

Can I manually reference a range in another worksheet?

Yes. Rather than selecting the other worksheet range with your mouse, you can type the range reference directly into your formula. Type the worksheet name, surrounded by single quotation marks (') if the name contains a space; type an exclamation mark (!); then type the cell or range address. Here is an example: **'Expenses 2013'!B2:B10**.

Can I reference a range in another workbook in my formula?

Yes. Open the workbook you want to reference, click the **Excel taskbar icon** (▣), and then click the other workbook to switch to it. Click the worksheet that has the range you want to reference, and then select the range. Click the **Excel taskbar icon** (▣), and then click the original workbook to switch back. Excel adds the workbook range reference to your formula.

Move or Copy a Formula

You can restructure or reorganize a worksheet by moving an existing formula to a different part of the worksheet. When you move a formula, Excel preserves the formula's range references.

Excel also enables you to make a copy of a formula, which is a useful technique if you require a duplicate of the formula elsewhere or if you require a formula that is similar to an existing formula. When you copy a formula, Excel adjusts the range references to the new location.

Move or Copy a Formula

Move a Formula

1. Click the cell that contains the formula you want to move.

2. Position the Excel mouse pointer (⊕) over any outside border of the cell. The pointer (⊕) changes to the Range Border (⬚).

3. Click and drag the cell to the new location. The Range Border (⬚) changes to the mouse pointer (⬚).

A. Excel displays an outline of the cell.

B. Excel displays the address of the new location.

4. Release the mouse button.

C. Excel moves the formula to the new location.

D. Excel does not change the formula's range references.

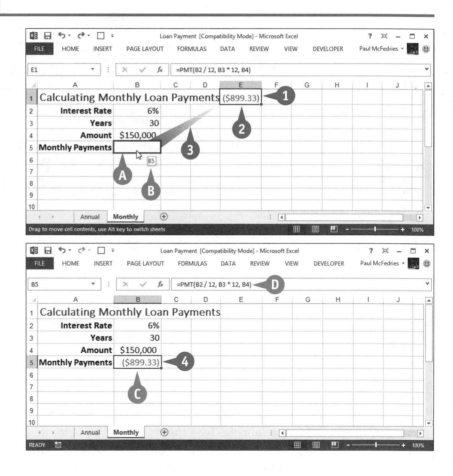

Copy a Formula

1. Click the cell that contains the formula you want to copy.

2. Press and hold Ctrl.

3. Position the mouse pointer (⊕) over any outside border of the cell; the pointer (⊕) becomes the Pointer Copy (⊳).

4. Click and drag the cell where you want the copy to appear.

E. Excel displays an outline of the cell.

F. Excel displays the address of the new location.

5. Release the mouse button.

6. Release Ctrl.

G. Excel creates a copy of the formula in the new location.

H. Excel adjusts the range references.

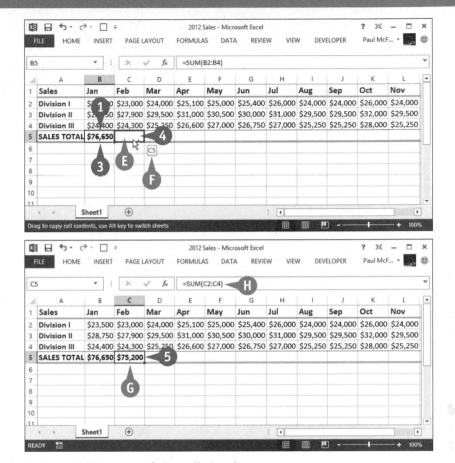

Note: To make multiple copies, drag the bottom-right corner of the cell. Excel fills the adjacent cells with copies of the formula. See the following section, "Switch to Absolute Cell References" for an example.

TIP

Why does Excel adjust the range references when I copy a formula?

When you make a copy of a formula, Excel assumes that you want that copy to reference different ranges than in the original formula. In particular, Excel assumes that the ranges you want to use in the new formula are positioned relative to the ranges used in the original formula, and that the relative difference is equal to the number of rows and columns you dragged the cell to create the copy.

Suppose your original formula references cell A1, and you make a copy of the formula in the cell one column to the right. Excel also adjusts the cell reference one column to the right, so it becomes B1 in the new formula. To learn how to control this behavior, see the following section, "Switch to Absolute Cell References."

Switch to Absolute Cell References

You can make some formulas easier to copy by switching to absolute cell references. When you use a regular cell address — called a *relative cell reference* — such as A1 in a formula, Excel adjusts that reference when you copy the formula to another location. To prevent that reference from changing, you must change it to the *absolute cell reference* format: A1.

See the first tip at the end of this section to learn more about the difference between relative and absolute cell references.

Switch to Absolute Cell References

1 Double-click the cell that contains the formula you want to edit.

2 Select the cell reference you want to change.

3 Press **F4**.

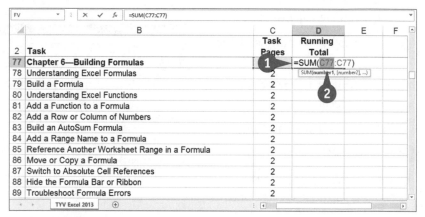

A Excel switches the address to an absolute cell reference.

4 Repeat Steps **2** and **3** to switch any other cell addresses that you require in the absolute reference format.

5 Click **Enter** (✓) or press **Enter**.

188

B Excel adjusts the formula.

6 Copy the formula.

Note: See the preceding section, "Move or Copy a Formula," to learn how to copy a formula.

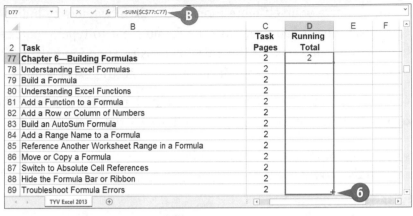

C Excel preserves the absolute cell references in the copied formulas.

TIPS

What is the difference between absolute and relative cell references?

Excel treats cell references in formulas as being relative to the formula's cell. If the formula in cell B5 references cell A1, Excel treats A1 as the cell four rows up and one column to the left. If you copy the formula to cell D10, the cell four rows up and one column to the left now refers to cell C6. In the copied formula, Excel changes A1 to C6. If the original formula refers to A1, then the copied formula in cell D10 also refers to A1.

How do I restore a cell address back to a relative cell reference?

Press F4 once to switch to the absolute cell reference format, such as A1. Press F4 again to switch to a mixed reference format that uses a relative column and absolute row (A$1). Press F4 a third time to switch to a mixed reference format that uses an absolute column and relative row ($A1). Press F4 a fourth time to return to the relative cell reference (A1).

Hide the Formula Bar or Ribbon

You can give yourself more room in the Excel window by hiding the Formula bar or Ribbon. This is a good idea if you never use the Formula bar to type or edit cell data, or never use its features, such as the Name box, or the Enter and Insert Function buttons. If you find that you need the Formula bar later, you can quickly restore it to the Excel window.

You can also gain more worksheet room by hiding the Ribbon. When you hide the Ribbon, Excel keeps the tabs visible, so you can still access the commands.

Hide the Formula Bar or Ribbon

Hide the Formula Bar

1 Click the **View** tab.

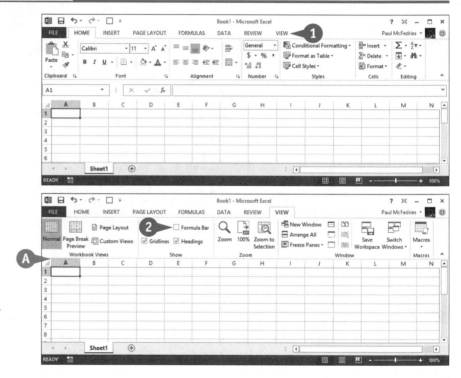

2 Click the selected **Formula Bar** check box (☑) and it is cleared (☐).

Ⓐ Excel removes the Formula bar from the window.

Note: To restore the Formula bar, repeat Steps 1 and 2. The empty check box (☐) is filled (☑).

Hide the Ribbon

1 Click **Unpin the Ribbon** (^).

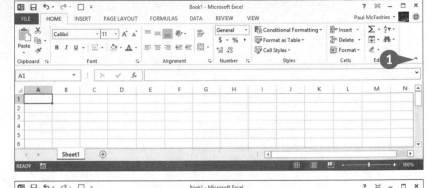

Ⓑ Excel hides the Ribbon.

Ⓒ Excel keeps the Ribbon tabs visible.

Note: To restore the Ribbon, click any tab, and then click **Pin the Ribbon** (↯).

Note: You can also hide and display the Ribbon by pressing `Ctrl`+`F1`.

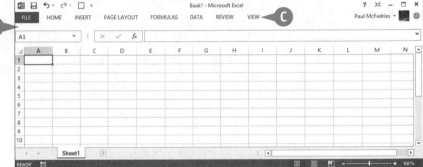

TIP

If I can only see part of a long entry in the Formula bar, can I fix it?
On the right side of the Formula bar, click the **Expand Formula Bar** button (⌄) or press `Ctrl`+`Shift`+`U` to increase the size of the Formula bar, as shown here. To enlarge it further, either click and drag the bottom edge of the Formula bar, or click the **Gallery Down** (⌄) or **Up** (⌃) scroll arrows to navigate the entry. Click the **Collapse Formula Bar** button (^) or press `Ctrl`+`Shift`+`U` to return the Formula bar to its normal state.

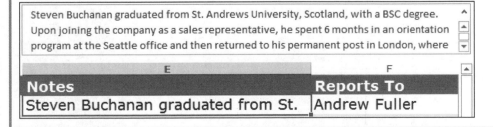

CHAPTER 9

Getting More Out of Formulas

If your spreadsheet contains formulas, there are tools and techniques that can help you get more out of those formulas. These include toggling between displaying formulas and results; monitoring a formula result; and troubleshooting formula errors.

Paste a Formula Result

You can control the output that a copied formula displays by pasting the formula's result rather than the actual formula.

After you copy a formula that uses relative cell references, when you paste the formula, Excel automatically adjusts the cell references. This automatic adjustment of cell references means that you always end up with a different formula after you paste the original. One way to avoid this is to use absolute cell references, as described in Chapter 8. Alternatively, if you are only interested in the formula result, you can paste the copied formula as a value.

Paste a Formula Result

1 Select the cell containing the formula you want to copy.

Note: This task uses a single cell, but the technique also works for a range of cells.

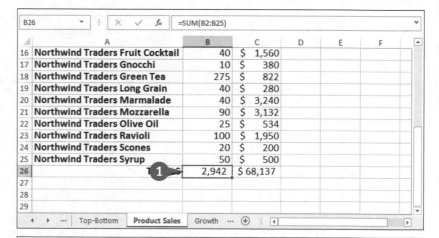

2 Click the **Home** tab.

3 Click **Copy** (🗐).

Note: You can also copy the selected cell by pressing Ctrl+C.

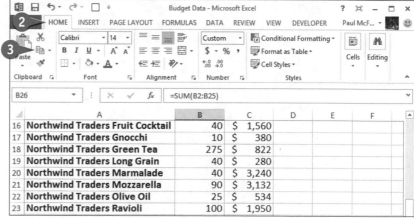

④ Click the cell where you want to paste the formula value.

⑤ Click the **Paste** drop-down arrow (☑).

⑥ Click **Paste Values** (🗒).

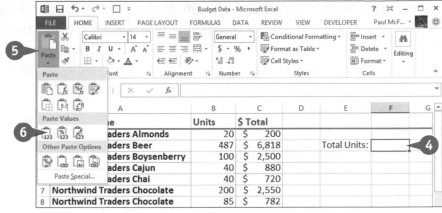

Ⓐ Excel pastes just the value of the formula, not the actual formula.

TIPS

Can I paste the result with formatting?
Yes. To include the original number format in the pasted cell, click the **Paste** drop-down arrow (☑), and then click **Values & Number Formatting** (🗒) instead. If you prefer to transfer all the original cell formatting, click the **Paste** drop-down arrow (☑), and then click **Values & Source Formatting** (🗒).

If I change the formula or its input values, does the pasted result change as well?
No. The pasted value will be incorrect if the formula changes in any way. To ensure that a particular cell always displays the current formula result, select the destination cell, press ⌨ =, click the original cell, and then press Enter. This simple formula tells Excel to always display the value of the original cell's formula.

Show Formulas Instead of Results

If you want to check a formula, you cannot do it by looking at the cell because Excel displays the formula result instead of the formula itself. You must click the cell to view the formula in the Formula bar. That works for a single cell, but what if you need to check all the formulas in a worksheet? You could click each cell that contains a formula, but that is impractical in a sheet with dozens of formulas. Instead, you can change the worksheet view to display the formulas in each cell rather than the formula results.

Show Formulas Instead of Results

1 Switch to the worksheet that contains the formulas you want to display.

2 Click the **File** tab.

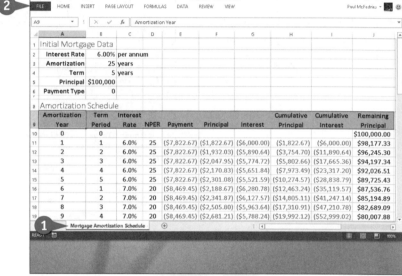

3 Click **Options**.

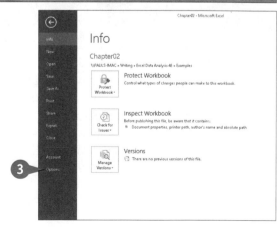

The Excel Options dialog box appears.

④ Click **Advanced**.

⑤ Click the empty **Show formulas in cells instead of their calculated results** check box (☐) and it is filled (☑).

⑥ Click **OK**.

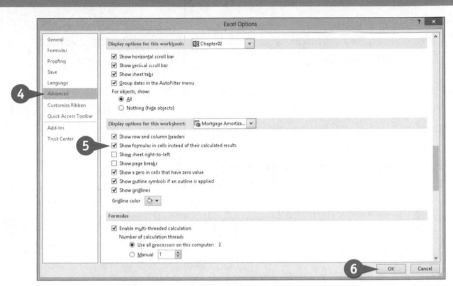

Ⓐ Excel displays the formulas instead of their results.

Note: You can also toggle the display between formulas and results by pressing Ctrl+ ~ .

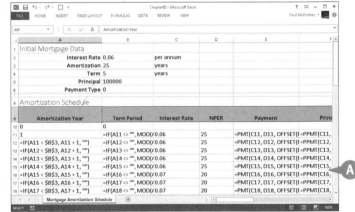

TIP

Is there are an easy way to view formulas in all worksheets?

The technique you learned in this section applies only to the current worksheet. If you want to view the formulas in every sheet in a workbook, run the following VBA macro:

```
Sub ToggleFormulasAndResults()
    Dim win As Window
    Dim wv As WorksheetView
    For Each win In ActiveWorkbook.Windows
        For Each wv In win.SheetViews
            wv.DisplayFormulas = Not wv.DisplayFormulas
        Next 'wv
    Next 'win
End Sub
```

See Chapter 25 to learn how to add and run a VBA macro in Excel.

Use a Watch Window to Monitor a Cell Value

When you build a spreadsheet, it is often useful to monitor a cell. For example, if a cell calculates the average of a range, you might want to monitor the average as the data changes to see if it reaches a particular value.

Monitoring a cell value is hard if the cell's formula resides in a different worksheet or off-screen in the current worksheet. Rather than navigating back and forth to check the value, use the Watch Window, which always stays on-screen. This way, no matter where you are within Excel, you can see the value of the cell.

Use a Watch Window to Monitor a Cell Value

1 Select the value you want to watch.

2 Click the **Formulas** tab.

3 Click **Watch Window**.

The Watch Window appears.

4 Click **Add Watch**.

The Add Watch dialog box appears.

A The selected cell appears in the reference box.

B If the cell is incorrect, click the cell you want to monitor.

5 Click **Add**.

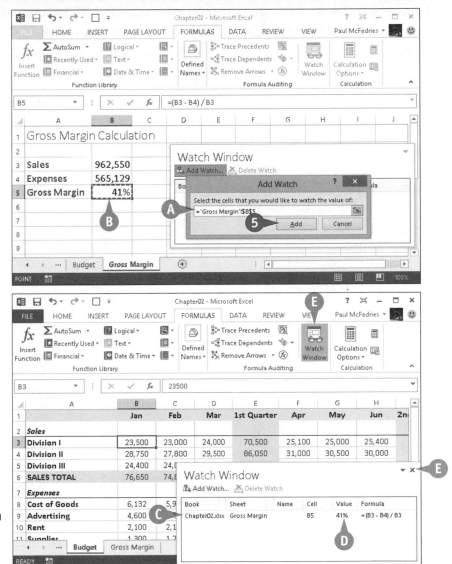

C Excel adds the cell to the Watch Window.

D The value of the cell appears here.

As you work with Excel, the Watch Window stays on top of the other windows so you can monitor the cell value.

E If the Watch Window gets in the way, you can hide it by either clicking **Close** (×) or by clicking **Watch Window** in the Formula tab.

TIPS

Can I only monitor one cell value at a time?

You are not restricted to monitoring just a single cell in the Watch Window. You can add as many watch items as you need. Note, too, that although you can use the Watch Window as a handy way to monitor a cell value, you can also use it to navigate. That is, if you double-click a watch item, Excel automatically selects the corresponding cell.

How do I remove an item from the Watch Window?

If you no longer need to monitor a particular cell value, you should delete the cell's watch item to reduce clutter in the Watch Window. Click the **Formulas** tab and then click **Watch Window** to open the Watch Window. Click the watch you no longer need, and then click **Delete Watch**. Excel removes the watch.

Create an Array Formula

If you repeat the same formula across a range, you can take advantage of *array formulas*, which are special formulas that generate multiple results. If your worksheet has expense totals in cells C11, D11, and E11, and a budget increase value in cell C3, you calculate the new budget values with the following formulas:

=C11 * (1 + C3)   =D11 * (1 + C3)   =E11 * (1 + C3)

Rather than typing these formulas separately, you can just type a single array formula:

{=C11:E11 * (1 + C3)}

Create an Array Formula

Create a Multicell Array Formula

① Select the range where you want the formula results to appear.

② Type the array formula.

③ Press Ctrl + Shift + Enter.

FV			× ✓ fx	=C11:E11 * (1 + C3)				
	A	B	C	D	E	F	G	H
3		**INCREASE**	3%					
4								
5		**2012 EXPENSES**	**January**	**February**	**March**			
6		**Advertising**	$4,600	$4,200	$5,200			
7		**Rent**	$2,100	$2,100	$2,100			
8		**Supplies**	$1,300	$1,200	$1,400			
9		**Salaries**	$16,000	$16,000	$16,500			
10		**Utilities**	$500	$600	$600			
11		**2012 TOTAL**	$24,500	$24,100	$25,800			
12								
13		**2013 BUDGET**	=C11:E11 * (1 + C3)			◀①		
14		**2013 TOTAL**						
15			②					

Excel Data Analysis 4E   Budget - 1st Quarter   ⊕

Ⓐ Excel enters the formula as an array formula and automatically adds braces around it.

Ⓑ Excel enters the results in the range you selected.

C13			× ✓ fx	{=C11:E11 * (1 + C3)} ◀Ⓐ				
	A	B	C	D	E	F	G	H
3		**INCREASE**	3%					
4								
5		**2012 EXPENSES**	**January**	**February**	**March**			
6		**Advertising**	$4,600	$4,200	$5,200			
7		**Rent**	$2,100	$2,100	$2,100			
8		**Supplies**	$1,300	$1,200	$1,400			
9		**Salaries**	$16,000	$16,000	$16,500			
10		**Utilities**	$500	$600	$600			
11		**2012 TOTAL**	$24,500	$24,100	$25,800			
12								
13		**2013 BUDGET**	$25,235	$24,823	$26,574	◀Ⓑ		
14		**2013 TOTAL**						
15								

Excel Data Analysis 4E   Budget - 1st Quarter   ⊕

Create a Single-Cell Array Formula

1. Select the cell where you want the formula result to appear.

2. Type the array formula.

3. Press Ctrl + Shift + Enter .

| FV | ▼ | : | × | ✓ | fx | =SUM(C11:E11 * (1 + C3)) |

▲	A	B	C	D	E	F	G	H
3		**INCREASE**	3%					
4								
5		**2012 EXPENSES**	**January**	**February**	**March**			
6		**Advertising**	$4,600	$4,200	$5,200			
7		**Rent**	$2,100	$2,100	$2,100			
8		**Supplies**	$1,300	$1,200	$1,400			
9		**Salaries**	$16,000	$16,000	$16,500			
10		**Utilities**	$500	$600	$600			
11		**2012 TOTAL**	$24,500	$24,100	$25,800			
12								
13		**2013 BUDGET**	$25,235	$24,823	$26,574			
14		**2013 TOTAL**	=SUM(C11:E11 * (1 + C3))	◀ 2				
15								

◀ ▶ ⋯ | Excel Data Analysis 4E ① Budget - 1st Quarter | ⊕ | : | ◀

C. Excel enters the formula as an array formula and automatically adds braces around it.

D. Excel enters the result in the cell you selected.

| C14 | ▼ | : | × | ✓ | fx | {=SUM(C11:E11 * (1 + C3))} ◀ C |

▲	A	B	C	D	E	F	G	H
3		**INCREASE**	3%					
4								
5		**2012 EXPENSES**	**January**	**February**	**March**			
6		**Advertising**	$4,600	$4,200	$5,200			
7		**Rent**	$2,100	$2,100	$2,100			
8		**Supplies**	$1,300	$1,200	$1,400			
9		**Salaries**	$16,000	$16,000	$16,500			
10		**Utilities**	$500	$600	$600			
11		**2012 TOTAL**	$24,500	$24,100	$25,800			
12								
13		**2013 BUDGET**	$25,235	$24,823	$26,574			
14		**2013 TOTAL**	$76,632	◀ D				
15								

◀ ▶ ⋯ | Excel Data Analysis 4E | **Budget - 1st Quarter** | ⊕ | : | ◀

TIPS

Why can I not delete or edit a cell within a multicell array formula's results?

It is important to remember that Excel treats multicell array formulas as a unit. This means that you cannot edit, move, or delete a single cell or any subset of cells within an array. If you need to work with an array, you must select the whole range. Note that you can select an array quickly by selecting one of its cells and pressing Ctrl + / .

How can I make a multicell array smaller?

To reduce the size of an array, select it, select the Formula bar, and then press Ctrl + Enter to change the entry to a normal formula. You can then select the smaller range and reenter the array formula.

Combine Two Ranges Arithmetically

When you build a spreadsheet, you may find that the data you use is not correct, or is not producing the answers you seek. For example, a particular range of numbers might need to be doubled, or a range's data may work better if every value is increased by 10.

You can solve this problem by creating a new range that has the factor you want to use to modify the original range, and then combining the two ranges using the appropriate arithmetic operation.

Combine Two Ranges Arithmetically

1 Create a range that includes the factor by which you want to modify the original range.

Note: The new range must be the same size and shape as the original range.

2 Select the original range.

3 Click the **Home** tab.

4 Click **Copy** (⎙).

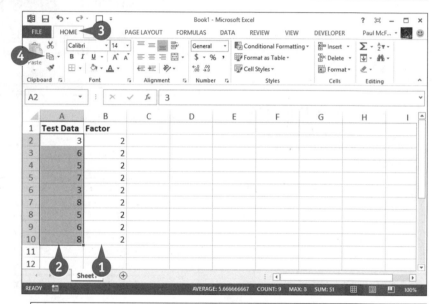

5 Select the range that contains the factors.

6 Click the **Paste** drop down arrow (⌄).

7 Click **Paste Special**.

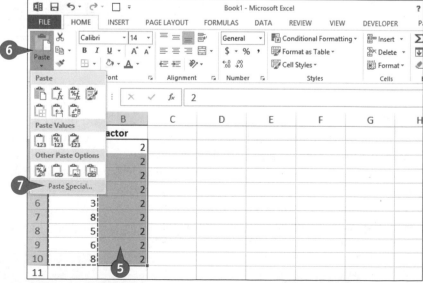

The Paste Special dialog box appears.

⑧ Click the empty radio button (○) of the arithmetic operation you want to use and it is filled (◉).

⑨ Click **OK**.

Ⓐ Excel combines the two ranges using the arithmetic operation you selected.

	A	B	C	D
1	**Test Data**	**Factor**		
2	3	6		
3	6	12		
4	5	10		
5	7	14		
6	3	6		
7	8	16		
8	5	10		
9	6	12		
10	8	16		
11			(Ctrl) ▾	
12				

TIPS

If my original data is in a column, does the range of factors also have to be in a column?

No. If your original data is in a column but your range of factors is in a row (or vice versa), you can still combine them arithmetically. Follow Steps **1** to **7** to open the Paste Special dialog box, and then select the arithmetic operation you want to use. Click the empty **Transpose** check box (□) and it is filled (☑). Click **OK**.

Do I have to use constants in the new range?

No. The new range can use whatever values you require.

Skip Data Tables When Calculating Workbooks

Because a data table (see Chapter 16) is an array, Excel treats it as a unit, so a worksheet recalculation means that the entire data table is always recalculated. This is not a big problem for a small data table with a few dozen formulas. However, it is not uncommon to have data tables with hundreds or even thousands of formulas, and these larger data tables can really slow down worksheet recalculation. To avoid this problem, you can configure Excel to skip data tables when it calculates worksheets.

Skip Data Tables When Calculating Workbooks

1 Click the **File** tab.

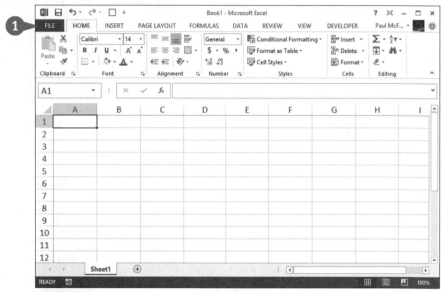

2 Click **Options**.

The Excel Options dialog box appears.

3 Click **Formulas**.

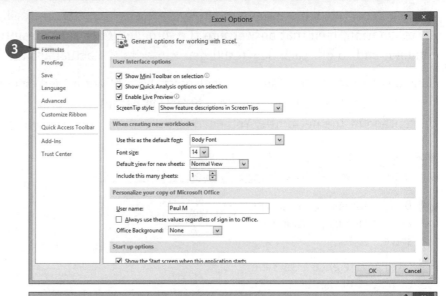

4 Click the empty **Automatic except for data tables** radio button (○) and it is filled (◉).

5 Click **OK**.

The next time you calculate a workbook, Excel bypasses the data tables.

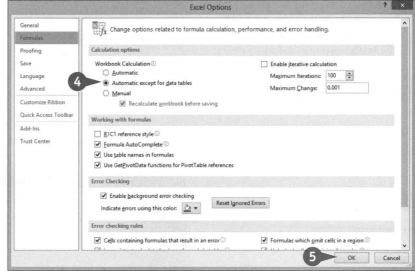

TIPS

How do I recalculate a data table?

To recalculate a data table, follow Steps **1** to **3**, and then click the filled **Automatic except for data tables** radio button (◉) and it is cleared (○). Click **OK**, and then recalculate the workbook. If you prefer to leave the **Automatic except for data tables** option selected, select any cell inside the data table, and then press F9 to recalculate.

Is there an easier way to toggle the skipping of data tables on and off?

Yes. If you often turn this option on and off, Excel offers a faster method for toggling this setting. Click the **Formulas** tab, click **Calculation Options** in the Calculation group, and then click the **Automatic Except for Data Tables** command. Alternatively, from the keyboard, press Alt+M, press X, and then press E.

Turn On Iterative Calculations

Some Excel calculations cannot derive the answer directly. Instead, you perform a preliminary calculation, feed that answer into the formula to get a new result, feed the new result into the formula, and so on. Each new result gets closer to the actual answer. This process is called *iteration*.

Consider a formula that calculates net profit by subtracting the amount paid in profit sharing from the gross profit. This is not simple subtraction because the profit sharing amount is calculated as a percentage of the net profit. You need to set up your formula, and then let Excel iterate the result.

Turn On Iterative Calculations

1 Build a formula that requires an iterative calculation to solve.

Ⓐ Circular reference arrows are displayed in the table.

Ⓑ In the **Formulas** tab, you can click **Remove Arrows** (🔏) to hide the circular reference arrows.

2 Click the **File** tab.

3 Click **Options**.

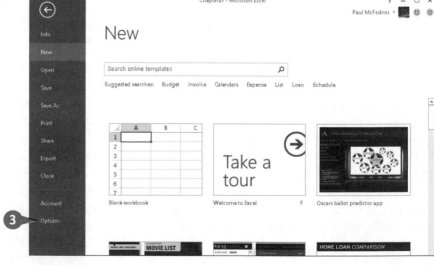

The Excel Options dialog box appears.

4 Click **Formulas**.

5 Click the empty **Enable iterative calculation** check box (□) and it is filled (☑).

C If Excel fails to converge on the solution, you can try typing a higher value in the **Maximum Iterations** text box.

D If you want a more accurate solution, you can try typing a smaller value in the **Maximum Change** text box.

6 Click **OK**.

Excel performs the iteration.

E The iterated result appears in the formula cell.

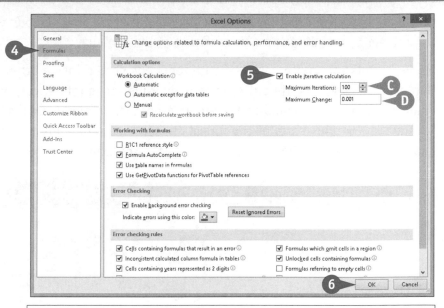

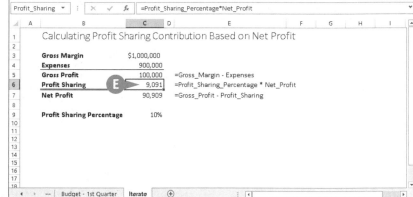

TIPS

Why does Excel display circular reference arrows when I set up an iterative calculation?

When you set up an iterative calculation, you are setting up a circular reference formula because there are terms on the left and right sides of the equal sign that depend on each other. In this section's example, the formula in C7 references the Profit_Sharing cell, which is C6. However, the Profit_Sharing cell references the Net_Profit cell, which is C7, so the references are circular.

What does the Maximum Change option do?

The Maximum Change value tells Excel how accurate you want your results to be. The smaller the number, the more accurate the calculation, but the longer the iteration takes.

Troubleshoot a Formula by Stepping Through Each Part

If you have a formula that is returning an inaccurate or erroneous result, you can troubleshoot the problem by stepping through each part of the formula.

Many formulas are quite complex, with functions nested inside other functions, multiple sets of parentheses, several different operators, multiple range references, and so on. You can use the Evaluate Formula command to help troubleshoot such formulas. This command enables you to step through the various parts of the formula to see the preliminary results returned by each part. By examining these interim results, you can often see where your formula goes awry.

Troubleshoot a Formula by Stepping Through Each Part

1 Select the cell that contains the formula you want to troubleshoot.

2 Click the **Formulas** tab.

3 Click **Evaluate Formula** (⑭).

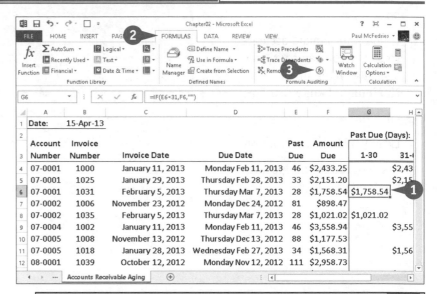

The Evaluate Formula dialog box appears.

Ⓐ Excel underlines the first expression that it will evaluate.

4 Click **Evaluate**.

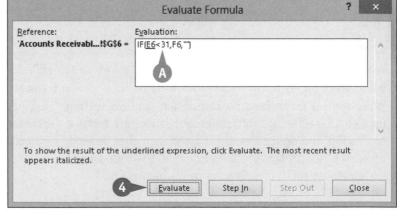

B Excel evaluates the underlined term, and then displays the result in italics.

C Excel underlines the next expression that it will evaluate.

5 Click **Evaluate**.

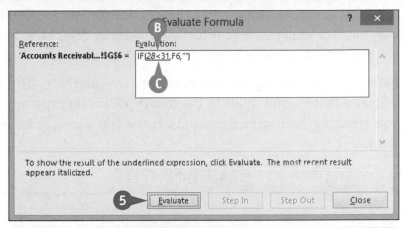

6 Repeat Step 5 to continue evaluating the formula's expressions.

Note: Continue evaluating the formula until you find the error or want to stop the evaluation.

D If you evaluate all the terms in the formula, Excel displays the result.

7 Click **Close**.

Note: If you still have trouble pinpointing the error, see the section "Audit a Formula to Locate Errors" later in this chapter.

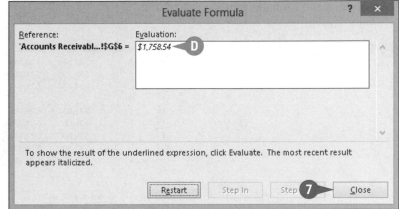

TIPS

I still do not see the error. What am I missing?

It is possible the error exists in one of the cells referenced by the formula. To check, when Excel underlines the cell reference, click **Step In** at the bottom of the Evaluate Formula dialog box. This tells Excel to display that cell's formula in the Evaluate Formula dialog box. You can then evaluate this secondary formula to look for problems. To return to the main formula, click **Step Out**.

Is there an easier way to check a particular part of a formula?

Yes. Open the formula cell for editing, and then select the expression that you want to evaluate. Either click the **Formulas** tab, and then click **Calculate Now** (⊞) in the Calculation group, or press F9. Excel evaluates the selected expression. Press Esc when you are done.

Display Text Instead of Error Values

If Excel encounters an error when calculating a formula, it often displays an error value as the result. For example, if your formula divides by zero, Excel indicates the error by displaying the value #DIV/0 in the cell.

Rather than displaying an error value, you can use the IFERROR function to test for an error and display a more useful result in the cell. IFERROR takes two arguments: expression is the formula you are using, and error_result is the text you want Excel to display if the formula produces an error.

Display Text Instead of Error Values

1 Select the range that contains the formulas you want to edit.

2 Press F2.

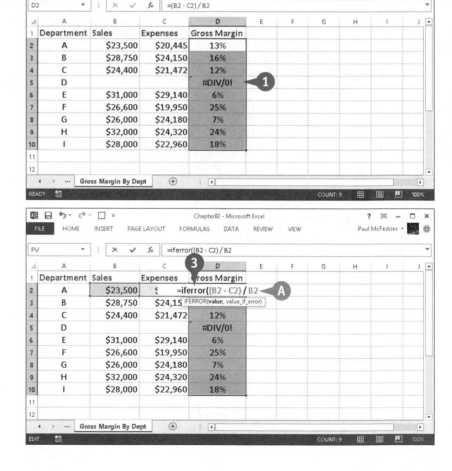

A Excel opens the first cell for editing.

3 After the formula's equal sign (=), type **iferror(**.

④ At the end of the formula, type a comma followed by the text (in quotation marks) that you want Excel to display in place of any error, followed by a closing parenthesis.

⑤ Press Ctrl + Enter.

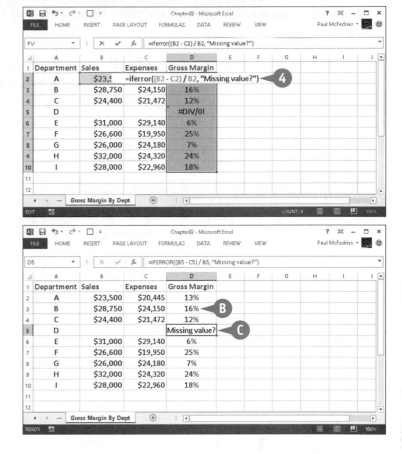

Ⓑ Excel displays the formula result in cells where there is no error.

Ⓒ Excel displays the text message in cells that generate an error.

TIP

What are the most common Excel error values?

The following six are the most common:

- #DIV/0. Your formula is dividing by zero. Check the divisor input cells for zero or blank values.

- #N/A. Your formula could not return a legitimate result. Check that your function arguments are appropriate.

- #NAME?. Your formula uses an unidentified range or function name. Double-check your names.

- #NUM!. Your formula uses a number inappropriately. Check the function arguments to make sure they use the correct data types.

- #REF#. Your formula contains a reference to an invalid cell, such as one that has been deleted. Restore the deleted cell or adjust the reference.

- #VALUE!. Your formula uses an inappropriate value in a function argument, such as a string instead of a number. Double-check your function arguments.

Check for Formula Errors in a Worksheet

You can take advantage of the background error checking in Excel to look for formula errors in a worksheet.

Excel's formula error checker is similar to Microsoft Word's grammar checker, in that it uses a set of rules to determine correctness, and it operates in the background to monitor your formulas. If it detects something wrong, it displays an *error indicator* — a green triangle — in the upper-left corner of the cell containing the formula. You can then use the associated smart tag to see a description of the error and to either fix or ignore the error.

Check for Formula Errors in a Worksheet

1. Examine your worksheet for a cell that displays the error indicator (⌐).

2. Click the cell.

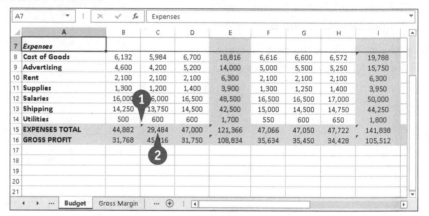

Ⓐ The error smart tag appears.

3. Move the mouse pointer (☒) over the smart tag.

Ⓑ Excel displays a description of the error.

4. Click the smart tag.

212

C Excel displays the smart tag options.

5 Click the command that fixes the formula.

Note: The name of the command depends on the error. You only see this command if Excel can fix the error.

D If the formula is not an error, you can click **Ignore Error** instead.

E Excel adjusts the formula.

F Excel removes the error indicator (ʳ) from the cell.

6 Repeat Steps **1** to **5** until you have checked all your worksheet formula errors.

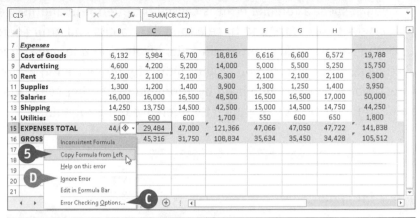

Can I customize the error checker?

Yes. To choose which rules you want enforced, click **File**, click **Options** to display the Excel Options dialog box, and then click the **Formulas** tab. (Alternatively, click an error smart tab, and then click **Error Checking Options**.) In the Error Checking Rules section, click the selected check box (☑) of any rule you do not want enforced and it is cleared (☐). Click **OK**.

Can I change the color of the error indicator?

Yes. This is a good idea if your workbook uses green colors for text or cell backgrounds, or if you have graphics that use a great deal of green. Click **File**, click **Options**, and then click the **Formulas** tab. In the Error Checking section, click the **Indicate errors using this color** drop-down arrow (☑), and then to click the color you prefer. Click **OK**.

Audit a Formula to Locate Errors

If you suspect a formula error is caused by an error in another cell, you can use Excel's auditing features to visualize and trace a formula's inputs and error sources. Auditing operates by creating *tracers* — arrows that point to the cells involved in a formula. Tracers can find three cell types: *Precedents* (cells that are directly or indirectly referenced in a formula), *dependents* (cells that are directly or indirectly referenced by a formula in another cell), and *errors* (cells that contain an error value, and are directly or indirectly referenced in a formula).

Audit a Formula to Locate Errors

Trace Precedents

1 Click the cell containing the formula with the precedents you want to trace.

2 Click the **Formulas** tab.

3 Click **Trace Precedents** (![icon]).

Ⓐ Excel adds a tracer arrow to each direct precedent.

4 Repeat Step **3** until you have added tracer arrows for all the formula's indirect precedents.

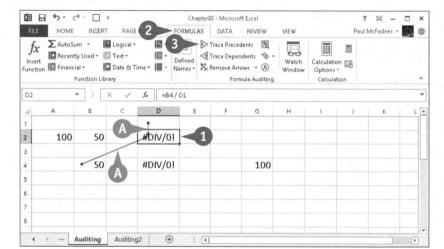

Trace Dependents

1 Click the cell containing the formula with the dependents you want to trace.

2 Click the **Formulas** tab.

3 Click **Trace Dependents** (![icon]).

Ⓑ Excel adds a tracer arrow to each direct dependent.

4 Repeat Step **3** until you have added tracer arrows for all the formula's indirect dependents.

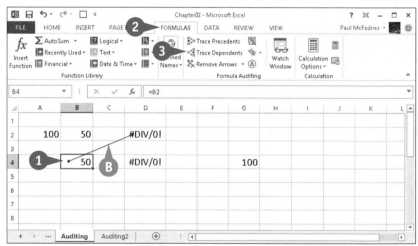

Trace Errors

1 Click the cell containing the error.

2 Click the **Formulas** tab.

3 Click **Remove Arrows** (🔀).

4 Click the **Error Checking** drop-down arrow ().

5 Click **Trace Error**.

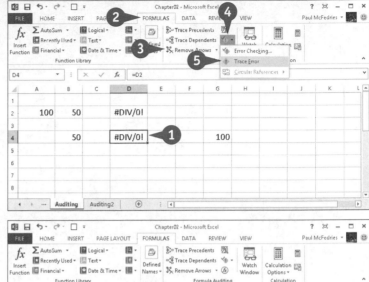

C Excel selects the cells that contain the original error.

D Excel displays tracer arrows showing the selected cells' precedents and dependents.

E A red tracer arrow indicates an error.

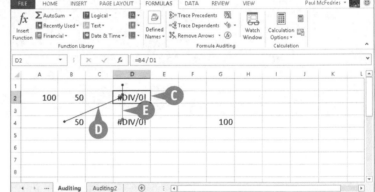

TIP

Is there a way to trace multiple errors?
You can use Error Checking to look for and trace errors. Click **Formulas**, and then click **Error Checking** (🔹). The Error Checking dialog box displays the first error, if any. You have the following choices:

- Trace Error: This button appears if the error is caused by an error in another cell. Click this button to display tracer arrows for the formula's precedents and dependents.
- Show Calculation Steps: This button appears if the error is caused by the cell's formula. Click this button to launch the Evaluate Formula feature, as described in the section "Troubleshoot a Formula by Stepping Through Each Part."
- Ignore Error: Click this button to bypass the error.

Click the **Previous** and **Next** buttons to navigate the worksheet errors.

CHAPTER 10

Manipulating Worksheets

An Excel worksheet is where you type your headings and data, and build your formulas. You spend most of your time in Excel operating within a worksheet, so you need to know how to navigate and perform worksheet tasks, such as renaming, moving, copying, and deleting.

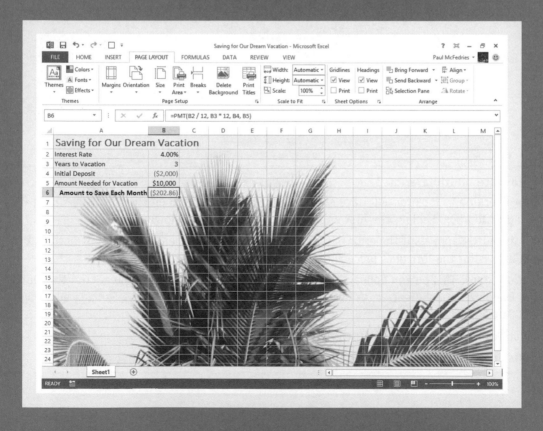

Navigate a Worksheet

You can use a few keyboard techniques that make it easier to navigate data after you type it into a worksheet.

It is usually easiest to use your mouse to click in the next cell you want to work with. If you are using Excel on a tablet or PC that has a touchscreen, then you can tap the next cell you want to use. However, if you are typing data, using the keyboard to navigate to the next cell is often faster because your hands do not have to leave the keyboard.

Keyboard Techniques for Navigating a Worksheet	
Press	**To move**
←	Left one cell
→	Right one cell
↑	Up one cell
↓	Down one cell
Home	To the beginning of the current row
Page down	Down one screen
Page up	Up one screen
Alt + Page down	One screen to the right
Alt + Page up	One screen to the left
Ctrl + Home	To the beginning of the worksheet
Ctrl + End	To the bottom-right corner of the used portion of the worksheet
Ctrl +arrow keys	In the direction of the arrow to the next nonblank cell if the current cell is blank, or to the last nonblank cell if the current cell is not blank

Rename a Worksheet

You can make your Excel workbooks easier to understand and navigate by providing each worksheet with a name that reflects the contents of the sheet.

Excel provides worksheets with generic names, such as Sheet1 and Sheet 2. You can change these to more descriptive names, such as Sales 2013, Amortization, or Budget Data. Note, however, that although worksheet names can include any combination of letters, numbers, symbols, and spaces, they cannot be longer than 31 characters.

Rename a Worksheet

① Display the worksheet you want to rename.

② Click the **Home** tab.

③ Click **Format**.

④ Click **Rename Sheet**.

Ⓐ You can also double-click the worksheet's tab.

Ⓑ Excel opens the worksheet name for editing and selects the text.

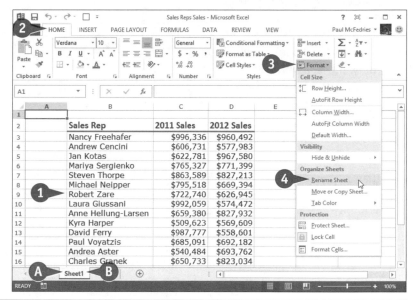

⑤ If you want to edit the existing name, press either ◄ or ► to deselect the text.

⑥ Type the new worksheet name.

⑦ Press **Enter**.

Excel assigns the new name to the worksheet.

Create a New Worksheet

When you create a new workbook, Excel includes a single worksheet you can use to build a spreadsheet model or store data. If you want to build a new model or store a different set of data, and this new information is related to the existing data in the workbook, you can create a new worksheet to hold the new information. Excel supports multiple worksheets in a single workbook, so you can add as many worksheets as you need for your project or model.

In most cases, you add a blank worksheet, but Excel also comes with several predefined templates.

Create a New Worksheet

Insert a Blank Worksheet

1. Open the workbook to which you want to add the worksheet.

2. Click the **Home** tab.

3. Click the **Insert** drop-down arrow (⌄).

4. Click **Insert Sheet**.

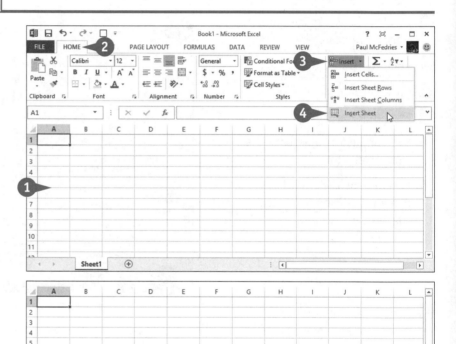

Ⓐ Excel inserts the worksheet.

Note: You can also insert a blank worksheet by pressing Shift + F11.

Ⓑ Another way to add a blank worksheet is to click the **Insert Worksheet** button (⊕).

Insert a Worksheet from a Template

1 Open the workbook to which you want to add the worksheet.

2 Right-click a worksheet tab.

3 Click **Insert**.

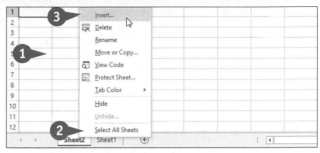

The Insert dialog box appears.

4 Click the **Spreadsheet Solutions** tab.

5 Click the type of worksheet you want to add.

C You can also click **Templates on Office.com** to download worksheet templates from the web.

6 Click **OK**.

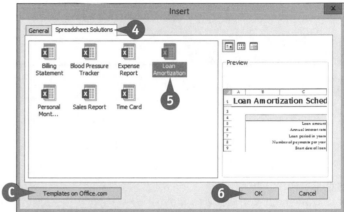

D Excel inserts the worksheet.

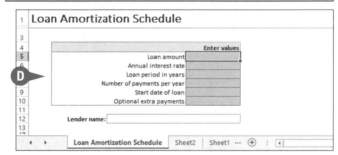

TIP

How do I navigate from one worksheet to another?

The easiest way is to click the tab of the worksheet you want to use. You can also click the following controls:

Control	Action
◄	Move to the previous worksheet.
►	Move to the next worksheet.
Ctrl + ◄	Move to the first worksheet.
Ctrl + ►	Move to the last worksheet.

Move a Worksheet

You can organize an Excel workbook and make it easier to navigate by moving your worksheets to different positions within the workbook. You can also move a worksheet to another workbook.

When you add a new worksheet to a workbook, Excel adds the sheet to the left of the existing sheets. However, it is unlikely that you will add each new worksheet in the order you want them to appear in the workbook. For example, in a budget-related workbook, you might prefer to have all the sales-related worksheets together, all the expense-related worksheets together, and so on.

Move a Worksheet

1 If you want to move the worksheet to another workbook, open that workbook, and then return to the current workbook.

2 Click the tab of the worksheet you want to move.

3 Click the **Home** tab.

4 Click **Format**.

5 Click **Move or Copy Sheet**.

Ⓐ You can also right-click the tab and then click **Move or Copy Sheet**.

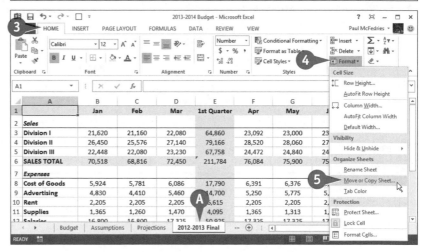

The Move or Copy dialog box appears.

6 If you want to move the sheet to another workbook, click the **To book** drop-down arrow (▾), and then click the workbook.

7 Use the **Before sheet** list to click a destination worksheet.

When Excel moves the worksheet, it appears to the left of the sheet you selected in Step **7**.

8 Click **OK**.

B Excel moves the worksheet.

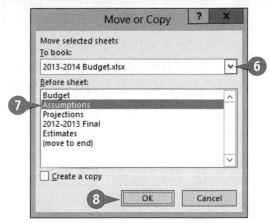

	A	B	C	D	E	F	G	H	I	
1		Jan	Feb	Mar	1st Quarter	Apr	May	Jun	2nd Quarter	
2	*Sales*									
3	**Division I**	21,620	21,160	22,080	64,860	23,092	23,000	23,368	69,460	23
4	**Division II**	26,450	25,576	27,140	79,166	28,520	28,060	27,600	84,180	28
5	**Division III**	22,448	22,080	23,230	67,758	24,472	24,840	24,610	73,922	24
6	**SALES TOTAL**	70,518	68,816	72,450	211,784	76,084	75,900	75,578	227,562	77
7	*Expenses*									
8	**Cost of Goods**	5,924	5,781	6,086	17,790	6,391	6,376	6,349	19,115	6,
9	**Advertising**	4,830	4,410	5,460	14,700	5,250	5,775	5,513	16,538	5,
10	**Rent**	2,205	2,205	2,205	6,615	2,205	2,205	2,205	6,615	2,
11	**Supplies**	1,365	1,260	1,470	4,095	1,365	1,313	1,470	4,148	1,
12	Salaries	16,800	16,800	17,325	50,925	17,325	17,325	17,850	52,500	17

Budget · 2012-2013 Final · Assumptions · Projections

TIP

Is there an easier way to move a worksheet within the same workbook?
You can use your mouse:

1 Move the mouse pointer (▷) over the tab of the worksheet.

2 Click and drag the worksheet tab to the new position within the workbook. The mouse pointer (▷) becomes the Move Worksheet pointer (▨).

A As you drag, an arrow shows the worksheet's position.

3 When you have the worksheet where you want it, drop the worksheet tab.

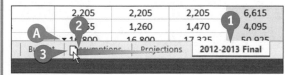

	2,205	2,205	2,205	6,615
	1,260	1,470	4,095
	16,800	16,800	17,325	50,925

Budget · Assumptions · Projections · 2012-2013 Final

Copy a Worksheet

Excel enables you to make a copy of a worksheet in the same workbook or in another one.

One of the secrets to productivity in Excel is not repeating work. If you have already created a worksheet and find that you need a second one that is similar, then you should not create the new worksheet from scratch. Instead, copy the existing worksheet, and then edit the new one as needed.

Copy a Worksheet

1 If you want to copy the worksheet to another workbook, open that workbook, and then return to the current workbook.

2 Click the tab of the worksheet you want to copy.

3 Click the **Home** tab.

4 Click **Format**.

5 Click **Move or Copy Sheet**.

Ⓐ You can also right-click the tab, and then click **Move or Copy Sheet**.

The Move or Copy dialog box appears.

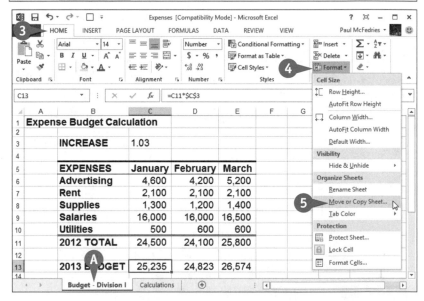

6 If you want to copy the sheet to another workbook, click the **To book** drop-down arrow (⌄), and then click the workbook.

7 Use the **Before sheet** list to click a destination worksheet.

When Excel copies the worksheet, the copy appears to the left of the sheet you selected in Step 7.

8 Click the empty **Create a copy** check box (☐) and it is filled (☑).

9 Click **OK**.

Ⓑ Excel copies the worksheet.

Ⓒ Excel gives the new worksheet the same name as the original, but with (2) appended.

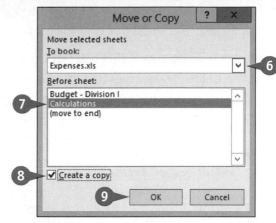

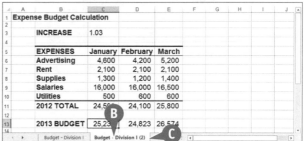

TIP

Is there an easier way to copy a worksheet within the same workbook?
You can use your mouse:

1 Move the mouse pointer (▷) over the tab of the workbook you want to copy.

2 Hold down **Ctrl**.

3 Click and drag the worksheet tab left or right. The mouse pointer (▷) becomes the Copy Worksheet pointer (▨).

Ⓐ As you drag, an arrow shows the worksheet position.

4 When the worksheet is where you want it, drop the tab.

Delete a Worksheet

If you have a worksheet that you no longer need, you can delete it from the workbook. This reduces the size of the workbook and makes the workbook easier to navigate.

You cannot undo a worksheet deletion, so check the worksheet contents carefully before proceeding with the deletion. To be extra safe, save the workbook before performing the worksheet deletion. If you delete the wrong sheet accidentally, close the workbook without saving your changes.

Delete a Worksheet

1 Click the tab of the worksheet you want to delete.

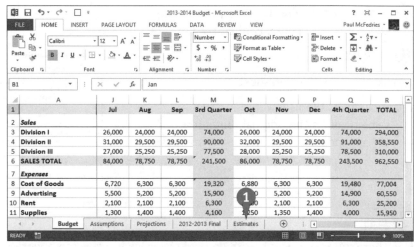

2 Click the **Home** tab.

3 Click the **Delete** drop-down arrow (⌄).

4 Click **Delete Sheet**.

Ⓐ You can also right-click the tab, and then click **Delete Sheet**.

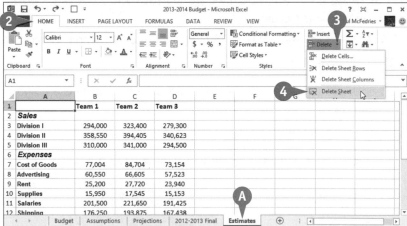

If the worksheet contains data, Excel asks you to confirm that you want to delete the worksheet.

5 Click **Delete**.

B Excel removes the worksheet.

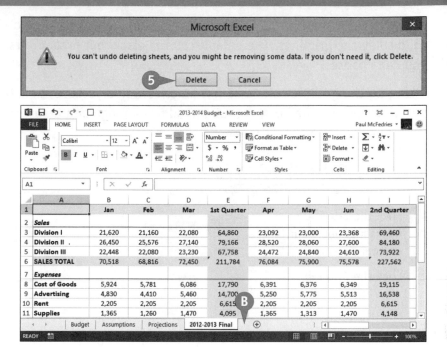

TIP

Do I have to delete multiple worksheets individually?

No. You can select all the sheets you want to remove, and then run the deletion. To select multiple worksheets, click the tab of one of the worksheets, hold down **Ctrl**, and then click the tabs of the other worksheets.

An easy way to select multiple worksheets for deletion is to right-click any worksheet tab, and then click **Select All Sheets**. Hold down **Ctrl**, and then click the tabs of the worksheets that you do not want to delete. After you select your worksheets, follow Steps **3** to **5** to delete them.

Change the Gridline Color

You can add some visual interest to your worksheet by changing the color that Excel uses to display the gridlines. The default color is black, but Excel offers a palette of 56 colors from which you can choose.

Changing the gridline color also has practical value because it enables you to differentiate between the gridlines and the borders that you add to a range or a table. See Chapter 5 to learn how to add borders to your worksheet ranges.

Change the Gridline Color

1 Click the tab of the worksheet you want to customize.

2 Click the **File** tab.

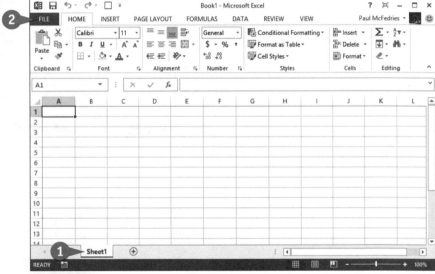

3 Click **Options**.

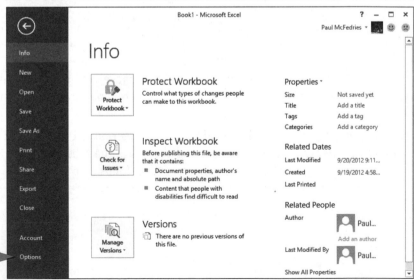

The Excel Options dialog box appears.

④ Click **Advanced**.

⑤ Scroll down to the **Display options for this worksheet** section.

⑥ Click the **Gridline color** drop-down arrow (☑).

⑦ Click the color you want to use.

⑧ Click **OK**.

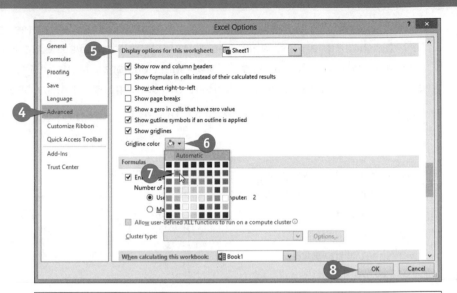

Ⓐ Excel displays the gridlines using the color you selected.

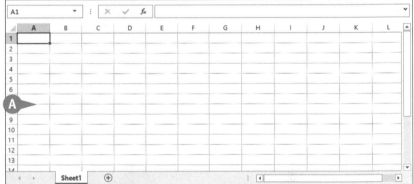

TIP

Can I change the gridline color for all the sheets in my workbook?

Yes. One method would be to follow the steps in this section for each worksheet in your workbook. However, an easier method is to first select all of the sheets in the workbook. To do this, right-click any worksheet tab and then click **Select All Sheets**.

You can now follow Steps 2 to 8 to apply the new gridline color to all your worksheets. Once you have done that, right-click any worksheet tab, and then click **Ungroup Sheets** to collapse the grouping.

Toggle Worksheet Gridlines On and Off

You can make your worksheet look cleaner and make the worksheet text easier to read by turning off the sheet gridlines. When you do this, Excel displays the worksheet with a plain white background, which often makes the worksheet easier to read. This is particularly true on a worksheet where you have added numerous borders to your ranges, as described in Chapter 5.

If you have trouble selecting ranges with the gridlines turned off, you can easily turn them back on.

Toggle Worksheet Gridlines On and Off

Turn Gridlines Off

1 Click the tab of the worksheet with which you want to work.

2 Click the **View** tab.

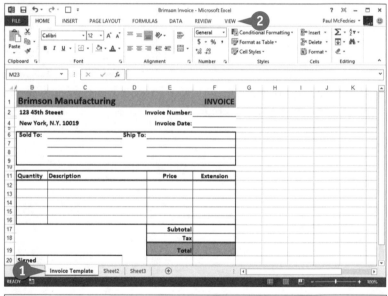

3 Click the selected **Gridlines** check box (☑) and it is cleared (☐).

Ⓐ Excel turns off the gridline display.

Turn Gridlines On

Ⓑ To turn gridlines back on, click the empty **Gridlines** check box (☐) and it is filled (☑).

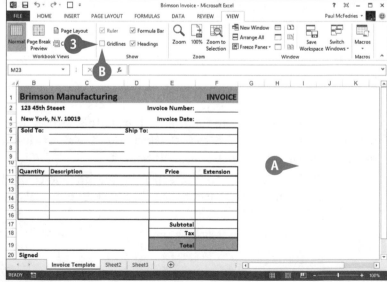

Toggle Worksheet Headings On and Off

You can give yourself a bit more room to work by turning off the worksheet's row headings — the numbers 1, 2, and so on to the left of the worksheet — and column headings — the letters A, B, and so on above the worksheet.

If you have trouble reading your worksheet or building formulas with the headings turned off, you can easily turn them back on.

Toggle Worksheet Headings On and Off

Turn Headings Off

1. Click the tab of the worksheet with which you want to work.

2. Click the **View** tab.

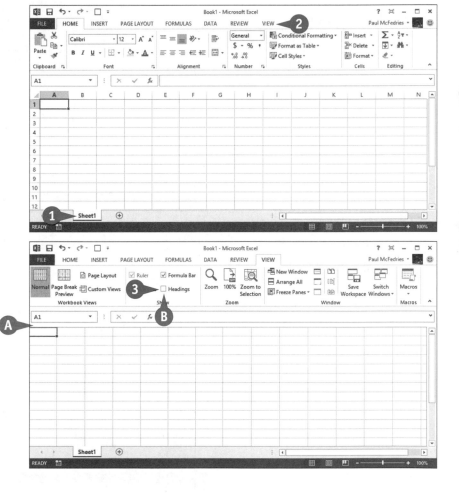

3. Click the selected **Headings** check box (☑) and it is cleared (☐).

Ⓐ Excel turns off the headings.

Turn Headings On

Ⓑ To turn headings back on, click the empty **Headings** check box (☐) and it is filled (☑).

Set the Worksheet Tab Color

You can make a workbook easier to navigate by color-coding the worksheet tabs. For example, if you have a workbook with sheets associated with several projects, you could apply a different tab color for each project. Similarly, you could format the tabs of incomplete worksheets with one color, and completed worksheets with another color.

Excel offers 10 standard colors and 60 colors associated with the current workbook theme. You can also apply a custom color if none of the standard or theme colors suits your needs.

Set the Worksheet Tab Color

1 Click the tab of the worksheet you want to format.

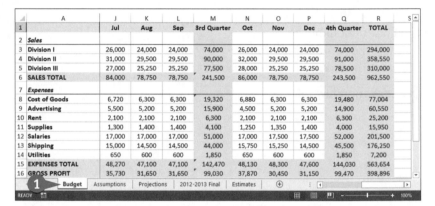

2 Click the **Home** tab.

3 Click **Format**.

4 Click **Tab Color**.

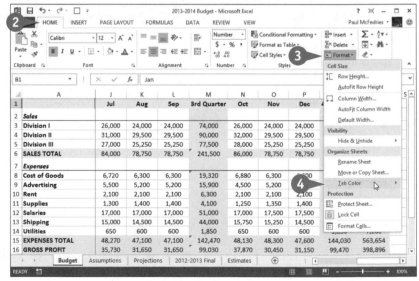

Excel displays the Tab Color palette.

⑤ Click the color you want to use for the current tab.

Ⓐ To apply a custom color, click **More Colors**, and then use the Colors dialog box to choose the color you want.

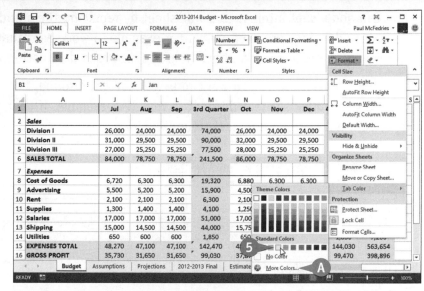

Ⓑ Excel applies the color to the tab.

Note: You can also right-click the tab, click **Tab Color**, and then click the color you want to apply.

Note: The tab color appears very faintly when the tab is selected, but the color appears quite strongly when any other tab is selected.

TIPS

If I want to apply the same color to several worksheets, do I have to format them individually?

No. You can select all the sheets you want to format and then apply the tab color. To select multiple worksheets, click the tab of one of the worksheets, hold down **Ctrl**, and then click the tabs of the other worksheets. After you have selected your worksheets, follow Steps 2 to 5 to apply the tab color to all the selected worksheets at once.

How do I remove a tab color?

If you no longer require a worksheet to have a colored tab, you can remove the color. Follow Steps 1 to 4 to select the worksheet and display the Tab Color palette, and then click **No Color**. Excel removes the color from the worksheet's tab.

Set the Worksheet Background

You can add visual interest to a worksheet by replacing the standard white sheet background with a photo, drawing, or other image. For example, a worksheet that tracks the amount needed for a future vacation could show a photo from the proposed destination as the background.

When choosing the image you want to use as the background, be sure to select a picture that will not make the worksheet text difficult to read. For example, if your sheet text is a dark color, choose a light-colored image as the background.

Set the Worksheet Background

1 Click the tab of the worksheet you want to customize.

2 Click the **Page Layout** tab.

3 Click **Background** ( ).

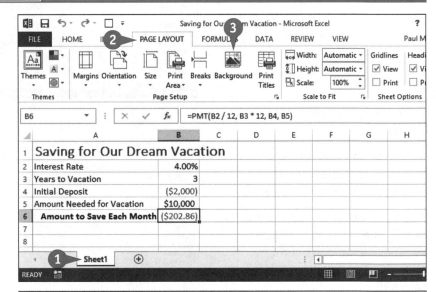

The Insert Pictures dialog box appears.

4 Click **From a file**.

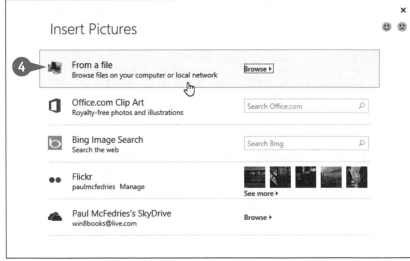

The Sheet Background dialog box appears.

⑤ Select the location of the image you want to use.

⑥ Click the image.

⑦ Click **Insert**.

Ⓐ Excel formats the worksheet background with the image you selected.

TIPS

How do I apply a background color instead of a background image?
Excel does not have a command that changes the background color of the entire worksheet. Instead, you must first select all the cells in the worksheet by clicking **Select All** (◢). Click the **Home** tab, click the **Fill Color** drop-down arrow (▾), and then click the color you want to use. Excel applies the color to the background of every cell.

How do I remove the background image from the worksheet?
If you find that having the background image makes it difficult to read the worksheet text, then you should remove the background. Click the tab of the worksheet, click **Page Layout**, and then click **Delete Background** (▨). Excel removes the background image from the worksheet.

Zoom In on or Out of a Worksheet

You can get a closer look at a portion of a worksheet by zooming in on that range. When you zoom in on a range, Excel increases the magnification of the range, which makes it easier to see the range data, particularly when the worksheet font is quite small.

On the other hand, if you want to get a sense of the overall structure of a worksheet, you can also zoom out. When you zoom out, Excel decreases the magnification, so you see more of the worksheet.

Zoom In on or Out of a Worksheet

1 Click the tab of the worksheet you want to zoom.

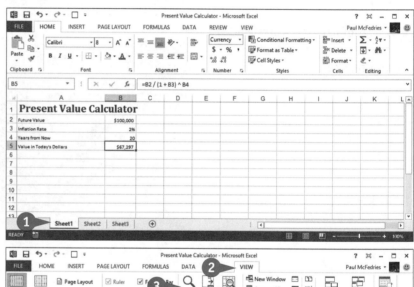

2 Click the **View** tab.

3 Click **Zoom** (🔍).

A You can also run the Zoom command by clicking the zoom level in the status bar.

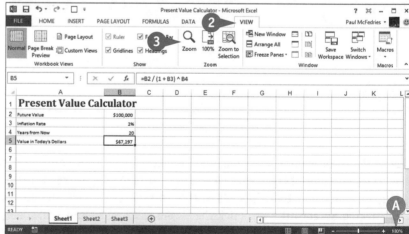

The Zoom dialog box appears.

④ Click the empty radio button (○) of the magnification level you want to use and it is filled (◉).

Ⓑ You can also click the empty **Custom** radio button (○) and it is filled (◉). Then, type a magnification level in the text box.

Note: Select a magnification level above 100% to zoom in on the worksheet; select a level under 100% to zoom out of the worksheet.

⑤ Click **OK**.

Excel changes the magnification level and redisplays the worksheet.

Ⓒ You can click **100%** ( ) to return to the normal zoom level.

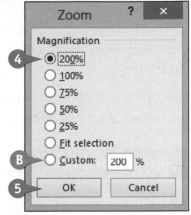

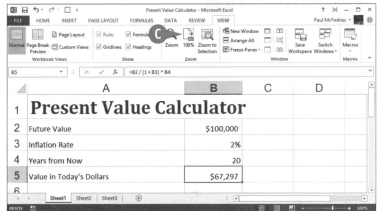

TIPS

How can I zoom in on a particular range?
Excel offers the Zoom to Selection feature that enables you to zoom in on a range quickly and easily. First, select the range that you want to magnify. Click the **View** tab, and then click **Zoom to Selection** ( ). Excel magnifies the selected range to fill the entire Excel window.

Is there an easier way to zoom in and out of a worksheet?
Yes, you can use the Zoom slider ( ), which appears on the far-right side of the Excel status bar. Drag the slider ( ) to the right to zoom in on the worksheet or to the left to zoom out. You can also click the **Zoom In** ( ) or **Zoom Out** ( ) buttons to change the magnification.

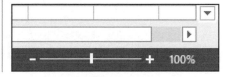

Split a Worksheet into Two Panes

You can make it easier to examine your worksheet data by splitting the worksheet into two scrollable panes, each of which shows different parts of the worksheet. This is useful if you have cell headings at the top of the worksheet that you want to keep in view as you scroll down the worksheet.

Splitting a worksheet into two panes is also useful if you want to keep some data or a formula result in view while you scroll to another part of the worksheet.

Split a Worksheet into Two Panes

1 Click the tab of the worksheet you want to split.

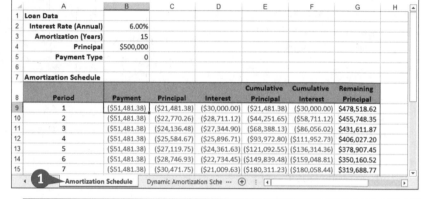

2 Select a cell in column A that is below the point where you want the split to occur.

For example, if you want to place the first five rows in the top pane, select cell A6.

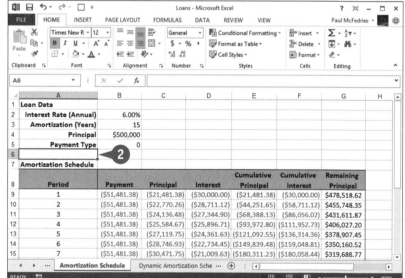

③ Click the **View** tab.

④ Click **Split** (⊟).

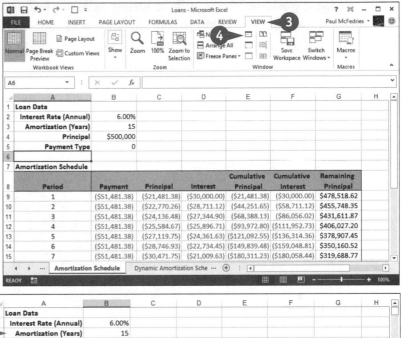

Ⓐ Excel splits the worksheet into two horizontal panes at the selected cell.

Ⓑ You can adjust the size of the panes by clicking and dragging the split bar up or down.

To remove the split, either click **Split** (⊟) again, or double-click the split bar.

TIPS

Can I split a worksheet into two vertical panes?
Yes. First, select a cell in the top row of the worksheet. Specifically, select the top cell in the column to the right of where you want the split to occur. For example, if you want to show only column A in the left pane, select cell B1. When you click **Split** (⊟), Excel splits the worksheet into two vertical panes.

Can I split a worksheet into four panes?
Yes. This is useful if you have four worksheet areas that you want to examine separately. First, select the cell where you want the split to occur. Note that this cell must not be in either row 1 or column A. When you click **Split** (⊟), Excel splits the worksheet into four panes. The cell you selected becomes the upper-left cell in the bottom-right pane.

Hide or Unhide a Worksheet

You can hide a worksheet so that it no longer appears in the workbook. This is useful if you need to show the workbook to other people, but the workbook contains a worksheet with sensitive or private data that you do not want others to see. You might also want to hide a worksheet if it contains unfinished work that is not ready for others to view.

To learn how to protect a workbook so that other people cannot unhide a worksheet, see Chapter 23.

Hide or Unhide a Worksheet

Hide a Worksheet

1. Click the tab of the worksheet you want to hide.

2. Click the **Home** tab.

3. Click **Format**.

4. Click **Hide & Unhide**.

5. Click **Hide Sheet**.

Ⓐ You can also right-click the worksheet tab, and then click **Hide Sheet**.

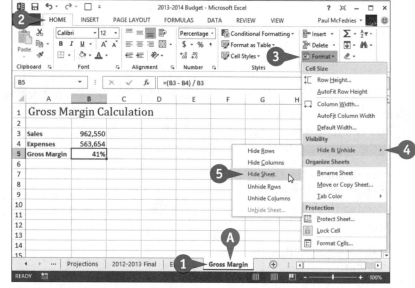

Ⓑ Excel temporarily removes the worksheet from the workbook.

240

Unhide a Worksheet

1 Click the **Home** tab.

2 Click **Format**.

3 Click **Hide & Unhide**.

4 Click **Unhide Sheet**.

ⓒ You can also right-click any worksheet tab, and then click **Unhide Sheet**.

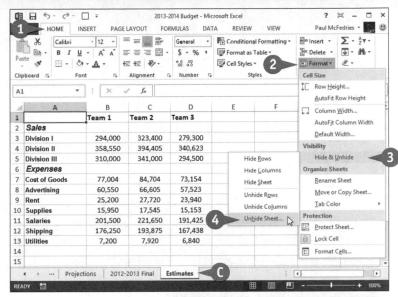

The Unhide dialog box appears.

5 Click the worksheet you want to restore.

6 Click **OK**.

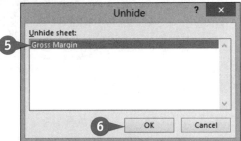

ⓓ Excel returns the worksheet to the workbook.

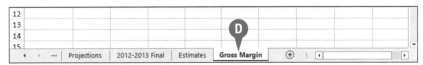

TIP

Do I have to hide multiple worksheets individually?

No. You can select all the sheets you want to work with, and then hide them. To select multiple worksheets, click the tab of one of the worksheets, hold down Ctrl, and then click the tabs of the other worksheets.

If your workbook has many worksheets and you want to hide most of them, right-click any worksheet tab, and then click **Select All Sheets**. Hold down Ctrl, and then click the tabs of the worksheets that you do not want to hide. After you select your worksheets, follow Steps **3** to **5** to hide all of them.

CHAPTER 11

Dealing with Workbooks

Everything you do in Excel takes place within a *workbook*, which is the standard Excel file. This chapter shows you how to get more out of workbooks by creating new files; saving, opening, and closing files; checking spelling; and more.

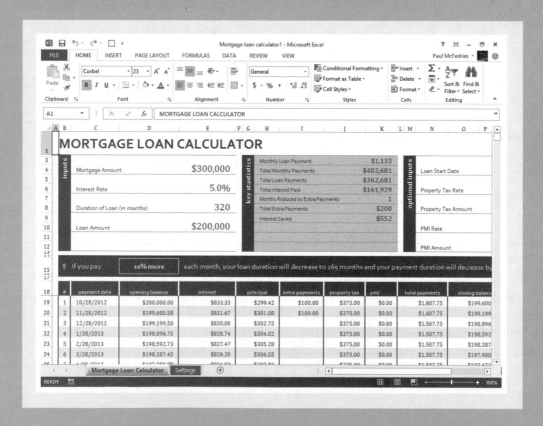

Create a New Blank Workbook

To perform new work in Excel, you need to create a new, blank Excel workbook first. When you launch Excel, it prompts you to create a new workbook and you can click Blank Workbook to start with a blank file that contains a single empty worksheet. However, for subsequent files you must use the File tab to create a new blank workbook.

If you prefer to create a workbook based on one of the Excel templates, see the following section, "Create a New Workbook from a Template."

Create a New Blank Workbook

1 Click the **File** tab.

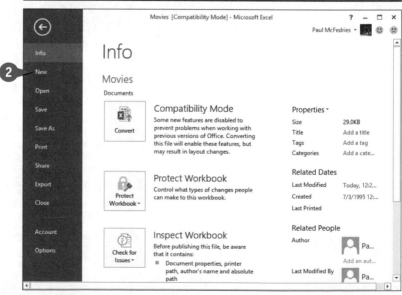

2 Click **New**.

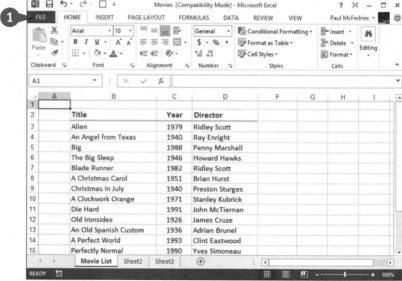

3 Click **Blank Workbook.**

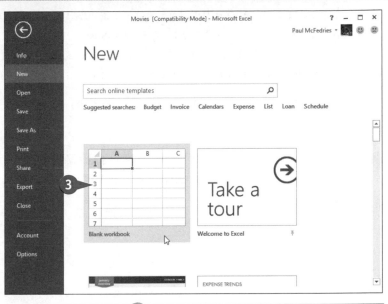

A Excel creates the blank workbook and displays it in the Excel window.

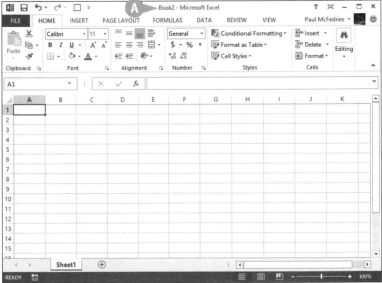

TIPS

Is there a faster method I can use to create a new workbook?
Yes. Excel offers a keyboard shortcut for faster workbook creation. From the keyboard, press Ctrl + N.

When I start Excel, how can I prevent it from removing the blank workbook it opens automatically?
Excel assumes that you want a fresh workbook when you start it, so it prompts you to create a new one. If you do not make any changes to the blank workbook and open an existing file, Excel assumes you do not want to use the new workbook and closes it. To prevent this, make a change to the blank workbook before opening another file.

Create a New Workbook from a Template

You can save time and effort by creating a new workbook based on one of the Excel template files. Each template includes a working spreadsheet model that contains predefined headings, labels, and formulas, as well as preformatted colors, fonts, styles, borders, and more. In many cases, you can use the new workbook as is and just fill in your own data.

Excel 2013 offers more than two dozen templates, and many more are available through Microsoft Office Online.

Create a New Workbook from a Template

1 Click the **File** tab.

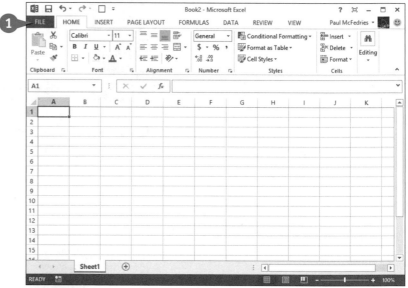

2 Click **New**.

Ⓐ To use an Office Online template, use the Search online templates text box to type a word or two that defines the type of template you want to use.

3 Click the template you want to use.

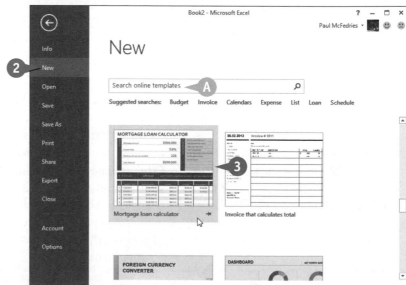

B A preview of the template appears.

4 Click **Create**.

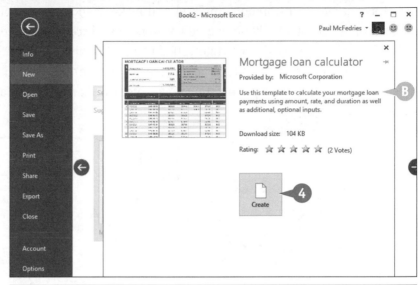

C Excel creates the new workbook and displays it in the Excel window.

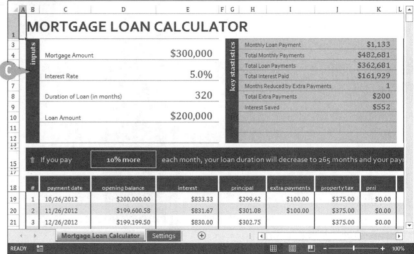

TIP

Can I create my own template?

Yes. If you have a specific workbook structure that you use frequently, you should save it as a template so that you do not have to re-create the same structure from scratch each time. Open the workbook, click **File**, and then click **Save as**. In the Save As dialog box, click **Computer**, and then click **Browse**. Click the **Save as type** drop-down arrow (⌄), and then click **Excel Template**. Type a name in the **File name** text box and then click **Save**. To use the template, click **File** and click **Open**; then, in the Open dialog box, click **Computer**, click **Browse**, and then click your template file.

Save a Workbook

After you create a workbook in Excel and make changes to it, you can save the document to preserve your work. When you edit a workbook, Excel stores the changes in your computer's memory, which is erased each time you shut down your computer. Saving the document preserves your changes on your computer's hard drive. To ensure that you do not lose any work if your computer crashes or Excel freezes up, you should save your work frequently: at least every few minutes.

Save a Workbook

① Click **Save** (💾).

You can also press Ctrl+S.

If you have saved the document previously, your changes are now preserved, and you do not need to follow the rest of the steps in this section.

The Save As tab appears.

② Click **Computer**.

③ Click **Browse**.

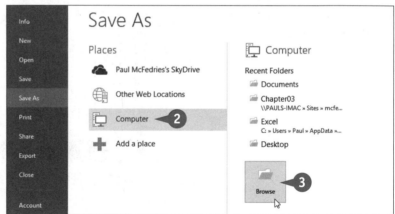

The Save As dialog box appears.

④ Select a folder in which to store the file.

⑤ Click in the **File name** text box and type the name that you want to use for the document.

⑥ Click **Save**.

Excel saves the file.

Note: To learn how to save a workbook in an older Excel format, see Chapter 22.

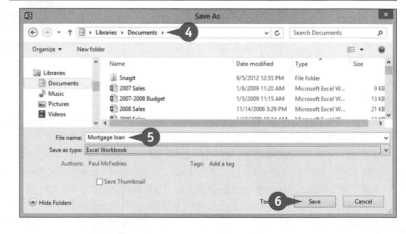

Open a Workbook

To view or make changes to an Excel workbook that you have saved in the past, you must open the workbook in Excel. To open a workbook, you must first locate it in the folder you used when you originally saved the file.

If you have used the workbook recently, you can save time by opening the workbook from the Excel Recent Workbooks menu, which displays a list of the 25 workbooks that you have used most recently.

Open a Workbook

1 Click the **File** tab (not shown).

2 Click **Open**.

The Open tab appears.

Ⓐ You can click **Recent Workbooks** to see a list of your recently used workbooks. If you see the file you want, click it, and then skip the rest of these steps.

3 Click **Computer**.

4 Click **Browse**.

You can also press Ctrl + O .

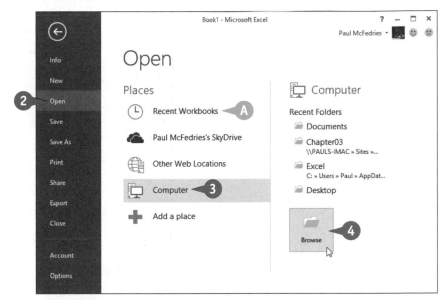

The Open dialog box appears.

5 Select the folder that contains the workbook you want to open.

6 Click the workbook.

7 Click **Open**.

The workbook appears in a window.

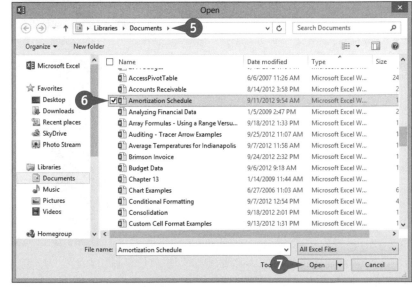

Specify Workbook Properties

Properties are data that describe or categorize a workbook. For example, the name of the person who created a workbook is a property for that file. Although properties such as the date a workbook was last modified are added automatically, Excel enables you to add your own properties. For example, you can add a title and comments about a workbook, and you can add one or more *tags*, which are keywords that reflect the content of the workbook.

Windows references such properties when you perform searches, so by specifying workbook properties you can make your Excel files easier to find.

Specify Workbook Properties

Specify Basic Properties

1. Open the workbook you want to modify.

2. Click the **File** tab.

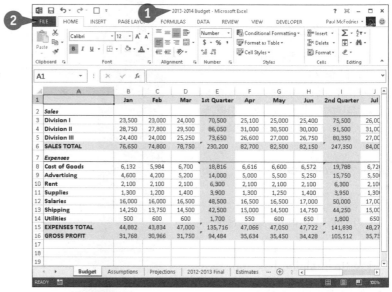

3. Click **Info**.

4. Click a property, and then type the value you want it to have.

5. Repeat Step 4 for each property you want to specify.

Excel adds the property data to the workbook.

Specify Advanced Properties

1 Click **Properties**.

2 Click **Advanced Properties**.

Excel opens the workbook's Properties dialog box with the Custom tab displayed.

3 Click the property you want to add.

Ⓐ If you do not see what you want, type it in the **Name** box.

4 Click the **Type** drop-down arrow (⌄), and then click the property data type.

5 Type the property value.

6 Click **Add**.

7 Repeat Steps 3 to 6 to add each property.

8 Click **OK**.

Excel adds the advanced properties to the workbook.

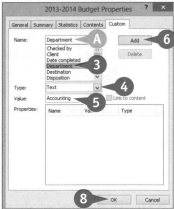

TIPS

Is there an easier way to add property values to a workbook?

Yes. You can view properties such as Comments, Keyboards, and Status in the Document Panel, which appears just above the workbook. In the Info tab, click **Properties** and then click **Show Document Panel**. Excel returns you to the workbook and opens the Document Panel.

Can I only access a workbook's properties from within Excel?

No. In File Explorer, right-click the workbook, and then click **Properties** to open the Properties dialog box. Click the **Details** tab to see the complete list of properties for the file. The **Property** column shows the name of each property. Use the controls in the **Value** column to change each property that can be edited, and then click **OK**.

Find Text in a Workbook

Most spreadsheet models require at most a screen or two in a single worksheet, so locating the text you want is usually not difficult. However, you might be working with a large spreadsheet model that takes up either multiple screens in a single worksheet or multiple worksheets. In such large workbooks, locating specific text can be difficult and time consuming. You can make this task easier and faster using the Excel Find feature, which searches the entire workbook in the blink of an eye.

Find Text in a Workbook

1 Click the **Home** tab.

2 Click **Find & Select**.

3 Click **Find**.

Note: You can also run the Find command by pressing Ctrl + F.

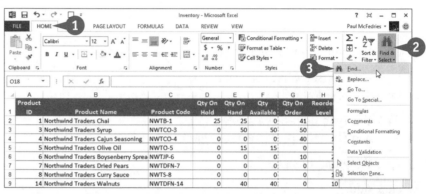

The Find and Replace dialog box appears.

4 Click in the **Find what** text box and type the text you want to find.

5 Click **Find Next**.

🅐 Excel selects the next cell that contains an instance of the search text.

Note: If the search text does not exist in the document, Excel displays a dialog box to let you know.

6 If the selected instance is not the one you want, click **Find Next** until Excel finds the correct instance.

7 Click **Close** to close the Find and Replace dialog box.

🅑 Excel leaves the cell selected.

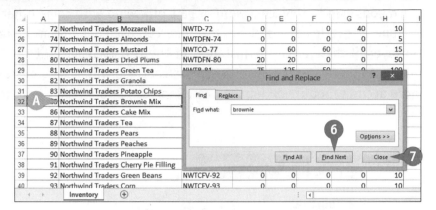

How can I get Excel to search the entire workbook, rather than just the current worksheet?

In the Find and Replace dialog box, click **Options** to expand the dialog box. Click the **Within** drop-down arrow (☑), and then click **Workbook**. This option tells Excel to examine the entire workbook for your search text.

When I search for a name, such as Bill, Excel also matches the non-name bill. Is there a way to fix this?

Yes. In the Find and Replace dialog box, click **Options** to expand the dialog box. Select the empty **Match case** check box (☐) and it is filled (☑). Excel now matches only the search text with the same mix of upper- and lowercase letters you specify in the **Find what** text box. If you type **Bill**, the program matches only *Bill* and not *bill*.

Replace Text in a Workbook

Do you need to replace a word or part of a word with some other text? If you only need to replace one or two instances of the text, you can usually perform the replacement quickly and easily. However, if there are many instances of the text to replace, it can take a long time. Also, the more instances there are, the more likely it is that you will make a mistake. You can save time and do a more accurate job if you let the Excel Replace feature replace the text for you.

Replace Text in a Workbook

1 Click the **Home** tab.

2 Click **Find & Select**.

3 Click **Replace**.

Note: You can also run the Replace command by pressing `Ctrl` + `H`.

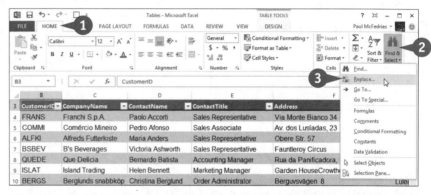

The Find and Replace dialog box appears.

4 In the **Find what** text box, type the text you want to find.

5 Click in the **Replace with** text box and type the text you want to use as the replacement.

6 Click **Find Next**.

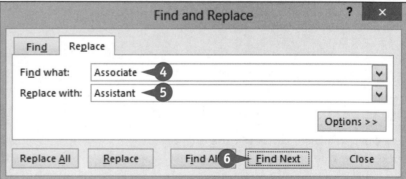

Ⓐ Excel selects the cell that contains the next instance of the search text.

Note: If the search text does not exist in the document, Excel displays a dialog box to let you know.

⑦ If the selected instance is not the one you want, click **Find Next** until Excel finds the correct instance.

⑧ Click **Replace**.

Ⓑ Excel replaces the selected text with the replacement text.

Ⓒ Excel selects the next instance of the search text.

⑨ Repeat Steps 7 and 8 until you have replaced all of the instances you want to replace.

⑩ Click **Close** to close the Find and Replace dialog box.

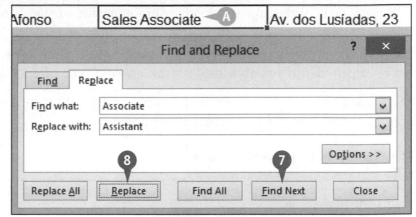

TIP

Is there a faster way to replace every instance of the search text with the replacement text?

Yes. In the Find and Replace dialog box, click **Replace All**. This tells Excel to replace every instance of the search text with the replacement text. However, you should exercise some caution with this feature because it may make some replacements that you did not intend. Click **Find Next** a few times to make sure the matches are correct.

Also, consider clicking **Options,** and then selecting the empty **Match case** check box (□) so it is filled (☑), as described in the preceding section, "Find Text in a Workbook."

Check Spelling and Grammar

Although Excel workbooks are mostly concerned with numbers, formulas, and data, a workbook that contains misspelled words might not be taken as seriously as one that is free of jarring typos. You can eliminate any text errors in your Excel workbooks by taking advantage of the spell-checker, which identifies potentially misspelled words and offers suggested corrections.

When the spell-checker flags a word as misspelled, you can correct the word, tell the spell-checker to ignore it, or add it to the spell-checker's dictionary.

Check Spelling and Grammar

① Click the **Review** tab.

② Click **Spelling** (ABC✓).

Note: You can also press F7.

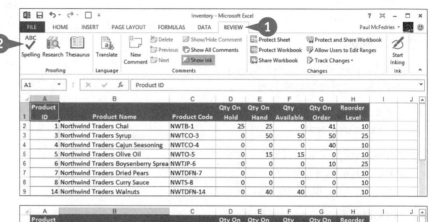

Ⓐ The Spelling dialog box appears and selects the cell that contains the first error.

③ Click the correction you want to use.

④ Click **Change**.

Ⓑ Click **Change All** to correct every instance of the error.

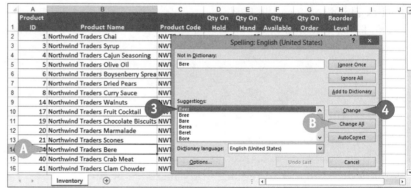

C The spell-checker displays the next error.

5 If you want to correct the word, repeat Step **4**.

D If you do not want to correct the word, click one of the following buttons:

Click **Ignore Once** to skip this instance of the error.

Click **Ignore All** to skip all instances of the error.

Click **Add to Dictionary** to include the word in the spell-checker's dictionary.

6 When the check is complete, click **OK**.

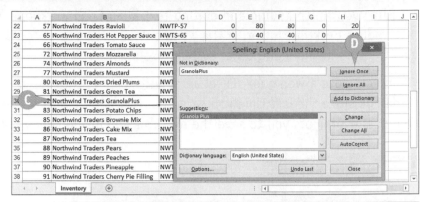

TIP

How can I remove a word that I added to the spell-checker's dictionary?

Follow these steps:

1 Click **File**.

2 Click **Options** to open the Excel Options dialog box.

3 Click **Proofing**.

4 Click **Custom Dictionaries** to open its dialog box.

5 Click **Edit Word List**.

6 Click the term you want to remove.

7 Click **Delete**.

8 Click **OK** to return to the Custom Dictionaries dialog box.

9 Click **OK** to return to the Excel Options dialog box.

10 Click **OK**.

Close a Workbook

When you finish adding and editing text in an Excel workbook, you should close the workbook to reduce desktop clutter. If the workbook is very large or contains many images, closing the file also frees up memory and other system resources.

When you close a workbook, Excel automatically checks to see if you have made changes to the workbook since the last time you saved it. If Excel determines that the workbook contains unsaved changes, it prompts you to save the file. To avoid losing your work, be sure to save the workbook.

Close a Workbook

1 Display the workbook you want to close.

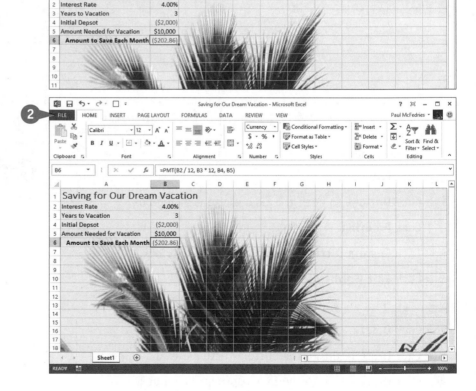

2 Click the **File** tab.

③ Click **Close**.

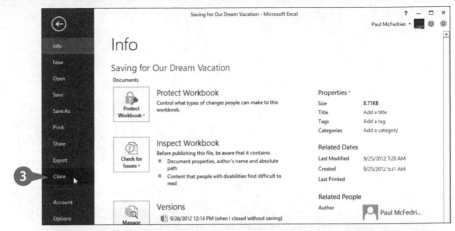

If you have unsaved changes in the workbook, Excel asks if you want to save your work.

④ Click **Save**.

Ⓐ If you do not want to preserve your changes, click **Don't Save**.

Ⓑ If you decide to keep the document open, click **Cancel**.

The program saves your work, and then closes the document.

TIP

Are there faster methods I can use to close a document?

Yes. You can also close a document using a keyboard shortcut or a mouse click. From your keyboard, press Ctrl + W to close the current document; then, with your mouse, click the **Close** button (×) in the upper-left corner of the document window.

CHAPTER 12

Managing Workbooks

To get the most out of Excel, you need to manage your workbook files, and this chapter shows you the best ways to do this. For example, you learn how to increase the number of recent workbooks that Excel displays, and how to open one or more workbooks automatically at start-up.

Increase the Number of Recent Documents

When you click the File tab and then click Recent, Excel displays a list of the workbooks that you have used most recently, and clicking an item in the list opens that workbook. The Recent list is therefore a quick way to open a file, but only if the workbook you want appears in that list.

To improve the chances that a workbook appears in the Recent list, you can increase the number of files that Excel displays. The default is 22, but you can specify a number as high as 50.

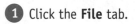

Increase the Number of Recent Documents

1 Click the **File** tab.

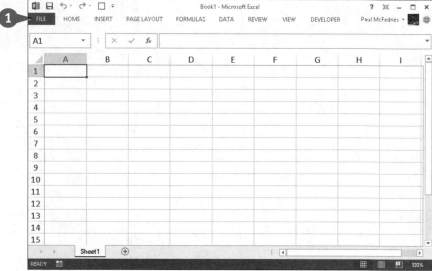

2 Click **Options**.

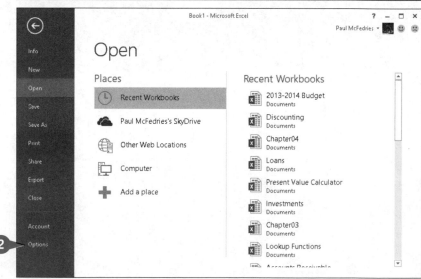

The Excel Options dialog box appears.

③ Click **Advanced.**

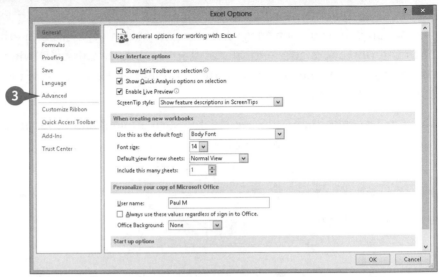

④ In the Display section, use the **Show this number of Recent Workbooks** text box to specify the number of recent workbooks you want to display.

⑤ Click **OK.**

The next time you click the **File** tab, then **Open**, and then **Recent Workbooks**, you see the number of recent workbooks that you specified.

TIPS

Can I remove or keep items in the Recent Workbooks list?

Yes. If a workbook that you use only rarely appears on the list, remove it by right-clicking the workbook, and then clicking **Remove from list**. If you want a particular workbook to always appear on the list, move the mouse pointer (⇘) over the file, and then click **Pin this item to the list** (⊣).

Are there any other ways to access recent workbooks?

Yes. If you are running Excel on Windows 8 or 7, you can take advantage of jump lists to open recent Excel workbooks. Pin the Excel icon to the taskbar as described in Chapter 1, and then right-click the icon to access the recent workbooks. You can also pin items to this list by moving the mouse pointer (⇘) over an item, and then clicking **Pin to this list** (⊣).

Open Workbooks Automatically at Start-up

You may often open the same few workbooks each time you start Excel. The Recent Workbooks list can help you open these files quickly, but an even easier method is to configure Excel to open the workbooks automatically at start-up. You do this by moving the workbooks to a folder that contains no other workbooks, and then configuring Excel to open every workbook in that folder automatically at start-up.

This task assumes that you have created such a folder and have moved into that folder the workbook files that you want to open automatically.

Open Workbooks Automatically at Start-up

1 Click the **File** tab.

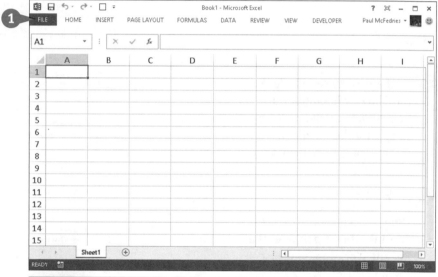

2 Click **Options**.

The Excel Options dialog box appears.

③ Click **Advanced**.

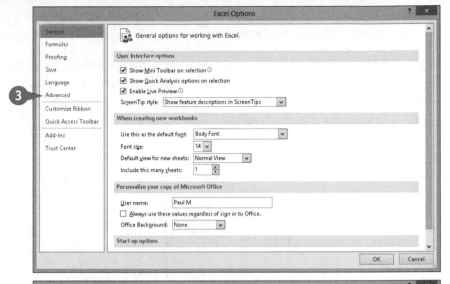

④ In the General section, use the **At startup, open all files in** text box to type the location of the folder that contains the workbooks you want Excel to open.

⑤ Click **OK**.

The next time you launch Excel, it automatically opens all the workbooks in the folder you specified.

TIP

What can I do if I am not sure of the folder location?

If you are not sure about the exact location of the folder you want to use, open File Explorer in Windows 8, or Windows Explorer in earlier versions of Windows, and navigate to the folder. In Windows 8, 7, or Vista, right-click the **Address** box and then click **Copy address**; in Windows XP, select the **Address** box text and then press Ctrl + C. You can then follow Steps 1 to 3, click in the **At startup, open all files in** text box, and paste the address by pressing Ctrl + V.

Create a Workspace of Workbooks

I f you have multiple workbooks that you always open as a group, you can save time by creating a workspace for those files and then opening the workspace when you need them.

If you have workbooks that you use regularly, opening all of them each time you need them can be inconvenient. To make this task easier, you can define a workspace that includes those files. A *workspace* is a special file that acts as a pointer to a collection of workbooks. When you open the workspace file, Excel automatically opens all the files contained in the workspace.

Create a Workspace of Workbooks

Create a Workspace

1. Open all the workbooks that you want to include in the workspace.

2. Close any workbooks that you do not want to include in the workspace.

3. Click the **View** tab.

4. Click **Save Workspace** (⊞).

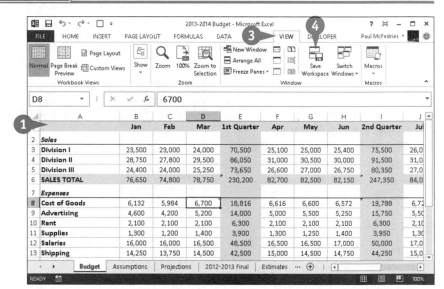

The Save Workspace dialog box appears.

5. Choose a location for the workspace file.

6. Use the **File name** text box to type a name for the workspace file.

7. Click **Save**.

Note: If any of your open workbooks have unsaved changes, Excel prompts you to save those changes. In each case, click **Save**.

Excel saves the workspace file.

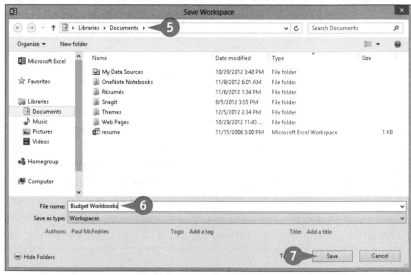

Open a Workspace

1 Click the **File** tab (not shown).

2 Click **Open**.

3 Click **Computer**.

4 Click **Browse**.

The Open dialog box appears.

5 Click the drop-down arrow ($\vee$), and select **Workspaces**.

6 Click the workspace file you want to open.

7 Click **Open**.

Excel opens each workbook that is part of the workspace.

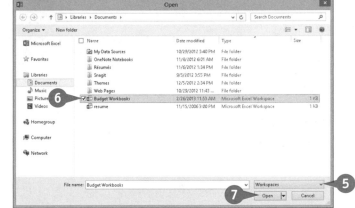

TIPS

Can I create more than one workspace file?

Yes. You do not need to restrict yourself to a single workspace file. For example, you can create a separate workspace file for each of your projects. This enables you to quickly switch from one set of workbooks to another, or even open multiple workspaces simultaneously.

Is there an easy way to close all the files in a workspace?

When you open a workspace or switch from one workspace to another, you usually want to close all the open workbooks to avoid cluttering the Excel window. Rather than close each workbook manually, customize the Quick Access Toolbar or the Ribbon with the Close All command, which closes all open files. See Chapter 1 to learn how to customize these Excel features.

Specify a New Default File Location

By default, when you save a new workbook, Excel displays your user profile's Documents folder in the Save As dialog box. Similarly, when you run the Open command, Excel displays your Documents folder in the Open dialog box automatically.

The folder that Excel displays automatically in the Save As and Open dialog boxes is called the *default file location*. If you store your Excel workbooks elsewhere, it is inconvenient to have to navigate to that folder before you can save or open a workbook. If you change the default file location to the other folder, it makes saving and opening more efficient.

Specify a New Default File Location

1 Click the **File** tab.

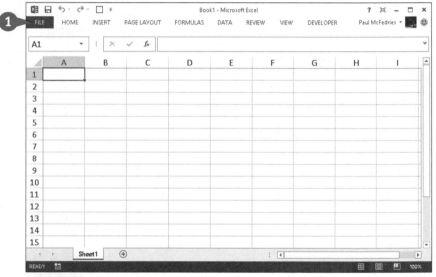

2 Click **Options**.

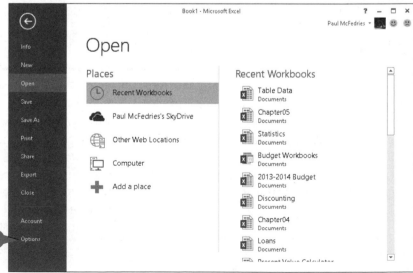

The Excel Options dialog box appears.

3 Click **Save**.

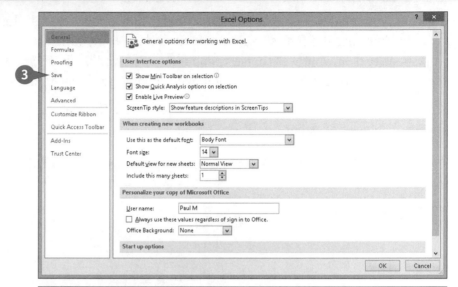

4 Use the **Default local file location** text box to type the path to the folder you want to use as the default.

5 Click **OK**.

6 Quit, and then restart Excel.

Excel now displays your folder automatically in the Save As and Open dialog boxes.

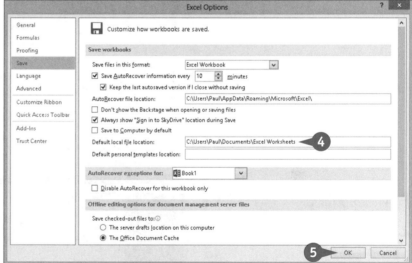

TIPS

How can I be sure to enter the correct file location?

Unfortunately, Excel does not offer a Browse button or similar feature to help you choose the folder you want to use as the default file location. If you are unsure of the exact location, you can copy and paste the correct location. To learn how, see the Tip in the section "Open Workbooks Automatically at Start-up" earlier in this chapter.

Can I use a network location as the default file location?

Yes. This must be a shared network folder, and you must have sufficient permissions to save files to the folder and make changes to the files in the folder. In the **Default local file location** text box, type a network address in the form *SERVER**Share*, where *SERVER* is the name of the network computer, and *Share* is the name of the shared folder.

Set the Default Font and Font Size for New Workbooks

When you create a workbook, Excel automatically applies certain formatting options, such as the font and the font size. The default is Body Font, which refers to the font used for regular worksheet text in whatever theme is applied to the workbook. If you would rather have the same font regardless of the theme, then you need to configure that font as the default.

You can also configure Excel with a default font size. The standard size is 11 points, but you can specify a larger or smaller size if you prefer.

Set the Default Font and Font Size for New Workbooks

1 Click the **File** tab.

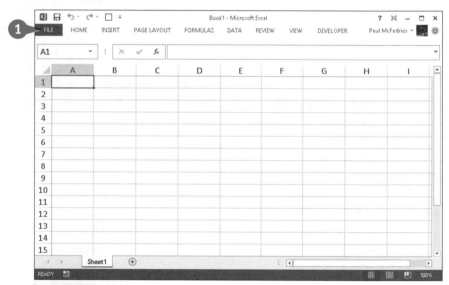

2 Click **Options**.

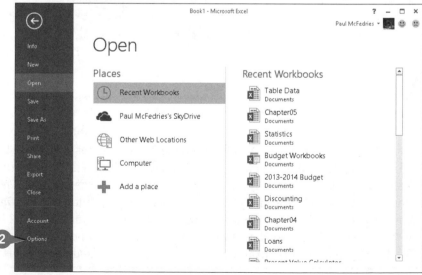

The Excel Options dialog box appears with the General tab displayed.

③ Click the **Use this as the default font** drop-down arrow (⌄), and then click and select the default font you want.

④ Click the **Font size** drop-down arrow (⌄), and then click the default size you want.

⑤ Click **OK**.

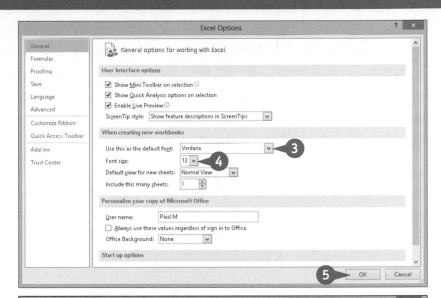

Excel warns you that the change will not go into effect until you restart the program.

⑥ Click **OK**.

⑦ Close and restart Excel.

All new workbooks that you create now use the font and font size that you specified.

TIPS

Can I apply a particular font only for certain worksheets?

Yes. Click **Select all** (◢) in the upper-left corner of the worksheet to select the entire sheet, click the **Home** tab, and then use the **Font** list to set the font for the sheet. If you prefer different fonts for headings and body text, then you can create a custom theme font, as described in Chapter 6.

How do I reset the fonts to the Excel default?

You can return the font and font size to the original Excel configuration by following Steps 1 and 2 in this section to display the General tab of the Excel Options dialog box. Click the **Use this as the default font** drop-down arrow (⌄), and then click **Body Font**. Click the **Font size** drop-down arrow (⌄), and then click **11**. Click **OK** to apply your changes.

Set the Default Number of Worksheets for New Workbooks

If you normally add worksheets to a new workbook, you can save time by configuring Excel to always include your preferred number of worksheets in each new file.

By default, Excel includes one blank worksheet in each new workbook that you create. However, you might find that you always use three, four, or more worksheets in most of your workbooks. If so, then you have to waste time adding the new sheets to the workbook. You can save time by telling Excel the number of worksheets you prefer to have in your new workbooks.

Set the Default Number of Worksheets for New Workbooks

1 Click the **File** tab.

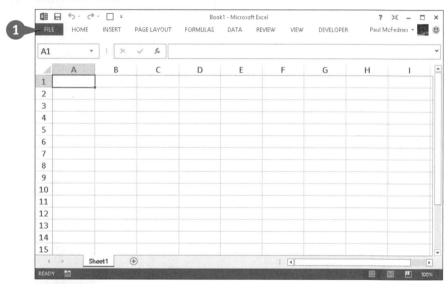

2 Click **Options**.

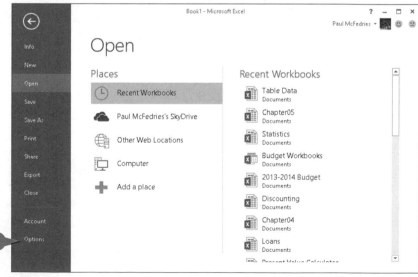

The Excel Options dialog box appears with the General tab displayed.

3 Use the **Include this many sheets** text box to specify the number of worksheets you want in each new workbook.

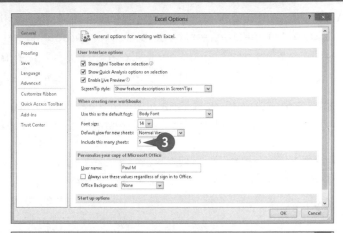

4 Click **OK**.

Each time you create a new workbook, Excel now includes the number of worksheets that you specified.

TIP

Is there a way to determine the number of sheets in each new workbook as I create them?
Excel does not have a feature that allows for this, but the following macro solves this problem by enabling you to specify the number of sheets you want in each new workbook:

```
Sub NewWorkbookWithCustomSheets()
    Dim currentSheets As Integer
    With Application
        currentSheets = .SheetsInNewWorkbook
        .SheetsInNewWorkbook = InputBox( _
            "How many sheets do you want " & _
            "in the new workbook?", , 3)
        Workbooks.Add
        .SheetsInNewWorkbook = currentSheets
    End With
End Sub
```

For more information about adding a macro to Excel, see Chapter 25.

Repair a Corrupted Workbook File

Excel workbooks rarely have problems and they generally open successfully. However, a hard drive error or memory error could create a problem that corrupts the file. When that happens and you try to open the workbook, Excel displays an error message telling you either that it does not recognize the file format or that the file is corrupted.

Whatever the cause, it is important that you do not lose any data, so Excel offers an Open and Repair command that first attempts to repair the file, and then to open the repaired workbook in Excel.

Repair a Corrupted Workbook File

1 Click the **File** tab.

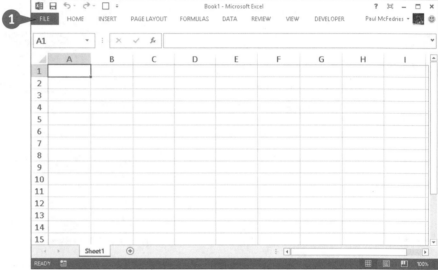

2 Click **Open**.

3 Click **Computer**.

4 Click **Browse**.

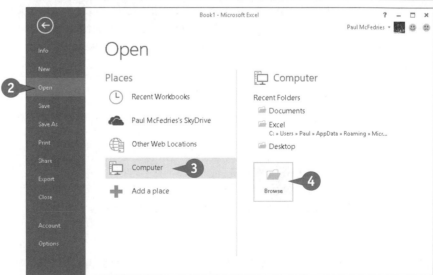

The Open dialog box appears.

5 Click the workbook you want to repair.

6 Click the **Open** drop-down arrow (⌄).

7 Click **Open and Repair**.

8 In the dialog box that appears, click **Repair**.

Excel repairs and then opens the file.

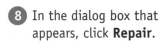

What do I do if Excel is unable to repair my workbook?

If Excel cannot repair the workbook, you may still be able to save the workbook's data. Follow Steps 1 to 7 to select the Open and Repair command. In the dialog box that appears, click **Extract Data**. In the dialog box that appears, click **Recover Formulas** if you want Excel to try to recover the workbook's formulas. If that does not work, follow Steps 1 to 7 again, click **Extract Data**, and then click **Convert to Values** instead; this tells Excel to convert all the formulas to their results. After Excel repairs the file, click **Close**.

Another way to recover some (or all) of your work is to open a previous version of the workbook, if one exists — see Chapter 23 for details.

Convert a Workbook to a PDF File

Although many people use Excel, not everyone does. If you want a non-Excel user to see your Excel data and results, you must find some way of sharing your workbook with that person.

One easy way to do this is by using a PDF file, which uses a near-universal file format that displays documents exactly as they appear in the original application, but can be configured to prevent people from making changes to the document. Most people have the Adobe Acrobat PDF reader on their PCs, but a free version can easily be obtained at www.adobe.com.

Convert a Workbook to a PDF File

1 Open the workbook you want to convert to PDF.

2 Click the **File** tab.

3 Click **Export**.

4 Click **Create PDF/XPS Document**.

5 Click **Create PDF/XPS**.

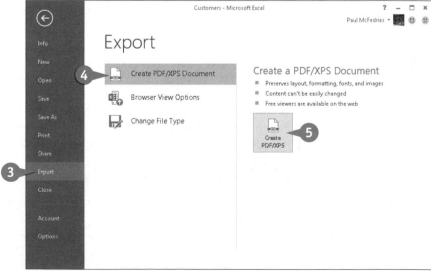

The Publish as PDF or XPS dialog box appears.

⑥ Choose a location for the file.

⑦ Type a name for the file.

⑧ Make sure the **Save as type** drop-down list shows **PDF**.

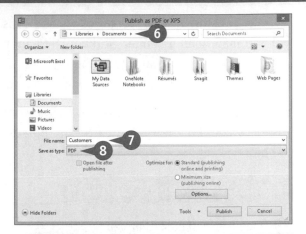

⑨ Click the empty **Standard** radio button (○) and it is filled (⦿).

Ⓐ If you will be sharing the PDF file online, create a smaller file by clicking the empty **Minimum Size** radio button (○) and it is filled (⦿).

⑩ Click **Publish**.

Excel publishes the file as a PDF.

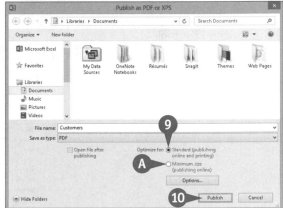

TIPS

Can I convert the whole workbook to a PDF file?
Yes. By default, Excel publishes only the current worksheet to PDF. If you want to publish the entire workbook instead, follow Steps 1 to 9 to open the Publish as PDF or XPS dialog box, and then set up the file. Click **Options** to open the Options dialog box, click the empty **Entire workbook** radio button (○) and it is filled (⦿). Click **OK**.

What is XPS?
XPS stands for XML Paper Specification. It uses XML (eXtensible Markup Language) for the document structure and the ZIP format for the document container file. So, it is based on open and available technologies, unlike PDF, which is a proprietary format owned by Adobe Systems. In the Publish as PDF or XPS dialog box, click the **Save as type** drop-down arrow (⌄), and then click **XPS Document**.

Create a Workbook Template

After you construct a workbook — add tabs, insert data and formulas, and format everything — you may need a similar workbook for another purpose. Rather than starting from scratch, you can use the Save As command (see the section "Create a New Workbook from an Existing File" later in this chapter) to create a new workbook based on the existing file.

However, if you need to use the existing workbook as the basis for many other workbooks, it is easier to convert the workbook to a template file. You can then create new workbooks based on that template.

Create a Workbook Template

1 Open the workbook that you want to save as a template.

2 Click the **File** tab.

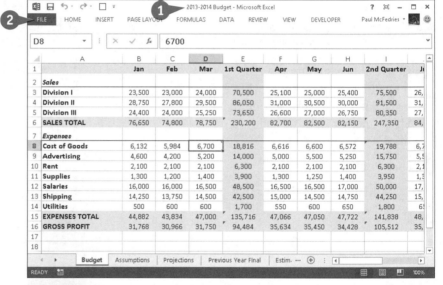

3 Click **Export**.

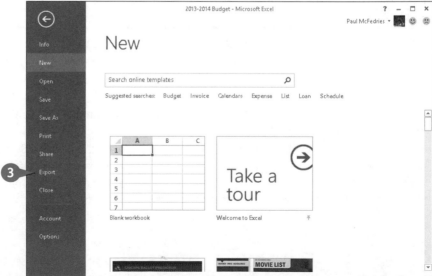

④ Click **Change File Type.**

⑤ Click **Template.**

⑥ Click **Save As.**

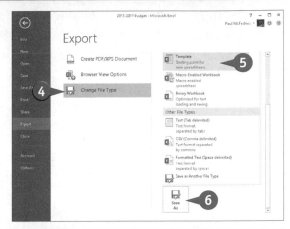

The Save As dialog box appears.

Ⓐ Excel automatically chooses Excel Template as the file type.

⑦ Select a location to save the template.

⑧ Use the **File name** text box to type a name for the template file.

⑨ Click **Save.**

Excel saves the workbook as a template file.

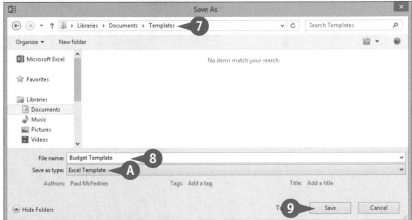

TIPS

How do I use my template?
First, make sure you have closed the new template file. Click the **File** tab, click **Open**, click **Computer**, and then click **Browse** to display the Open dialog box. Navigate to the folder that contains your template, right-click the template file, and then click **New.**

Are there other types of template files I can create?
In the Save As dialog box, the **Save as type** list offers three types of templates. The **Excel Template** file type creates a template compatible with Excel 2013, 2010, and 2007. If your workbook includes macros and you want them in your template, choose **Excel Macro-Enabled Template.** If you require a template file compatible with earlier versions of Excel, choose **Excel 97-2003 Template.**

Create a New Workbook from an Existing File

One of the secrets of Excel productivity is to minimize the number of times you have to "reinvent the wheel." That is, you should not create a new workbook from scratch if you already have an existing workbook that contains some or all of the data, formulas, or formatting that you require in the new file.

The easiest way to do this is to open the original file and then use the Save As command to create a copy of the workbook either under a different name or in a different location.

Create a New Workbook from an Existing File

1 Open the original workbook.

2 Click the **File** tab.

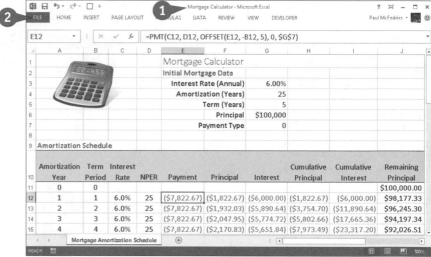

3 Click **Save As**.

4 Click **Computer**.

5 Click **Browse**.

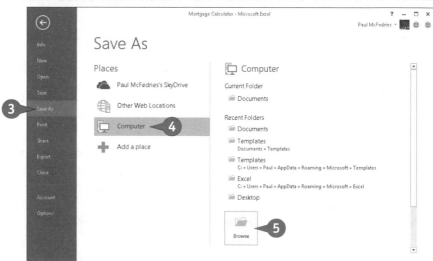

The Save As dialog box appears.

6 Choose a location for the new file.

7 Use the **File name** text box to name the new file.

Note: You must change the location, filename, or both to avoid overwriting the original workbook.

8 Click **Save**.

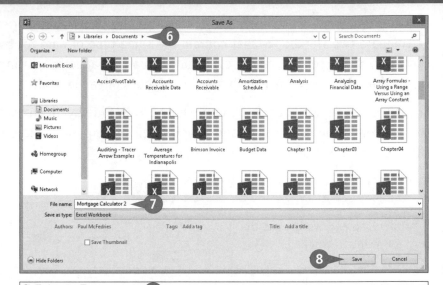

Excel closes the original workbook and then saves the new workbook.

A Excel opens the new workbook.

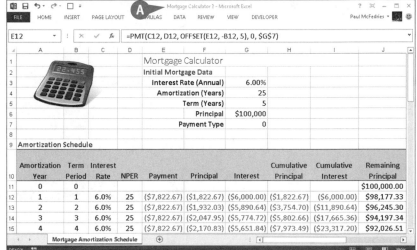

TIP

Can I use the Save As command to make a backup copy of a workbook?
Yes, Save As can operate as a rudimentary backup procedure. Follow the steps in this section to create a copy of the original workbook with the same name as the original, but store the copy in a different location. Good places to choose are a second hard drive, a USB flash drive, or a memory card. Remember, too, that after you complete the Save As steps, the *backup copy* will be open in the program. Be sure to close the copy and then reopen the original.

Compare Two Workbooks Side by Side

It is often useful to compare the contents of two workbooks. For example, you might want to compare two workbooks that contain the same type of data for two different departments. Similarly, if you sent a copy of a workbook to a colleague for editing, you might want to compare the original and the copy to see what changes your colleague made.

To help compare workbooks, Excel offers the View Side by Side command, which displays two workbooks beside each other, and as you scroll through one, Excel automatically scrolls through the other by the same amount.

Compare Two Workbooks Side by Side

1 Open the two workbooks that you want to compare.

Note: It does not matter if you also have other workbooks open at the same time.

2 Switch to one of the workbooks that you want to compare.

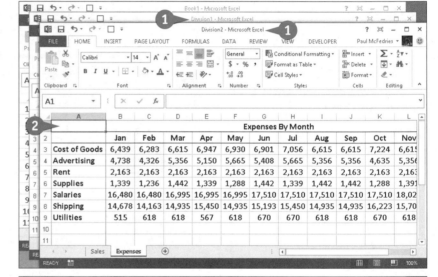

3 Click the **View** tab.

4 Click **View Side by Side** (⬚).

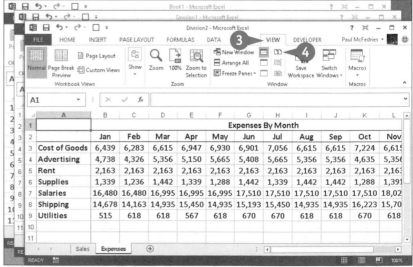

The Compare Side by Side dialog box appears.

⑤ Click the other workbook that you want to use in the comparison.

⑥ Click **OK**.

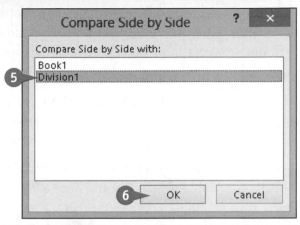

Ⓐ Excel arranges the windows of the two workbooks so that you can compare them.

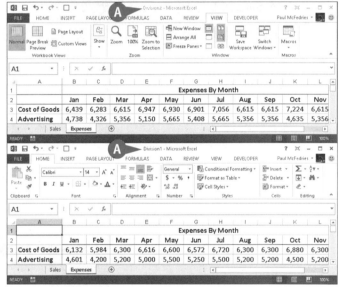

TIPS

Can I disable the automatic scrolling?

By default, Excel configures the View Side by Side feature with *synchronous scrolling*: When you scroll vertically or horizontally in one window, Excel automatically scrolls the other window by the same amount in the same direction. To keep one window in the same position while you scroll the other, click the **View** tab, and then click to turn off the **Synchronous Scrolling** (🔳) command.

How can I compare two workbooks that are tiled vertically instead of horizontally?

Despite the name, the View Side by Side command tiles the workbooks horizontally, not vertically, as you might expect. Unfortunately, you cannot configure View Side by Side to arrange the workbook windows vertically. You can arrange them that way manually, but you do not get the synchronous scrolling feature.

Check for Features Not Supported by Earlier Versions of Excel

Each new version of Excel includes new features, and some of these features introduce functionality that is incompatible with earlier versions of Excel. For example, Excel 2013 introduces several new worksheet functions, while Excel 2010 introduced sparklines and slicers. These features are not supported by earlier versions of Excel.

At best, these incompatible features can cause your workbook to appear different to other people; at worst, they can cause errors. If you will be distributing a workbook to users of earlier versions of Excel, use the Compatibility Checker to look for incompatible features in the workbook.

Check for Features Not Supported by Earlier Versions of Excel

1 Open the workbook you want to check.

2 Click the **File** tab.

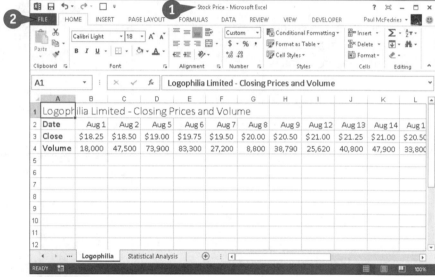

3 Click **Info**.

4 Click **Check for Issues**.

5 Click **Check Compatibility**.

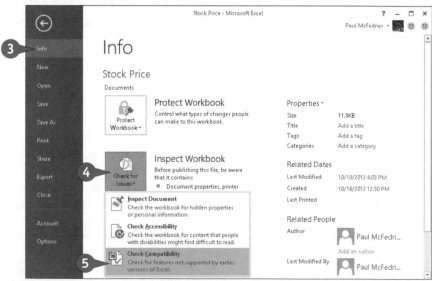

The Compatibility Checker appears.

6 Click the **Select versions to show** drop-down arrow (☑).

7 Click an Excel version if you do not want to see compatibility issues for that version.

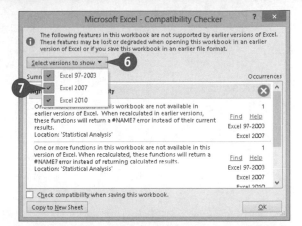

A Excel displays the workbook's compatibility issues.

B To see the specific cell, range, or object that has the problem, you can click **Find**.

8 Click **OK**.

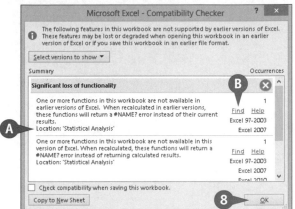

TIP

Is there an easy way to check compatibility as I work on my spreadsheet?
Yes. If you have other changes to make to the workbook before distributing the file, you may prefer to check compatibility as you go along. Rather than running the steps in this section every time, follow Steps 1 to 5 to open the Compatibility Checker. Click the empty **Check compatibility when saving this workbook** check box (☐) and it is filled (☑).

Excel then checks for incompatible features automatically each time you save the workbook. If it finds incompatible items, Excel displays the Compatibility Checker to let you know. Note the problematic items and click **Continue** to save the document.

CHAPTER 13

Formatting Workbooks

Excel offers several settings that enable you to control the look of a workbook, including the workbook colors, fonts, and special effects. You can also apply a workbook theme and add a header and footer to a workbook.

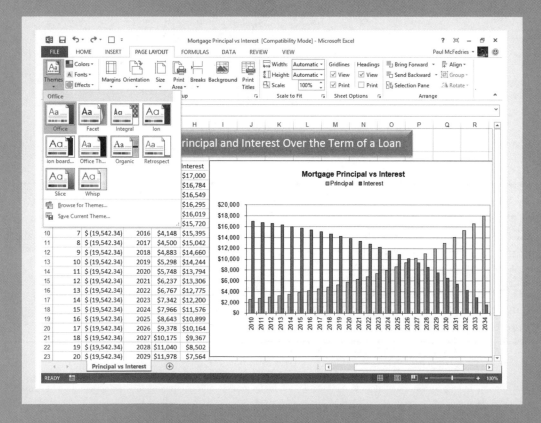

Modify Workbook Colors

You can give your workbook a new look by selecting a different color scheme. Each color scheme affects a dozen workbook elements, including the workbook's text colors, background colors, border colors, chart colors, and more. Excel offers more than 20 color schemes. However, if none of these predefined schemes suits your needs, you can also create your own custom color scheme.

To get the most out of the Excel color schemes, you must apply styles to your ranges, as described in Chapter 5.

Modify Workbook Colors

1 Open or switch to the workbook you want to format.

2 Click the **Page Layout** tab.

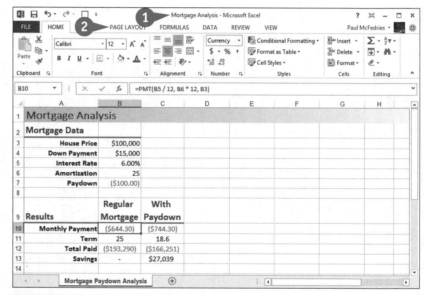

3 Click **Colors** (■).

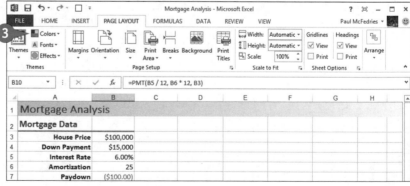

4 Click the color scheme you want to apply.

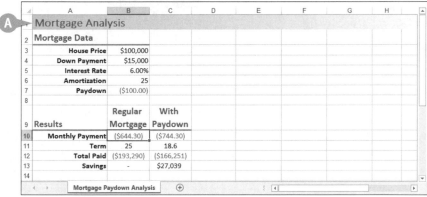

A Excel applies the color scheme to the workbook.

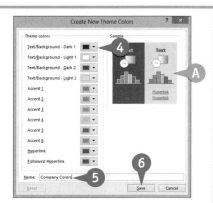

	A	B	C	D	E	F	G	H
1	Mortgage Analysis							
2	Mortgage Data							
3	House Price	$100,000						
4	Down Payment	$15,000						
5	Interest Rate	6.00%						
6	Amortization	25						
7	Paydown	($100.00)						
8								
9	Results	Regular Mortgage	With Paydown					
10	Monthly Payment	($644.30)	($744.30)					
11	Term	25	18.6					
12	Total Paid	($193,290)	($166,251)					
13	Savings	-	$27,039					
14								

TIP

Can I create my own color scheme?

Yes. Follow these steps:

1 Click the **Page Layout** tab.

2 Click **Colors** (▣).

3 Click **Customize Colors**.

The Create New Theme Colors dialog box appears.

4 Click each **Theme Color** drop-down arrow (☑), and then click the color you want.

A The Sample area shows what your theme colors look like.

5 Type a name for the custom color scheme.

6 Click **Save**.

Set Workbook Fonts

You can add visual appeal to your workbook by selecting a different font scheme. Each font scheme has two defined fonts: a *heading font* for the titles and headings, and a *body font* for the regular worksheet text. Excel offers more than 20 font schemes. However, if none of the predefined schemes is suitable, you can create a custom font scheme.

To get the most out of the Excel font schemes, particularly the heading fonts, you must apply styles to your ranges, as described in Chapter 5.

Set Workbook Fonts

1 Open or switch to the workbook you want to format.

2 Click the **Page Layout** tab.

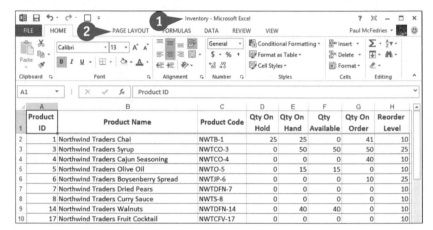

3 Click **Fonts** (A).

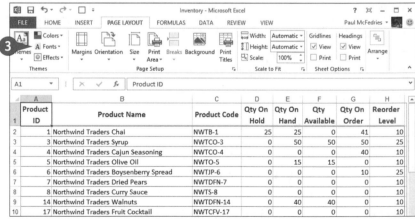

④ Click the font scheme you
want to apply.

Ⓐ Excel applies the heading
font to the workbook's
headings.

Ⓑ Excel applies the body font
to the workbook's regular
text.

Product ID	Product Name	Product Code	Qty On Hold	Qty On Hand	Qty Available	Qty On Order	Reorder Level
1	Northwind Traders Chai	NWTB-1	25	25	0	41	10
3	Northwind Traders Syrup	NWTCO-3	0	50	50	50	25
4	Northwind Traders Cajun Seasoning	NWTCO-4	0	0	0	40	10
5	Northwind Traders Olive Oil	NWTO-5	0	15	15	0	10
6	Northwind Traders Boysenberry Spread	NWTJP-6	0	0	0	10	25
7	Northwind Traders Dried Pears	NWTDFN-7	0	0	0	0	10
8	Northwind Traders Curry Sauce	NWTS-8	0	0	0	0	10
14	Northwind Traders Walnuts	NWTDFN-14	0	40	40	0	10
17	Northwind Traders Fruit Cocktail	NWTCFV-17	0	0	0	0	10
19	Northwind Traders Chocolate Biscuits Mix	NWTBGM-19	0	0	0	20	5
20	Northwind Traders Marmalade	NWTJP-6	0	0	0	40	10
21	Northwind Traders Scones	NWTBGM-21	0	0	0	0	5
34	Northwind Traders Beer	NWTB-34	23	23	0	0	15
40	Northwind Traders Crab Meat	NWTCM-40	0	0	0	120	30

TIP

Can I create my own font scheme?
Yes. Follow these steps:

① Click the **Page Layout** tab.

② Click **Fonts** (Ⓐ).

③ Click **Customize Fonts**.

The Create New Theme Fonts dialog box
appears.

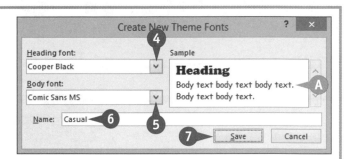

④ Click the **Heading font** drop-down arrow (▾)
and select a font.

⑤ Click the **Body font** drop-down arrow (▾), and select a font.

Ⓐ The Sample area shows a preview.

⑥ Type a name for the custom font scheme.

⑦ Click **Save**.

Choose Workbook Effects

You can enhance the look of your workbook by selecting a different effect scheme. The effect scheme applies to charts and graphic objects. Each scheme defines a border and fill style, and an added effect, such as a drop shadow or glow. Excel offers more than 20 effect schemes.

To get the most out of the Excel effect schemes, you must apply a style to your chart, as described in Chapter 18, or to your graphic object, as described in Chapter 19.

Choose Workbook Effects

1 Open or switch to the workbook you want to format.

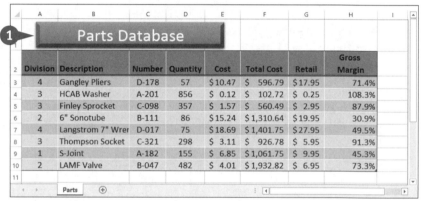

2 Click the **Page Layout** tab.

3 Click **Effects** (⬤).

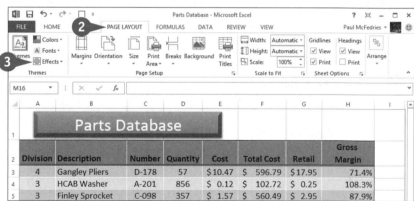

④ Click the effect scheme you want to apply.

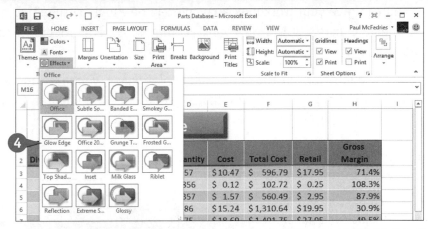

🅐 Excel applies the effect scheme to the workbook's charts and graphics.

TIPS

Can I create a custom effect scheme?
No. Unlike with the color schemes and font schemes described earlier in this chapter, Excel does not have a feature that enables you to create your own effect scheme.

Why are all effect schemes the same color?
The color you see in the effect schemes depends on the color scheme you applied to your workbook. If you apply a different color scheme (described in the "Modify Workbook Colors" section earlier in this chapter), you see a different color in the effect schemes. To use a custom effect color, create a custom color scheme, and then change the Accent 1 color to the one you want.

Apply a Workbook Theme

You can give your workbook a completely new look by selecting a different workbook theme. Each theme consists of the workbook's colors, fonts, and effects. Excel offers 10 predefined workbook themes.

To get the most out of the Excel workbook themes, you must apply styles to your ranges, as described in Chapter 5; to your charts, as described in Chapter 18; and to your graphic objects, as described in Chapter 19.

Apply a Workbook Theme

1 Open or switch to the workbook you want to format.

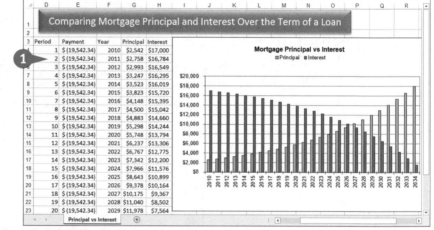

2 Click the **Page Layout** tab.

3 Click **Themes** (⬛).

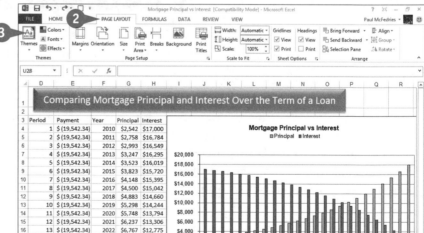

④ Click the workbook theme you want to apply.

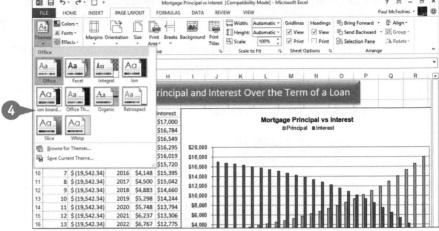

Ⓐ Excel applies the theme to the workbook.

Note: After you apply the theme, the new font size might require you to adjust the column widths to see your data properly.

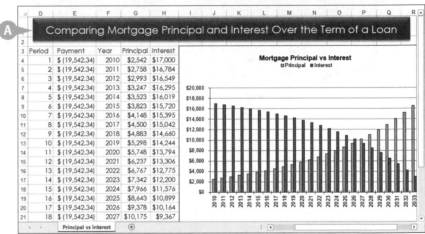

TIP

Can I create my own workbook theme?

Yes. Follow these steps:

① Format the workbook with a color scheme, font scheme, and effect scheme, as described in the previous three sections.

② Click the **Page Layout** tab.

③ Click **Themes** (⊞).

④ Click **Save Current Theme**.

The Save Current Theme dialog box appears.

⑤ Type a name for the custom theme.

⑥ Click **Save**.

Add a Workbook Header

If you will be printing a workbook, you can enhance the printout by building a custom header that includes information such as the page number, date, filename, or even a picture.

The *header* is an area on the printed page between the top of the page text and the top margin. Excel offers a number of predefined header items that enable you to add data to the workbook header quickly. If none of the predefined header items suits your needs, Excel also offers tools that make it easy to build a custom header.

Add a Workbook Header

1 Click the **View** tab.

2 Click **Page Layout** ( ).

Excel switches to Page Layout view.

Ⓐ You can also click the status bar's **Page Layout** button ( ).

3 Click the **Click to add header** text.

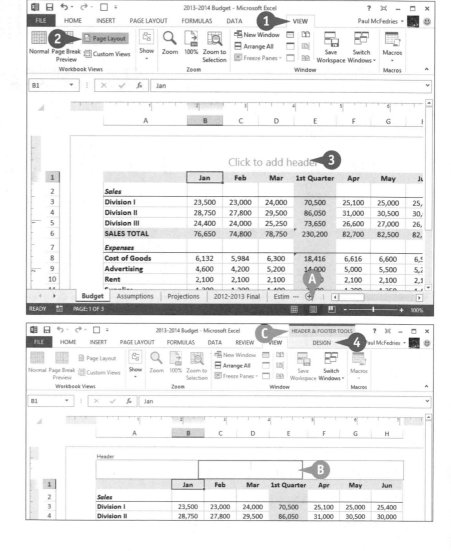

Ⓑ Excel opens the header area for editing.

Ⓒ Excel adds the **Header & Footer Tools** tab.

4 Click the **Design** tab.

5 Type your text in the header.

6 If you want to include a predefined header item, click **Header,** and then click the item.

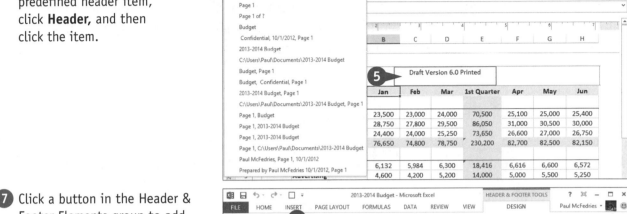

7 Click a button in the Header & Footer Elements group to add that element to the header.

D Excel inserts a code into the header, such as &[Date] for the Current Date element, as shown here.

8 Repeat Steps **5** to **7** to build the header.

9 Click outside the header area.

Excel applies the header. When you are in Page Layout view, you see the current values for elements such as the date.

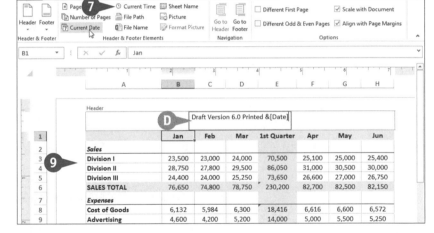

TIP

Can I have multiple headers in a workbook?

Yes. You can have a different header and footer on the first page, which is useful if you want to add a title or explanatory text to the first page. In the Design tab, click the empty **Different First Page** check box (□) and it is filled (☑).

You can also have different headers and footers on the even and odd pages of the printout, such as showing the filename on the even pages and the page numbers on the odd pages. In the **Design** tab, click the empty **Different Odd & Even Pages** check box (□) and it is filled (☑).

Add a Workbook Footer

If you will be printing a workbook, you can enhance the printout by building a custom footer that includes information such as the current page number, the total number of pages, the worksheet name, and more.

The *footer* is an area on the printed page between the bottom of the page text and the bottom margin. Excel offers a number of predefined footer items that enable you to add data to the workbook footer quickly. If none of the predefined footer items suits your needs, Excel also offers tools that make it easy to build a custom footer.

Add a Workbook Footer

1 Click the **View** tab.

2 Click **Page Layout** (🔲).

Excel switches to Page Layout view.

Ⓐ You can also click the **Page Layout** button (🔲).

3 Click the **Click to add header** text.

Note: If you scroll to the bottom of the page and click the **Click to add footer** text, you can skip Step **6**.

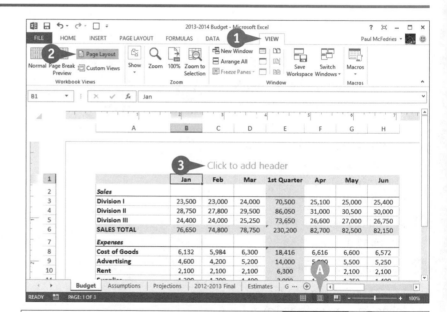

Ⓑ Excel adds the **Header & Footer Tools** tab.

4 Click the **Design** tab.

5 Click **Go to Footer** (🔳).

Ⓒ Excel opens the footer area for editing.

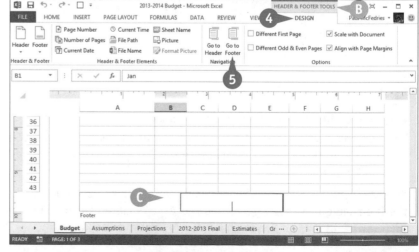

6 Type your text in the footer.

7 If you want to include a predefined footer item, click **Footer,** and then click the item.

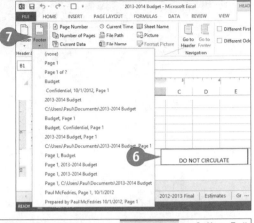

8 Click a button in the Header & Footer Elements group to add that element to the footer.

D Excel inserts a code into the footer, such as &[Pages] for the Number of Pages element, as shown here.

9 Repeat Steps 6 to 8 to build the footer.

10 Click outside the footer area.

Excel applies the footer. When you are in Page Layout view, you see the current values for elements such as the page number.

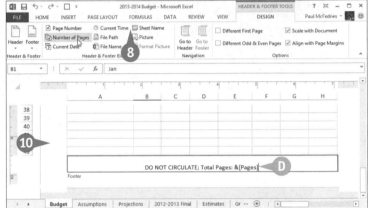

TIP

Can I view my headers and footers before I print the workbook?

Yes. Follow these steps:

1 Click the **File** tab.

2 Click **Print**.

A The right side of the Print tab shows you a preview of the workbook printout.

B The header appears here.

C The footer appears here.

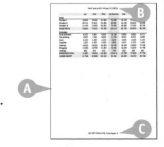

CHAPTER 14

Printing Workbooks

If you want to distribute hard copies of one or more worksheets or an entire workbook, you can use the Excel Print feature. Before you print, you can adjust print-related options such as the margins, page orientation, and paper size.

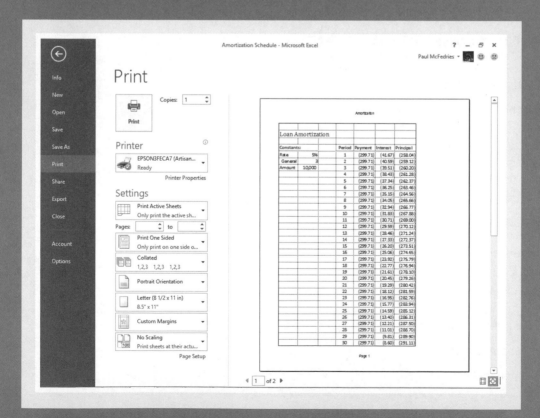

Adjust Workbook Margins

You can get more space on the printed page to display your worksheet data by using smaller page margins. The *margins* are the blank areas that surround the printed data. For example, if you find that Excel is printing extra pages because your data is a bit too wide or a bit too long to fit on a single page, you can reduce either the left and right margins or the top and bottom margins.

If you or another person will be writing notes on the printouts, consider using wider margins to allow more room for the notes.

Adjust Workbook Margins

Using the Ribbon

1 Open the workbook you want to print.

2 Click the **Page Layout** tab.

3 Click **Margins** (▦).

Ⓐ If you see a margin setting you want to use, click it, and skip the remaining steps.

4 Click **Custom Margins**.

The Page Setup dialog box appears with the Margins tab selected.

5 Use the spin boxes to specify the margin sizes in inches.

Note: Do not make the margins too small or your document may not print properly. Most printers cannot handle margins smaller than about 0.25 inch, although you should consult your printer manual to confirm this. In particular, see if your printer offers a borderless printing option.

6 Click **OK**.

Excel adjusts the margin sizes.

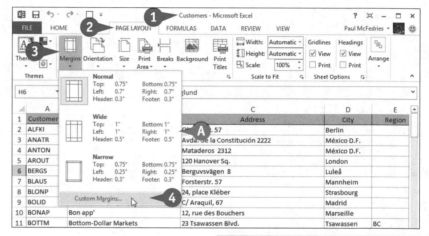

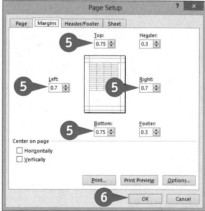

Using the Ruler

1. Open the workbook you want to print.

2. Click **Page Layout** (▣).

3. Move the mouse pointer (▷) over the right edge of the ruler's left margin area, and it becomes the Left/Right margin pointer (↔).

4. Click and drag the edge of the margin to set the left margin width.

5. Click and drag the left edge of the right margin area to set the margin width.

6. Move the mouse pointer (▷) over the bottom edge of the ruler's top margin area, and it becomes the Top/Bottom Margin pointer (↕).

7. Click and drag the edge of the margin to set the top margin width.

8. Click and drag the top edge of the bottom margin area (not shown) to set the bottom margin width.

TIPS

Can I center the text on the page after increasing margin sizes?

Yes. Follow Steps **1** to **4** in the "Using the Ribbon" subsection. Click the empty **Horizontally** check box (□) and it is filled (☑). Click the empty **Vertically** check box (□) and it is filled (☑). Click **OK**.

What are the header and footer margins?

The header margin is the space between the workbook header and the top of the page, and the footer margin is the space between the workbook footer and the bottom of the page. In the **Margins** tab of the Page Setup dialog box, use the **Header** and **Footer** spin boxes to set these.

Change the Page Orientation

You can improve the look of your printout by changing the page orientation to suit your data. The page orientation determines whether Excel prints more rows or columns on a page. Portrait orientation is taller, so it prints more rows; landscape orientation is wider, so it prints more columns.

Choose the orientation based on your worksheet data. If your worksheet has many rows and only a few columns, choose portrait; if it has many columns but just a few rows, choose landscape.

Change the Page Orientation

1 Open the workbook you want to print.

2 Click the **Page Layout** tab.

3 Click **Orientation** (🖼).

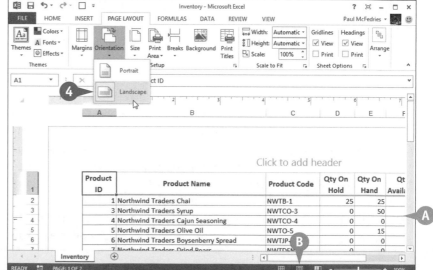

4 Click the orientation you want to use.

Ⓐ Excel adjusts the orientation.

Ⓑ Click **Page Layout** (▣) to see the orientation.

Insert a Page Break

You can control what data appears on each printed page by inserting a page break in your worksheet. A *page break* is a location within a worksheet where Excel begins a new printed page. Excel normally inserts its own page breaks based on the number and height of rows in the sheet, the number and width of the sheet columns, the margin widths, and the page orientation.

A vertical page break starts a new page at a particular column; a horizontal page break starts a new page at a particular row.

Insert a Page Break

1 Open the workbook you want to print.

2 Select the cell to the right of and below where you want the vertical and horizontal page breaks to appear.

Note: Select a cell in row 1 to create just a vertical page break; select a cell in column A to create just a horizontal page break.

3 Click the **Page Layout** tab.

4 Click **Breaks** (⊨).

5 Click **Insert Page Break**.

⬤ Excel inserts the page breaks and indicates them with thicker lines.

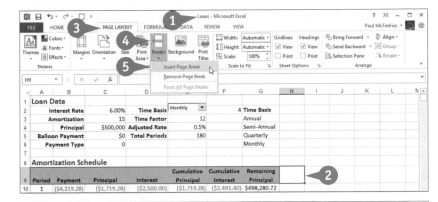

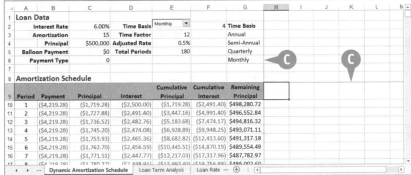

Choose a Paper Size

You can customize your print job by choosing the appropriate paper size for your printout. For example, if your worksheet has many rows, you might prefer to print it on a longer sheet of paper, such as a legal-size page (8-1/2 inches wide × 14 inches long). Similarly, if your worksheet has many columns, you might also want to use a longer sheet of paper, but switch to landscape mode, as described in the section "Change the Page Orientation" earlier in the chapter.

Check your printer manual to make sure your printer can handle the paper size you select.

Choose a Paper Size

1 Open the workbook you want to print.

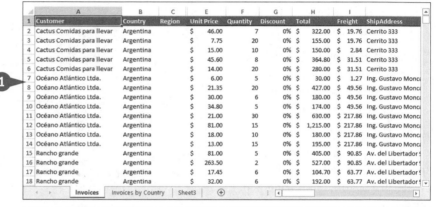

2 Click the **Page Layout** tab.

3 Click **Size** (⊤̄F).

A If you see a page size you want to use, click it, and skip the rest of these steps.

4 Click **More Paper Sizes**.

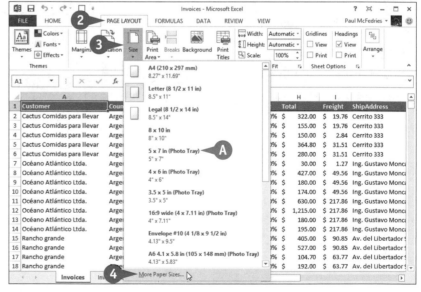

The Page Setup dialog box appears with the **Page** tab selected.

⑤ Click the **Paper size** drop-down arrow (☑), and then click the size you want to use.

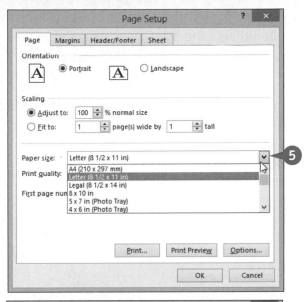

⑥ Click **OK**.

Excel uses the new paper size option when you print the workbook.

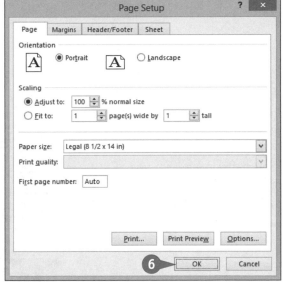

TIP

Is there a way to ensure that all my worksheet columns fit onto a single page?
Yes. Try selecting a wider page size as described in this section. You can also reduce the left and right margins (see the section "Adjust Workbook Margins" earlier in this chapter). Alternatively, switch to the landscape orientation (see the section "Change the Page Orientation" earlier in this chapter). You can also follow Steps 1 to 4 to display the Page Setup dialog box with the **Page** tab selected. Click the empty **Fit to** radio button (○) and it is filled (◉). Set the **page(s) wide by** spin box to 1. Set the **tall** spin box to a number large enough that all of your printed rows will fit on a single page. (If you do not know the correct number, click **Print Preview** to check.) Click **OK**.

Set the Print Area

You can control the cells that Excel includes in the printout by setting the print area for the worksheet. The print area is a range of cells that you select. When Excel prints the workbook, it only prints the cells within the print area.

You normally define a single range of cells as the print area, but it is possible to set up two or more ranges as the print area. See the first Tip on the next page for more information.

Set the Print Area

1 Open the workbook you want to print.

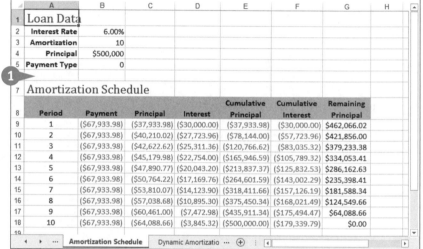

2 Select the range that you want to print.

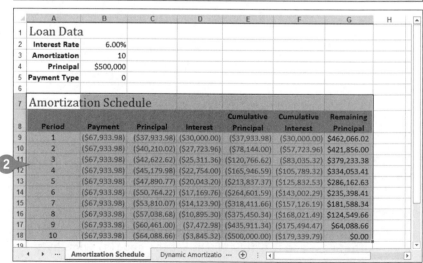

③ Click the **Page Layout** tab.

④ Click **Print Area** ( ).

⑤ Click **Set Print Area**.

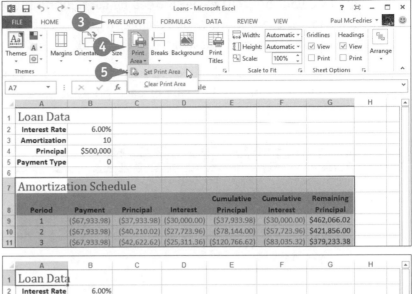

Ⓐ Excel displays a border around the print area.

When you print the worksheet, Excel prints only the cells within the print area.

TIPS

Can I define two different ranges as the print area?

Yes. The easiest way to do this is to follow the steps in this section to set the first range as the print area. Next, select the second range, click the **Page Layout** tab, click **Print Area** ( ), and then click **Add to Print Area**. You can repeat this procedure to add as many ranges as you require to the print area.

How do I remove an existing print area?

To set a new print area, you do not need to remove the existing one. Select the range you want to use, and then follow Steps **3** to **5**. Excel replaces the original print area with the new one. If you no longer want a print area defined, click the **Page Layout** tab, click **Print Area** ( ), and then click **Clear Print Area**.

Configure Titles to Print on Each Page

You can make your printout easier to read by configuring the worksheet to print the range titles on each page of the printout. For example, if your data has a row of headings at the top, you can configure the worksheet to display those headings at the top of each printout page.

Similarly, if your data has a column of headings at the left, you can configure the worksheet to display those headings on the left side of each printout page.

Configure Titles to Print on Each Page

1 Open the workbook you want to print.

2 Click the tab of the worksheet you want to configure.

3 Click the **Page Layout** tab.

4 Click **Print Titles** (⊞).

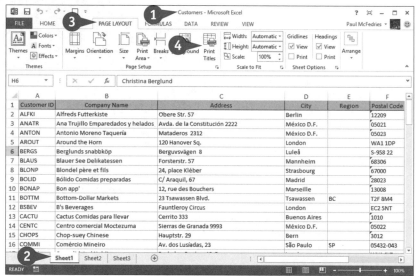

Excel opens the Page Setup dialog box with the **Sheet** tab displayed.

5 Click inside the **Rows to repeat at top** range box.

6 Click **Collapse Dialog** (⊞).

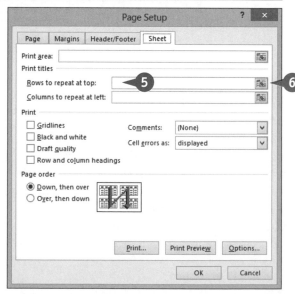

Ⓐ Excel collapses the Page Setup dialog box.

The mouse pointer (⌖) becomes row select (→).

⑦ Use row select (→) and click the row that you want at the top of each printed page.

If you want more than one row repeated at the top of each page, use row select (→) and click the last row that you want to repeat.

⑧ Click **Restore Dialog** (▦).

Ⓑ The address of the row appears in the **Rows to repeat at top** box.

⑨ Click **OK**.

Excel displays the selected row at the top of each page when printed.

TIP

How do I configure my worksheet to print a column of headings on each page?

If your headings appear in a column rather than a row, you can still configure the sheet to print them on each page. Follow these steps:

① Follow Steps **1** to **4** to open the Page Setup dialog box with the **Sheet** tab displayed.

② Click inside the **Columns to repeat at left** range box.

③ Click **Collapse Dialog** (▦).

④ Use column select (↓) and click the column you want on the left of each printed page.

⑤ Click **Restore Dialog** (▦).

⑥ Click **OK**.

Preview a Printout

You can save time and paper by using the Print Preview feature to examine your printout on-screen before you send it to the printer. You can use Print Preview to make sure settings such as margins, page orientation, page breaks, print areas, and sheet titles all result in the printout you want.

If you see a problem in the preview, you can use the Print Preview screen to adjust some printout options.

Preview a Printout

1 Open the workbook you want to print.

2 Click the tab of the worksheet you want to preview.

3 Click the **File** tab.

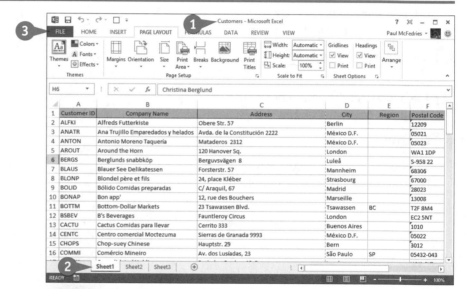

4 Click **Print**.

The Print window appears.

Ⓐ Excel displays a preview of the printout.

Note: If you do not see the preview, click **Show Print Preview**.

5 Click **Print Preview Next Page** (▶) to scroll through the printout pages.

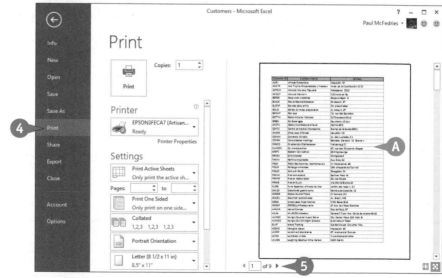

6 Click **Print Preview Previous Page**
(◂) to return to a printout page.

B You can click the **Page Orientation**
drop-down arrow (☑) to change the
page orientation.

C You can click the **Page Size** drop-
down arrow (☑) to change the page
size.

D You can click the **Margins** drop-
down arrow (☑) to change the
margins.

7 When you are done, click **Back** (◉)
to return to the workbook.

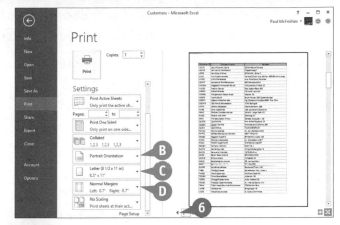

TIP

Can I fine-tune the margins in Print Preview?
Yes. The **Margins** list only offers a few predefined margin sets. To
define custom margins in Print Preview, follow these steps:

1 Click **Show Margins** (▭).

A Print Preview augments the preview with lines that indicate the
margins.

2 Click and drag a line to adjust that margin.

Print a Workbook

When you need a hard copy of your document, either for your files or to distribute to someone else, you can send the document to your printer.

This section assumes that you have a printer connected to your computer and that the printer is turned on. Also, before printing you should check that your printer has enough paper (and that it is the right size) to complete the print job.

Print a Workbook

① Open the workbook you want to print.

② If you only want to print a single worksheet, click the tab of that worksheet.

Note: To print multiple worksheets, hold down Ctrl and click the top of each sheet you want to print.

③ Click the **File** tab.

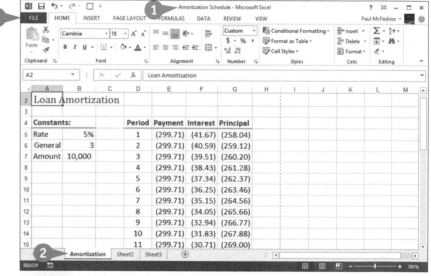

④ Click **Print**.

Note: You can also press Ctrl + P.

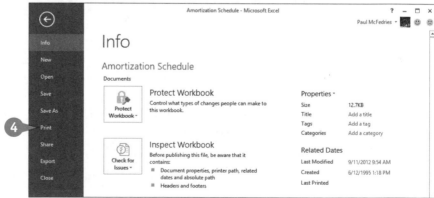

The Print window appears.

⑤ Type the number of copies you want to print in the **Copies** text box.

Ⓐ If you have more than one printer, click the **Printer** drop-down arrow (⌄), and then click the printer you want to use.

Ⓑ By default, **Print Active Sheets** appears in the **Print What** list, which tells Excel to print only the selected sheets. If you want to print all sheets in the workbook, click the **Print What** drop-down arrow (⌄), and then click **Print Entire Workbook**.

⑥ Click **Print**.

Excel prints the document.

Ⓒ The printer icon (🖨) appears in the taskbar's notification area while the document prints.

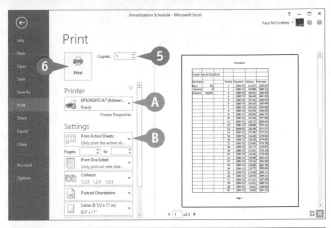

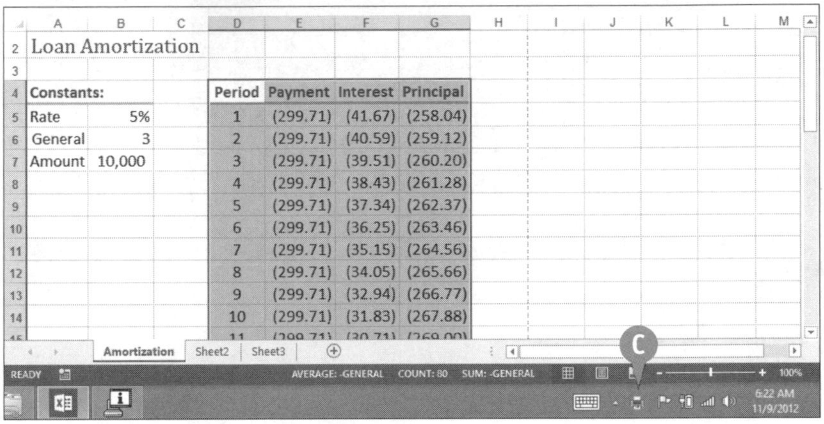

	A	B	C	D	E	F	G
2	Loan Amortization						
4	Constants:			Period	Payment	Interest	Principal
5	Rate	5%		1	(299.71)	(41.67)	(258.04)
6	General	3		2	(299.71)	(40.59)	(259.12)
7	Amount	10,000		3	(299.71)	(39.51)	(260.20)
8				4	(299.71)	(38.43)	(261.28)
9				5	(299.71)	(37.34)	(262.37)
10				6	(299.71)	(36.25)	(263.46)
11				7	(299.71)	(35.15)	(264.56)
12				8	(299.71)	(34.05)	(265.66)
13				9	(299.71)	(32.94)	(266.77)
14				10	(299.71)	(31.83)	(267.88)

TIPS

Is there a faster way to print?
Yes. If you want to print a single copy of the selected worksheet, the Excel Quick Print command sends it to your default printer. Click the **More arrow** (�) in the Quick Access Toolbar, and then click **Quick Print** to add this command to the toolbar. You can then click **Quick Print** (🖨) and print a worksheet without having to go through the Print window.

Can I print just part of a worksheet?
Yes, you can tell Excel to print just a range. Begin by selecting the range(s) you want to print. (See Chapter 3 to learn how to select a range.) Follow Steps 3 and 4 to open the Print window, and then choose the number of copies. Click the **Print What** drop-down arrow (⌄), and then click **Print Selection**. Click **Print**.

CHAPTER 15

Working with Tables

The forte of Excel is spreadsheet work, of course, but its row-and-column layout also makes it a natural flat-file database manager. That is, instead of typing data, and then using the Excel tools to build formulas and analyze that data, you can also use Excel simply to store data in a special structure called a table.

Understanding Tables

In Excel, a *table* is a rectangular range of cells used to store data. The table is a collection of related information with an organizational structure that makes it easy to find or extract data from its contents.

To get the most out of Excel tables, you need to understand a few basic concepts, such as how a table is like a database, the advantages of tables, and how they help with data analysis.

A Table Is a Database

A table is a type of database where the data is organized into rows and columns: Each column represents a database field, which is a single type of information, such as a name, address, or phone number; each row represents a database record, which is a collection of associated field values, such as the information for a specific contact.

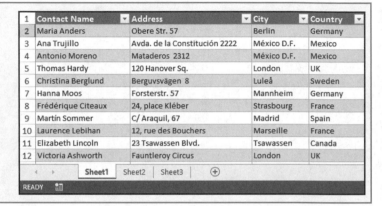

Advantages of a Table

A table differs from a regular Excel range in that Excel offers a set of tools that makes it easier for you to work with the data within a table. As you see in this chapter, these tools make it easy to convert existing worksheet data into a table, add new records and fields to a table, delete existing records and fields, insert rows to show totals, and apply styles.

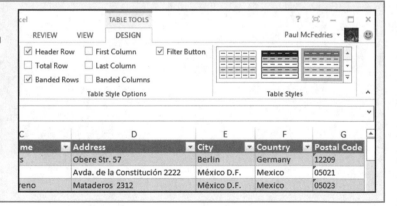

Data Analysis

Tables are also useful tools for analyzing your data. For example, as you see in Chapter 17, you can easily use a table as the basis of a PivotTable, which is a special object for summarizing and analyzing data. In Chapter 16, you also learn how to sort table records and how to filter table data to show only specific records.

Get to Know Table Features

Although a table looks much like a regular Excel range, it offers a number of features that differentiate it from a range. To understand these differences and make it as easy as possible to learn how to build and use tables, you need to know the various features in a typical table, such as the table rows and columns, the table headers, and the filter buttons.

Ⓐ Table Column

Contains one type of information (such as names). Each column is the equivalent of a database field.

Ⓑ Column Headers

The names you assign to table columns. These specify the type of data, and are always found in the first row of the table.

Ⓒ Table Cell

An item in a table column that represents one instance of that column's data (such as a name). Each cell is equivalent to a database field value.

Ⓓ Table Row

A collection of associated table cells, such as the data for a single contact. Each row is the equivalent of a database record.

Ⓔ Column Filter Button

A feature that gives you access to a set of commands that perform various actions on a column, such as sorting or filtering the column data.

Convert a Range to a Table

In Excel 2013, you cannot create a table from scratch, and then fill it with data. You must first create a range that includes at least some of the data you want in your table, and then convert that range to a table.

Note that you do not need to input all of your data before converting the range to a table. Once you have the table, you can add new rows and columns as needed, as described later in this chapter. However, it is best to decide up front whether you want your table to have column headers.

Convert a Range to a Table

1 Click a cell within the range that you want to convert to a table.

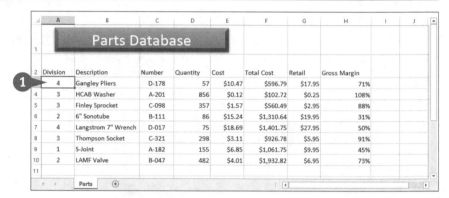

2 Click the **Insert** tab.

3 Click **Table** (⊞).

Note: You can also choose the Table command by pressing **Ctrl** + **T**.

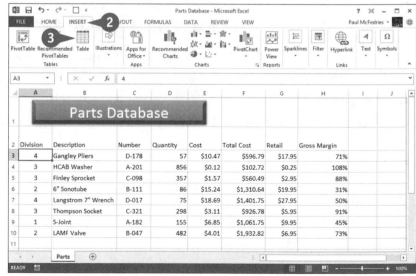

The Create Table dialog box appears.

Ⓐ Excel selects the range that it will convert to a table.

Ⓑ To change the range, click **Collapse Dialog** (▦), drag the mouse pointer (⊕) over the new range, and then click **Restore Dialog** (▥).

④ If your range has labels you want to use as column headers, click the empty **My table has headers** check box (☐) and it is filled ☑).

⑤ Click **OK**.

Excel converts the range to a table.

Ⓒ Excel applies a table format to the range.

Ⓓ The Table Tools contextual tab appears.

Ⓔ Filter buttons appear in each column heading.

⑥ Click the **Design** tab to see the Excel table design tools.

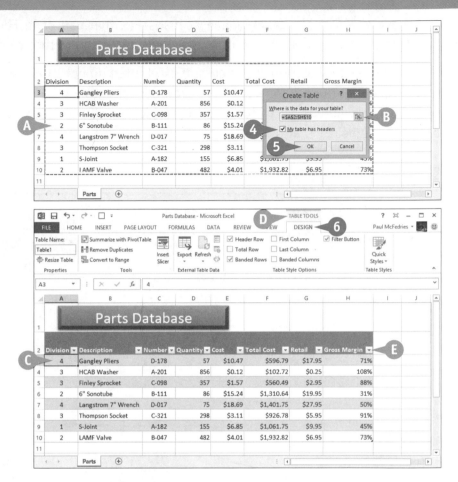

TIPS

Do I need to add labels to the top of each column before converting my range to a table?
No. Follow Steps 1 to 3 to display the Create Table dialog box, and then click the selected **My table has headers** check box (☑) and it is cleared (☐). Click **OK** and Excel converts the range to a table, and automatically adds headers to each column. These headers use the generic names Column1, Column2, and so on.

If I selected the wrong range for my table, is there a way to tell Excel the correct range?
Yes, although you cannot change the location of the headers. To redefine the range used in the table, first select any cell in the table. Under the Table Tools contextual tab, click the **Design** tab, and then click **Resize Table** (▦) to open the Resize Table dialog box. Drag the mouse pointer (⊕) over the new range, and then click **OK**.

Select Table Data

To work with part of a table, you must first select that part of it. For example, if you want to apply a format to an entire column or copy an entire row, select that column or row.

The normal range-selection techniques in Excel often do not work well with a table. For example, selecting an entire worksheet column or row does not work because no table uses up an entire worksheet column or row. Instead, Excel provides tools for selecting a column (just the data, or the data and the header), a row, or the entire table.

Select Table Data

Select a Table Column

1. Click any cell in the column you want to select.

2. Right-click the selected cell.

3. Click **Select**.

4. Click **Table Column Data**.

   Excel selects all the column's data cells.

Select a Table Column and Header

1. Click any cell in the column you want to select.

2. Right-click the selected cell.

3. Click **Select**.

4. Click **Entire Table Column**.

   Excel selects the column's data and header.

Select a Table Row

1. Click any cell in the row you want to select.

2. Right-click the selected cell.

3. Click **Select**.

4. Click **Table Row**.

   Excel selects all the data within the row.

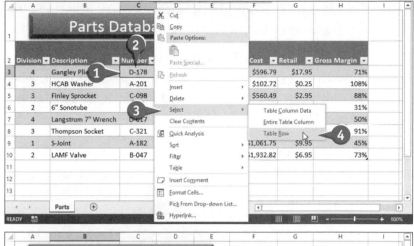

Select the Entire Table

1. Click any cell within the table.

2. Press **Ctrl** + **A**.

   Excel selects the entire table.

Division	Description	Number	Quantity	Cost	Total Cost	Retail	Gross Margin
4	Gangley Pliers	D-178	57	$10.47	$596.79	$17.95	71%
3	HCAB Washer	A-201	856	$0.12	$102.72	$0.25	108%
3	Finley Sprocket	C-098	357	$1.57	$560.49	$2.95	88%
2	6" Sonotube	B-111	86	$15.24	$1,310.64	$19.95	31%
4	Langstrom 7" Wrench	D-017	75	$18.69	$1,401.75	$27.95	50%
3	Thompson Socket	C-321	298	$3.11	$926.78	$5.95	91%
1	S-Joint	A-182	155	$6.85	$1,061.75	$9.95	45%
2	LAMF Valve	B-047	482	$4.01	$1,932.82	$6.95	73%

TIP

Can I select multiple columns or rows in a table?

Yes. First, select one cell in each of the columns that you want to include in your selection. If the columns are not side-by-side, click the first cell and then hold down **Ctrl** as you click each of the other cells. Right-click any selected cell, click **Select**, and then click **Table Column Data** (or **Entire Table Column** if you also want to include the column headers in the selection).

To select two or more table rows, first select one cell in each of the rows that you want to include in your selection. Again, if the rows are not adjacent, click the first cell and then hold down **Ctrl** as you click each of the other cells. Right-click any selected cell, click **Select**, and then click **Table Row**.

Insert a Table Row

You can add a new record to your Excel table by inserting a new row. You can insert a row either within the table or at the end of the table.

Once you type the initial set of data into your table, you will likely add most new records within the table by inserting a new row above a current one. However, when you are in the initial data entry phase, you will most likely prefer to add new records by adding a row to the end of the table.

Insert a Table Row

① Select a cell in the row below which you want to insert the new row.

② Click the **Home** tab.

③ Click **Insert** (⊞).

④ Click **Insert Table Rows Above**.

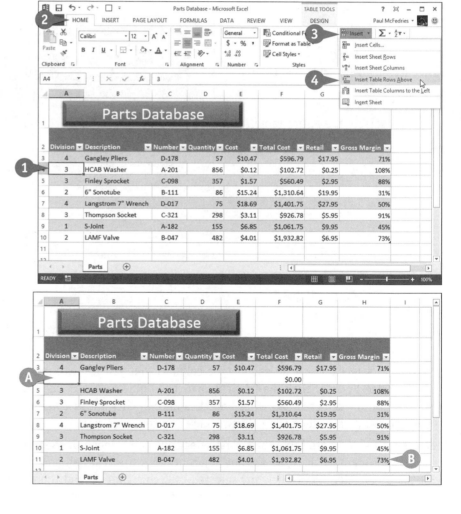

Ⓐ Excel inserts the new row.

Ⓑ To insert a new row at the end of the table, select the lower-right table cell, and then press Tab.

Insert a Table Column

You can add a new field to your Excel table by inserting a new column. You can insert a column either within or at the end of a table.

To make data entry easier and more efficient, you should decide in advance all the fields you want to include in the table. However, if later on you realize you forgot a particular field, you can still add it to the table. Inserting a table column is also useful if you imported or inherited the data from elsewhere and you see that the data is missing a field that you require.

Insert a Table Column

1 Select a cell in the column to the left of which you want to insert the new column.

A If you want to insert the new column at end of the table, select a cell in the last table column.

2 Click the **Home** tab.

3 Click **Insert** (⊞).

4 Click **Insert Table Columns to the Left**.

To insert a column at the end of the table instead, click **Insert Table Columns to the Right** (not shown).

B Excel inserts the new column.

5 Name the new field by editing the column header.

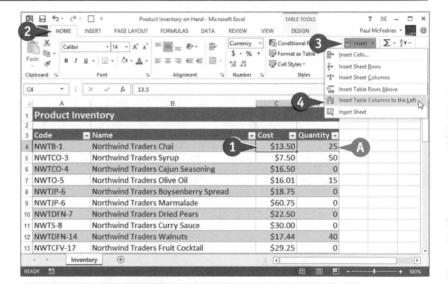

Delete a Table Row

If your table contains a record that includes inaccurate, outdated, or unnecessary data, you should delete that row to preserve your table's data integrity.

An Excel table is a repository of data that you can use as a reference source or to analyze or summarize the data. However you use the table, it is only as beneficial as its data is accurate, so you should take extra care to ensure the data you input is correct. If you find that an entire record is inaccurate or unnecessary, Excel enables you to delete that row quickly.

Delete a Table Row

1 Select a cell in the row you want to delete.

Note: To delete multiple rows, select a cell in each row you want to delete.

2 Click the **Home** tab.

3 Click **Delete** (🔲✕).

4 Click **Delete Table Rows**.

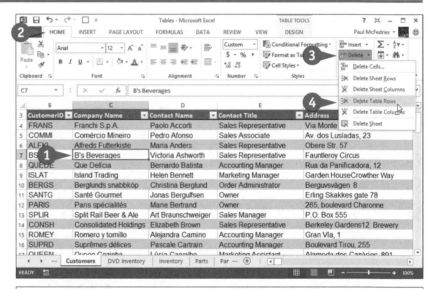

Ⓐ Excel deletes the row.

Delete a Table Column

If your table contains a field that you do not require, you should delete that column to make your table easier to work with and manage.

As you see later in this chapter and in Chapter 16, you analyze and summarize your table information based on the data in one or more fields. If your table contains a field that you never look at and that you never use for analysis or summaries, consider deleting that column to reduce table clutter and make your table easier to navigate.

Delete a Table Column

1. Select a cell in the column you want to delete.

Note: To delete multiple columns, select a cell in each column you want to delete.

2. Click the **Home** tab.

3. Click **Delete** (📇).

4. Click **Delete Table Columns**.

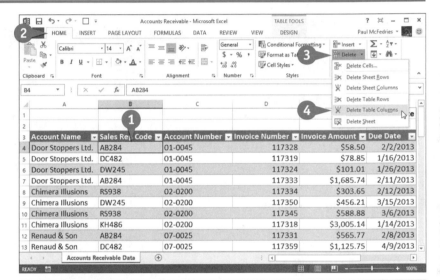

A. Excel deletes the column.

Add a Column Subtotal

You can get more out of your table data by summarizing a field with a subtotal that appears at the bottom of the column.

Although the word *subtotal* implies that you are summing the numeric values in a column, Excel uses the term more broadly. That is, a subtotal can be not only a numeric sum, but also an average, a maximum or minimum, or a count of the values in the field. You can also choose more esoteric subtotals, such as a standard deviation or variance.

Add a Column Subtotal

1 Select all the data in the column you want to total.

Note: See the section "Select Table Data" earlier in the chapter to learn how to select column data.

2 Click the **Quick Analysis** smart tag (⊞).

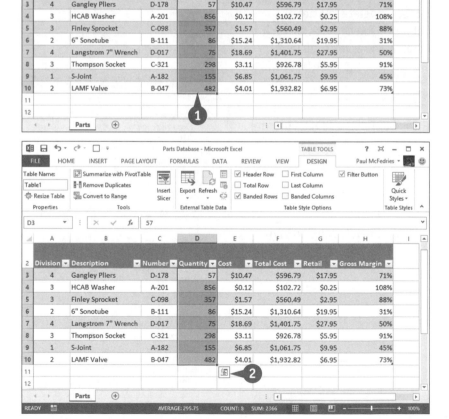

The Quick Analysis options appear.

③ Click **Totals**.

④ Click the type of calculation you want to use.

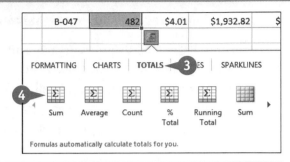

Ⓐ Excel adds a Total row to the bottom of the table.

Ⓑ Excel inserts a SUBTOTAL function to perform the calculation you chose in Step 4.

Ⓒ Click the cell's drop-down arrow (⌄) to choose a different type of subtotal.

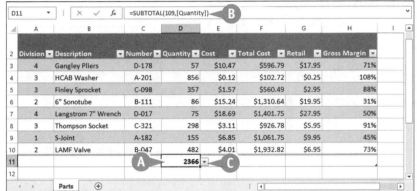

TIP

Is there a quick way to insert a total row in my table?

Yes. If the column you want to total is the last one in the table, you can add the total row and include a SUBTOTAL function:

① Click any cell.

② Click the **Design** tab.

③ Click the empty **Total Row** check box (☐) and it is filled (☑).

Ⓐ Excel inserts a row named Total at the bottom.

Ⓑ Excel adds a SUBTOTAL function below the last column.

④ Click the cell's drop-down arrow (⌄), and then click the type of subtotal you want.

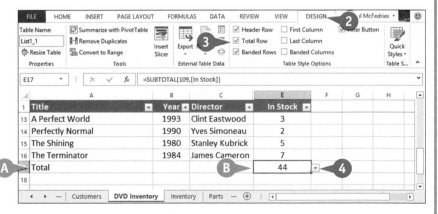

Convert a Table to a Range

If you no longer require the Excel table tools, you can convert a table to a normal range.

Tables are extremely useful, but they can occasionally be bothersome. If you click a table cell, click the Design tab, and then click a cell outside the table, Excel automatically switches to the Home tab. If you then click a table cell again, Excel switches back to the Design tab. If you are not using the table features in the Design tab, this behavior can be annoying, but you can prevent it from happening by converting the table to a normal range.

Convert a Table to a Range

1 Click a cell inside the table.

2 Click the **Design** tab.

3 Click **Convert to Range** (⬚).

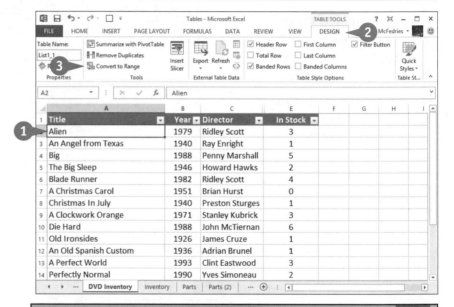

Excel asks you to confirm.

4 Click **Yes**.

Excel converts the table to a normal range.

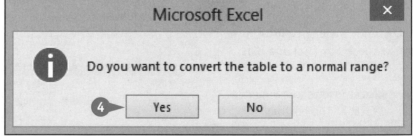

Apply a Table Style

You can give an Excel table more visual appeal and make it easier to read by applying a table style.

A table style is a combination of formatting options that Excel applies to 13 different table elements, including the first and last columns, the header row, the total row, and the entire table. For each element, Excel applies one or more of the following formatting options: the font, including the typeface, style, size, color, and text effects; the border; and the background color and fill effects.

Apply a Table Style

1. Click a cell inside the table.

2. Click the **Design** tab.

3. Click the **Table Styles** Gallery arrow (⩶).

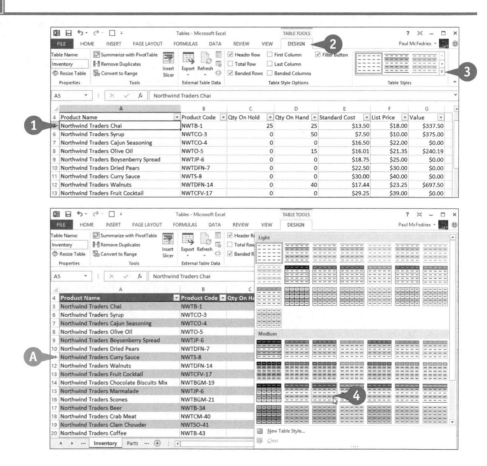

The Table Styles gallery appears.

4. Click the table style you want to use.

Ⓐ Excel applies the style to the table.

Resize a Table

If your current table coordinates no longer accurately reflect the data, you can fix this by *resizing* the table, and providing Excel with the correct coordinates.

When you insert new rows and columns or delete existing rows and columns, Excel automatically adjusts the table's coordinates. However, if you originally selected the wrong range for your table, or if you have pasted new data into the worksheet, you can update Excel with the new table coordinates by resizing the table. Note, however, that you cannot change the location of the table headers.

Resize a Table

1 Click a cell inside the table.

2 Click the **Design** tab.

3 Click **Resize Table** (⊕).

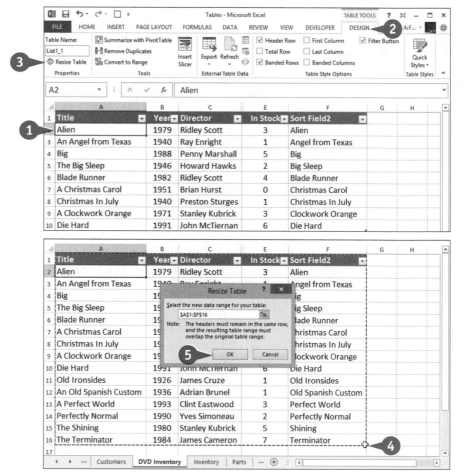

The Resize Table dialog box appears.

4 Drag the mouse pointer (✛) over the new range.

5 Click **OK**.

Excel adjusts the table coordinates to include the data you selected.

Rename a Table

If you have multiple tables in a worksheet or workbook, you can make it easier to tell them apart and navigate between them by assigning each a meaningful name.

When you create a table, Excel provides a generic name, such as Table1. Renaming tables with labels that reflect their contents can help you navigate them because you can select one by name using Excel's Name Box. Using meaningful names also helps with table-related functions, such as SUMIF and COUNTIF, because you can easily understand references, such as Parts[Division], which refers to the Division column with a table named Parts.

Rename a Table

1 Click a cell inside the table.

2 Click the **Design** tab.

3 Use the **Table Name** text box to type the name you want to use.

4 Press Enter .

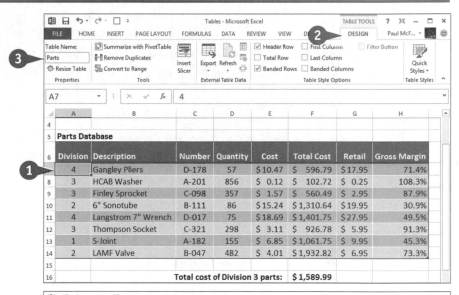

Excel updates the table name.

A Excel also updates any formulas that include references to the table.

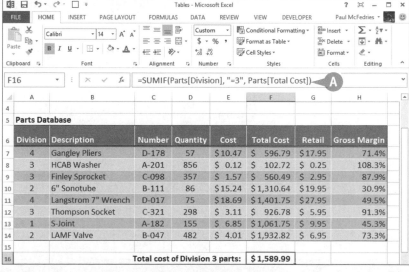

CHAPTER 16

Analyzing Data

You can get more out of Excel by performing *data analysis*, which is the application of tools and techniques to organize, study, and reach conclusions about a specific collection of information. In this chapter, you learn data analysis techniques such as sorting and filtering a range, creating data tables, and using subtotals and scenarios.

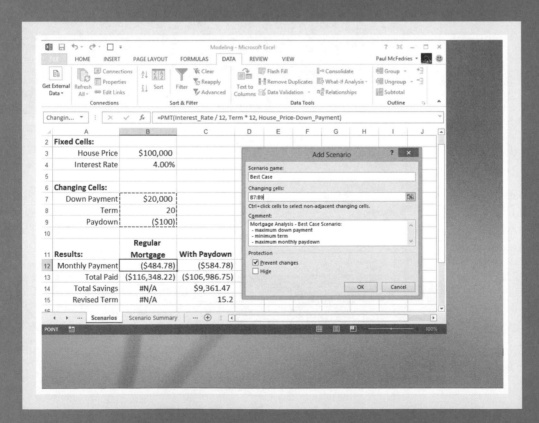

Sort a Range or Table

You can make a range easier to read and analyze by sorting the data based on the values in one or more columns.

You can sort the data in either ascending or descending order. An ascending sort arranges the values alphabetically from A to Z, or numerically from smallest to largest; a descending sort arranges the values alphabetically from Z to A, or numerically from largest to smallest.

Sort a Range or Table

1. Click any cell in the range you want to sort.

2. Click the **Data** tab.

3. Click **Sort** (⬇).

The Sort dialog box appears.

4. Click the **Sort by** drop-down arrow (⌄), and then click the field you want to use for the main sort level.

5. Click the **Order** drop-down arrow (⌄), and then click a sort order for the field.

6. To sort on another field, click **Add Level**.

(A) Excel adds another sort level.

(7) Click the **Then by** drop-down arrow ([v]), and then click the field you want to use for the sort level.

(8) Click the **Order** drop-down arrow ([v]), and then click a sort order for the field.

(9) Repeat Steps 6 to 8 to add more sort levels as needed.

(10) Click **OK**.

(B) Excel sorts the range.

TIPS

Is there a faster way to sort a range?

Yes, as long as you only need to sort your range on a single column. First, click in any cell inside the column you want to use for the sort. Click the **Data** tab, and then click one of the following buttons in the Sort & Filter group: Sort Ascending (↑) or Sort Descending (↓).

How do I sort a range using the values in a row instead of a column?

You can tell Excel to sort a range from left to right based on the values in one or more rows. Follow Steps 1 to 3 to display the Sort dialog box. Click **Options** to display the Sort Options dialog box. Click the empty **Sort left to right** radio button (○) and it is filled (●). Click **OK**.

Filter a Range or Table

You can analyze table data much faster by only viewing those table records that you want to work with. In Excel, this is called *filtering* a range.

The easiest way to filter a range is to use the Filter buttons, each of which presents you with a list of check boxes for each unique value in a column. You filter the data by activating the check boxes for the rows you want to see. If you have converted the range to a table, as described in Chapter 15, the Filter buttons for each column are displayed automatically.

Filter a Range or Table

Display the Filter Buttons

Note: If you are filtering a table, you can skip directly to the "Filter the Data" subsection.

1 Click inside the range.

2 Click the **Data** tab.

3 Click **Filter** (⊤).

Ⓐ Excel adds a Filter button (⌄) to each field.

Filter the Data

1 Click the **Filter button** (⌄) for the field you want to use as the filter.

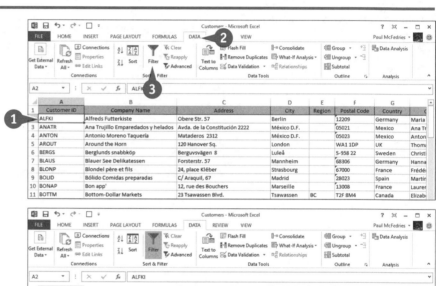

ⓑ Excel displays a list of the unique values in the field.

② Click the empty check box (☐) for each value you want to see and it is filled (☑).

ⓒ You can toggle all check boxes on and off by clicking **Select All**.

③ Click **OK**.

ⓓ Excel filters the table to show only those records that have the field values you selected.

ⓔ Excel displays the number of records found.

ⓕ The field's drop-down list displays a filter icon (▼).

To remove the filter, click the **Data** tab, and then click **Clear** (▼; not shown).

TIP

Can I create filters that are more sophisticated?
Yes, *quick filters* enable you to specify criteria for a field:

① Click the **Filter button** (▼) for the field you want to be the filter.

② Click **Number Filters**.

Note: If it is a date field, click **Date Filters**; if it is a text field, click **Text Filters**.

③ Click the filter you want.

④ Type the value you want.

⑤ Click **OK**.

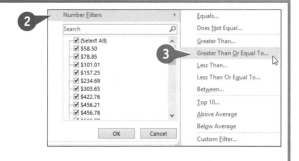

Calculate a Conditional Sum

In your data analysis, you might need to sum only those values that satisfy some condition. You can do this using the SUMIF function, which sums only those cells in a range that meet the condition you specify. SUMIF takes three arguments: range, the range of cells you want to use to test the condition; criteria, a text string that specifies which cells in range to sum; and the optional sum_range, the range from which you want the sum values to be taken. Excel sums only those cells in sum_range that correspond to the cells in range that meet the criteria.

Calculate a Conditional Sum

1 In the cell where you want the result to appear, type **=sumif(**.

2 Type the range argument.

3 Type a comma (,), and then the criteria argument.

Note: Enclose the criteria argument in double quotation marks.

4 If required, type a comma (,), and then the sum_range argument.

Note: If you omit sum_range, Excel uses range for the sum.

5 Type **)**.

6 Click **Enter** (✓) or press **Enter**.

Ⓐ Excel displays the conditional sum in the cell.

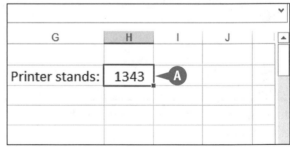

Note: You can use the question mark (?) and asterisk (*) wildcards when creating your condition. ? matches a single character; * matches multiple characters.

Calculate a Conditional Count

When analyzing data, you might need to count the items in a range, a task normally handled by the COUNT function. However, in some cases you might need to count only those values that meet a condition. You can do this by using the COUNTIF function. COUNTIF counts only those cells in a range that meet the condition you specify. COUNTIF takes two arguments: range, the range of cells you want to use to test the condition; and criteria, a text string that determines which cells in range to count.

Calculate a Conditional Count

1 In the cell where you want the result to appear, type **=countif(**.

2 Type the range argument.

3 Type a comma (,), and then the criteria argument.

Note: Enclose the criteria argument in double quotation marks.

4 Type **)**.

5 Click **Enter** (✓) or press **Enter**.

Ⓐ Excel displays the conditional count in the cell.

Note: You can use the question mark (?) and asterisk (*) wildcards when creating your condition. ? matches a single character; * matches multiple characters.

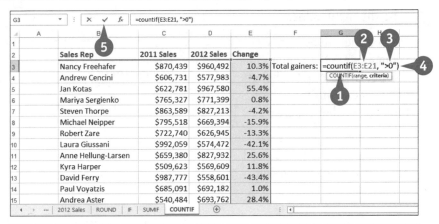

Create a Data Table

If you are interested in studying the effect a range of values has on the formula, you can set up a *data table*. It consists of the formula you are using and multiple input values for that formula. Excel automatically creates a solution to the formula for each different input value.

Do not confuse data tables with the Excel tables that you learn about in Chapter 15. A data table is a special range that Excel uses to calculate multiple solutions to a formula.

Create a Data Table

① Type the input values:

To type the values in a column, start the column one cell down and one to the left of the cell containing the formula, as shown here.

To type the values in a row, start the row one cell up and one to the right of the cell containing the formula.

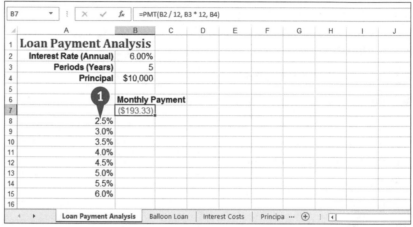

② Select the range that includes the input values and formula.

③ Click the **Data** tab.

④ Click **What-If Analysis** (▦).

⑤ Click **Data Table**.

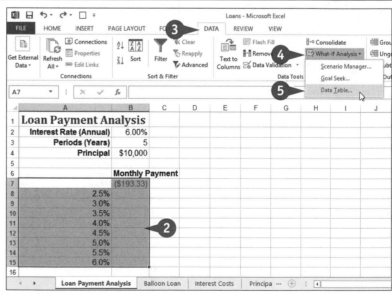

The Data Table dialog box appears.

6 Specify the formula cell you want to use as the data table's input cell:

If the input values are in a column, type the input cell's address in the **Column input cell** text box.

If you typed the input values in a row, type the input cell's address in the **Row input cell** text box.

7 Click **OK**.

A Excel displays the results.

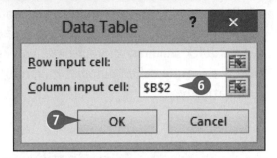

TIPS

What is what-if analysis?

The technique called *what-if analysis* is perhaps the most basic method for analyzing worksheet data. With what-if analysis, you first calculate a formula D, based on the input from variables A, B, and C. You then say, "What happens to the result if I change the value of variable A?," "What happens if I change B or C?," and so on.

Why do I get an error when I try to delete part of the data table?

Data table results are created as an *array formula*, which is a special formula that Excel treats as a unit. This means that you cannot move or delete part of the results. If you need to work with the data table results, you must first select the entire results range.

Summarize Data with Subtotals

Although you can use formulas and worksheet functions to summarize your data in various ways, including sums, averages, counts, maximums, and minimums, if you are in a hurry, or if you just need a quick summary of your data, you can get Excel to do most of the work for you. The secret here is a feature called *automatic subtotals*, which are formulas that Excel adds to a worksheet automatically.

Summarize Data with Subtotals

① Click a cell within the range you want to subtotal.

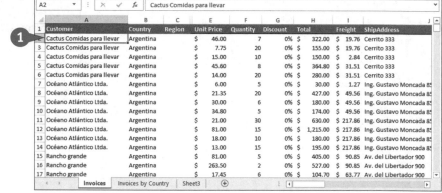

② Click the **Data** tab.

③ Click **Subtotal** (▦).

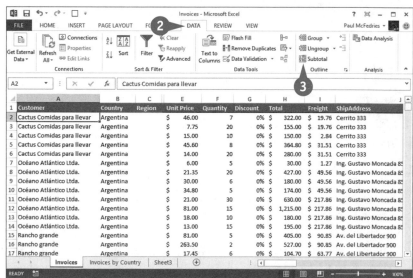

The Subtotal dialog box appears.

④ Click the **At each change in** drop-down arrow (⌄), and then click the column you want to use to group the subtotals.

⑤ In the **Add subtotal to** list, click the empty check box (☐) for the column you want to summarize and it is filled (☑).

⑥ Click **OK**.

Ⓐ Excel calculates the subtotals and adds them into the range.

Ⓑ Excel adds outline symbols to the range.

Note: See the next section, "Group Related Data," to learn more about outlining in Excel.

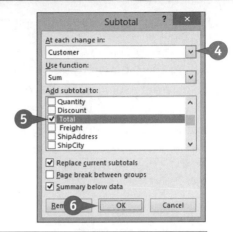

TIPS

Do I need to prepare my worksheet to use subtotals?

Yes. Excel sets up automatic subtotals based on data groupings in a selected field. For example, if you ask for subtotals based on the Customer field, Excel runs down the Customer column and creates a new subtotal each time the name changes. To get useful summaries, you need to sort the range on the field containing the data groupings in which you are interested.

Can I only calculate totals?

No. The word *subtotal* here is a bit misleading because you can summarize more than just totals. You can also count values, calculate the average of the values, determine the maximum or minimum value, and more. To change the summary calculation, follow Steps 1 to 4, click the **Use function** drop-down arrow (⌄), and then click the function you want to use for the summary.

Group Related Data

You can control a worksheet range display by grouping the data based on the worksheet formulas and data.

Grouping the data creates a worksheet outline, which you can use to "collapse" sections of the sheet to display only summary cells, or "expand" hidden sections to show the underlying detail. Note that when you add subtotals to a range as described in the preceding section, "Summarize Data with Subtotals," Excel automatically groups the data and displays the outline tools.

Group Related Data

Create the Outline

1. Display the worksheet you want to outline.

2. Click the **Data** tab.

3. Click the **Group** drop-down arrow ($\boxed{\vee}$).

4. Click **Auto Outline**.

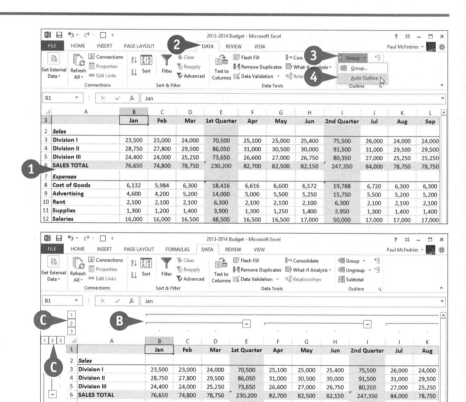

A Excel outlines the worksheet data.

B Excel uses level bars to indicate the grouped ranges.

C Excel displays level symbols to indicate the various levels of the detail that are available in the outline.

Use the Outline to Control the Range Display

1 Click a **Collapse** symbol (−) to hide the range indicated by the level bar.

D You can also collapse multiple ranges that are on the same outline level by clicking the appropriate level symbol.

E Excel collapses the range.

2 Click the **Expand** symbol (+) to view the range again.

F You can also show multiple ranges that are on the same outline level by clicking the appropriate level symbol.

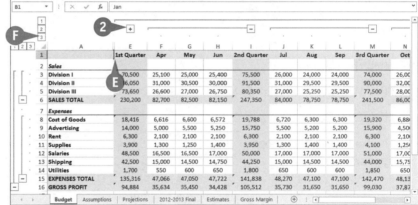

TIP

Do I have to prepare my worksheet before I can group the data?

Yes. Not all worksheets can be grouped, so you need to make sure your worksheet is a candidate for outlining. First, the worksheet must contain formulas that reference cells or ranges directly adjacent to the formula cell. Worksheets with SUM functions that subtotal cells above or to the left are particularly good candidates for outlining.

Second, there must be a consistent pattern to the direction of the formula references. For example, a worksheet with formulas that always reference cells above or to the left can be outlined. Excel will not outline a worksheet with, say, SUM functions that reference ranges above and below a formula cell.

Analyze Data with Goal Seek

If you already know the formula result you want, but you must find an input value that produces that result, you can use the Excel Goal Seek tool to solve the problem. You tell Goal Seek the final value you need and which variable to change, and it finds a solution for you.

For example, you might know that you want to have $50,000 saved to purchase new equipment five years from now, so you need to calculate how much to invest each year.

Analyze Data with Goal Seek

1 Set up your worksheet model.

Note: See the first Tip at the end of this section to learn more about setting up a worksheet for Goal Seek.

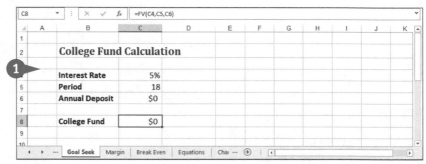

2 Click the **Data** tab.

3 Click **What-If Analysis** (🔣).

4 Click **Goal Seek**.

The Goal Seek dialog box appears.

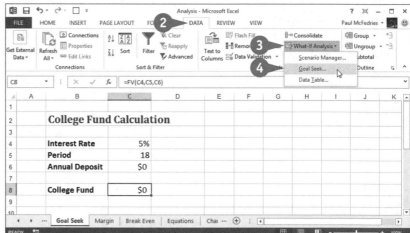

⑤ Click inside the **Set cell** box.

⑥ Click the cell that contains the formula with which you want Goal Seek to work.

⑦ Use the **To value** text box to type the value that you want Goal Seek to find.

⑧ Click in the **By changing cell** box.

⑨ Click the cell that you want Goal Seek to modify.

⑩ Click **OK**.

Ⓐ Goal Seek adjusts the changing cell value until it reaches a solution.

Ⓑ The formula now shows the value you typed in Step **7**.

⑪ Click **OK**.

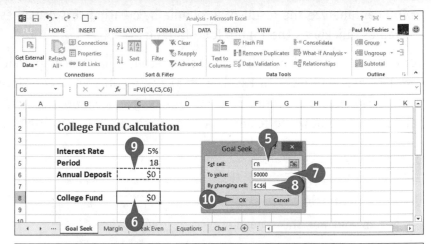

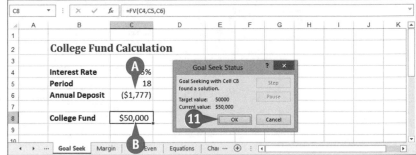

TIPS

How do I set up my worksheet to use Goal Seek?

First, set up one cell as the *changing cell*, which is the value that Goal Seek will manipulate to reach the goal. Type an initial value (such as 0) into the cell. Second, set up the other input values for the formula and give them proper initial values. Third, create a formula for Goal Seek to use to reach the goal.

What other types of problems can Goal Seek solve?

One is called a *break-even analysis*, in which you determine the number of units you need to sell so that your total profits are 0. In this case, the changing cell is the number of units sold and the formula is the profit calculation. You can also use Goal Seek to determine which price (the changing cell) is required to return a particular profit margin (the formula).

Analyze Data with Scenarios

You can analyze the result of a formula by creating sets of values that enable you to use those values quickly as the inputs for a formula.

For example, one set of values might represent a best-case approach, while another might represent a worst-case approach. In Excel, each of these coherent sets of input values — known as *changing cells* — is called a *scenario*. By creating multiple scenarios, you can easily apply these different value sets to analyze how the result of a formula changes under different conditions.

Analyze Data with Scenarios

Create a Scenario

1 Set up your worksheet model.

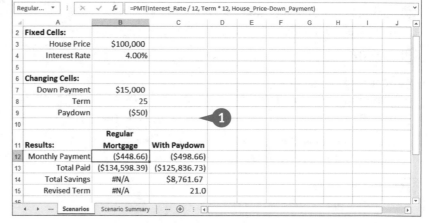

2 Click the **Data** tab.

3 Click **What-If Analysis** (📊).

4 Click **Scenario Manager**.

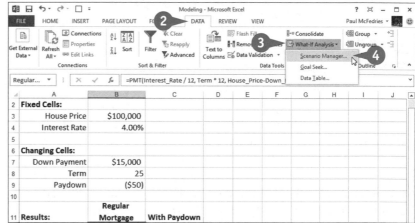

The Scenario Manager dialog box appears.

5 Click **Add**.

The Add Scenario dialog box appears.

6 Type a name for the scenario.

7 Click in the **Changing cells** box.

8 Select the cells you want to change in the scenario.

9 Type a description for the scenario.

10 Click **OK**.

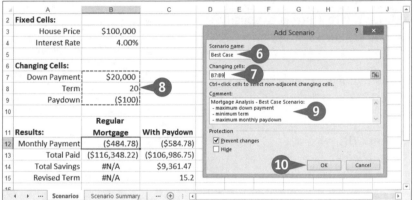

TIPS

Are there any restrictions on the changing cells?
When you are building a worksheet model for use with scenarios, make sure that each changing cell is a constant value. If you use a formula for a changing cell, Excel replaces that formula with a constant value defined in the scenario, so you lose your formula.

Do I need to add a description to each scenario?
Yes. As you see in the next section, once you have one or more scenarios defined, they appear in the Scenario Manager. For each scenario, you also see its changing cells and description. The description is often very useful, particularly if you have several scenarios defined, so be sure to write a detailed description in Step **9** to help you differentiate your scenarios later on.

continued ▶

Excel stores your scenarios in the Scenario Manager. You can use the Scenario Manager to perform a number of scenario-related tasks. For example, you can select one of your scenarios and then click a button to display the scenario's values in your worksheet. You can also use the Scenario Manager to edit existing scenarios and to delete scenarios you no longer need.

Analyze Data with Scenarios (continued)

The Scenario Values dialog box appears.

⑪ Use the text boxes to specify a value for each changing cell.

Ⓐ To add more scenarios, click **Add,** and then repeat Steps **6** to **11**.

⑫ Click **OK**.

⑬ Click **Close**.

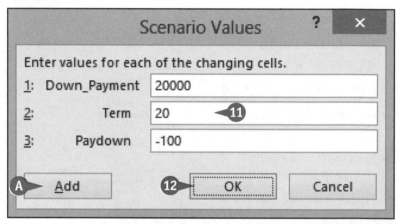

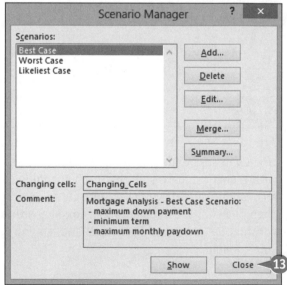

Display Scenarios

1 Click the **Data** tab.

2 Click **What-If Analysis** (📑).

3 Click **Scenario Manager**.

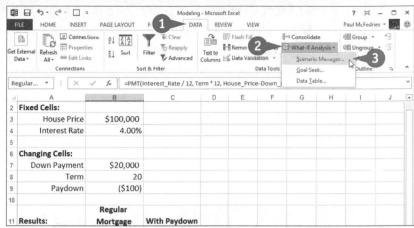

The Scenario Manager dialog box appears.

4 Click the scenario you want to display.

5 Click **Show**.

Ⓑ Excel enters the scenario values into the changing cells and displays the formula result.

6 Repeat Steps 4 and 5 to display other scenarios.

7 Click **Close**.

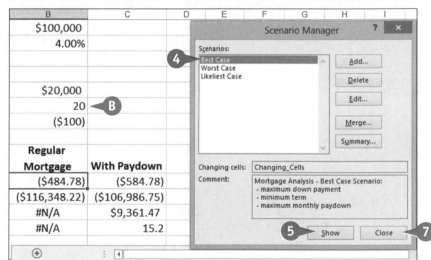

TIPS

How do I edit a scenario?

If you need to make changes to a scenario, you can edit the name, the changing cells, the description, and the scenario's input values. Click the **Data** tab, click **What-If Analysis** (📑), and then click **Scenario Manager**. In the Scenario Manager dialog box, click the scenario you want to modify, and then click **Edit**.

How do I remove a scenario?

If you have a scenario that you no longer need, delete it to reduce clutter in the Scenario Manager. Click the **Data** tab, click **What-If Analysis** (📑), and then click **Scenario Manager**. Click the scenario you want to delete. Note that Excel does not ask you to confirm the deletion, so double-check that you have selected the correct scenario. Click **Delete**, and then click **Close**.

Remove Duplicate Values from a Range or Table

You can make your Excel data more accurate for analysis by removing duplicate records. Duplicate records throw off calculations by including the same data two or more times. To prevent this, you should delete duplicate records. However, rather than looking for duplicates manually, you can use the Remove Duplicates command, which quickly finds and removes duplicates in even the largest ranges or tables.

Before you use the Remove Duplicates command, you must decide what defines a duplicate record in your data. That is, does every field have to be identical or is it enough that only certain fields are identical?

Remove Duplicate Values from a Range or Table

1 Click a cell inside the range or table.

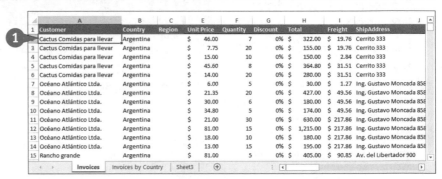

2 Click the **Data** tab.

3 Click **Remove Duplicates** (▯▯).

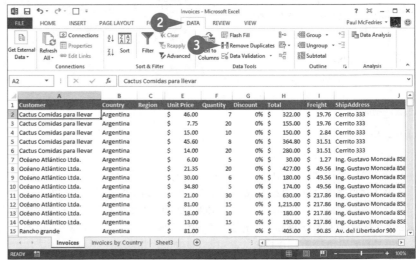

The Remove Duplicates dialog box appears.

4 Select the empty check box (□) beside each field in which you want Excel to check for duplication values and it is filled (☑).

Note: Excel does not give you a chance to confirm the deletion of the duplicate records, so be sure you want to do this before proceeding.

5 Click **OK**.

Excel deletes any duplicate records it finds.

A Excel tells you the number of duplicate records it deleted.

6 Click **OK**.

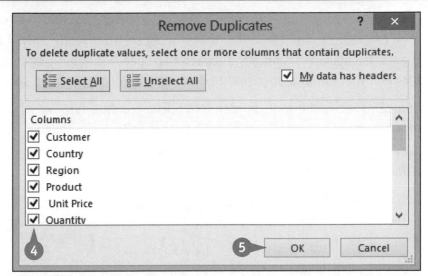

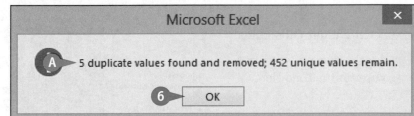

TIPS

If I have many columns, is there a quick way to check for duplicates based on just a couple of fields?

Yes. Click **Unselect All** in the Remove Duplicates dialog box, and all selected check boxes (☑) are cleared (□). You can then click the empty check boxes (□) of only those you want Excel to use, and they are filled (☑).

Can I remove duplicates even if my range does not have column headers?

Yes. Follow Steps 1 to 3 to open the Remove Duplicates dialog box, and then make sure the **My data has headers** check box is deselected (□). Select the empty check boxes (□) labeled Column A, Column B, and so on to choose the columns in which you want Excel to check for duplicate values and they are filled (☑). Click **OK**.

Highlight Cells That Meet Some Criteria

A *conditional format* is formatting that Excel applies only to cells that meet the criteria you specify. For example, you can tell Excel to apply the formatting only if a cell's value is greater or less than some specified amount, between two specified values, or equal to some value. You can also look for cells that contain specified text, dates that occur during a specified timeframe, and more.

You can specify the font, border, and background pattern, which helps to ensure that the cells that meet your criteria stand out from the other cells in the range.

Highlight Cells That Meet Some Criteria

1 Select the range with which you want to work.

2 Click the **Home** tab.

3 Click **Conditional Formatting** (⊞).

4 Click **Highlight Cells Rules**.

5 Click the operator you want to use for the condition.

A dialog box appears, the name of which depends on the operator you chose in Step 5.

6 Type the value you want to use for the condition.

Ⓐ You can also click **Collapse Dialog** (⬚), click a worksheet cell, and then click **Restore Dialog** (⬚).

Depending on the operator, you may need to specify two values.

7 Click this drop-down arrow (⌄), and then click the formatting you want to use.

Ⓑ To create your own format, click **Custom Format**.

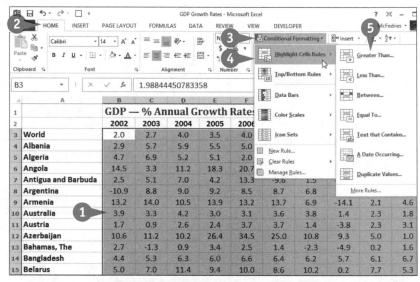

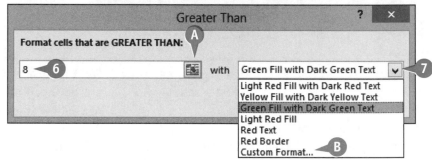

8 Click **OK**.

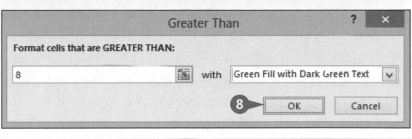

C Excel applies the formatting to cells that meet the condition you specified.

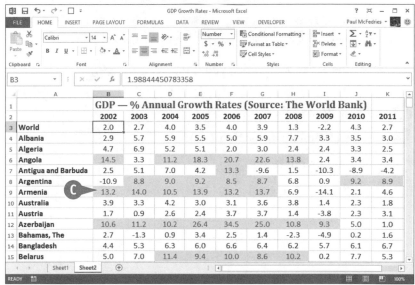

TIPS

Can I set up more than one conditional format on a range?

Yes. You can set up one condition for cells that are greater than some value, and a separate condition for cells that are less than some other value. You can apply unique formats to each condition. Follow Steps **1** to **8** to configure the new condition.

How do I remove a conditional format?

If you no longer require a conditional format, you can delete it. Follow Steps **1** to **3** to select the range and display the Conditional Formatting drop-down menu, and then click **Manage Rules**. Excel displays the Conditional Formatting Rules Manager dialog box. Click the conditional format you want to remove and then click **Delete Rule**.

Highlight the Top or Bottom Values in a Range

When analyzing worksheet data, it is often useful to look for items that stand out from the norm. For example, you might want to know which sales reps sold the most last year, or which departments had the lowest gross margins.

You can do this by setting up *top/bottom rules*, where Excel applies a conditional format to those items that are at the top or bottom of a range of values. For the top or bottom values, you can specify a number, such as the top 5 or 10, or a percentage, such as the bottom 20 percent.

Highlight the Top or Bottom Values in a Range

1 Select the range with which you want to work.

2 Click the **Home** tab.

3 Click **Conditional Formatting** (▦).

4 Click **Top/Bottom Rules**.

5 Click the type of rule you want to create.

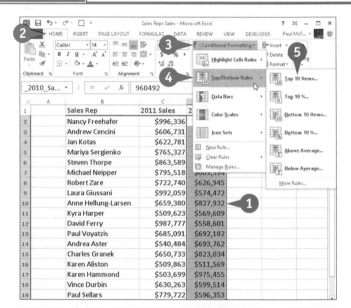

A dialog box appears, whose name depends on the type of rule you clicked in Step 5.

6 Type the value you want to use for the condition.

7 Click this drop-down arrow (▾), and then click the formatting you want to use.

Ⓐ To create your own format, click **Custom Format**.

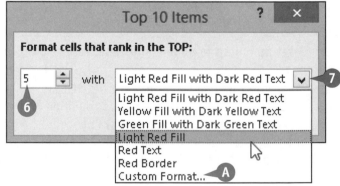

8 Click **OK**.

B Excel applies the formatting to cells that meet the condition you specified.

B	C	D
Sales Rep	2011 Sales	2012 Sales
Nancy Freehafer	$996,336	$960,492
Andrew Cencini	$606,731	$577,983
Jan Kotas	$622,781	$967,580
Mariya Sergienko	$765,327	$771,399
Steven Thorpe	$863,589	$827,213
Michael Neipper	$795,518	$669,394
Robert Zare	$722,740	$626,945
Laura Giussani	$992,059	$574,472
Anne Hellung-Larsen	$659,380	$827,932
Kyra Harper	$509,623	$569,609
David Ferry	$987,777	$558,601
Paul Voyatzis	$685,091	$692,182
Andrea Aster	$540,484	$693,762
Charles Granek	$650,733	$823,034
Karen Aliston	$509,863	$511,569
Karen Hammond	$503,699	$975,455
Vince Durbin	$630,263	$599,514
Paul Sellars	$779,722	$596,353

TIPS

Can I highlight cells that are above or below the average?

Yes, Excel also enables you to create top/bottom rules based on the average value in the range. First, follow Steps 1 to 4 to select the range and display the Top/Bottom Rules menu. Then click either **Above Average** to format those values that exceed the range average, or **Below Average** to format those values that are less than the range average.

How do I remove a top/bottom rule?

If you no longer require a top/bottom rule, you can delete it. Follow Steps 1 to 3 to select the range and display the Conditional Formatting drop-down menu. Click **Clear Rules**, and then click **Clear Rules from Selected Cells**. Excel removes the rule from the range.

Analyze Cell Values with Data Bars

In some data analysis scenarios, you might be interested more in the relative values within a range than the absolute values. For example, if you have a table of products that includes a column showing unit sales, how do you compare the relative sales of all the products?

This sort of analysis is often easiest if you visualize the relative values. You can do that by using *data bars*. Data bars are a data visualization feature that applies colored, horizontal bars to each cell in a range of values, and these bars appear "behind" the values in the range.

Analyze Cell Values with Data Bars

1 Select the range with which you want to work.

2 Click the **Home** tab.

3 Click **Conditional Formatting** (▦).

4 Click **Data Bars**.

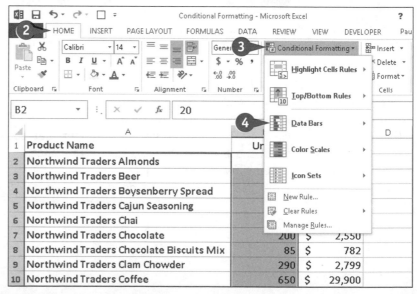

5 Click the fill type of data bars you want to create:

A Gradient Fill data bars begin with a solid color, and then gradually fade to a lighter color.

B Solid Fill data bars are a solid color.

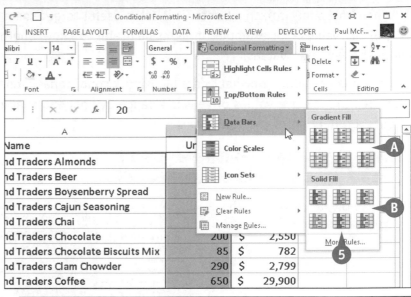

C Excel applies the data bars to each cell in the range.

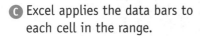

TIPS

How do data bars work?

The length of the data bar that appears in each cell depends on the value in that cell: The larger the value, the longer the data bar. The cell with the highest value has the longest data bar, and the cell with the lowest value has the shortest. The lengths of the data bars in the other cells reflect each cell's value.

How do I delete data bars from a range?

If you no longer require the data bars, you can remove them. Follow Steps **1** to **3** to select the range and display the Conditional Formatting drop-down menu, and then click **Manage Rules**. Excel displays the Conditional Formatting Rules Manager dialog box. Click the data bar rule you want to remove, click **Delete Rule**, and then click **OK**.

Analyze Cell Values with Color Scales

When analyzing worksheet data, it is often useful to get some idea about the overall distribution of the values. For example, it might be useful to know whether a range has a lot of low values and just a few high values.

You can analyze your worksheet data by using a conditional format called *color scales*. A color scale compares the relative values of cells in a range by applying shading to each cell, where the shading color is a reflection of the cell's value.

Analyze Cell Values with Color Scales

1 Select the range with which you want to work.

2 Click the **Home** tab.

3 Click **Conditional Formatting** (⊞).

4 Click **Color Scales**.

5️⃣ Click the color scale that has the color scheme you want to apply.

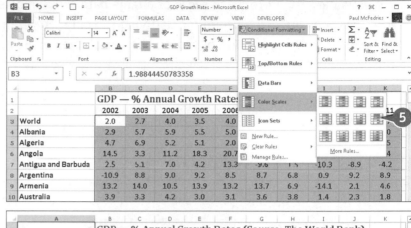

🅐 Excel applies the color scales to each cell in the range.

TIPS

In what other situations are color scales useful?

Besides showing patterns, color scales can also tell you whether your data includes any *outliers*, values that are much higher or lower than all or most of the others. Similarly, you can also use color scales to make value judgments about your data. For example, high sales and low numbers of product defects are good, whereas low margins and high employee turnover rates are bad.

When should I use a three-color scale versus a two-color scale?

If your goal is to look for outliers or make value judgments about your data, go with a three-color scale because outliers stand out more, and you can assign your own values to the colors (such as positive, neutral, and negative). Use a two-color scale when you want to look for patterns in the data, because a two-color scale has less contrast.

Analyze Cell Values with Icon Sets

When you are trying to make sense of a large data set, symbols that have common or well-known associations are often useful for clarifying the data. For example, for most people a check mark means something is good or finished or acceptable, whereas an X means something is bad or unfinished or unacceptable; a green circle is positive, whereas a red circle is negative (think traffic lights).

Excel puts these and many other symbolic associations to good use with the *icon sets* feature. You use icon sets to visualize the relative values of cells in a range.

Analyze Cell Values with Icon Sets

1. Select the range with which you want to work.

2. Click the **Home** tab.

3. Click **Conditional Formatting** (⬚).

4. Click **Icon Sets**.

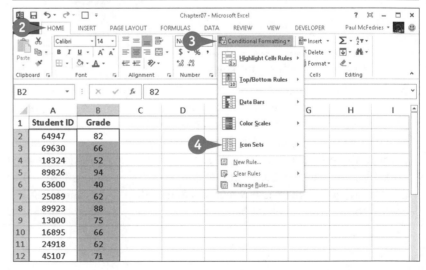

5 Click the type of icon set you want to apply.

The categories include Directional, Shapes, Indicators, and Ratings.

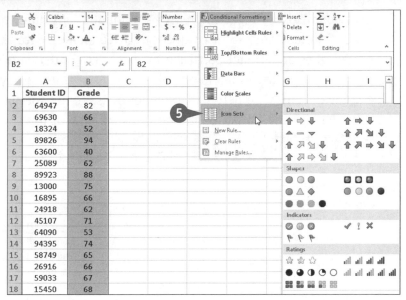

A Excel applies the icons to each cell in the range.

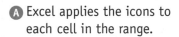

TIPS

How do icon sets work?

With icon sets, Excel adds a particular icon to each cell in the range, and that icon tells you something about the cell's value relative to the rest of the range. For example, the highest values might be assigned an upward-pointing arrow, the lowest values a downward-pointing arrow, and the values in between a horizontal arrow.

How do I use the different icon set categories?

The Excel icon sets come in four categories: Directional, Shapes, Indicators, and Ratings. Use Directional icon sets for indicating trends and data movement; use Shapes icon sets for pointing out the high (green) and low (red) values; use Indicators to add value judgments; and use Ratings to show where each cell resides in the overall range of data values.

Create a Custom Conditional Formatting Rule

Excel's conditional formatting rules — highlight cells rules, top/bottom rules, data bars, color scales, and icon sets — offer an easy way to analyze data through visualization. However, these predefined rules do not suit particular types of data or data analysis. The icon sets assume that higher values are more positive than lower values, but that is not always true; in a database of product defects, lower values are better than higher ones. To get the type of data analysis you prefer, you can create a custom conditional formatting rule and apply it to your range.

Create a Custom Conditional Formatting Rule

1 Select the range with which you want to work.

	Workgroup	Group Leader	Defects	Units	% Defective
1	Product Defects				
2	Workgroup	Group Leader	Defects	Units	% Defective
3	A	Hammond	8	969	0.8%
4	B	Hammond	4	815	0.5%
5	C	Hammond	14	1,625	0.9%
6	D	Hammond	3	1,453	0.2%
7	E	Hammond	9	767	1.2%
8	F	Hammond	10	1,023	1.0%
9	G	Hammond	15	1,256	1.2%
10	H	Hammond	8	781	1.0%
11	L	Bolter	7	1,109	0.6%
12	M	Bolter	8	1,021	0.8%
13	N	Bolter	6	812	0.7%
14	O	Bolter	11	977	1.1%
15	P	Bolter	5	1,182	0.4%
16	Q	Bolter	7	961	0.7%
17	R	Bolter	12	689	1.7%
18	T	Bolter	19	1,308	1.5%

Student Grades   **Product Defects**   (+)

2 Click the **Home** tab.

3 Click **Conditional Formatting** (🔳).

4 Click **New Rule**.

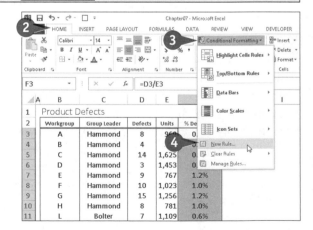

The New Formatting Rule dialog box appears.

5 Click the type of rule you want to create.

6 Edit the rule's style and formatting.

The controls you see depend on the rule type you selected.

A With Icon Sets, click **Reverse Icon Order** if you want to reverse the normal icon assignments, as shown here.

7 Click **OK**.

B Excel applies the conditional formatting to each cell in the range.

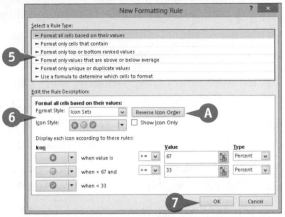

2	Workgroup	Group Leader	Defects	Units	% Defective
3	A	Hammond	8	969	0.8%
4	B	Hammond	4	815	0.5%
5	C	Hammond	14	1,625	0.9%
6	D	Hammond	3	1,453	0.2%
7	E	Hammond	9	767	1.2%
8	F	Hammond	10	1,023	1.0%
9	G	Hammond	15	1,256	1.2%
10	H	Hammond	8	781	1.0%
11	L	Bolter	7	1,109	0.6%
12	M	Bolter	8	1,021	0.8%
13	N	Bolter	6	812	0.7%
14	O	Bolter	11	977	1.1%
15	P	Bolter	5	1,182	0.4%
16	Q	Bolter	7	961	0.7%
17	R	Bolter	12	689	1.7%
18	T	Bolter	19	1,308	1.5%

◀ ▶ ⋯ | Student Grades | **Product Defects** | **B**

TIPS

How do I modify a custom conditional formatting rule?
Follow Steps 1 to 3 to select the range and display the Conditional Formatting drop-down menu, and then click **Manage Rules**. Excel displays the Conditional Formatting Rules Manager dialog box. Click the rule you want to modify and then click **Edit Rule**.

How do I remove a custom rule?
Follow Steps 1 to 3 to select the range and display the Conditional Formatting drop-down menu, click **Clear Rules**, and then click **Clear Rules from Selected Cells**. If you have multiple custom rules defined for a worksheet and no longer require them, you can remove all of them. Click the **Home** tab, click **Conditional Formatting**, click **Clear Rules**, and then click **Clear Rules from Entire Sheet**.

Consolidate Data from Multiple Worksheets

It is common to distribute similar worksheets to multiple departments to capture budget numbers, inventory values, survey data, and so on. Those worksheets must then be combined into a summary report showing company-wide totals. This is called *consolidating* the data.

Rather than doing this manually, Excel can consolidate your data automatically. You can use the Consolidate feature to consolidate the data either by position or by category. In both cases, you specify one or more source ranges (the ranges that contain the data you want to consolidate) and a destination range (the range where the consolidated data will appear).

Consolidate Data from Multiple Worksheets

Consolidate by Position

1 Create a new worksheet that uses the same layout (including row and column headers) as the sheets you want to consolidate.

2 Open the workbooks that contain the worksheets you want to consolidate.

3 Select the upper-left corner of the destination range.

4 Click the **Data** tab.

5 Click **Consolidate** (⊟ᵃ).

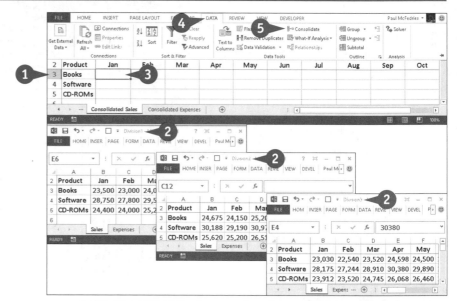

The Consolidate dialog box appears.

6 Click the **Function** drop-down arrow (⌄), and then click the summary function you want to use.

7 Click inside the **Reference** text box.

8 Select one of the ranges you want to consolidate.

9 Click **Add**.

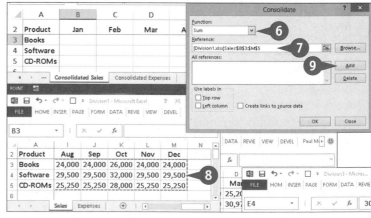

Ⓐ Excel adds the range to the All References list.

⑩ Repeat Steps 7 to 9 to add all of the consolidation ranges.

⑪ Click **OK**.

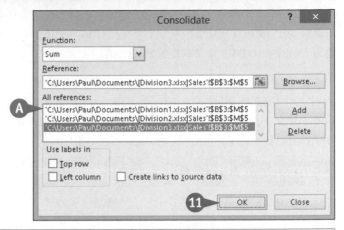

Ⓑ Excel consolidates the data from the source ranges and displays the summary in the destination range.

TIP

Is there an easy way to update the consolidation if the source data changes?

If the source data changes, then you probably want to reflect those changes in the consolidation worksheet. Rather than running the entire consolidation again, click the empty **Create links to source data** check box (☐) in the Consolidate dialog box and it is filled (☑). This enables you to update the consolidation worksheet by clicking the **Data** tab and then clicking **Refresh All**.

This also means that Excel creates an outline in the consolidation sheet, and you can use that outline to see the detail from each of the source ranges. See the section "Group Related Data" earlier in this chapter to learn more about outlines in Excel.

continued ▶

I f the worksheets you want to summarize do not use the same layout, you need to tell Excel to consolidate the data *by category*. This method consolidates the data by looking for common row and column labels in each worksheet.

For example, suppose you are consolidating sales and Division A sells software, books, and videos; Division B sells books and CD-ROMs; and Division C sells books, software, videos, and CD-ROMs. When you consolidate this data, Excel summarizes the software from Divisions A and C, the CD-ROMs from Divisions B and C, and the books from all three.

Consolidate Data from Multiple Worksheets (continued)

Consolidate by Category

1 Create a new worksheet for the consolidation.

2 Open the workbooks that contain the worksheets you want to consolidate.

3 Select the upper-left corner of the destination range.

4 Click the **Data** tab.

5 Click Consolidate (⊞→◻).

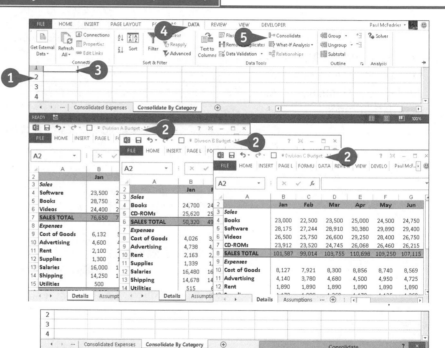

The Consolidate dialog box appears.

6 Click the **Function** drop-down arrow (☑), and then click the summary function you want to use.

7 Click inside the **Reference** text box.

8 Select one of the ranges you want to consolidate.

Note: Be sure to include the row and column labels in the range.

9 Click **Add**.

Ⓐ Excel adds the range to the All references list.

⑩ Repeat Steps **7** to **9** to add all of the consolidation ranges.

⑪ If you have labels in the top row of each range, click the empty **Top Row** check box (☐) and it is filled (☑).

⑫ If you have labels in the left-column row of each range, click the empty **Left column** check box (☐) and it is filled (☑).

⑬ Click **OK**.

Ⓑ Excel consolidates the data from the source ranges and displays the summary in the destination range.

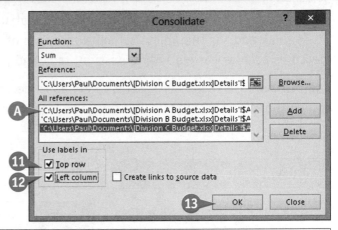

	A	B	C	D	E	F	G	H	I	J	
1		Jan	Feb	Mar	Apr	May	Jun	Jul	Aug	Sep	Oct
2	Sales										
3	Software	51,675	50,244	52,910	55,480	54,890	54,800	56,380	52,910	52,910	
4	Books	76,450	74,550	78,000	82,500	81,250	81,420	83,800	78,220	78,220	
5	Videos	50,900	49,750	51,850	55,850	55,400	53,500	55,500	53,750	53,750	
6	CD-ROMs	49,532	48,720	51,258	53,998	54,810	54,303	54,810	51,258	51,258	
7	SALES TOTAL	228,557	223,264	234,018	247,828	246,350	244,023	250,490	236,138	236,138	2!
8	Expenses										
9	Cost of Goods	18,285	17,861	18,721	19,826	19,708	19,522	20,039	18,891	18,891	
10	Advertising	13,478	12,306	15,236	14,650	16,115	15,383	16,115	15,236	15,236	
11	Rent	6,153	6,153	6,153	6,153	6,153	6,153	6,153	6,153	6,153	
12	Supplies	3,809	3,516	4,102	3,809	3,663	4,102	3,809	4,102	4,102	
13	Salaries	46,880	46,880	48,345	48,345	48,345	49,810	49,810	49,810	49,810	
14	Shipping	41,753	40,288	42,485	43,950	42,485	43,218	43,950	42,485	42,485	
15	Utilities	1,465	1,758	1,758	1,612	1,758	1,905	1,905	1,758	1,758	
16	EXPENSES TOTAL	131,822	128,762	136,800	138,345	138,227	140,091	141,781	138,435	138,435	1
17	GROSS PROFIT	38,150	37,475	38,033	44,046	44,019	42,420	44,132	37,202	37,202	

Consolidated Expenses | **Consolidate By Category**

TIP

What happens if the source data layout changes?

If the layout of the source data changes, then you must run the consolidation again.

If you consolidated by position, then before you can rerun the consolidation, you must first adjust the layout of the consolidation worksheet to match the changes to the source data. (You do not need to do this if you consolidated by category.)

No matter which consolidation method you used, before you run the consolidation again, you must delete the existing source ranges. Click the **Data** tab, and then click **Consolidate** (▤) to display the Consolidate dialog box. For each source range, click the range in the **All references** list and then click **Delete**.

Load the Analysis ToolPak

You can get access to a number of powerful statistical analysis tools by loading the Analysis ToolPak add-in. The Analysis ToolPak consists of 19 statistical tools that calculate statistical measures such as correlation, regression, rank and percentile, covariance, and moving averages.

You can also use the analysis tools to generate descriptive statistics (such as median, mode, and standard deviation), random numbers, and histograms.

Load the Analysis ToolPak

1 Click the **File** tab (not shown).

2 Click **Options**.

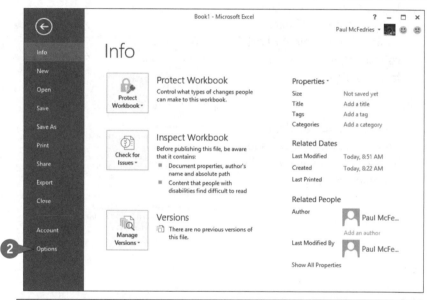

The Excel Options dialog box appears.

3 Click **Add-Ins**.

4 In the Manage list, click **Excel Add-ins**.

5 Click **Go**.

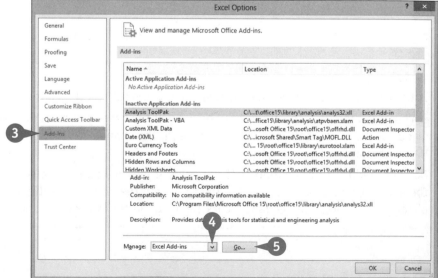

The Add-Ins dialog box appears.

6 Click the empty **Analysis ToolPak** check box (☐) and it is filled (☑).

7 Click **OK**.

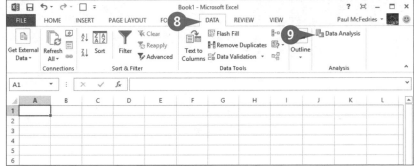

Excel loads the Analysis ToolPak add-in.

8 Click the **Data** tab.

9 Click **Data Analysis** (📊) to access the Analysis ToolPak tools.

TIP

How do I use the statistical tools?
The steps vary by tool, but you can follow these general steps:

1 Click the **Data** tab.

2 Click **Data Analysis** (📊).

The Data Analysis dialog box appears.

3 Click the tool you want.

4 Click **OK**.

Excel displays a dialog box for the tool.

5 Fill in the dialog box (the controls vary by tool).

6 Click **OK**.

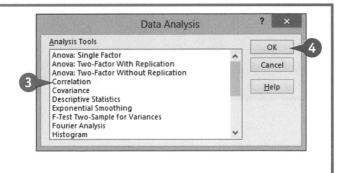

CHAPTER 17

Analyzing Data with PivotTables

A PivotTable is a powerful data analysis tool that automatically groups large amounts of data into smaller, more manageable categories. In this chapter, you learn how to create PivotTables, edit them, pivot them, format them, calculate with them, and much more.

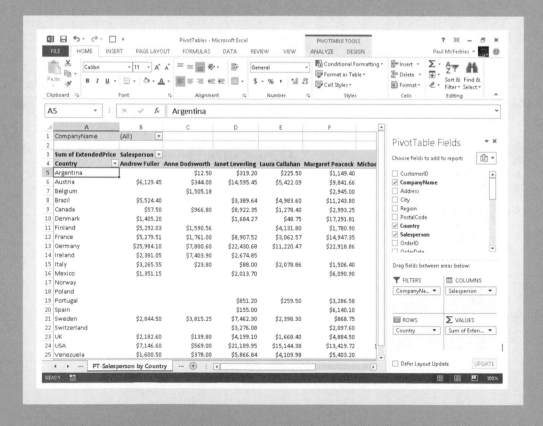

Understanding PivotTables

Tables and external databases can contain thousands of records. Analyzing that much data can be a nightmare without the right tools. Excel offers a powerful data analysis tool called a *PivotTable*, which enables you to summarize hundreds of records in a concise tabular format. You can then manipulate the layout of — or *pivot* — the table to see different views of your data.

PivotTables help you analyze large amounts of data by performing three operations: Grouping the data into categories, summarizing the data using calculations, and filtering the data to show only the records with which you want to work.

Grouping

A PivotTable is a powerful data-analysis tool because it automatically groups large amounts of data into smaller, more manageable categories. Suppose you have a data source with a Region field in which each cell contains one of four values: East, West, North, and South. The original data may contain thousands of records, but if you build your PivotTable using the Region field, the resulting table has only four rows — one for each of the four Region values in your data.

Sum of Quantity	Column Labels ▾		
Row Labels ▾	1 Free with 10	Extra Discount	Grand Total
0-200	186.00	203.00	389.00
200-400	429.00	430.00	859.00
400-600	638.00	619.00	1257.00
600-800	363.00	286.00	649.00
800-1000	440.00	791.00	1231.00
1000-1200	473.00	632.00	1105.00
1200-1400	429.00	293.00	722.00
1400-1600	473.00	120.00	593.00
1600-1800	110.00	254.00	364.00
1800-2000	132.00	274.00	406.00
2000-2200	275.00		275.00
Grand Total	3948.00	3902.00	7850.00

Summarizing

Excel also displays summary calculations for each group. The default calculation is Sum, which means for each group Excel totals all the values in some specified field. For example, if your data has a Region field and a Sales field, a PivotTable can group the unique Region values and display the total of the Sales values for each one. Other summary calculations include Count, Average, Maximum, Minimum, and Standard Deviation.

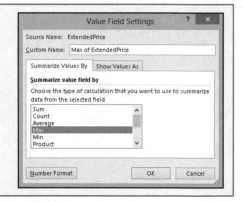

Filtering

A PivotTable also enables you to view just a subset of the data. For example, by default the PivotTable's groupings show all the unique values in the field. However, you can manipulate each grouping to hide those that you do not want to view. Each PivotTable also comes with a filter area that enables you to apply a filter to the entire PivotTable.

Advertisement	Direct mail	▾	
Sum of Net_$	Column Labels ▾		
Row Labels ▾	1 Free with 10	Extra Discount	Grand Total
Copy holder	1196.58	1130.64	2327.22
Glare filter	3293.40	2360.54	5653.94
Mouse pad	2991.45	2469.91	5461.36
Printer stand	2070.81	1679.94	3750.75
Grand Total	9552.24	7641.03	17193.27

Explore PivotTable Features

You can get up to speed with PivotTables very quickly after you learn a few key concepts. You need to understand the features that make up a typical PivotTable, particularly the four areas — row, column, data, and page — to which you add fields from your data.

You also need to understand some important PivotTable terminology that you will encounter throughout this book, including terms such as *source data*, *pivot cache*, and *summary calculation*.

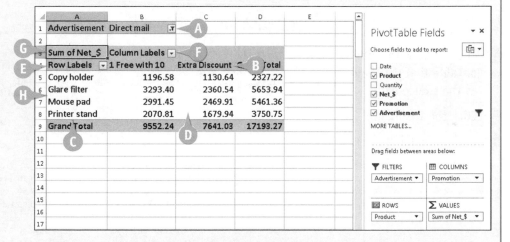

Ⓐ Filter

Displays a drop-down list with the unique values from a field. When you select one, Excel filters the results to include only the records that match that value.

Ⓑ Column Area

Displays horizontally the unique values from a field in your data.

Ⓒ Row Area

Displays vertically the unique values from a field in your data.

Ⓓ Data Area

Displays the results of the calculation that Excel applied to a numeric field in your data.

Ⓔ Row Field Header

Identifies the field contained in the row area. Also used to filter the field values that appear in the row area.

Ⓕ Column Field Header

Identifies the field contained in the column area. Also used to filter the field values that appear in the column area.

Ⓖ Data Field Header

Specifies both the calculation (such as Sum) and the field (such as Invoice Total) used in the data area.

Ⓗ Field Items

The unique values for the field added to the particular area.

Build a PivotTable from an Excel Range or Table

If the data you want to analyze exists as an Excel range or table, you can use the PivotTable command to easily build a PivotTable report based on your data. You need only specify the location of your source data and then choose the location of the resulting PivotTable.

Excel creates an empty PivotTable in a new worksheet or in the location you specify. Excel also displays the PivotTable Fields pane, which contains four areas: FILTERS, COLUMNS, ROWS, and VALUES. To complete the PivotTable, you must populate some or all of these areas with one or more fields from your data.

Build a PivotTable from an Excel Range or Table

1. Click a cell within the range or table that you want to use as the source data.

2. Click the **Insert** tab.

3. Click **PivotTable** (📊).

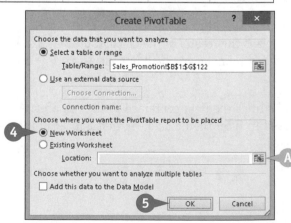

The Create PivotTable dialog box appears.

4. Click the empty **New Worksheet** radio button (○); it is filled (◉).

Ⓐ If you want to place the PivotTable in an existing location, click the empty **Existing Worksheet** radio button (○); it is filled (◉). Then, use the **Location** range box to select the worksheet and cell where you want the PivotTable to appear.

5. Click **OK**.

B Excel creates a blank PivotTable.

C Excel displays the PivotTable Fields pane.

6 Click and drag a field and drop it inside the ROWS area.

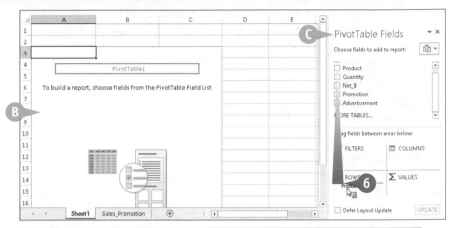

D Excel adds the field's unique values to the PivotTable's row area.

7 Click and drag a numeric field and drop it inside the VALUES area.

E Excel sums the numeric values based on the row values.

8 If desired, click and drag fields and drop them in the COLUMNS and FILTERS areas.

Each time you drop a field in an area, Excel updates the PivotTable to include the new data.

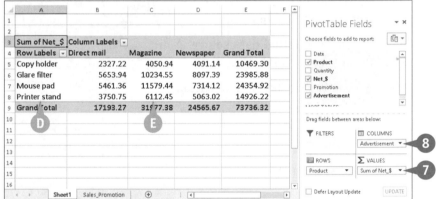

TIPS

Are there faster ways to build a PivotTable?
Yes. In the PivotTable Fields list, click the empty check box (☐) for a text or date field; it is filled (☑) and Excel adds the field to the ROWS area. Click the empty check box (☐) for a numeric field; it is filled (☑) and Excel adds the field to the VALUES area. You can also right-click a field, and then click the area that you want to use.

For what is the FILTERS box used?
To add a filter field to the PivotTable, which enables you to display a subset of the data that consists of one or more unique values from the filter field. For more details, see the section "Apply a PivotTable Filter" later in this chapter.

Create a PivotTable from External Data

You can create a PivotTable using an external data source, which enables you to build reports from extremely large datasets and from relational database systems.

The data you are analyzing might not exist in an Excel range or table, but outside of Excel in a relational database management system (RDBMS) such as Microsoft Access or SQL Server. With these programs, you can set up a table, query, or other object that defines the data with which you want to work. You can then build your PivotTable based on this external data source.

Create a PivotTable from External Data

1 Press **Alt**+**D**, and then press **P**.

The PivotTable and PivotChart Wizard - Step 1 of 3 dialog box appears.

2 Select the empty **External data source** radio button (○); it is filled (⊙).

3 Select the empty **PivotTable** radio button (○); it is filled (⊙).

4 Click **Next**.

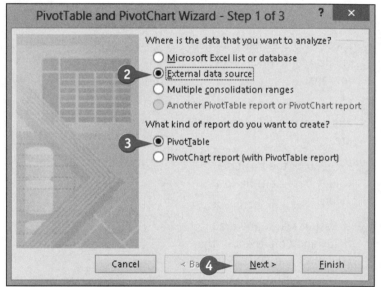

The PivotTable and PivotChart Wizard - Step 2 of 3 dialog box appears.

5 Click **Get Data**.

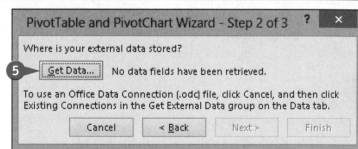

The Choose Data Source dialog box appears.

6 Click the type of data source you want to use.

7 Click **OK**.

The Select Database dialog box appears.

8 Click the folder that contains the database.

9 Click the database.

10 Click **OK**.

The Query Wizard - Choose Columns dialog box appears.

11 Click the table or column you want to use as the source data for your PivotTable.

12 Click **Add** (⟩).

Ⓐ The table's fields appear in this list.

13 Click **Next**.

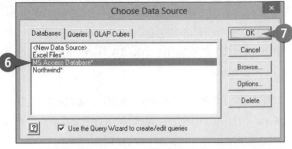

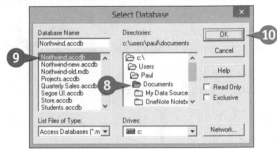

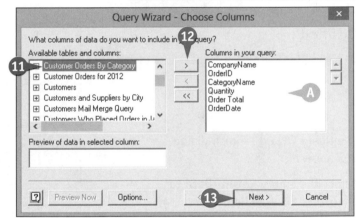

TIP

How can I create a data source?
In Excel, click the **Data** tab, click **Get External Data**, click **From Other Sources**, and then click **From Microsoft Query**. In the Choose Data Source dialog box, click **New Data Source**. Click the filled Use the Query Wizard to Create/Edit Queries check box (☑) so it is cleared (☐), and then click **OK**. In the Create New Data Source dialog box, type a name for your data source, select the database driver that your data source requires, and then click **OK**.

continued ▶

This section assumes that you have already defined the appropriate data source and do not want to work with Microsoft Query directly. Note, too, that Steps 14 and 15 skip over the Query Wizard dialog boxes that enable you to filter and sort the external data because that is not usually pertinent for a PivotTable.

The other assumption made in this section is that you do not want the external data to be imported to Excel. Rather, in this section, the external data resides only in the new PivotTable; you do not see the actual data in your workbook.

Create a PivotTable from External Data (continued)

The Query Wizard - Filter Data dialog box appears.

14 Click **Next**.

The Query Wizard - Sort Order dialog box appears.

15 Click **Next** (not shown).

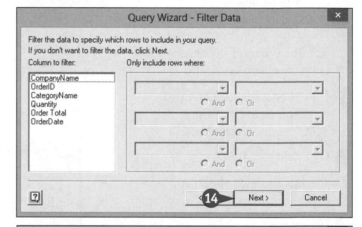

The Query Wizard - Finish dialog box appears.

16 Select the empty **Return Data to Microsoft Excel** radio button (○); it is filled (⊙).

17 Click **Finish**.

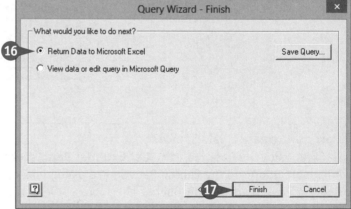

Excel returns you to the PivotTable and PivotChart Wizard - Step 2 of 3 dialog box.

18 Click **Finish**.

Excel creates an empty PivotTable.

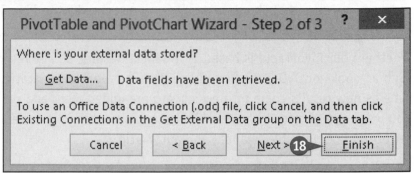

A The fields available in the table or query that you chose in Step 11 appear in the PivotTable Fields pane.

19 Click and drag fields from the PivotTable Fields pane and drop them in the PivotTable areas.

B Excel summarizes the external data in the PivotTable.

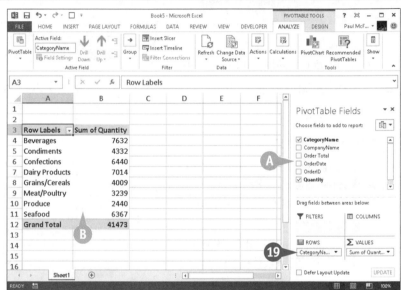

TIPS

Are there any drawbacks to using external data?
The most common drawback is that you often have no control over the actual external file. For example, if you attempt to refresh the PivotTable, Excel may display an error message. If you suspect the problem is a change to the database login data, click **OK** to display the Login dialog box, and find out the new login name and password from the database administrator.

What can I do if I receive an error when I try to refresh a PivotTable based on external data?
The problem may also be that the database file has been moved or renamed. Click **OK** in the error message, and then click **Database** in the Login dialog box. You can then use the Select Database dialog box to find and select the database file.

Refresh PivotTable Data

You can ensure that the data analysis represented by the PivotTable remains up to date by refreshing the PivotTable.

Whether your PivotTable is based on financial results, survey responses, or a database of collectibles such as books or DVDs, the underlying data is probably not static. That is, the data changes over time as new results come in, new surveys are undertaken, and new items are added to the collection. You will need to refresh the PivotTable to ensure that it is current. Excel offers two methods for refreshing a PivotTable: manual and automatic.

Refresh PivotTable Data

Refresh Data Manually

1. Click any cell inside the PivotTable.

2. Click the **Analyze** tab.

3. Click **Refresh** ( ).

   You can also press Alt + F5.

Ⓐ To update every PivotTable in the workbook, click the **Refresh** drop-down arrow ( ), and then click **Refresh All**.

   You can also update all PivotTables by pressing Ctrl + Alt + F5.

   Excel updates the PivotTable data.

Refresh Data Automatically

1. Click any cell inside the PivotTable.

2. Click the **Analyze** tab.

3. Click **PivotTable** ( ).

4. Click **Options**.

Note: You can also right-click any cell in the PivotTable and then click PivotTable Options.

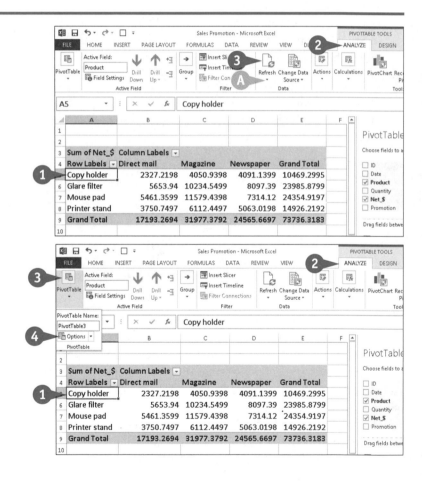

The PivotTable Options dialog
box appears.

5 Click the **Data** tab.

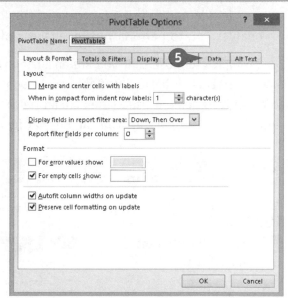

6 Click the empty **Refresh data
when opening the file** check
box (☐); it is filled (☑).

7 Click **OK**.

Excel applies the refresh options.

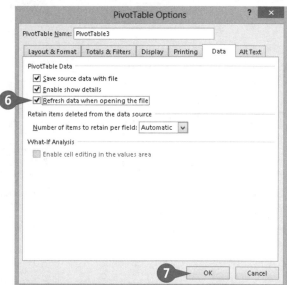

TIPS

Can I automatically refresh a PivotTable more frequently?
Yes. If your PivotTable is based on external data, you can set
up a schedule to refresh it at a specified interval. Click any
cell inside the PivotTable, click the **Analyze** tab, click the
Refresh drop-down arrow (☑), and then click **Connection
Properties**. Select the empty **Refresh every** check box (☐);
it is filled (☑). Use the spin box to specify the refresh
interval in minutes.

**Is there a drawback to using a
refresh schedule?**
Yes. When you set up an automatic
refresh, you might prefer not to have the
source data updated too frequently.
Depending on where the data resides and
how much data you are working with,
the refresh could take some time, which
may slow down the rest of your work.

Add Multiple Fields to the Row or Column Area

You can add multiple fields to any of the PivotTable areas. This is a powerful technique that enables you to perform further analysis of your data by viewing the data differently.

For example, suppose that you are analyzing the results of a sales campaign that ran several types of advertisements. A basic PivotTable might show you the sales for each Product (the row field) according to the Advertisement used (the column field). You might also be interested in seeing the breakdown in sales for each promotion. You can do that by adding the Promotion field to the row area.

Add Multiple Fields to the Row or Column Area

Add a Field to the ROWS Area

1 Click a cell within the PivotTable.

2 Click the empty check box (☐) of the text or date field that you want to add; it is filled (☑).

A Excel adds the field to the ROWS box.

B Excel adds the field's unique values to the PivotTable's row area.

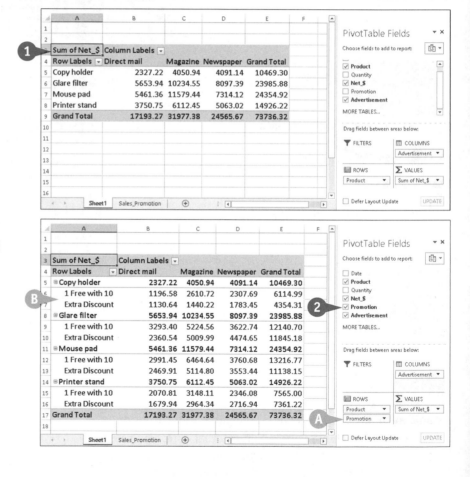

386

Add a Field to the ROWS or COLUMNS Area

1 Click a cell within the PivotTable.

2 In the PivotTable Fields list, click and drag the field that you want to add, and then drop it in either the ROWS or COLUMNS box.

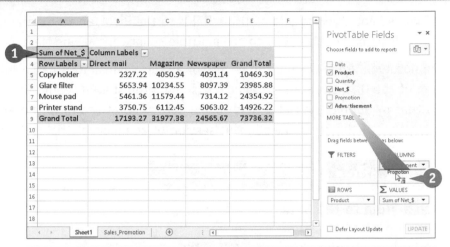

C Excel adds the field to the ROWS or COLUMNS box.

D Excel adds the field's unique values to the PivotTable's row or column area.

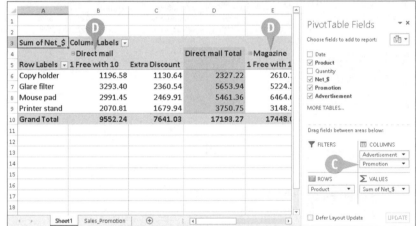

TIPS

Can I change the field positions within the row or column area?

Yes. After you add a second field to the row or column area, you can change the field positions to change the PivotTable view. In the PivotTable Field List, use the ROWS or COLUMNS box to click and drag the button of the field you want to move, and then drop the field above or below an existing field button.

Can I only add two fields to the row or column area?

No, Excel does not restrict you to just two fields in the row or column area. Depending on your data analysis requirements, you are free to add three, four, or more fields to the row area or to the column area.

Add Multiple Fields to the Data Area

Excel enables you to add multiple fields to the PivotTable's data area, which enhances your analysis by enabling you to see multiple summaries at one time.

Suppose you are analyzing the results of a sales campaign. A basic PivotTable might show you the sum of the Quantity sold. You might also be interested in seeing the net dollar amount sold. You can do that by adding the Net $ field to the data area, as shown in the example in this section. You can use either of the techniques in this section to add multiple fields to the data area.

Add Multiple Fields to the Data Area

Add a Field to the Data Area with a Check Box

1 Click a cell within the PivotTable.

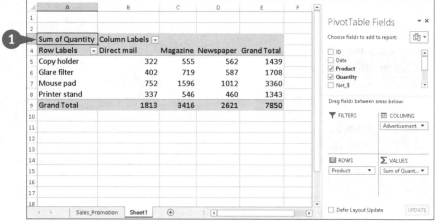

2 Select the empty check box (☐) of the field you want to add to the data area; it is filled (☑).

Ⓐ Excel adds a button for the field to the VALUES box.

Ⓑ Excel adds the field to the PivotTable's data area.

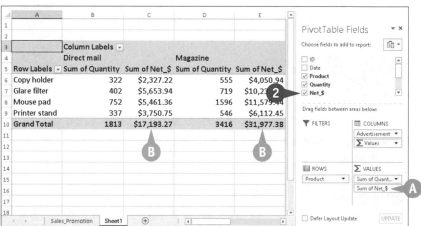

Add a Field to the Data Area by Dragging

1 Click a cell within the PivotTable.

2 In the PivotTable Fields pane, click and drag the field you want to add and drop it in the VALUES box.

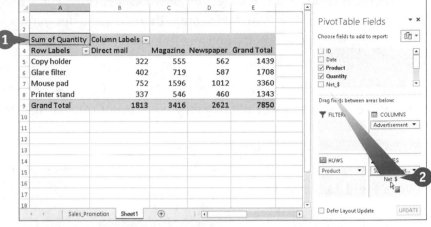

C Excel adds the field to the PivotTable's data area.

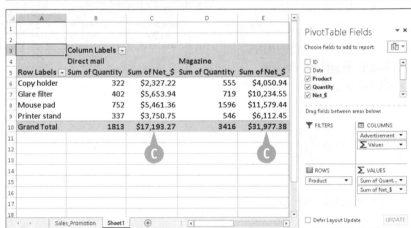

TIPS

Why does Excel add a Values button to the COLUMNS box?

When you add a second field to the data area, Excel moves the labels (for example, Sum of Quantity and Sum of Net $) into the column area for easier reference. Excel also adds a Values button in the COLUMNS box section of the PivotTable Fields pane, so you can pivot the values within the report. For more information, see the section "Move a Field to a Different Area."

Can I only add two fields to the row or column area?

No, Excel does not restrict you to just two fields in the data area. You are free to add three, four, or more data fields to enhance your analysis of the data.

Move a Field to a Different Area

A PivotTable is not a static collection of worksheet cells. You can move a PivotTable's fields from one area of the PivotTable to another. This enables you to view your data from different perspectives, which can greatly enhance the analysis of the data. Moving a field within a PivotTable is called *pivoting* the data.

The most common way to pivot the data is to move fields between the row and column areas. However, you can also pivot data by moving a row or column field to the filter area.

Move a Field to a Different Area

Move a Field between the Row and Column Areas

1 Click a cell within the PivotTable.

2 Click and drag a COLUMNS field button and drop it within the ROWS box.

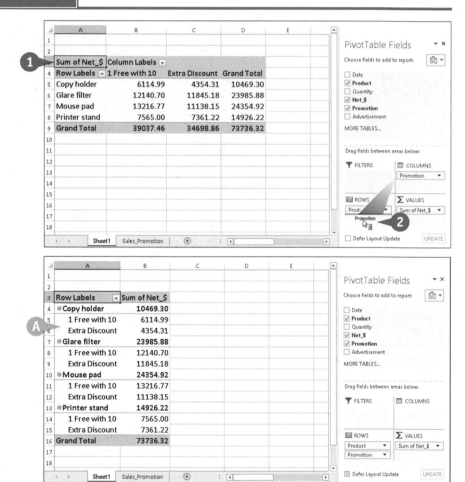

A Excel displays the field's values within the row area.

You can also drag a field button from the ROWS box area and drop it within the COLUMNS box.

Move a Row or Column Field to the Filters Area

1. Click a cell within the PivotTable.

2. Click and drag a field from the ROWS box and drop it within the FILTERS box.

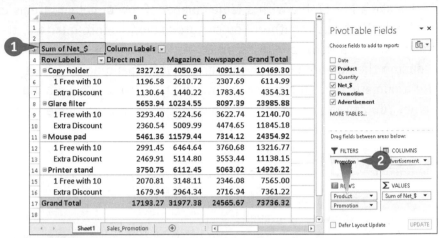

B. Excel moves the field button to the report filter.

You can also drag a field button from the COLUMNS box and drop it within the FILTERS box.

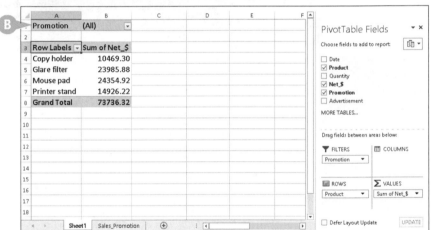

TIP

Can I move a field to the PivotTable's data area?

Yes. You can move any row, column, or filter field to the PivotTable's data area. This may seem strange because row, column, and page fields are usually text values, and the default data area calculation is Sum. How can you sum text values? You cannot, of course. Instead, Excel's default PivotTable summary calculation for text values is Count. Therefore, if you drag the Promotion field and drop it inside the data area, Excel creates a second data field named Count of Promotion.

Group PivotTable Values

To make a PivotTable with a large number of row or column items easier to work with, you can group the items together. You can group months into quarters, thus reducing the number of items from twelve to four. A report that lists dozens of countries can group them by continent, thus reducing the number of items to four or five, depending on where the countries are located. If you use a numeric field in the row or column area, you may have hundreds of items, one for each numeric value. You can improve the report by creating just a few numeric ranges.

Group PivotTable Values

1 Click any item in the numeric field that you want to group.

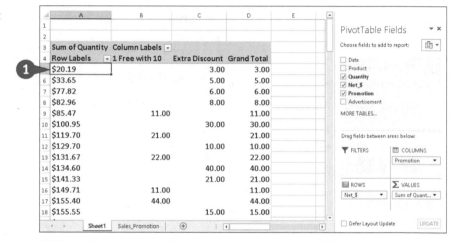

2 Click the **Analyze** tab.

3 Click **Group**.

4 Click **Group Field**.

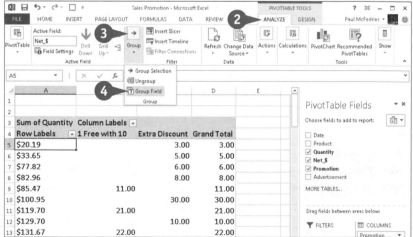

The Grouping dialog box appears.

5 Type the starting numeric value.

A Click the empty **Starting at** and **Ending at** check boxes (☐). They are filled (☑), and Excel extracts the minimum and maximum values of the numeric items, and places them in the text boxes.

6 Type the ending numeric value.

7 Type the size that you want to use for each grouping.

8 Click **OK**.

B Excel groups the numeric values.

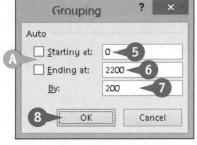

3	Sum of Quantity	Column Labels ▾		
4	Row Labels ▾	1 Free with 10	Extra Discount	Grand Total
5	0-200	186.00	203.00	389.00
6	200-400	429.00	430.00	859.00
7	400-600	638.00	619.00	1257.00
8	600-800	363.00	286.00	649.00
9	800-1000	440.00	791.00	1231.00
10	1000-1200	473.00	632.00	1105.00
11	1200-1400	429.00	293.00	722.00
12	1400-1600	473.00	120.00	593.00
13	1600-1800	110.00	254.00	364.00
14	1800-2000	132.00	274.00	406.00
15	2000-2200	275.00		275.00
16	**Grand Total**	**3948.00**	**3902.00**	**7850.00**
17				

TIPS

How do I group date and time values?
Click any item in the date field that you want to group. Click the **Analyze** tab, click **Group**, and then click **Group Field**. In the Grouping dialog box, type the start date or time and the end date or time. In the **By** list, click the type of grouping that you want, such as **Months** or **Quarters**. Click **OK**.

How do I group text values?
You must create custom groups. Begin by selecting the items that you want to include in a group. Click the **Analyze** tab, click **Group**, and then click **Group Selection**. Click the group label, type a new name for the group, and then press Enter. Repeat for each custom group that you want to create.

Apply a PivotTable Filter

By default, each PivotTable displays a summary for all the records in your source data. However, there may be situations in which you need to focus more closely on some aspect of the data. You can focus on a specific item from one of the source data fields by taking advantage of the PivotTable's filter field.

For example, suppose you are dealing with a PivotTable that summarizes data from a sales promotion by showing the net amount sold by product and promotion. To break down this summary by advertisement, you could add that field to the filter area.

Apply a PivotTable Filter

Apply a Report filter

1. Add a field to the FILTERS box.

2. Click the drop-down arrow (⌄) in the filter field.

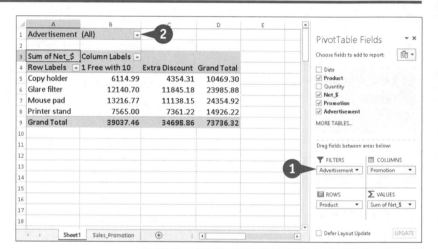

Excel displays a list of the report filter field values.

3. Click the item that you want to use as a filter.

Ⓐ If you want to display data for two or more report filters, click the empty **Select Multiple Items** check box (☐); it is filled (☑). Repeat Step 3 to select the other filters.

4. Click **OK**.

B Excel filters the PivotTable to show only the data for the item that you selected.

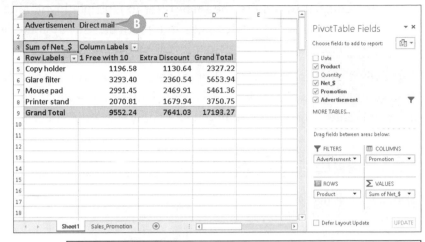

Remove the Filter

1 Click the **Filter** icon (⊤) in the report filter field.

Excel displays a list of the report filter field values.

2 Click **All**.

3 Click **OK**.

Excel removes the filter from the PivotTable.

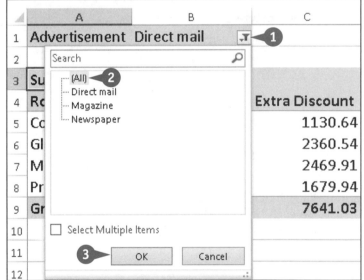

TIP

Can I add multiple fields to the filter area?

Yes. This enables you to apply multiple filters to the data. For example, suppose you have a PivotTable that summarizes sales promotion data by showing the total amount sold for each product, and that you have a filter field with Advertisement data that enables you to isolate the sales by product for a specific type of advertising used in the promotion. You could extend your analysis to look at the advertisement-specific sales by product for individual promotions.

To do this, add the Promotion field as a second field in the FILTERS box and then use the steps in this section to choose a specific advertisement and a specific promotion. It does not matter which order the fields appear in the filter because the filtering comes out the same in the end.

Filter a PivotTable with a Slicer

It is not unusual to require the same filter in multiple PivotTable reports. For example, if you are a sales manager responsible for sales in a particular set of countries, then you might often need to filter PivotTables to show data from just those countries.

If you have to apply the same filter repeatedly, then the process becomes inefficient. To combat this, you can use a *slicer*. A slicer is very similar to a report filter, except that it is independent of any PivotTable. This means that you can apply the same slicer to multiple PivotTables.

Filter a PivotTable with a Slicer

1 Click a cell inside the PivotTable with which you want to work.

2 Click the **Analyze** tab.

3 Click **Insert Slicer** (⊞).

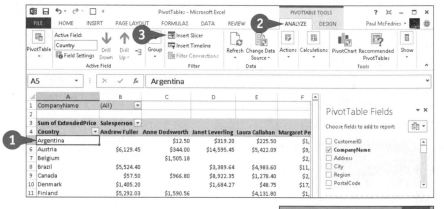

The Insert Slicers dialog box appears.

4 Select the empty check box (☐) beside each field for which you want to create a slicer and it is filled (☑).

5 Click **OK**.

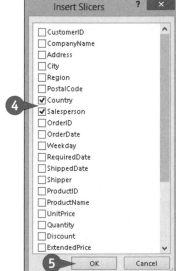

Ⓐ Excel displays one slicer for each field you selected.

Ⓑ The Slicer Tools contextual tab appears when a slicer has the focus.

Ⓒ You can use the controls in the Options tab to customize each slicer.

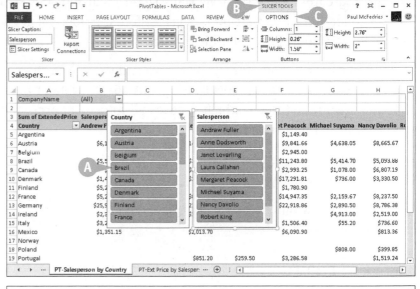

⑥ Click a field item that you want to include in your filter.

⑦ If you want to include multiple items in your filter, hold down Ctrl and click each item.

Ⓓ Excel filters the PivotTable based on the field items you selected in each slicer.

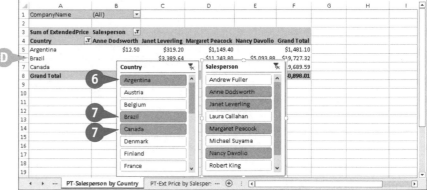

TIPS

Is there an easier way to locate items in a slicer?
If a field contains many items, you may have to scroll a long way to find the one you want. It is often easier in this case to configure the slicer to display its items in multiple columns. Click the title of the slicer to select it, click the **Options** tab, and then use the **Columns** text box to set the number of columns.

How can I get rid of a slicer that is cluttering the PivotTable window?
Right-click the slicer, and then click **Remove *Slicer*** (where *Slicer* is the name of the slicer, which is usually the field name). If you only want to hide the slicer temporarily, click any slicer, click **Options**, and then click **Selection Pane.** This displays the Selection and Visibility task pane. Click the eye icon beside the slicer to hide it.

Apply a PivotTable Style

You can greatly reduce the time you spend formatting your PivotTables if you apply a style, which is a collection of formatting options — fonts, borders, and background colors — that Excel defines for different areas of a PivotTable.

Excel defines more than 80 PivotTable styles, divided into three categories: Light, Medium, and Dark. The Light category includes Pivot Style Light 16, the default formatting applied to PivotTable reports that you create, and None, which removes all formatting from the PivotTable. You can also create your own PivotTable style format.

Apply a PivotTable Style

1 Click any cell within the PivotTable you want to format.

2 Click the **Design** tab.

3 In the PivotTable Styles group, click the **More** button (☰).

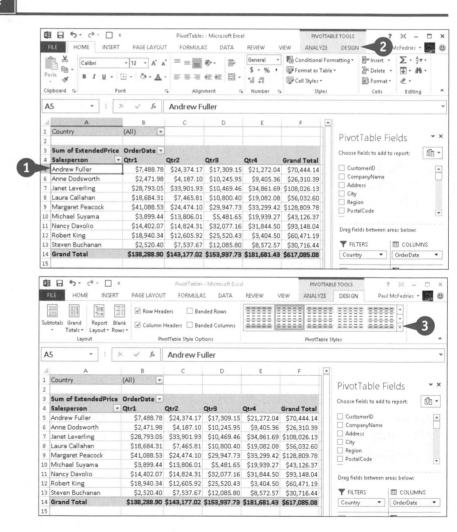

Ⓐ The PivotTable Styles gallery appears.

Note: When you hover the mouse pointer (⬚) over a style, Excel temporarily formats the PivotTable with that style.

④ Click the style you want to apply.

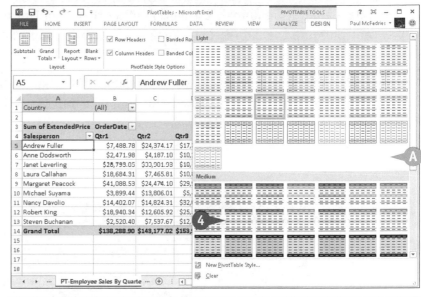

Ⓑ Excel applies the style.

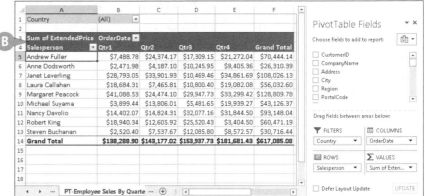

TIP

How can I define my own PivotTable style?
If none of the predefined PivotTable styles is the look that you want, you can define one yourself by creating your own custom PivotTable style.

You can format 25 PivotTable elements, including the entire table, the page field labels and values, the first column, the header row, the Grand Total row, and the Grand Total column.

Follow Steps **1** to **3** to display the PivotTable Styles gallery, and then click **New PivotTable Style**. In the New PivotTable Style dialog box, type a name for your custom style. Click each element that you want to format, click **Format**, use the Format Cells dialog box to select the formatting you want to use, and then click **OK**.

Change the PivotTable Summary Calculation

If your data analysis requires a calculation other than Sum (for numeric data) or Count (for text), you can configure the data field to use any of the other nine summary calculations built into Excel.

These calculations include Average, which calculates the mean value in a numeric field; Max, which displays the largest value in a numeric field; Min, which displays the smallest value in a numeric field; Product, which multiplies the values in a numeric field; and Count Nums, which displays the total number of numeric values in the source field.

Change the PivotTable Summary Calculation

1 Click any cell in the data field.

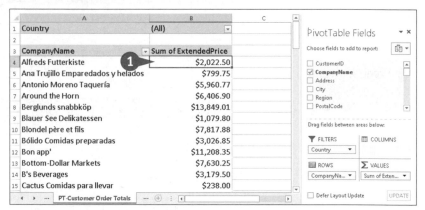

2 Click the **Analyze** tab.

3 Click **Active Field**.

4 Click **Field Settings**.

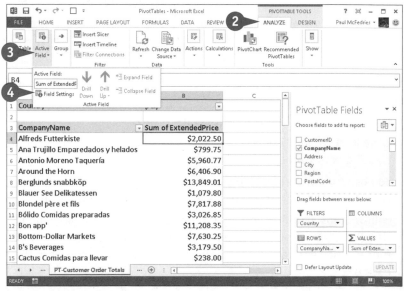

The Value Field Settings dialog box appears with the Summarize Values By tab displayed.

5 Click the summary calculation you want to use.

6 Click **OK**.

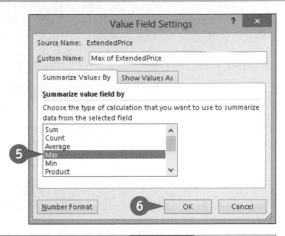

A Excel recalculates the PivotTable results.

B Excel renames the data field label to reflect the new summary calculation.

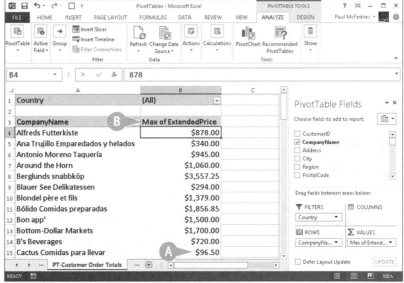

My PivotTable results do not look correct. Why?
Check the summary calculation that Excel has applied to the field to see if it is using Count instead of Sum. If the data field includes one or more text cells or one or more blank cells, Excel defaults to the Count summary function instead of Sum.

How do I change the summary calculation for a subtotal?
To change the subtotal summary calculation, click any cell in the outer field, click the **Analyze** tab, click **Active Field**, and then click **Field Settings**. Select the empty **Custom** radio button (○) and it is filled (◉). Click the summary calculation you want to use for the subtotals. Click **OK**.

Customize the PivotTable Fields Pane

You can customize the layout of the PivotTable Fields pane. You can choose the Field Section and Areas Section Side-By-Side option, which is useful if your source data has many fields.

Excel also offers the Fields Section Only option, which is useful if you add fields to the PivotTable by right-clicking the field name and then clicking the area to which you want the field to be added. The two Areas Section Only options are useful if you have finished adding fields to the PivotTable and you want to concentrate on moving fields between the areas and filtering the fields.

Customize the PivotTable Fields Pane

1. Click any cell inside the PivotTable.

2. Click **Tools** (⌗).

Ⓐ Excel displays the list of PivotTable Fields pane options.

3. Click the option you want to use.

Ⓑ Excel customizes the PivotTable Field List based on your selection.

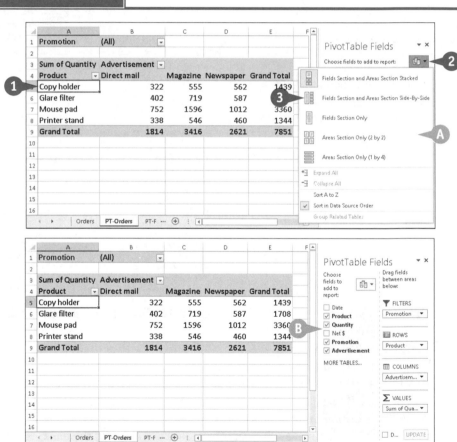

Create a PivotChart from a PivotTable

You can create a PivotChart directly from an existing PivotTable. This saves times because you do not have to configure the layout of the PivotChart or any other options.

A *PivotChart* is a graphical representation of the values in a PivotTable. However, a PivotChart goes far beyond a regular chart because it comes with many of the same capabilities as a PivotTable. These include hiding items, filtering data using the report area, and refreshing the PivotChart to account for changes in the underlying data. Also, if you move fields from one area of the PivotTable to another, the PivotChart changes accordingly.

Create a PivotChart from a PivotTable

1 Click any cell in the PivotTable.

2 Press F11.

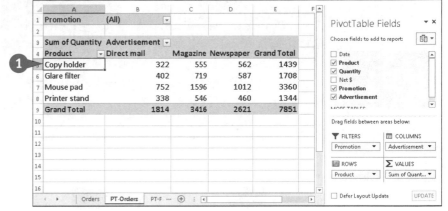

A Excel creates a new chart sheet and displays the PivotChart.

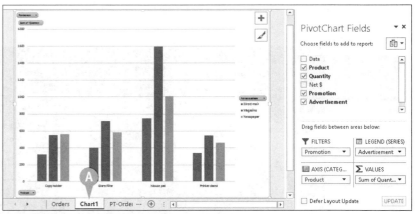

CHAPTER 18

Visualizing Data with Charts

You can take a worksheet full of numbers and display them as a chart. Visualizing your data in this way makes the data easier to understand and analyze. To help you see your data exactly the way you want, Excel offers a wide variety of chart types, and a large number of chart options.

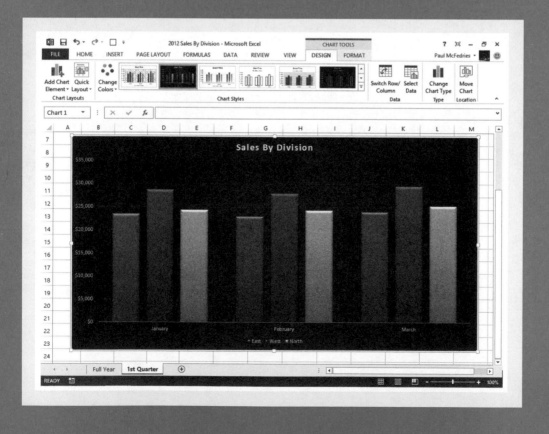

Examine Chart Elements

One of the best ways to analyze your worksheet data — or get your point across to other people — is to display your data visually in a *chart*, which is a graphic representation of spreadsheet data. As the data in the spreadsheet changes, the chart also changes to reflect the new numbers.

You have dozens of different chart formats to choose from, and if none of the built-in Excel formats is just right, you can further customize these charts to suit your needs. To get the most out of charts, you need to familiarize yourself with the basic chart elements.

A Category Axis

The axis that contains the category groupings (usually the X axis).

B Chart Title

The title of the chart.

C Data Marker

A symbol that represents a specific data value. The symbol used depends on the chart type.

D Data Series

A collection of related data values. Normally, the marker for each value in a series has the same pattern.

E Data Value

A single piece of data, also called a *data point*.

F Gridlines

Optional horizontal and vertical extensions of the axis tick marks. These lines make data values easier to read.

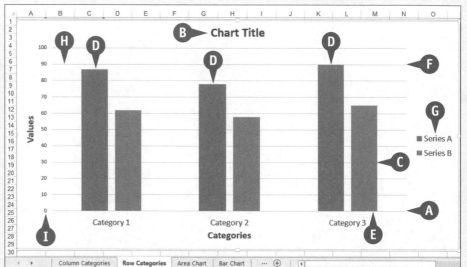

G Legend

A guide that shows the colors, patterns, and symbols used by the markers for each data series.

H Plot Area

The area bounded by the category and value axes. It contains the data points and gridlines.

I Value Axis

The axis that contains the data values (usually the Y axis).

Understanding Chart Types

Excel offers 11 types of charts, including column, bar, line, and pie charts. The type you should use depends on the type of data, and how you want to present it visually.

Understanding Chart Types

Chart Type	Description
Area chart	Shows the relative contributions over time that each data series makes to the whole picture.
Bar chart	Compares distinct items, or shows single items at distinct intervals. Often shows categories along the vertical axis and values along the horizontal.
Bubble chart	Similar to an XY chart, except there are three data series. In the third series, the individual plot points are displayed as bubbles.
Column chart	Like a bar chart, it compares distinct items, or shows single items at distinct intervals. Laid out with categories along the horizontal axis and values along the vertical.
Doughnut chart	Like a pie chart, it shows the proportion of the whole contributed by each value in a data series. You can also plot multiple data series.
Line chart	Shows how a data series changes over time. The category (X) axis usually represents a progression of even increments and the series points are plotted on the value (Y) axis.
Pie chart	Shows the proportion of the whole contributed by each value in a single data series. The whole is represented as a circle; each value is displayed as a proportional slice of the circle.
Radar chart	Makes comparisons within a data series and between data series relative to a center point. Each category is shown with a value axis extending from the center point.
Stock chart	Designed to plot stock-market prices, such as daily high, low, and closing values.
Surface chart	Analyzes two sets of data and determines the optimum combination of the two.
XY (or Scatter) chart	Shows the relationship between numeric values in two different data series. Can also plot a series of data pairs in XY coordinates.

Create a Chart

You can create a chart from your Excel worksheet data with just a few mouse clicks. Excel offers nearly 100 default chart configurations, so there should always be a type that best visualizes your data. If you prefer to let Excel suggest a chart type based on your data, see the following section, "Create a Recommended Chart."

Regardless of which chart type you choose, you can change to a different chart type at any time. See "Select a Different Chart Type" later in this chapter.

Create a Chart

1 Select the data that you want to visualize in a chart.

A If your data includes headings, be sure to include those in the selection.

2 Click the **Insert** tab.

3 Click a chart type.

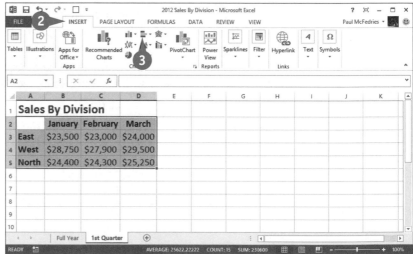

B Excel displays a gallery of configurations for the chart type.

4 Click the chart configuration you want to use.

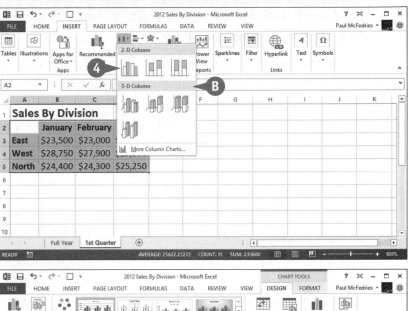

C Excel inserts the chart.

The sections in the rest of this chapter show you how to configure, format, and move the chart.

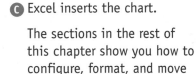

Is there a way to create a chart on a separate sheet?

Yes. You can use a special workbook sheet called a *chart sheet*. If you have not yet created your chart, select the worksheet data, right-click any worksheet tab, and then click **Insert** to display the Insert dialog box. Click the **General** tab, click **Chart**, and then click **OK**. Excel creates a new chart sheet and inserts the chart.

If you have already created your chart, you can move it to a separate chart sheet. See the Tip in the section "Move or Resize a Chart" later in this chapter.

Create a Recommended Chart

You can make it easier and faster to create a chart by choosing from one of the chart configurations recommended by Excel.

With close to 100 possible chart configurations, the Excel chart tools are certainly comprehensive. However, that can be an overwhelming number of choices if you are not sure which type would best visualize your data. Rather than wasting a great deal of time looking at dozens of different chart configurations, the Recommended Charts command examines your data, and then narrows down the possible choices to about 10 configurations that would work.

Create a Recommended Chart

1 Select the data that you want to visualize in a chart.

A If your data includes headings, be sure to include them in the selection.

2 Click the **Insert** tab.

3 Click **Recommended Charts**.

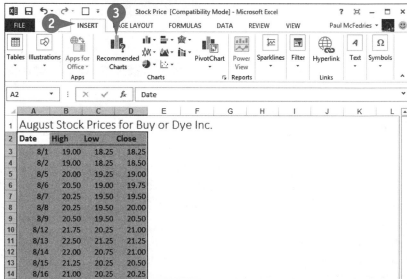

The Insert Chart dialog box appears with the Recommended Charts tab displayed.

④ Click the chart type you want to use.

Ⓑ A preview of the chart appears here.

⑤ Click **OK**.

Ⓒ Excel inserts the chart.

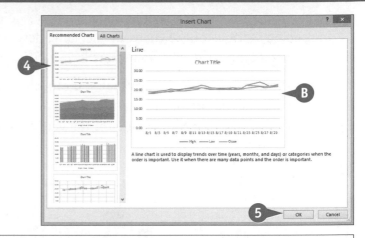

TIP

Is there a faster way to insert a recommended chart?

Yes, you can use the Quick Analysis feature in Excel:

① Select the data that you want to visualize in a chart, including the headings, if any.

② Click the **Quick Analysis** Smart Tag (📄).

③ Click **Charts**.

Excel displays the chart types recommended for your data.

④ Click the chart type you want to use.

Excel inserts the chart.

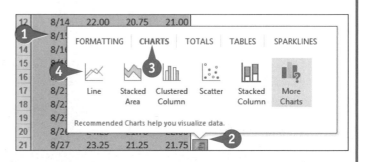

Add Chart Titles

You can make your chart easier to understand by adding chart titles, which are labels that appear in specific sections of the chart. By including descriptive titles, you make it easier for other people to see at a glance what your chart is visualizing.

There are three types of chart titles that you can add. The first type is the overall chart title, which usually appears at the top of the chart. You can also add a title for the horizontal axis to describe the chart categories, as well as a title for the vertical axis, which describes the chart values.

Add Chart Titles

1. Click the chart.
2. Click the **Design** tab.
3. Click **Add Chart Element**.
4. Click **Chart Title**.
5. Click **Above Chart**.

   Ⓐ Excel adds the title box.
6. Type the title.

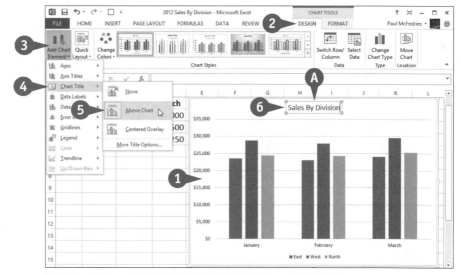

7. Click **Add Chart Element**.
8. Click **Axis Titles**.
9. Click **Primary Horizontal**.

   Ⓑ Excel adds the title box.
10. Type the title.
11. Click **Add Chart Element**.
12. Click **Axis Titles**.
13. Click **Primary Vertical**.

    Ⓒ Excel adds the title box.
14. Type the title.

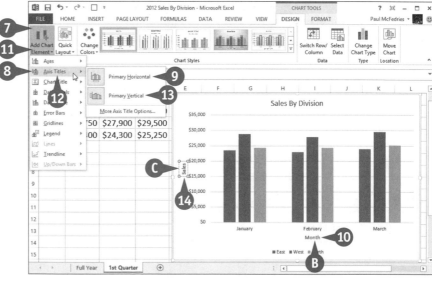

Add Data Labels

You can make your chart easier to read by adding data labels. A *data label* is a small text box that appears in or near a data marker and displays the value of that data point.

Excel offers several position options for the data labels, and these options depend on the chart type. For example, with a column chart, you can place the data labels within or above each column. For a line chart, you can place the labels to the left or right, or above or below, the data marker.

Add Data Labels

1 Click the chart.

2 Click the **Design** tab.

3 Click **Add Chart Element**.

4 Click **Data Labels**.

5 Click the position you want to use for the data labels.

Note: Remember that the position options you see depend on the chart type.

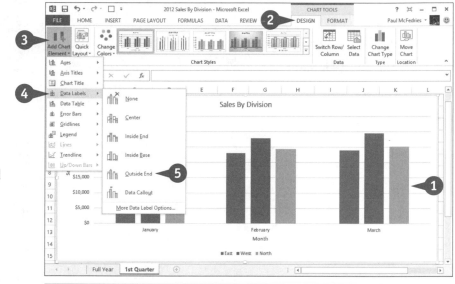

Ⓐ Excel adds the labels to the chart.

Position the Chart Legend

You can change the position of the chart *legend*, which identifies the colors associated with each data series in the chart. The legend is a crucial chart element for interpreting and understanding your chart, so it is important that you place it in the best position. For example, you might find the legend easier to read if it appears to the right of the chart. Alternatively, if you want more horizontal space to display your chart, you can move the legend above or below the chart.

Position the Chart Legend

1. Click the chart.

2. Click the **Design** tab.

3. Click **Add Chart Element**.

4. Click **Legend**.

5. Click the position you want to use for the legend.

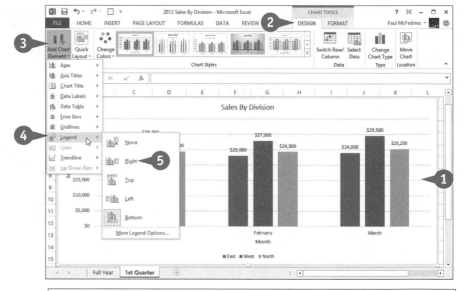

Ⓐ Excel moves the legend.

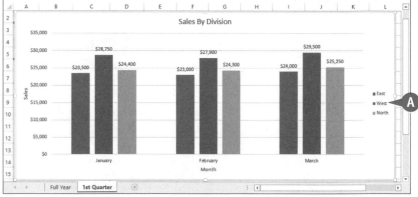

Display Chart Gridlines

You can make your chart easier to read and analyze by adding gridlines. Horizontal gridlines extend from the vertical (value) axis, and are useful with area, bubble, and column charts. Vertical gridlines extend from the horizontal (category) axis, and are useful with bar and line charts. *Major gridlines* are gridlines associated with the *major units* (the values you see displayed on the vertical and horizontal axes), while *minor gridlines* are gridlines associated with the *minor units* (values between each major unit).

Display Chart Gridlines

1 Click the chart.

2 Click the **Design** tab.

3 Click **Add Chart Element**.

4 Click **Gridlines**.

5 Click the horizontal gridline option you prefer.

Ⓐ Excel displays the horizontal gridlines.

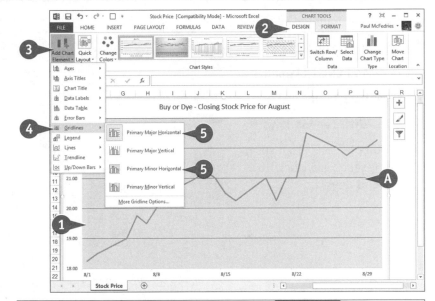

6 Click **Add Chart Element**.

7 Click **Gridlines**.

8 Click the vertical gridline option you prefer.

Ⓑ Excel displays the vertical gridlines.

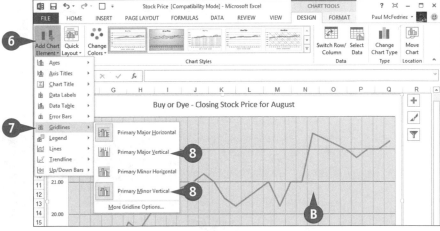

Display a Data Table

You can make it easier for yourself and others to interpret your chart by adding a data table. A *data table* is a tabular grid where each row is a data series from the chart, each column is a chart category, and each cell is a chart data point.

Excel gives you the option of displaying the data table with or without *legend keys*, which are markers that identify each series.

Display a Data Table

1 Click the chart.

2 Click the **Design** tab.

3 Click **Add Chart Element**.

4 Click **Data Table**.

5 Click **With Legend Keys**.

Ⓐ If you prefer not to display the legend keys, click **No Legend Keys**.

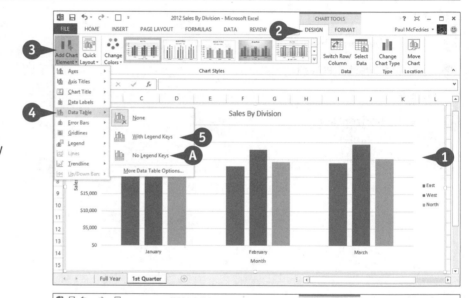

Ⓑ Excel adds the data table below the chart.

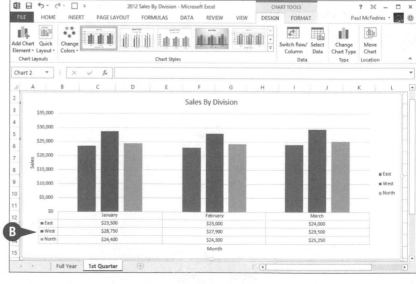

Change the Chart Layout and Style

You can quickly format your chart by applying a different chart layout and chart style. The chart layout includes elements such as the titles, data labels, legend, gridlines, and data table. The Quick Layouts feature in Excel enables you to apply these elements in different combinations with just a few mouse clicks. The chart style represents the colors used by the chart data markers and background.

Change the Chart Layout and Style

1. Click the chart.

2. Click the **Design** tab.

3. Click **Quick Layout**.

4. Click the layout you want to use.

Ⓐ Excel applies the layout.

5. Click the **Chart Styles** More arrow (⩒).

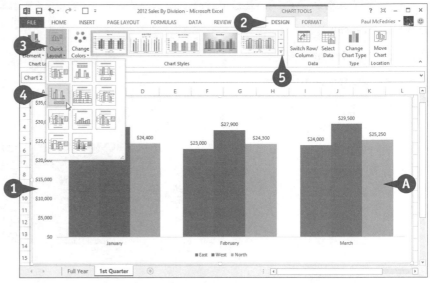

6. Click the chart style you want.

Ⓑ Excel applies the style to the chart.

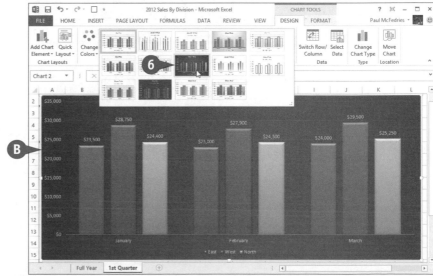

Select a Different Chart Type

If the current chart type is not showing your data in the best way, you can change the chart type. This enables you to experiment, not only with the 10 chart types, but also with the nearly 100 chart type configurations.

For example, if you are graphing a stock's high, low, and closing prices, a line chart shows you each value, but a stock chart gives you a better sense of the daily price movements. If you are using a bar chart to show the relative size of the components that make up something, you would more readily visualize the data by switching to a pie chart.

Select a Different Chart Type

1. Click the chart.

2. Click the **Design** tab.

3. Click **Change Chart Type**.

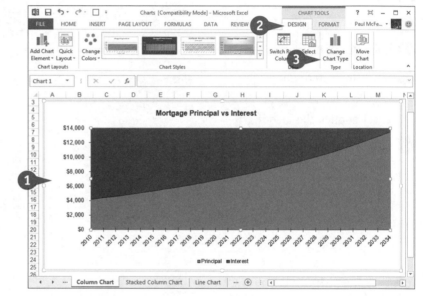

The Change Chart Type dialog box appears.

4. Click the chart type you want to use.

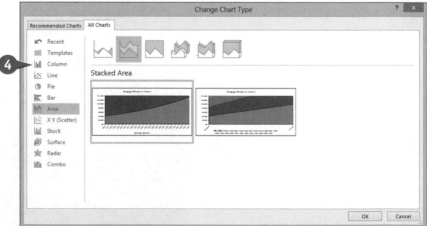

Excel displays the chart type configurations.

5 Click the subcategory and configuration you want to use.

6 Click **OK**.

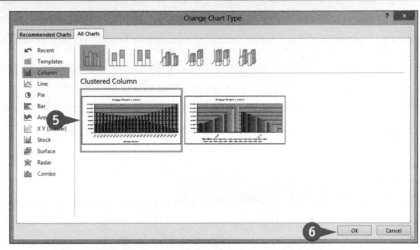

A Excel applies the new chart type.

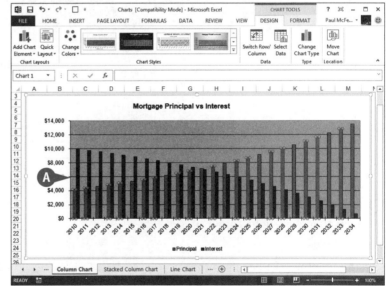

TIP

Can I save the chart type and formatting so that I can reuse it later on a different chart?
Yes. You do this by saving your work as a chart template. Follow the steps in this section and in the previous few sections of this chapter to set the chart type, titles, labels, legend position, gridlines, layout, and style. Right-click the chart's plot area or background, click **Save as Template**, type a name for the template, and then click **Save**. To reuse the template, follow Steps 1 to 3, click **Templates**, click your template, and then click **OK**.

Change the Chart Source Data

In Excel, a chart's *source data* is the original range used to create the chart. You can keep your chart up to date and accurate by adjusting the chart when its source data changes.

You normally do this when the structure of the source data changes. For example, if the source range adds a row or column, you can adjust the chart to include the new data. However, you do not need to make any adjustments if just the data within the original range changes. In such cases, Excel automatically adjusts the chart to display the new data.

Change the Chart Source Data

1 Click the chart to select it.

Ⓐ Excel selects the chart's source data.

2 Move the mouse pointer (✛) over the lower-right corner of the range.

The pointer (✛) becomes the Left/Right Margin pointer (↔).

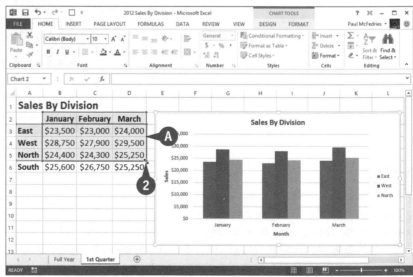

③ Click and drag the Left/Right Margin pointer (↔) until the selection includes all the data you want included in the chart.

Ⓑ Excel displays a blue outline to show you the new selection.

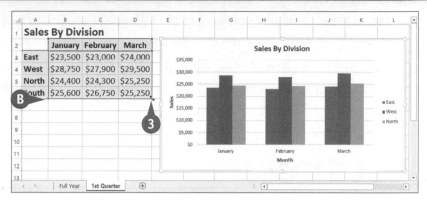

④ Release the mouse button.

Ⓒ Excel redraws the chart to include the new data.

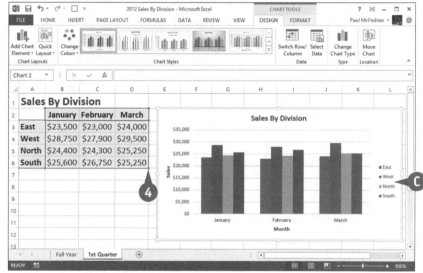

TIPS

Is there a way to swap the chart series with the chart categories without modifying the source data?

Yes. Excel has a feature that enables you to switch the row and column data, which swaps the series and categories without affecting the source data. First, click the chart to select it, and then click the **Design** tab. Click **Switch Row/Column** (🖾). Excel swaps the series and categories. Click **Switch Row/Column** (🖾) again to return to the original layout.

Is there a way to remove a series from a chart without deleting the data from the source range?

Yes. You can use the Select Data Source dialog box in Excel to remove individual series. Click the chart to select it, and then click the **Design** tab. Click **Select Data** (🖾) to open the Select Data Source. In the **Legend Entries (Series)** list, click the series you want to delete, and then click **Remove**. Click **OK**.

Move or Resize a Chart

You can move a chart to another part of the worksheet. This is useful if the chart is blocking the worksheet data or if you want the chart to appear in a particular part of the worksheet.

You can also resize a chart. For example, if you find that the chart is difficult to read, making the chart bigger often solves the problem. Similarly, if the chart takes up too much space on the worksheet, you can make it smaller.

Move or Resize a Chart

Move a Chart

1. Click the chart.

   Ⓐ Excel displays a border around it.

2. Move the mouse pointer (▷) over the chart border.

   The pointer (▷) becomes the pointer range border (✣).

Note: Do not position the mouse pointer over a corner or the middle of any side of the border.

3. Click and drag the chart border to the desired location.

4. Release the mouse button.

   Ⓑ Excel moves the chart.

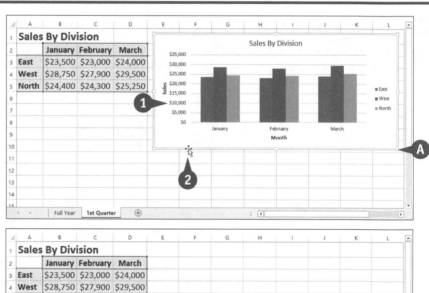

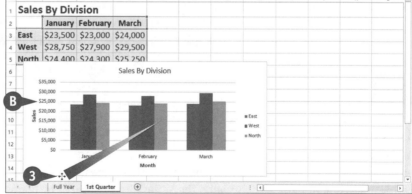

Resize a Chart

1 Click the chart.

C Excel displays a border around it.

D The border includes sizing handles.

2 Move the mouse pointer (◹) over a sizing handle.

The pointer (◹) becomes the Resize Chart Pointer Horizontal (⟷), Vertical (↕), or Corner (⤡).

3 Click and drag the handle.

E Excel displays a gray outline of the new chart size.

4 Release the mouse button.

F Excel resizes the chart.

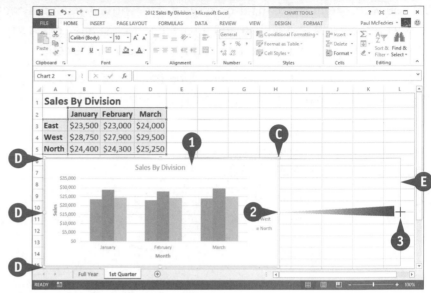

TIPS

Can I move a chart to a separate sheet?
Yes. If your chart already exists on a worksheet, you can move it to a new sheet. Click the chart, click the **Design** tab, and then click **Move Chart** to open the Move Chart dialog box. Select the empty **New sheet** radio button (○) and it is filled (◉). In the **New sheet** text box, type a name for the new sheet, and then click **OK**.

How do I delete a chart?
How you delete a chart depends on whether your chart exists as an object on a worksheet or in its own sheet. If the chart is on a worksheet, click the chart, and then press [Del]. If the chart exists on a separate sheet, right-click the sheet tab, click **Delete Sheet**, and then click **Delete**.

423

Add a Sparkline to a Cell

If you want a quick visualization of your data without having a chart take up a large amount of worksheet space, you can add a sparkline to a single cell. A *sparkline* is a small chart that visualizes a row or column of data and fits inside a single cell.

Excel offers three types of sparklines: Line (similar to a line chart), Column (similar to a column chart), and Win/Loss (for data that includes positive and negative values).

Add a Sparkline to a Cell

1 Select the row or column of data you want to visualize.

2 Click the **Insert** tab.

3 Click the type of sparkline you want to create.

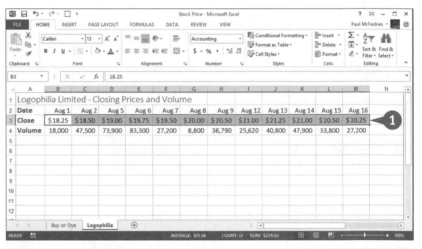

The Create Sparklines dialog box appears.

④ Click inside the **Location Range** box.

⑤ Click the cell where you want the sparkline to appear.

⑥ Click **OK**.

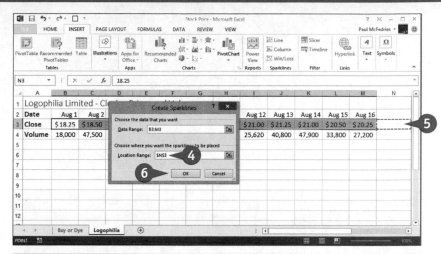

Ⓐ Excel adds the sparkline to the cell.

Ⓑ Excel displays the Sparkline Tools tab.

Ⓒ Use the tools in the Design tab to format your sparkline.

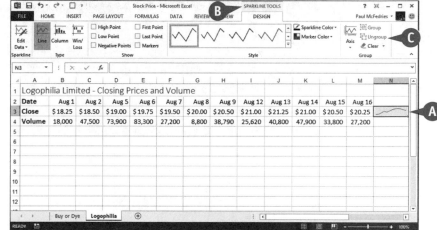

TIP

Can I add a sparkline to multiple rows or columns at once?
Yes. To do this, first select the rows or columns of data that you want to visualize. Follow Steps 2 and 3 to open the Create Sparklines dialog box and place the cursor inside the **Location Range** box. Select a single cell for each row or column that you have selected. For example, if you have selected five rows, select five cells. Click **OK**. Excel adds a sparkline for each selected row or column.

CHAPTER 19

Working with Worksheet Graphics

This chapter shows you how to enhance your Excel worksheets by incorporating shapes, clip art, pictures, or WordArt and SmartArt images.

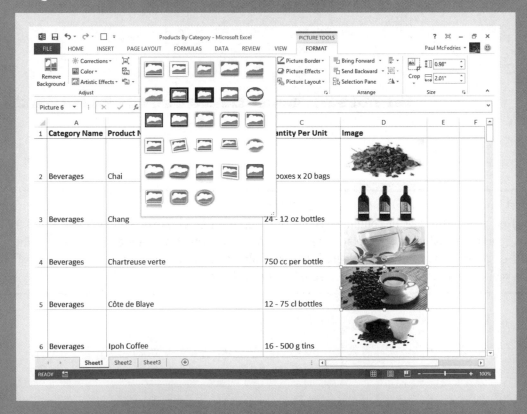

Draw a Shape

You can add visual appeal or enhance the readability of your worksheets by adding one or more shapes. The Excel Shapes gallery comes with more than 150 predefined objects called *shapes* (or sometimes *AutoShapes*) that enable you to quickly and easily draw anything from simple geometric figures such as lines, rectangles, and ovals, to elaborate items such as starbursts, flowchart symbols, and callout boxes. You can add these shapes to a worksheet either to enhance the aesthetics of your data or to help other people read and understand your work.

Draw a Shape

1 Display the worksheet on which you want to draw the shape.

2 Click the **Insert** tab.

3 Click **Illustrations**.

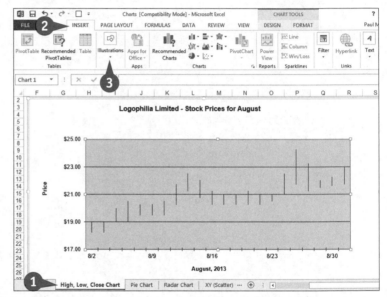

4 Click **Shapes**.

5 Click the shape you want to draw.

The mouse pointer ( ) becomes the pointer fill (+).

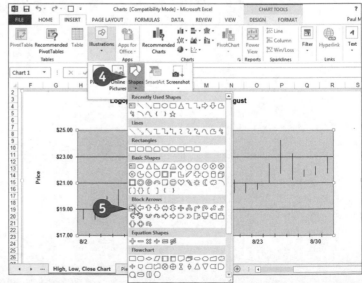

6 Click and drag the mouse pointer fill (**+**) to draw the shape.

7 When the shape is the size you want, release the mouse button.

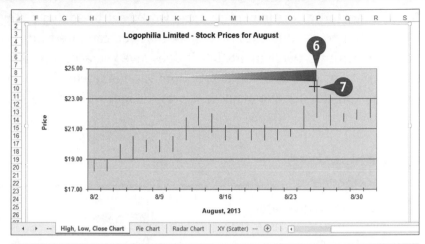

A The program draws the shape and adds edit handles around the shape's edges.

Note: If you need to move or resize the shape, see the section "Move or Resize a Graphic" later in this chapter.

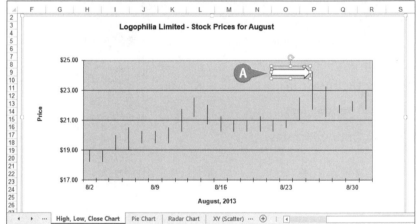

TIPS

Is there an easy way to draw a perfect circle or square?
Yes. Excel offers an easy technique for drawing circles and squares. Hold down the Shift key as you click and drag the shape to constrain the shape into a perfect circle or square. When you finish drawing the shape, release the Shift key.

Can I add text to a shape?
Yes. You can add text to the interior of any two-dimensional shape (that is, any shape that is not a line). After you draw the shape, right-click it, click **Edit Text**, and then type your text inside the shape. You can use the Home tab's Font controls to format the text. When you finish, click outside of the shape.

Insert Clip Art

You can improve the look of an Excel worksheet by adding a clip art image to the sheet. *Clip art* refers to small images or artwork that you can insert into your documents. Excel 2013 does not come with its own clip art, but it does give you access to the Office.com clip art collection, which contains thousands of images from various categories, such as business, people, nature, and symbols. You can use any of these clip art images without charge.

Insert Clip Art

1 Display the worksheet on which you want to insert the clip art image.

2 Click the cell where you want the upper-left corner of the image to appear.

3 Click the **Insert** tab.

4 Click **Illustrations**.

5 Click **Online Pictures**.

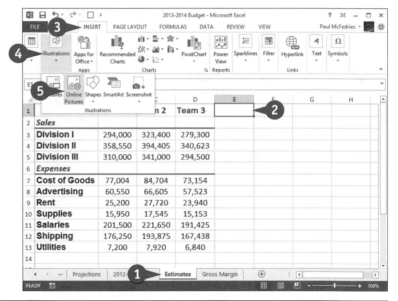

The Insert Pictures window appears.

6 Click **Office.com Clip Art**.

7 Use the **Search Office.com** text box to type a word that describes the kind of clip art image you want to insert.

8 Click **Search** (🔍).

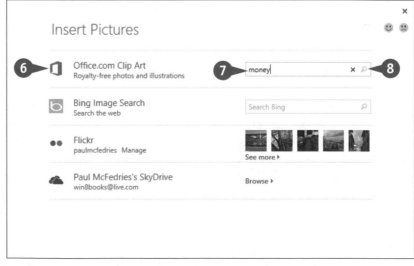

Ⓐ Excel displays a list of clip art images that match your search term.

⑨ Click the clip art image you want to use.

⑩ Click **Insert**.

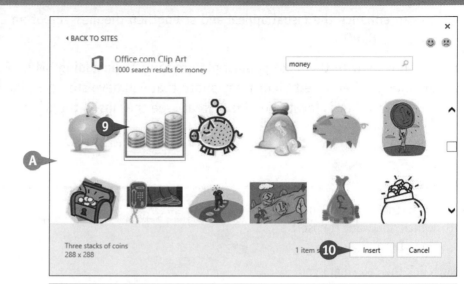

Ⓑ Excel inserts the clip art.

Note: If you need to move or resize the clip art, see the section "Move or Resize a Graphic" later in this chapter.

	A	B	C	D
1		Team 1	Team 2	Team 3
2	*Sales*			
3	**Division I**	294,000	323,400	279,300
4	**Division II**	358,550	394,405	340,623
5	**Division III**	310,000	341,000	294,500
6	*Expenses*			
7	**Cost of Goods**	77,004	84,704	73,154
8	**Advertising**	60,550	66,605	57,523
9	**Rent**	25,200	27,720	23,940
10	**Supplies**	15,950	17,545	15,153
11	**Salaries**	201,500	221,650	191,425
12	**Shipping**	176,250	193,875	167,438
13	**Utilities**	7,200	7,920	6,840
14				

Budget | Assumptions | Projections | 2012-2013 Final | Estima ...

TIPS

Is there an easier way to locate the clip art image that I want?
Yes. You can use a web browser to locate clip art images directly using the Office.com website. Navigate to http://office.microsoft.com/en-us/images/ and then click an image category, such as Business or People. Next, filter the images by media type and image size. For clip art, you should click **Illustration** in the Media Type list and **All** in the Image Size list.

Can I insert other online images?
Yes. Follow Steps **1** to **5**, and then use the Bing Image Search option to find the picture. If your Flickr account is connected to Windows 8, you can use the Flickr option to choose a photo. If you are using a Microsoft account with Windows 8, you can use the SkyDrive option to select an image from your SkyDrive.

Insert a Photo

You can enhance the visual appeal and strengthen the message of an Excel worksheet by adding a photo to the file.

Excel can work with the most popular picture formats, including BMP, JPEG, TIFF, PNG, and GIF. This means that you can insert almost any photo that you have stored on your computer. If you want to insert a photo that is located online instead, see the tips in the previous section "Insert Clip Art."

Insert a Photo

1 Open the worksheet in which you want to insert the photo.

2 Click the cell where you want the upper-left corner of the photo to appear.

3 Click the **Insert** tab.

4 Click **Illustrations**.

5 Click **Pictures**.

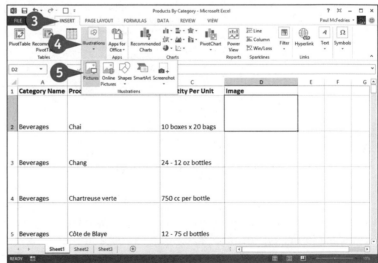

The Insert Picture dialog box appears.

6 Open the folder that contains the photo you want to insert.

7 Click the photo.

8 Click **Insert**.

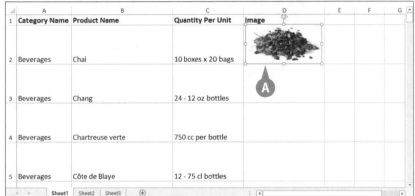

A Excel inserts the photo into the worksheet.

Note: If you need to move or resize the photo, see the section "Move or Resize a Graphic" later in this chapter.

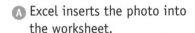

TIPS

Can I remove a distracting background from my photo?

Yes. Excel comes with a Background Removal feature that can eliminate the background in most photos. Click the photo, click the **Format** tab, and then click **Remove Background** (🖼). If part of the foreground is in the removal color, click **Mark Areas to Keep,** and then click and drag a line through the part you want to retain. When you are finished, click **Keep Changes**.

Can I reduce the size of a workbook that has many photos?

Yes. You can use the Compress Pictures feature. Click any image in the workbook, click the **Format** tab, and then click **Compress Pictures** (🖼). Click the selected **Apply only to this picture** check box (☑) and it is cleared (☐). Click an empty **Target output** radio button (○) and it is filled (◉). Click **OK**.

Insert WordArt

You can add some pizzazz to your Excel workbooks by inserting a WordArt image. A WordArt image is a graphic object that contains text stylized with shadows, outlines, reflections, and other predefined effects.

WordArt images enable you to apply sophisticated and fun effects to text with just a few mouse clicks. However, some of the more elaborate WordArt effects can make text difficult to read, so make sure that whatever WordArt image you use does not detract from your worksheet message.

Insert WordArt

1 Open the worksheet in which you want to insert the WordArt image.

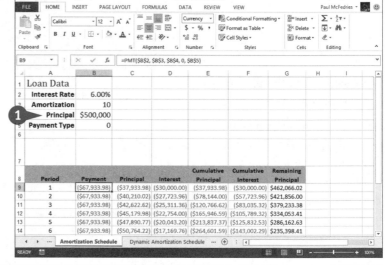

2 Click the **Insert** tab.

3 Click **Text**.

4 Click **WordArt**.

The WordArt gallery appears.

5 Click the WordArt style you want to use.

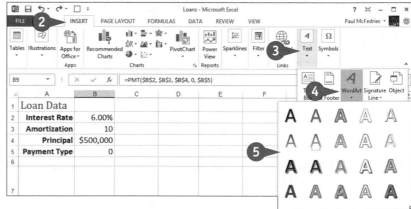

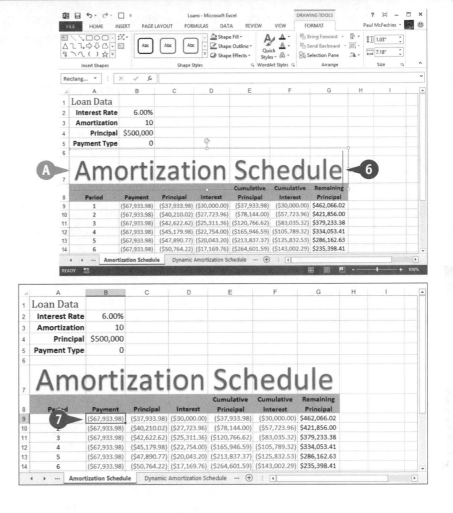

Ⓐ The WordArt image appears in the worksheet.

⑥ Type the text that you want to appear in the WordArt image.

⑦ Click outside the image to set it.

Note: You will likely have to move the WordArt image into position; see the section "Move or Resize a Graphic" later in this chapter.

TIPS

Can I change the default WordArt formatting?
Yes. Click the WordArt image to select it, and then use the Home tab's Font controls to adjust the WordArt text font. Click the **Format** tab. In the WordArt Styles group, use the **Text Fill** (⊿), **Text Outline** (⊿), and **Text Effects** (⊿) galleries to format the WordArt image. You can also use the Quick Styles gallery to select a different WordArt style.

Can I make my WordArt text run vertically?
Yes. Click the WordArt image to select it. Click the **Format** tab, and then click the dialog box launcher (⌐) in the **WordArt Styles** group. In the Format Shape task pane, click **Text Options,** and then click the **Textbox** icon (⎀). Click the **Text direction** drop-down arrow (⌄), and then click **Stacked.** Click **Close**, and Excel displays the WordArt text vertically.

Insert SmartArt

You can add a SmartArt graphic to a workbook to help present information in a compact, visual format. A SmartArt graphic is a collection of *nodes* — shapes with some text inside — that enables you to convey information visually.

For example, you can use a SmartArt graphic to present a company organization chart, the progression of steps in a workflow, the parts that make up a whole, and much more.

Insert SmartArt

1 Open the worksheet in which you want to insert the SmartArt image.

2 Click the **Insert** tab.

3 Click **Illustrations.**

4 Click **SmartArt**.

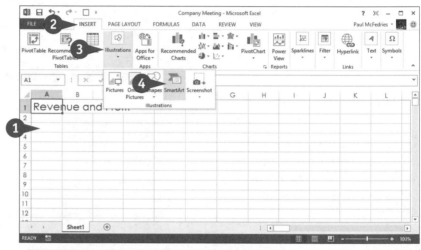

The Choose a SmartArt Graphic dialog box appears.

5 Click a SmartArt category.

6 Click the SmartArt style you want to use.

7 Click **OK**.

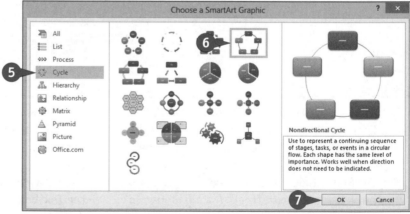

Ⓐ The SmartArt graphic appears in the document.

Ⓑ You use the Text pane to type the text for each node and to add and delete nodes.

⑧ Click a node in the Text pane.

⑨ Type the text that you want to appear in the node.

Ⓒ The text appears automatically in the associated shape.

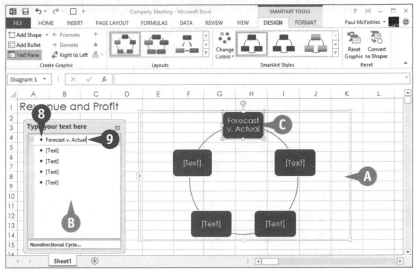

⑩ Repeat Steps **8** and **9** to fill in the other nodes in the SmartArt graphic.

Ⓓ You can click **Text Pane** (⊞) to hide the Text pane.

Note: You will likely have to move the SmartArt graphic into position; see the section "Move or Resize a Graphic."

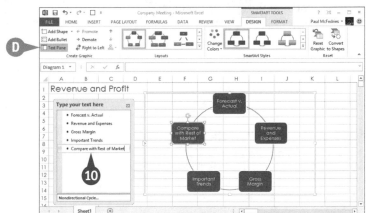

TIPS

How do I add a node to my SmartArt graphic?
First, decide where you want the node to appear in the image. That is, decide which existing node you want the new node to come before or after. Click the existing node, click the **Design** tab, click the **Add Shape** drop-down arrow (⊡), and then click **Add Shape After**. (If you want the new node to appear before the existing node, click **Add Shape Before**.)

Can I use shapes other than the ones supplied in the default SmartArt graphics?
Yes. Begin by clicking the node you want to change. Click the **Format** tab, and then click the **Change Shape** drop-down arrow (⊡) to display the Shapes gallery. Click the shape you want to use. Excel updates the SmartArt graphic node with the new shape.

Move or Resize a Graphic

To ensure that a graphic is ideally placed within an Excel worksheet, you can move the graphic to a new location or you can resize the graphic in its current location. For example, you might want to move or resize a graphic so that it does not cover existing worksheet text. Similarly, you might want to move or resize a graphic so that it is positioned near a particular worksheet element or fits within an open worksheet area. You can move or resize any graphic, including shapes, clip art, pictures, WordArt images, and SmartArt graphics.

Move or Resize a Graphic

Move a Graphic

1 Move the mouse pointer (⬉) over an edge of the graphic you want to move.

The mouse pointer (⬉) becomes the Move graphic (✥).

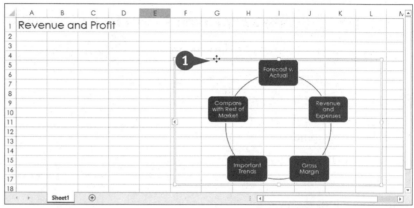

2 Drag the graphic to the location you prefer.

A Excel moves the graphic to the new location.

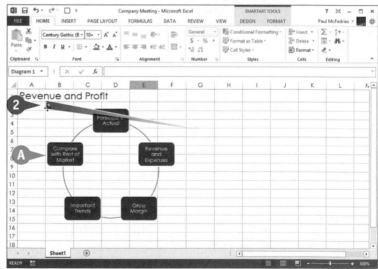

Resize a Graphic

1 Click the graphic.

B Sizing handles appear.

2 Move the mouse pointer (⇖) over a sizing handle.

C Use a left or right handle to adjust the width; the mouse pointer (⇖) becomes the Horizontal chart pointer (⟷).

D Use a top or bottom handle to adjust the height; the mouse pointer (⇖) becomes the Vertical chart pointer (↕).

E Use a corner handle to adjust the two sides adjacent to the corner; the mouse pointer (⇖) becomes the Corner chart pointer (⤢).

3 Drag the sizing handle; the mouse pointer (⇖) becomes the pointer fill (**+**).

4 Release the mouse button when the handle is in the position you want.

F Excel resizes the graphic.

5 Repeat Steps **2** to **4** to resize other sides of the graphic, as necessary.

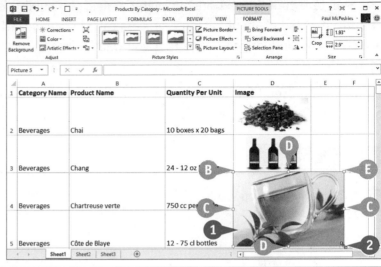

TIP

Can I rotate a graphic?

Yes. Most graphic objects come with a rotate handle. Follow these steps:

1 Move the mouse pointer (⇖) over the rotate handle; the pointer (⇖) becomes **Rotate Graphic** (↻).

2 Click and drag the rotate handle clockwise or counterclockwise to rotate the graphic.

3 Release the mouse button when the graphic is in the position you want.

Crop a Picture

If a picture contains extraneous material near the outside edges of the image, you can often cut out those elements using a process called *cropping*. When you crop a picture, you specify a rectangular area of the image that you want to keep. Excel discards everything outside of the rectangle.

Cropping is a useful feature because it can help viewers focus on the subject of a picture. Cropping is also useful for removing extraneous elements that appear on or near the edges of a photo.

Crop a Picture

1. Click the picture you want to crop.

2. Click the **Format** tab.

3. Click the **Crop** button ( ).

Ⓐ Crop handles appear around the picture.

④ Click and drag a crop handle.

The Excel mouse pointer (⊕) becomes pointer fill (✛).

Ⓑ Click and drag a side handle to crop that side.

Ⓒ Click and drag a corner handle to crop the two sides adjacent to the corner.

⑤ Release the mouse button when the handle is in the position you want.

⑥ Click the **Crop** button (🖼).

Excel turns off the Crop feature.

Ⓓ Excel crops the picture.

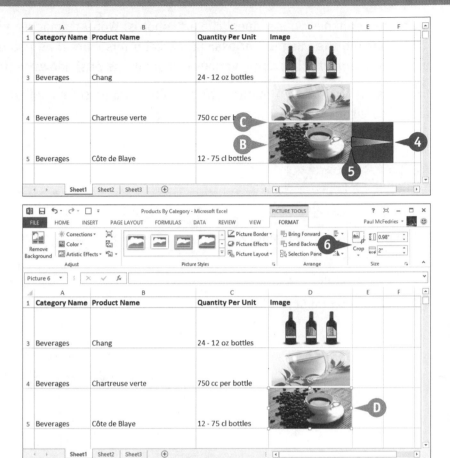

TIPS

If I have a picture with the main element in the middle, is it possible to crop in all directions at once to keep just that middle element?

Yes. You normally crop one side at a time by clicking and dragging a side crop handle, or two sides at a time by clicking and dragging a corner crop handle. To crop all four sides at once, hold down the `Ctrl` key, and then click and drag any corner crop handle.

Can I crop a picture to a particular aspect ratio or shape?

Yes. If you know the aspect ratio (the ratio of the width to the height) you want, click the **Crop** drop-down arrow (⌄), click **Aspect Ratio**, and then click the ratio, such as 3:5 or 4:6. If you prefer to crop to a shape, such as an oval or arrow, click the **Crop** drop-down arrow (⌄), click **Crop to Shape**, and then click the shape.

Format a Picture

You can enhance your shapes, clip art, photos, WordArt images, and SmartArt graphics by formatting the images. For example, Excel offers more than two dozen picture styles, which are predefined formats that apply various combinations of shadows, reflections, borders, and layouts.

Excel also offers a dozen picture effects, which are preset combinations of special effects such as glows, soft edges, bevels, and 3-D rotations.

Format a Picture

Apply a Picture Style

1. Click the picture you want to format.

2. Click the **Format** tab.

3. Click the **Picture Styles** More arrow (⩯).

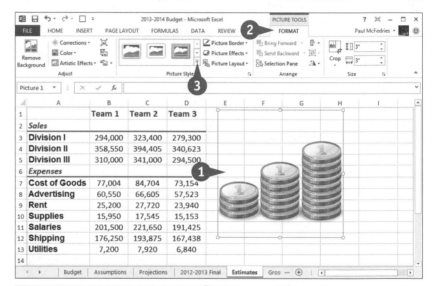

Ⓐ Excel displays the Picture Styles gallery.

4. Click the picture style you want to use.

Ⓑ Excel applies the style to the picture.

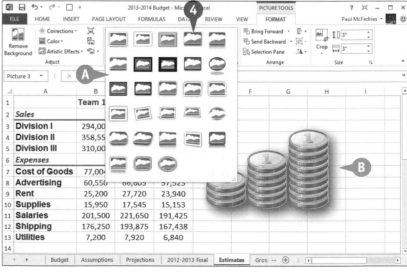

Apply a Picture Effect

1 Click the picture you want to format.

2 Click the **Format** tab.

3 Click the **Picture Effects** button (<img>).

Note: If the image is a shape, the **Picture Effects** button (<img>) is **Shape Effects**.

4 Click **Preset**.

5 Click the effect you want to apply.

C Excel applies the effect to the picture.

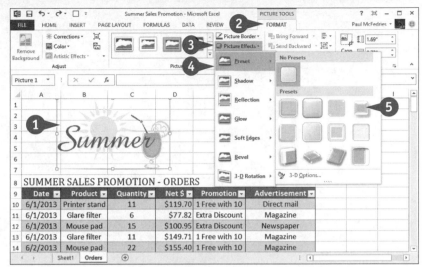

TIPS

I applied a style to a picture, but now I want to change the picture to something else. Do I have to start over?

No. You can simply replace the existing picture with the other picture, and Excel preserves the style so you do not have to repeat your work. Click the existing picture, click the **Format** tab, and then click the **Change Picture** button (<img>). Select the new picture you want to use and then click **Insert**.

If I do not like the formatting I applied to a picture, can I return it to its original look?

Yes. If you have not performed any other tasks since applying the formatting, click **Undo** (<img>) until Excel has removed the formatting. Alternatively, click **Picture Effects** (<img>), click **Preset**, and then click the icon in the **No Presets** section. To reverse all the changes you have made to a picture since you inserted the image, click the picture, click **Format**, and then click **Reset Picture** (<img>).

CHAPTER 20

Importing Data into Excel

Excel offers a number of tools that enable you to import external data into the program. Excel can access a wide variety of external data types. However, this chapter focuses on the six most common types: Data source files, Access tables, Word tables, text files, web pages, and XML files.

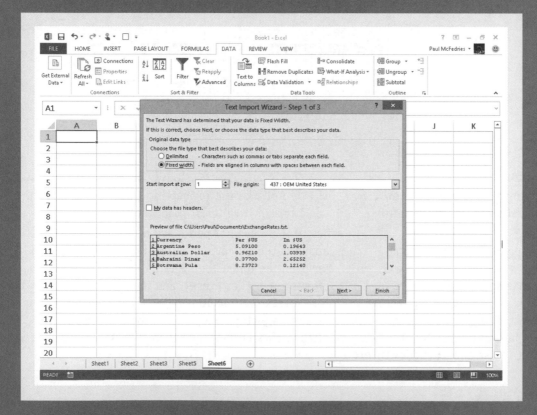

Understanding External Data

External data is data that resides outside of Excel in a file, database, server, or website. You can import external data directly into an Excel PivotTable or worksheet for additional types of data analysis.

Before you learn the specifics of importing external data into your Excel workbooks, you need to understand the various types of external data that you are likely to encounter. For the vast majority of applications, external data comes in one of the following six formats: data sources, Access tables, Word tables, text files, web pages, and XML files.

Data Source File

In Chapter 21, you learn about Open Database Connectivity (ODBC) data sources, which give you access to data residing in databases such as Access and dBase, or on servers such as SQL Server and Oracle. However, there are many other data-source types that connect to specific objects in a data source. For more information, see the section "Import Data from a Data Source."

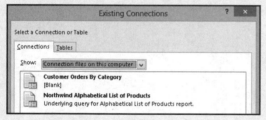

Access Table

Microsoft Access is the Office suite's relational database management system, and so it is often used to store and manage the bulk of the data used by a person, team, department, or company. For more information, see the section "Import Data from an Access Table."

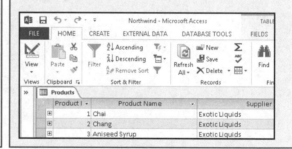

Word Table

Some simple data is often stored in a table embedded in a Word document. You can only perform so much analysis on that data within Word, and so it is often useful to import the data from the Word table into an Excel worksheet. For more information, see the section "Import Data from a Word Table."

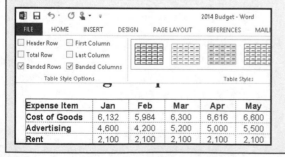

Text File

Text files often contain useful data. If that data is formatted properly — for example, where each line has the same number of items, all separated by spaces, commas, or tabs — then it is possible to import that data into Excel for further analysis. For more information, see the section "Import Data from a Text File."

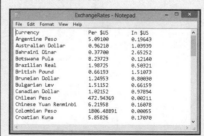

Web Page

People and companies often store useful data on web pages that reside either on the Internet or on company intranets. This data is often a combination of text and tables, but you cannot analyze web-based data in any meaningful way in your web browser. Fortunately, Excel enables you to create a web query that lets you import text and tables from a web page. For more information, see the section "Import Data from a Web Page."

XML

XML — Extensible Markup Language — is redefining how data is stored. This is reflected in the large number of tools that Excel now has for dealing with XML data, particularly tools for importing XML data into Excel. For more information, see the section "Import Data from an XML File."

Access to External Data

To use external data, you must have access to it. This usually means knowing at least one of the following: the location of the data or the login information required to authorize your use of the data.

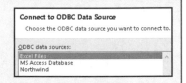

Location

To access external data, you must at least know where it is located. Here are the most common possibilities: in a file on your computer; in a file on your network; on a network server, particularly as part of a large, server-based database management system, such as SQL Server or Oracle; on a web page; and on a web server.

Login

Knowing where the data is located is probably all that you require if you are dealing with a local file or database or, usually, a web page. However, after you start accessing data remotely — on a network, database server, or web server — you will also require authorization to secure that access. See the administrator of the resource to obtain a username or login ID as well as a password.

Import Data from a Data Source

You can quickly import data into just about any format by importing the data from a defined data source file.

In this section, you learn how to import data from a *data connection file*. This is a data source that connects you to a wide variety of data, including ODBC, SQL Server, SQL Server OLAP Services, Oracle, and web-based data retrieval services. You can also read the Tip to learn how to create a data connection file.

Import Data from a Data Source

1 Click the **Data** tab.

2 Click **Get External Data**.

3 Click **Existing Connections**.

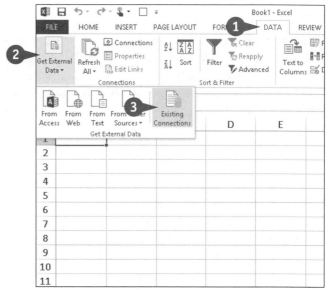

The Existing Connections dialog box appears.

4 Click the data source you want to import.

5 Click **Open**.

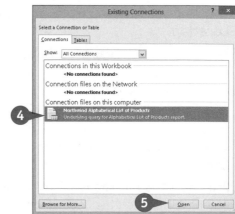

The Import Data dialog box appears.

6 Click the empty **Table** radio button (○) and it is filled (●).

A To import the data directly into a PivotTable, click the empty **PivotTable Report** radio button (○) and it is filled (●).

7 Select the empty **Existing worksheet** radio button (○) and it is filled (●).

8 Click the cell where you want the imported data to appear.

B To import the data to a new sheet, click the empty **New worksheet** radio button (○) and it is filled (●).

9 Click **OK**.

Excel imports the data into the worksheet.

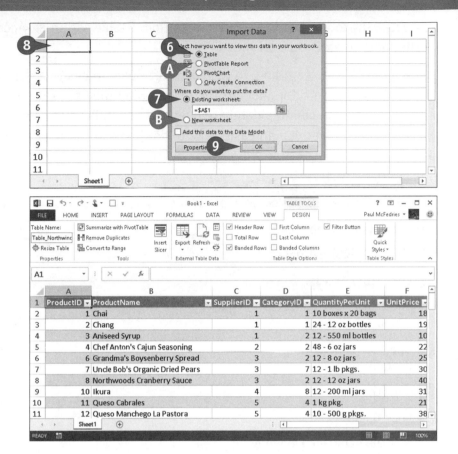

TIP

How do I create a data connection file?

To create your own data connection (.odc) file, click the **Data** tab, click **Get External Data**, click **From Other Sources**, and then click **From Data Connection Wizard.** Click the data source you want, and then click **Next**.

The next steps depend on the data source. For example, for Microsoft SQL Server or Oracle, you specify the server name or address and your server login data. Similarly, for ODBC DSN (Database Source Name), you choose the ODBC data source, specify the location of the file, and select the table or query to which you want to connect.

When you get to the Import Data dialog box, click **OK** to import the data or click **Cancel** if you just want to create the data source file for now.

Import Data from an Access Table

I f you want to use Excel to analyze data from a table within an Access database, you can import
the table to an Excel worksheet.

In Chapter 21, you learn how to use Microsoft Query to create a database query to extract records
from a database, to filter and sort the records, and then to return the results to Excel. Chapter 21
also covers how to create a database query for any ODBC data source, including an Access database.
However, Excel gives you an easier way to do this: You can import the table directly from the Access
database.

Import Data from an Access Table

1 Click the **Data** tab.

2 Click **Get External Data**.

3 Click **From Access**.

The Select Data Source
dialog box appears.

4 Open the folder that
contains the database.

5 Click the file.

6 Click **Open**.

Note: If the Data Link Properties
dialog box appears, make sure
the login information is correct
and then click **Test Connection**
until you can connect, then click
OK.

The Select Table dialog box
appears.

7 Click the table or query you
want to import.

8 Click **OK**.

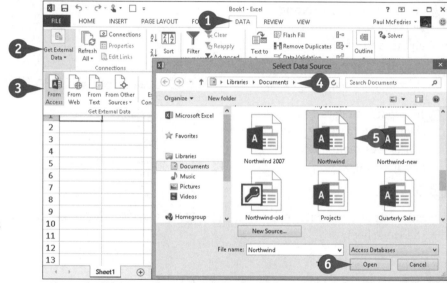

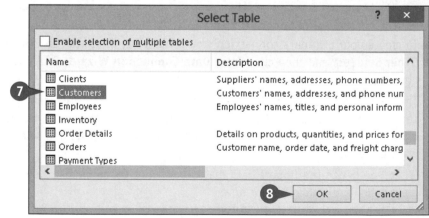

The Import Data dialog box appears.

9 Click the empty **Table** radio button (○) and it is filled (◉).

A To import the data directly into a PivotTable, click the empty **PivotTable Report** radio button (○) and it is filled (◉).

10 Select the empty **Existing worksheet** radio button (○) and it is filled (◉).

11 Click the cell where you want the imported data to appear.

B To import the data to a new sheet, click the empty **New worksheet** radio button (○) and it is filled (◉).

12 Click **OK**.

Excel imports the data to the worksheet.

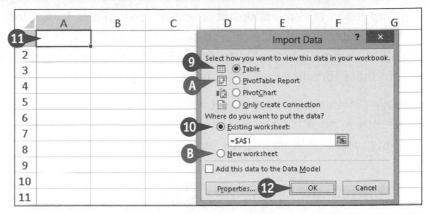

TIP

How can I stop the incessant password prompt?
To avoid this, tell Excel to save the database password along with the external data. Click the **Data** tab, click the **Refresh All** drop-down arrow (▾), and then click **Connection Properties.** In the Connection Properties dialog box, click the **Definition** tab, then click the empty **Save password** check box (□) and it is filled (☑). Click **Yes**, and then click **OK**.

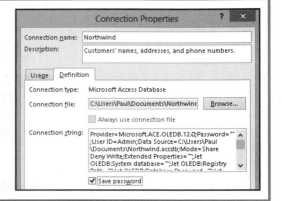

Import Data from a Word Table

Word tables are collections of rows, columns, and cells that look like Excel ranges. You can insert fields into Word table cells to perform calculations. In fact, Word fields support cell references, built-in functions such as SUM and AVERAGE, and operators such as addition (+) and multiplication (*), to build formulas that calculate results based on the table data.

However, even the most powerful Word formulas cannot perform the tasks available to you in Excel, which offers much more sophisticated data analysis tools. Therefore, to analyze your Word table data properly, you should import the table into an Excel worksheet.

Import Data from a Word Table

1. Launch Microsoft Word and open the document that contains the table.

2. Click a cell inside the table you want to import.

3. Click the **Layout** tab.

4. Click **Select**.

5. Click **Select Table**.

A You can also select the table by clicking the table selection handle.

6. Click the **Home** tab.

7. Click **Copy** (🗐).

   You can also press Ctrl + C.

   Word copies the table to the Clipboard.

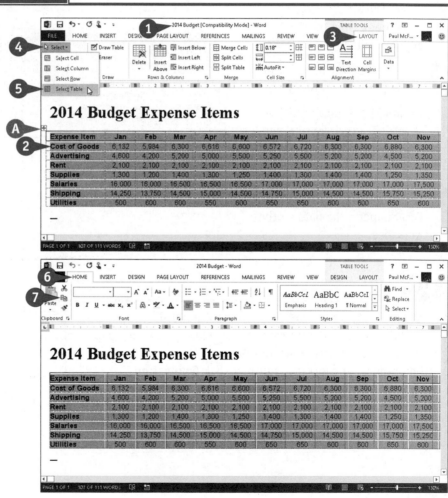

8 Switch to the Excel workbook into which you want to import the table.

9 Click the cell where you want the table to appear.

10 Click the **Home** tab.

11 Click **Paste** (▯).

You can also press Ctrl+V.

Excel pastes the Word table data.

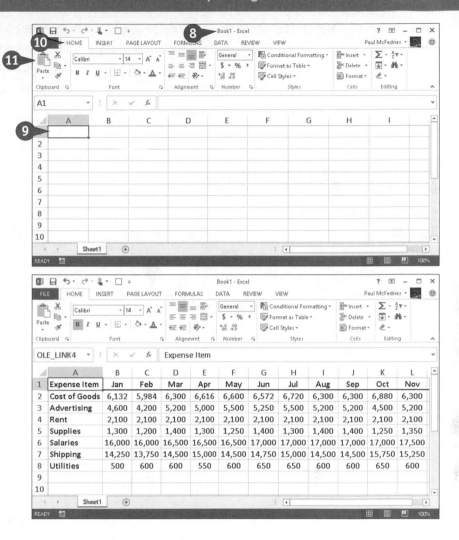

TIP

If I make changes to the Word data, are they reflected in the Excel data?

No. If this is a concern, a better approach is to shift the data's container application from Word to Excel. That is, after you paste the table data into Excel, copy the Excel range, switch to Word, click the **Home** tab, click the **Paste** drop-down arrow (▯), and then click **Paste Special**.

In the Paste Special dialog box, click **HTML Format** in the **As** list, click the empty **Paste link** radio button (○) and it is filled (⦿). Click **OK**, and the resulting table is linked to the Excel data. This means that any changes you make to the data in Excel appear in the Word table automatically. However, if you change the data in Word, you cannot update the original data in Excel.

Import Data from a Text File

Today, most data resides in some kind of special format: an Excel workbook, an Access database, on a web page, and so on. However, it is still relatively common to find data stored in simple text files because it is a universal format — it works on any system and a wide variety of programs. You can analyze the data contained in certain text files by importing the data into an Excel worksheet.

However, you can only import *delimited* or *fixed-width* text files. See the first Tip in this section to learn more.

Import Data from a Text File

Start the Text Import Wizard

1 Click the cell where you want the imported data to appear.

2 Click the **Data** tab.

3 Click **Get External Data**.

4 Click **From Text**.

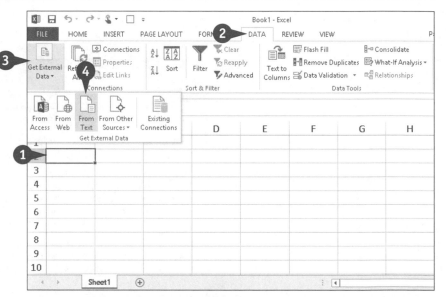

The Import Text File dialog box appears.

5 Open the folder that contains the text file.

6 Click the text file.

7 Click **Import**.

The Text Import Wizard – Step 1 of 3 dialog box appears.

Note: For delimited text, continue with Import Delimited Data; for fixed-width text, skip to Import Fixed-Width Data.

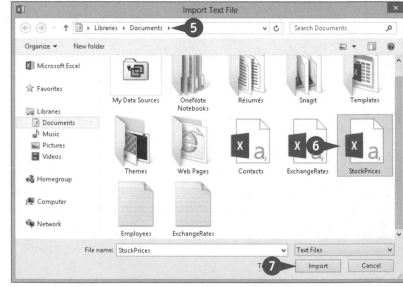

Import Delimited Data

1. Click the empty **Delimited** radio button (○) and it is filled (◉).

2. Use the **Start import at row** spin box to set the first row you want to import.

3. If the first import row is column headers, click the empty **My data has headers** check box (□) and it is filled (☑).

4. Click **Next**.

   The Text Import Wizard – Step 2 of 3 dialog box appears.

5. Click the empty check box (□) beside the delimiter character your data uses and it is filled (☑).

(A) If you choose the correct delimiter, the data appears in separate columns.

6. Click **Next**.

   The Text Import Wizard – Step 3 of 3 dialog box appears.

Note: To complete this section, follow the steps under "Finish the Text Import Wizard."

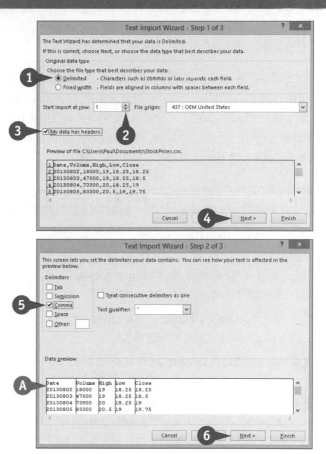

TIP

What are delimited and fixed-width text files?

A *delimited* text file uses a text structure in which each item on a line of text is separated by a character called a *delimiter*. The most common text delimiter is the comma (,). A delimited text file is imported into Excel by treating each line of text as a record and each item between the delimiter as a field.

A *fixed-width* text file uses a text structure in which all of the items on a line of text use a set amount of space — say, 10 or 20 characters — and these fixed widths are the same on every line of text. A fixed-width text file is imported into Excel by treating each line of text as a record and each fixed-width item as a field.

continued ▶

Import Data from a Text File (continued)

If you are importing data that uses the fixed-width structure, you must tell Excel where the separation between each field occurs.

In a fixed-width text file, each column of data is a constant width. The Text Import Wizard is usually quite good at determining the width of each column and, in most cases, the wizard automatically sets up *column break lines*, which are vertical lines that separate one field from the next. However, titles or introductory text at the beginning of the file can impair the wizard's calculations. Make sure the proposed break lines are accurate.

Import Data from a Text File (continued)

Import Fixed-Width Data

Note: You need to have run through the steps under "Start the Text Import Wizard" before continuing with this section.

1. Click the empty **Fixed width** radio button (○); it is filled (◉).

2. Use the **Start import at row** spin box to set the first row you want to import.

3. If the first import row consists of column headers, click the empty **My data has headers** check box (□); it is filled (☑).

4. Click **Next**.

   The Text Import Wizard – Step 2 of 3 dialog box appears.

5. Click and drag a break line to set the width of each column.

   To create a break line, you can click the ruler at the point where you want the break to appear.

   To delete a break line, you can double-click it.

6. Click **Next**.

   The Text Import Wizard – Step 3 of 3 dialog box appears.

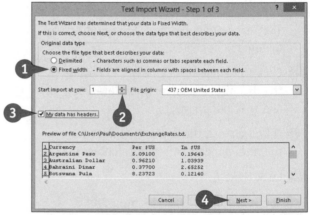

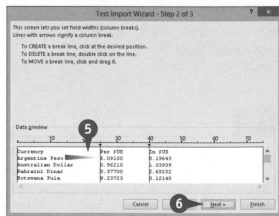

Finish the Text Import Wizard

1 Click a column.

2 Click the empty radio button (○) of the data format you want to apply to the column and it is filled (◉).

Ⓐ If you select the Date option, you can use this drop-down list to select the date format your data uses.

3 Repeat Steps 1 and 2 to set the data format for all of the columns.

4 Click **Finish**.

The Import Data dialog box appears.

5 Click the empty **Existing worksheet** radio button (○); it is filled (◉).

Ⓑ If you want the data to appear in a new sheet, click the empty **New worksheet** radio button (○); it is filled (◉).

6 Click **OK**.

Excel imports the data to the worksheet.

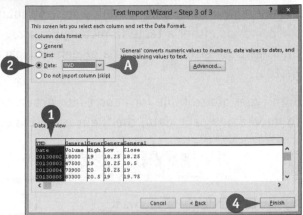

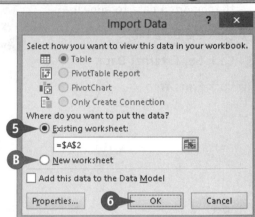

TIPS

What do I do when my data uses a comma instead of a dot as the decimal separator?

To import such data, click **Advanced** in the Text Import Wizard – Step 3 of 3 dialog box to display the Advanced Text Import Settings dialog box. Click the **Decimal separator** drop-down arrow (▾), and then click the text's decimal separator. You can also click the **Thousands separator** drop-down arrow (▾), and then click the text's thousands separator.

If I make a mistake when importing a text file, do I have to start over?

No. Click any cell in the imported data, click the **Data** tab, click the **Refresh All** drop-down arrow (▾), and then click **Connection Properties**. Click the **Definition** tab, and then click **Edit Query**. The Import Text File dialog box appears. Click the file you want, and then click **Import**. Excel launches the Import Text Wizard so you can run through the options again.

Import Data from a Web Page

Data is often available on web pages. Although this data is usually text, some web page data comes as either a table (a rectangular array of rows and columns) or as preformatted text (text that has been structured with a predefined spacing used to organize data into columns with fixed widths).

Both types are suitable for import into Access so that you can perform more extensive data analysis. To import web page data, the file must reside on your computer or on your network.

Import Data from a Web Page

1 Click the cell where you want the imported data to appear.

2 Click the **Data** tab.

3 Click **Get External Data**.

4 Click **From Web**.

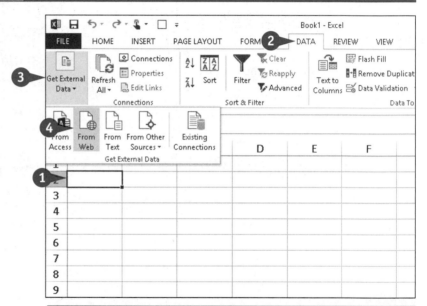

The New Web Query dialog box appears.

5 Type the address of the web page.

6 Click **Go**.

Ⓐ Excel loads the page into the dialog box.

7 Click the **Select Table** icon (⬛) beside the table that you want to import.

Ⓑ Excel selects the table.

8 Click **Import**.

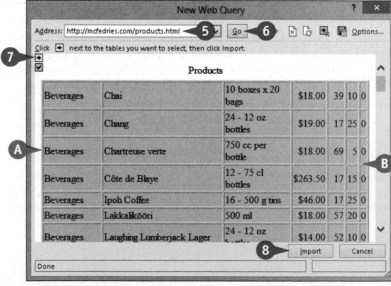

The Import Data dialog box appears.

9 Click the empty **Existing worksheet** radio button (○) and it is filled (◉).

C If you want the data to appear in a new sheet, click the empty **New worksheet** radio button (○) and it is filled (◉).

10 Click **OK**.

Excel imports the data to the worksheet.

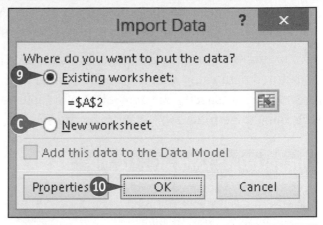

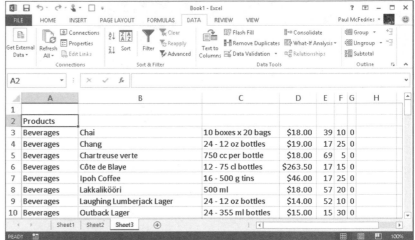

TIP

Are there other ways to import a web page into Excel?

Yes. Excel gives you two other methods for creating web queries. Both of these alternative methods assume that you already have the web page open in Internet Explorer:

- Right-click the page and then click **Export to Microsoft Excel**.
- Copy the web page text, switch to Excel, and then paste the text. When the Paste Options smart tag appears, click the smart tag drop-down arrow (⌄), and then click **Refreshable Web Query**.

Each of these methods opens the New Web Query dialog box and automatically loads the web page. If you want to save the web query for future use in other workbooks, click **Save Query** (🖫) in the New Web Query dialog box, and then use the Save Workspace dialog box to save the query file.

Import Data from an XML File

You can analyze data that currently resides in XML format by importing that data into Excel and then manipulating and analyzing the resulting table.

XML or *extensible markup language*, is a standard that enables the management and sharing of structured data using simple text files. These XML files organize data using *tags,* among other elements, that specify the equivalent of a table name and field names. Because XML is just text, if you want to perform data analysis on the XML file, you must import the XML file into an Excel table.

Import Data from an XML File

1. Click the cell where you want the imported data to appear.

2. Click the **Data** tab.

3. Click **Get External Data**.

4. Click **From Other Sources**.

5. Click **From XML Data Import**.

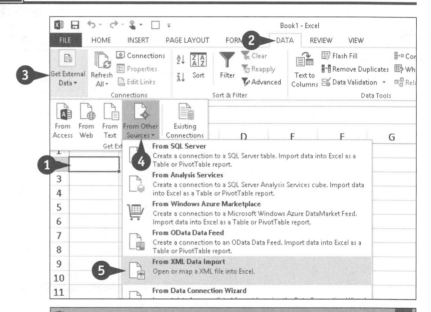

The Select Data Source dialog box appears.

6. Select the folder that contains the XML file you want to import.

7. Click the XML file.

8. Click **Open**.

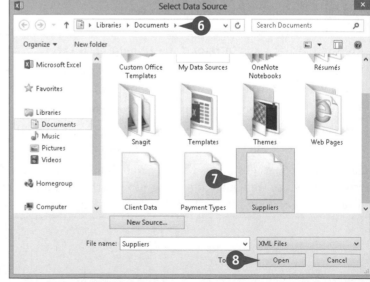

460

Note: If you see a dialog box that says there is a problem with the data, click **OK**.

The Import Data dialog box appears.

9 Click the empty **XML table in existing worksheet** radio button (○) and it is filled (●).

10 Click **OK**.

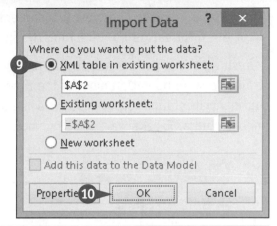

Excel imports the data into the worksheet as an XML table.

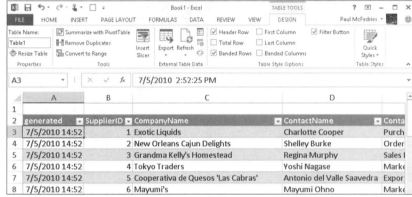

TIPS

What does an XML file look like?

An XML file is a text file that uses a specific structure. Here is a simple XML example that constitutes a single record in a table named *Products*:

```
<Products>
<ProductName>Chai</ProductName>
<CompanyName>Exotic Liquids</CompanyName>
<ContactName>Charlotte Cooper</
ContactName>
</Products>
```

Can I remove a field in the XML table?

Yes. Right-click the XML table, click **XML**, and then click **XML Source** to display the XML Source pane. The XML Source pane displays a list of the fields — called *elements* in the XML table. To remove an element, right-click it, and then click **Remove element**. To add an element back into the XML list, right-click the element and then click **Map element**.

Refresh Imported Data

External data often changes; you can ensure that you are working with the most up-to-date version of the information by refreshing the imported data.

Refreshing the imported data means retrieving the most current version of the source data. This is a straightforward operation most of the time. However, it is possible to construct a query that accesses confidential information or destroys some or all of the external data. Therefore, when you refresh imported data, Excel always lets you know the potential risks and asks if you are sure the query is safe.

Refresh Imported Data

Refresh Non-Text Data

1 Click any cell inside the imported data.

2 Click the **Data** tab.

3 Click the **Refresh All** drop-down arrow (⌄).

4 Click **Refresh**.

Note: You can also refresh the current data by pressing Alt + F5.

To refresh all the imported data in the current workbook, you can click Refresh All, or press Ctrl + Alt + F5.

Excel refreshes the imported data.

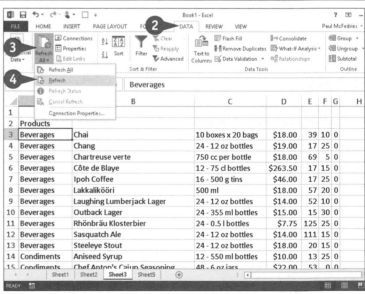

Refresh Text Data

1. Click any cell inside the imported text data.

2. Click the **Data** tab.

3. Click the **Refresh All** drop-down arrow (⌄).

4. Click **Refresh**.

Note: You can also refresh the current data by pressing Alt + F5.

The Import Text File dialog box appears.

5. Open the folder that contains the text file.

6. Click the text file.

7. Click **Import**.

Excel refreshes the imported text data.

TIPS

Is there an easier way to refresh data regularly?
In most cases, you can set up a schedule that automatically refreshes the data at a specified interval. Follow Steps 1 to 3 under "Refresh Non-Text Data," and then click **Connection Properties**. Click the empty **Refresh Every** check box (☐) and it is filled (☑). Use the spin box to specify the refresh interval in minutes (not every type of imported data supports this feature).

Why does my refresh not seem to be working?
The refresh may take a long time. To check the status of the refresh, follow Steps 1 to 3 under "Refresh Non-Text Data," and then click **Refresh Status** to display the External Data Refresh Status dialog box. Click **Close** to continue the refresh. If the refresh is taking too long, follow Steps 1 to 3 again, and then click **Cancel Refresh**.

Separate Cell Text into Columns

You can make imported data easier to analyze by separating the text in each cell into two or more columns of data.

An imported data column may contain multiple items of data. In imported contact data, for example, a column might contain each person's first and last name, separated by a space. This is problematic when sorting the contacts by last name, so you need to organize the names into separate columns. Excel makes this easy with the Text to Columns feature, which examines a column of data, and then separates it into two or more columns.

Separate Cell Text into Columns

1 Insert a column to the right of the column you want to separate.

Note: If the data will separate into three or more columns, you can insert as many new columns as you need to hold the separated data.

2 Select the data you want to separate.

3 Click the **Data** tab.

4 Click **Text to Columns** (📋).

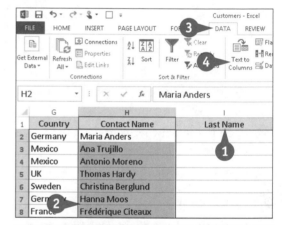

The Convert Text to Columns Wizard – Step 1 of 3 dialog box appears.

5 Click the empty **Delimited** radio button (○) and it is filled (⊙).

6 Click **Next**.

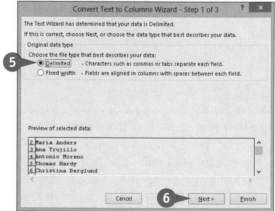

⑦ Click the empty check box (☐) beside the delimiter character that your text data uses and it is filled (☑).

Ⓐ If you choose the correct delimiter, the data appears in separate columns.

⑧ Click **Next**.

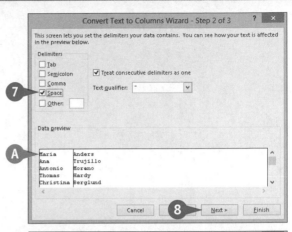

⑨ Click a column.

⑩ Click to select the data format you want Excel to apply to the column.

Ⓑ If you clicked the empty **Date** radio button (○), you can use this list to select the format your data uses.

⑪ Repeat Steps **9** and **10** to set the data format for all columns.

⑫ Click **Finish**.

Excel asks if you want to replace the contents of the destination cells.

⑬ Click **OK** (not shown).

Excel separates the data.

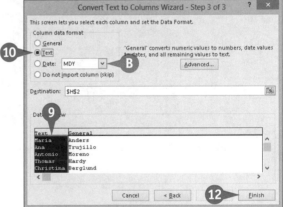

TIPS

What do I do if my column contains fixed-width text?

Follow Steps **1** to **4** to start the Convert Text to Columns Wizard. Click the empty **Fixed width** radio button (○) and it is filled (⊙). Click **Next**, and then click and drag a break line to set the width of each column. Click **Next** and follow Steps **9** to **13** to complete the wizard.

Does Excel always create only one extra column from the data?

Not always. For example, in a column of contact names, if any of those names use three words, Excel assumes that you want to create two extra columns for all the data. Unfortunately, this might cause Excel to overwrite some of your existing data. Therefore, before separating data into columns, check the data to see exactly how many columns Excel will create.

CHAPTER 21

Querying Data Sources

If you want to build a table or a PivotTable using a sorted, filtered subset of an external data source, you must use Microsoft Query to specify the sorting and filtering options, and the subset of the source data with which you want to work.

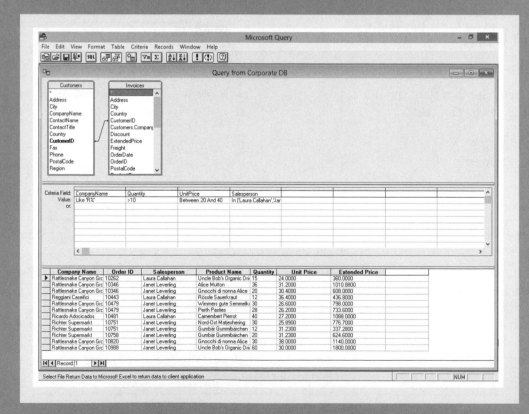

Understanding Microsoft Query

Microsoft Query is a special program that you can use to perform all the database query tasks mentioned in this section. You can use Microsoft Query to create data sources, add tables to a query, specify fields, filter records using criteria, and sort records. You can also save your queries as query files so that you can reuse them later. If you start Microsoft Query from within Excel, you can return the query records to Excel and use them in a table or PivotTable.

Data Source

All database queries require two things at the very beginning: access to a database, and an Open Database Connectivity (ODBC) data source for the database installed on your computer. ODBC is a database standard that enables a program to connect to and manipulate a data source. You learn how to create a new data source in the section "Define a Data Source."

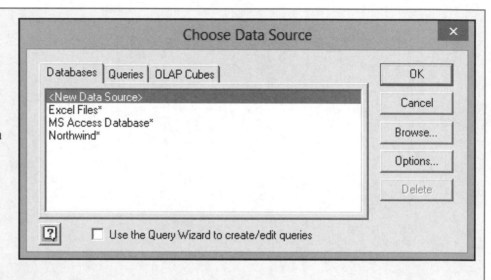

Database Query

Database queries make a large database more manageable by enabling you to perform three tasks: Selecting the tables and fields with which you want to work, filtering the records so that you only get the records you want, and sorting the data that you are extracting.

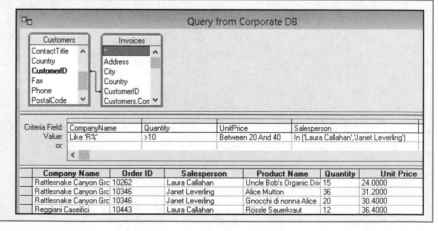

Query Criteria

You can specify the filtering portion of a database query by specifying one or more *criteria*. These are usually logical expressions that, when applied to each record in the query's underlying table, return either a true or false result. Every record that returns a true result is included in the query; every record that returns a false result is filtered out of the query. For example, if you only want to work with records where the Country field is equal to USA, you can set up criteria to do this.

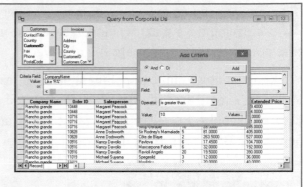

Criteria Operators

The following table lists the operators you can use to build your criteria expressions:

Operator	Value in the Field
Equals (=)	Is equal to a specified value.
Does not equal (<>)	Is not equal to a specified value.
Is greater than (>)	Is greater than a specified value.
Is greater than or equal to (≥=)	Is greater than or equal to a specified value.
Is less than (<)	Is less than a specified value.
Is less than or equal to (≤=)	Is less than or equal to a specified value.
Is one of	Is included in a group of values.
Is not one of	Is not included in a group of values.
Is between	Is between (and including) one value and another.
Is not between	Is not between (and does not include) one value and another.
Begins with	Begins with the specified characters.
Does not begin with	Does not begin with the specified characters.
Ends with	Ends with the specified characters.
Does not end with	Does not end with the specified characters.
Contains	Contains the specified characters.
Does not contain	Does not contain the specified characters.
Like	Matches a specified pattern.
Not like	Does not match a specified pattern.
Is Null	Is empty.
Is Not Null	Is not empty.

Define a Data Source

Before you can do any work in Microsoft Query, you must select the data source that you want to use. If you have a particular database that you want to query, you can define a new data source that points to the appropriate file or server.

Most data sources point to database files. For example, the relational database management program Microsoft Access uses file-based databases. You can also create data sources based on text files and Excel workbooks. However, some data sources point to server-based databases. For example, SQL Server and Oracle run their databases on special servers.

Define a Data Source

1. Click the **Data** tab.

2. Click Get **External Data**.

3. Click **From Other Sources**.

4. Click **From Microsoft Query**.

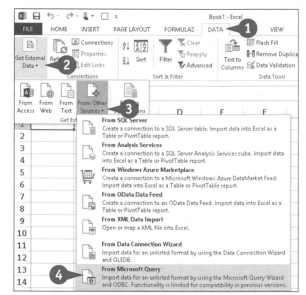

The Choose Data Source dialog box appears.

5. Click **New Data Source**.

6. Click the selected **Use the Query Wizard to create/edit queries** check box (☑) and it is cleared (☐).

7. Click **OK**.

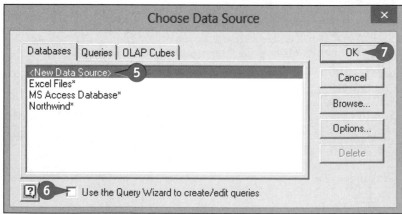

The Create New Data Source dialog box appears.

8 Type a name for your data source.

9 Click the **Select a driver for the type of of database you want to access** drop-down arrow (☑), and then click the database driver that your data source requires.

10 Click **Connect**.

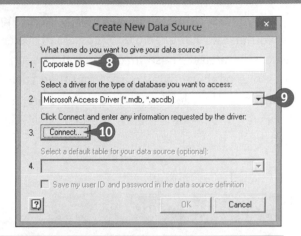

The dialog box for the database driver appears.

Note: The steps that follow show you how to set up a data source for a Microsoft Access database.

11 Click **Select**.

TIP

How do I set up an SQL Server data source?

Many businesses store data on the Microsoft SQL Server database system. This is a powerful server-based system that can handle the largest databases and thousands of users. To define a data source for an SQL Server installation on your network or some other remote location, first follow Steps **1** to **8**.

In the drop-down list of database drivers, click **SQL Server**. Click **Connect** to display the SQL Server Login dialog box. Ask your SQL Server database administrator for the information you require to complete this dialog box.

Type the name or remote address of the SQL Server in the **Server** text box, type your SQL Server login ID and password, and then click **OK**. Perform Steps **16** and **17** later in this section to complete the SQL Server data source.

continued ▶

Define a Data Source (continued)

The Choose Data Source dialog box often shows predefined data sources created by programs that you install. For example, Microsoft Office creates two default data sources: Excel Files and MS Access Database. These incomplete data sources do not point to a specific file. Instead, when you click one of these data sources and then click **OK,** Microsoft Query prompts you for the name and location of the file. These data sources are useful if you often switch the files that you are using. However, if you want a data source that always points to a specific file, follow the steps in this section.

Define a Data Source (continued)

The Select Database dialog box appears.

⑫ Open the folder that contains the database.

⑬ Click the database file.

⑭ Click **OK.**

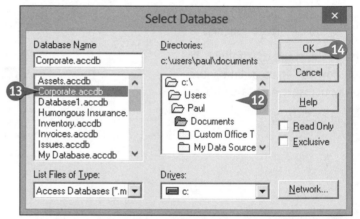

Excel returns you to the database driver's dialog box.

Ⓐ If you must provide a login name and password to access the database, click **Advanced** to display the Set Advanced Options dialog box. Type the login name and password and then click **OK.**

⑮ Click **OK.**

Excel returns you to the Create New Data Source dialog box.

B If you specified a login name and password as part of the data source, click the empty **Save my user ID and password in the data source definition** check box (☐) and it is filled (☑). This saves the login data.

16 Click **OK**.

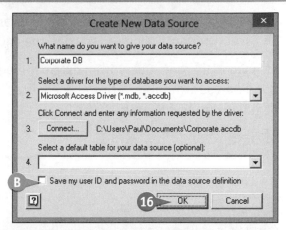

You are returned to the Choose Data Source dialog box.

17 Click **Cancel** to bypass the steps for importing the data.

Note: You will learn how to perform these steps in the rest of this chapter.

You can now use the data source in Microsoft Query.

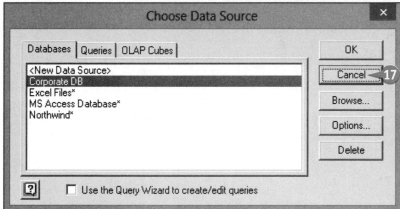

TIPS

Is there an advantage to selecting a default table in my data source?
Yes. In the Create New Data Source dialog box, you can click the **Select a default table for your data source** drop-down arrow (☑), and then click a table from the Access database. When you do this, each time you start a new query based on this data source, Microsoft Query automatically adds the default table to the query, thus saving you several steps.

Can I delete a data source?
Yes. If you have a data source that you no longer use, you should delete it to ensure that only usable data sources appear in the Choose Data Source dialog box. Follow Steps 1 to 4 to display the Choose Data Source dialog box. Click the data source, and then click the **Delete** button. When Microsoft Query asks you to confirm the deletion, click **Yes**.

Start Microsoft Query

To create a query that defines the fields and records that you want to return to and work with in Excel, you must begin by starting the Microsoft Query program.

Although Microsoft Query is an external program, you always start it from within Excel. That way, the data you configure with the query is automatically returned to Excel so that you can immediately begin analyzing the data.

Start Microsoft Query

1. Click the **Data** tab.

2. Click Get **External Data**.

3. Click **From Other Sources**.

4. Click **From Microsoft Query**.

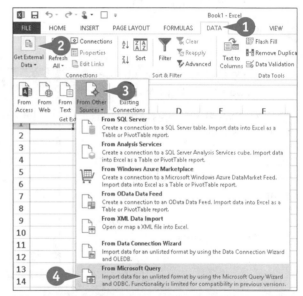

The Choose Data Source dialog box appears.

5. Click the data source with which you want to work.

6. Click the selected **Use the Query Wizard to create/edit queries** check box (☑) and it is cleared (☐).

7. Click **OK**.

The Microsoft Query window and the Add Tables dialog box appear.

Note: To learn how to use the Add Tables dialog box, see the section "Add a Table to a Query."

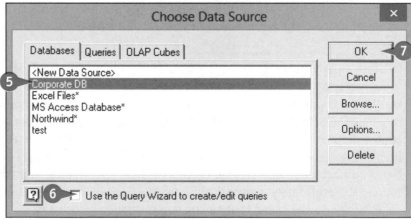

474

Tour the Microsoft Query Window

You can get the most out of Microsoft Query if you understand the layout of the screen and what each part of the Microsoft Query window represents.

Although you have not yet created a query using the Microsoft Query program, it is worthwhile to pause now and look at the various elements that make up the Microsoft Query window. Do not worry if what you currently see on your screen does not look like the window shown in this section. By the time you finish this chapter, you will have seen and worked with all the elements shown here.

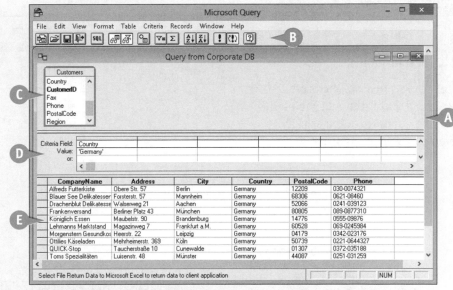

Ⓐ Query Window

Here, you create, edit, and preview the results. The window is divided into three panes: Table, criteria, and results.

Ⓑ Toolbar

The toolbar contains buttons that give you one-click access to many of the most useful features in Microsoft Query.

Ⓒ Table Pane

This displays one list for each table you add to the query. Each list shows the fields that are part of the table.

Ⓓ Criteria Pane

Here, you define the criteria that filter the records you want to return to Excel.

Ⓔ Query Results

As you change the aspects of a query, Microsoft Query updates this pane (also called the *data grid*) to show the effect of your changes.

Add a Table to a Query

With your data source created and Microsoft Query started, the next step is to add a table to the query.

In a database, a *table* is a two-dimensional arrangement of rows and columns that contain data. The columns are *fields* that represent distinct categories of data, and the rows are *records* that represent individual sets of field data. In some database management systems, the actual database files are tables. However, in most systems, each database contains a number of tables. Therefore, your first Microsoft Query task, in most cases, is to select the table with which you want to work.

Add a Table to a Query

1 Click **Table**.

2 Click **Add Tables**.

Note: When you start Microsoft Query from Excel, the Add Tables dialog box appears automatically, so you can skip Steps 1 and 2.

The Add Tables dialog box appears.

Ⓐ You can also open this dialog box by clicking **Add Tables** (🔲).

3 Click the table you want to add.

4 Click **Add**.

Ⓑ Microsoft Query adds the table to the table pane.

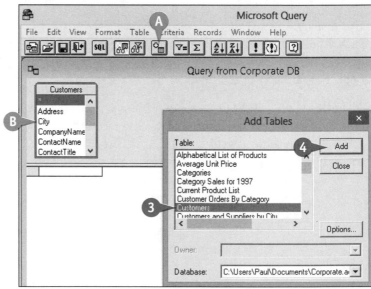

⑤ Repeat Steps 3 and 4 if you want to add multiple, related tables to the query.

Ⓒ If the tables are related, Microsoft Query displays a join line that connects the common fields.

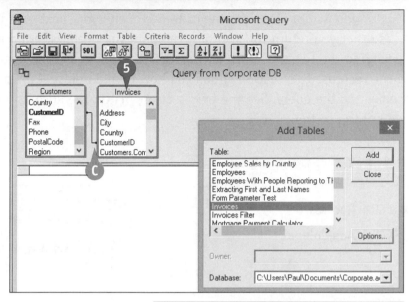

⑥ Click **Close**.

You are now ready to add fields to the query, as described in the next section.

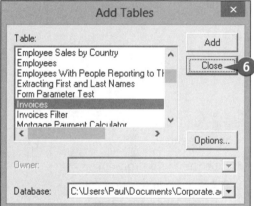

TIPS

Can I join two tables myself?
Yes. Click **Table,** and then click **Joins** to display the Joins dialog box. Click the **Left** drop-down arrow (⌄), and then click the common field from one of your tables. Click the **Right** drop-down arrow (⌄), and then click the common field from the other table. Click the **Operator** drop-down arrow (⌄), and then click =. Click **Add** and then click **Close**.

How do I remove a table from my query?
To remove a table from the query, first click the table in the table pane. Click **Table** and then click **Remove Table**. Alternatively, click the table and then press Delete. Microsoft Query deletes the table list. If you added fields from the table to the criteria pane or the results pane, Microsoft Query removes those fields as well.

Add Fields to a Query

After you add one or more tables to the query, your next step is to filter the resulting records so that you return to Excel only the data you need. Filtering the records involves two tasks: Specifying the fields with which you want to work and specifying the criteria you want to apply to the records. This section shows you how to add fields — or *columns*, as Microsoft Query calls them — to the query. See the next section, "Filter the Records with Query Criteria," to learn how to add criteria to the query.

Add Fields to a Query

1 Click **Records**.

2 Click **Add Column**.

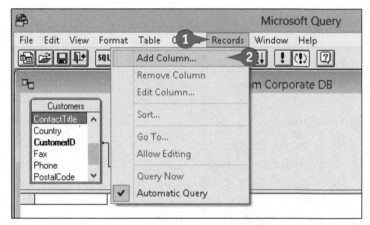

The Add Column dialog box appears.

3 Click the **Field** drop-down arrow (⌄), and then click the field you want to add.

A If you want to use a different field name, type it in the **Column heading** text box.

4 Click **Add**.

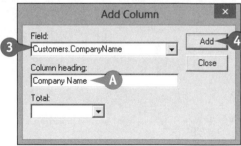

B Microsoft Query adds the field to the results pane.

C You can also either double-click a field name in a table list, or click and drag a field name in a table list and drop it inside the results pane.

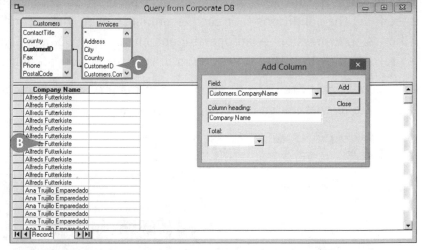

5 Repeat Steps 3 and 4 until you have added all the fields that you want to appear in the query.

6 Click **Close**.

Note: To change where a field appears in the data grid, first click the field heading to select the entire field. Then click and drag the field heading to the left or right and drop the field into the new position.

TIPS

What is the asterisk that appears at the top of each table list?

The asterisk (*) item represents all the fields in the table. So, if you know that you want to include in your query every field from a particular table, you do not need to add the fields individually. Instead, you can add the asterisk "field" to the query.

How do I remove a field from my query?

If you no longer need a field in the query, you should delete it from the data grid. Click the field heading or click any cell in the field; note that Microsoft Query does not ask for confirmation when you delete a field, so be sure you click the correct field. Click **Records** and then click **Remove Column** (or just press Delete).

Filter the Records with Query Criteria

To display the specific records that you want to return to Excel, you must filter the records by specifying the conditions that each record must meet. These conditions are called *criteria*, each of which is an expression — an operator and one or more values — applied to a specific field. Only those records for which the expression returns a true answer are included in the query results.

If you use multiple criteria, you can include in the results those records that match *all* the criteria, or those records that match *any one* of the criteria.

Filter the Records with Query Criteria

1. Click **Show/Hide Criteria** (⬚).

Ⓐ Microsoft Query displays the criteria pane.

2. Click **Criteria**.

3. Click **Add Criteria**.

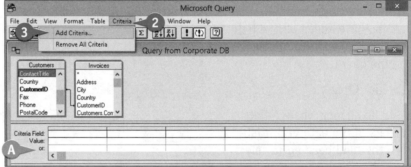

The Add Criteria dialog box appears.

4. Click the **Field** drop-down arrow (⌄), and then click the field to which you want the criteria applied.

5. Click the **Operator** drop-down arrow (⌄), and then click the operator you want to use.

6. Type the value or values for the criteria.

Ⓑ To use a value from the selected field, you can click **Values**, click the value you want to use, and then click **OK**.

7. Click **Add**.

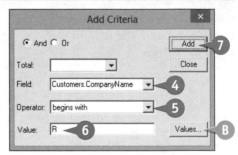

C Microsoft Query adds the criteria to the criteria pane.

D Microsoft Query filters the results to show only those records that satisfy the criteria.

Note: If you do not want to specify multiple criteria, skip to Step 10.

8 To add another criterion and display records that meet all the criteria you specify, click the empty **And** radio button (○) and it is filled (◉).

E To display records that meet at least one of the criteria you specify, click the empty **Or** radio button (○) and it is filled (◉).

9 Repeat Steps 3 to 7 until you have added all the criteria that you want to appear in the query.

10 Click **Close**.

F Microsoft Query filters the records to show only those that match your criteria.

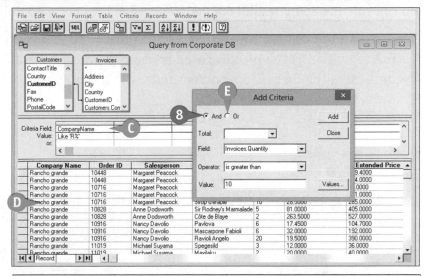

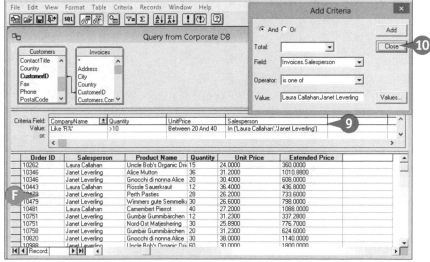

TIPS

How do I make changes to the criteria?
To change the field to which a criteria expression applies, use the criteria pane to click the field name, click the **Query** drop-down arrow (⯆) that appears, and then click the field you want to use. To change the criteria expression, either edit the expression directly in the criteria pane, or double-click the expression to display the Edit Criteria dialog box.

How do I delete a criterion from the query?
Click the bar just above the field name to select the entire criterion; note that Microsoft Query does not ask for confirmation when you delete a criterion, so be sure you click the correct one. Then press **Delete**. If you want to remove all the criteria and start over, click **Criteria,** and then click **Remove All Criteria**.

Sort Query Records

You can sort the query results on one or more fields to get a good look at your data.

You can sort the records either in ascending order (0 to 9, A to Z) or descending order (9 to 0, Z to A). You can also sort the records based on more than one field. In this case, Microsoft Query sorts the records using the first field, and then sorts within those results on the second field.

Sort Query Records

1 Click **Records**.

2 Click **Sort**.

The Sort dialog box appears.

3 Click the **Column** drop-down arrow (▼), and then click the field you want to sort.

4 To select a sort order, click the empty **Ascending** or **Descending** radio button (○) and it is filled (◉).

5 Click **Add**.

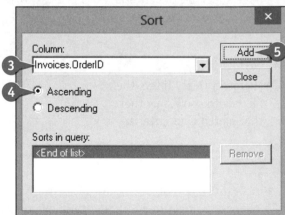

A Microsoft Query sorts the records in the results pane.

B Microsoft Query adds the sort to the Sorts in query list.

6 Repeat Steps 3 to 5 until you have added all the sorts that you want to use.

7 Click **Close**.

Microsoft Query sorts the records.

If you only want to sort the query results on a single field, you can click any cell in that field and then click one of the following icons:

C Click **Sort Ascending** (↑) to sort the field in ascending order.

D Click **Sort Descending** (↓) to sort the field in descending order.

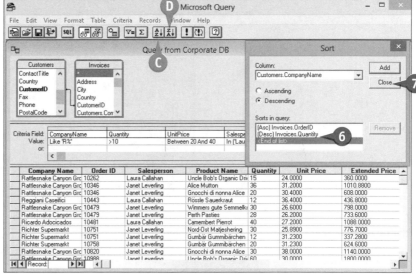

TIPS

Is there an easier way to sort on multiple fields?
You can use the toolbar to sort multiple fields. Organize the fields in the results pane so that they are side by side in the order in which you want to apply the sort. Click and drag the mouse pointer (↖) from the heading of the first sort field to the heading of the last. Finally, click either **Sort Ascending** (↑) or **Sort Descending** (↓).

How do I remove a sort that I no longer need?
Click **Records** and then click **Sort** to display the Sort dialog box. In the Sorts in query list, click the sort that you want to delete, and then click **Remove**.

Return the Query Results

After you finish adding fields to the query, filtering the data using criteria, and sorting the data, you are ready to return the results to Excel for use in your worksheet.

To manipulate or analyze the query data, you need to return the query results to Excel, and then start a new table or PivotTable based on those results. If you think you will reuse the query at a later date, you should save the query before returning the results. This section also shows you how to save and open Microsoft Query files.

Return the Query Results

1 Click **File**.

Ⓐ You can combine Steps 1 and 2 by clicking **Return Data** (⬚).

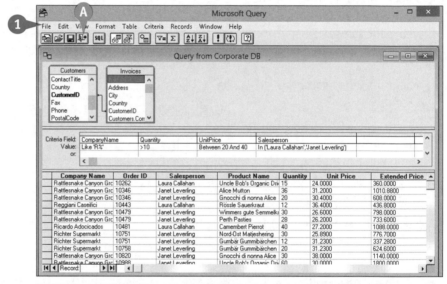

2 Click **Return Data to Microsoft Excel**.

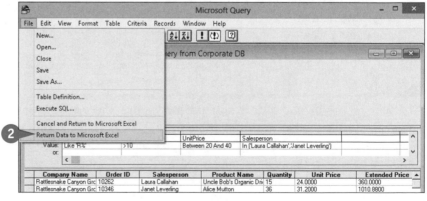

The Import Data dialog box appears.

3 Click the empty **Table** radio button (○) and it is filled (◉).

B If you want to create a PivotTable, click the empty **PivotTable Report** radio button (○) and it is filled (◉).

4 Click the empty **Existing worksheet** radio button (○) and it is filled (◉).

5 Click the cell where you want the imported data to appear.

C If you want the data to appear in a new sheet, click the empty **New worksheet** radio button (○) and it is filled (◉).

6 Click **OK**.

D Excel imports the query data into the worksheet.

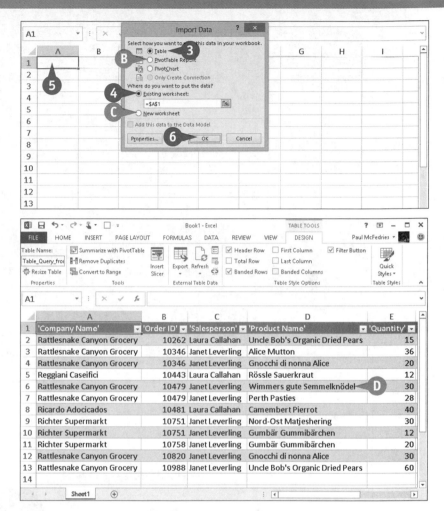

TIPS

How do I make changes to the query?

Click any cell in the table (or PivotTable), click the **Design** tab, click the **Refresh All** drop-down arrow (▾), and then click **Connection Properties** to open the Connection Properties dialog box. Click the **Definition** tab and then click the **Edit Query** button. This starts Microsoft Query and loads the query results. Make your changes, and then return the data to Excel.

How do I save and reuse a query?

To save a query using Microsoft Query, click **File**, and then click **Save** to display the Save As dialog box. Select the folder in which you want to store the query file, type a filename, and then click **Save**. To use the query file, start Microsoft Query, click **File**, click **Open** to display the Open Query dialog box, click the query file, and then click **Open**.

CHAPTER 22

Collaborating with Others

If you want to collaborate with other people on a workbook, Excel gives you several ways to do this, including adding comments, sharing a workbook, and even working on a spreadsheet online. You can also control your collaborations by protecting worksheet data and tracking the changes that others make.

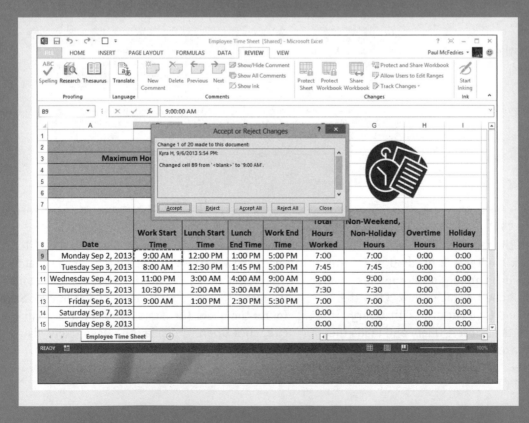

Add a Comment to a Cell

If you have received a workbook from another person, you can provide feedback to that person by adding a comment to a cell in the workbook. A comment is often the best way to provide corrections, questions, critiques, and other feedback because it does not change anything on the actual worksheet.

Each comment is attached to a particular cell and Excel uses a comment indicator to mark which cells have comments. When you view a comment, Excel displays the comment in a balloon.

Add a Comment to a Cell

Add a Comment

1 Click the cell on which you want to comment.

2 Click the **Review** tab.

3 Click **New Comment** (🗊).

Note: You can also right-click the cell and then click **Insert Comment**.

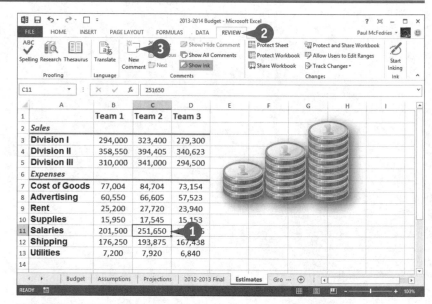

Excel displays a comment balloon.

Ⓐ Excel precedes the comment with your Excel username.

4 Type your comment.

5 Click outside the comment balloon.

Ⓑ Excel adds a comment indicator (◥) to the top-right corner of the cell.

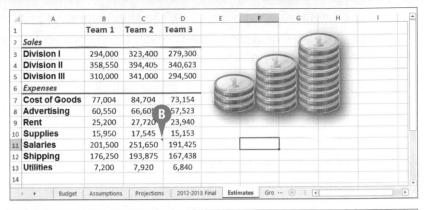

View a Comment

① Move the mouse pointer (☼) over the cell.

Ⓒ Excel displays the comment in a balloon.

Ⓓ In the Review tab, you can also click **Next** (☐) and **Previous** (☐) to run through the comments.

Ⓔ In the Review tab, you can also click **Show All Comments** (☐) to display every comment at once.

TIPS

Can I edit or remove a comment?

Yes. To edit an existing comment, click the cell that contains the comment, click the **Review** tab, click **Edit Comment** (☐) to open the comment in a balloon, and then edit the balloon text. To remove a comment, click the cell that contains the comment, click the **Review** tab, and then click **Delete Comment** (☐).

How do I change my Excel username?

Your username is important because it tells other people who added the comments. If your username consists of only your first name or initials, you can change it. Click **File,** and then click **Options** to open the Excel Options dialog box. Click the **General** tab, edit the name in the **User name** text box, and then click **OK** (this does not change your username in existing comments).

Protect a Worksheet's Data

If you will be distributing a workbook to other people, you can enable the options in Excel for safeguarding worksheet data by activating the sheet's protection feature. You can also configure the worksheet to require a password to unprotect it.

To safeguard worksheet data, you can either unlock only those cells that users are allowed to edit, or you can configure a range to require a password before it can be edited.

Protect a Worksheet's Data

1 Display the worksheet you want to protect.

2 Click the **Review** tab.

3 Click **Protect Sheet** (▦).

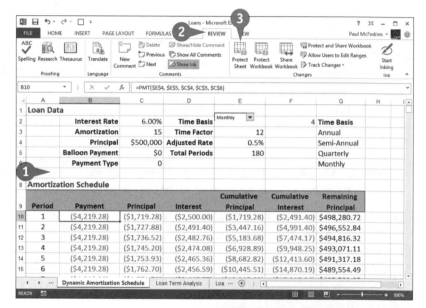

Excel displays the Protect Sheet dialog box.

4 Make sure the **Protect worksheet and contents of locked cells** check box is selected (☑).

5 Type a password in the **Password to unprotect sheet** text box.

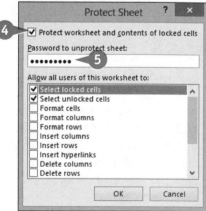

6 Click the empty check box (☐) beside each action that you want to allow unauthorized users to perform and it is filled (☑).

7 Click **OK**.

Excel asks you to confirm the password.

8 Type the password.

9 Click **OK**.

If you want to make changes to a worksheet, click the **Review** tab, click **Unprotect Sheet** (🔲), type the unprotect password, and then click **OK**.

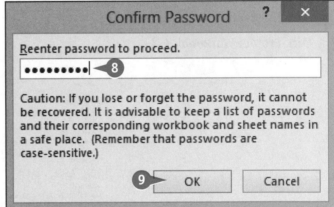

TIPS

When I protect a worksheet, can I allow users to edit some of the cells?

Yes. This is useful when you have a data entry area or other range you want people to be able to edit, but you do not want them to alter other parts of the worksheet. Unprotect the sheet if it is protected, select the range you want to unlock, click **Home**, click **Format**, and then click **Lock Cell** to turn off that option for the selected range.

When I protect a worksheet, can I configure a range to require a password before a user can edit the range?

Yes. First, unprotect the sheet if necessary. Select the range you want to protect, click the **Review** tab, and then click **Allow Users to Edit Ranges**. Click **New** in the Allow Users to Edit Ranges dialog box to open the New Range dialog box. Type a title for the range, type a password in the **Range** text box, and then click **OK**. When prompted to retype the password, do so, and then click **OK**.

Protect a Workbook's Structure

You can prevent unwanted changes to a workbook by activating protection for the workbook's structure. You can also configure the workbook to require a password to unprotect it.

Protecting a workbook's structure means preventing users from inserting new worksheets, renaming or deleting existing worksheets, moving or copying worksheets, hiding and unhiding worksheets, and more. See the tips at the end of this section to learn which commands Excel disables when you protect a workbook's structure.

Protect a Workbook's Structure

1 Display the workbook you want to protect.

2 Click the **Review** tab.

3 Click **Protect Workbook** (⊞).

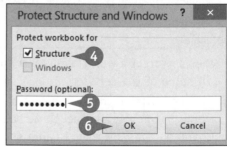

Excel displays the Protect Structure and Windows dialog box.

4 Click the empty **Structure** check box (☐) and it is filled (☑).

5 Type a password in the **Password** text box, if required.

6 Click **OK**.

If you specified a password,
Excel asks you to confirm it.

7 Type the password.

8 Click **OK**.

A Excel disables most
worksheet-related commands
on the Ribbon.

B Excel disables most
worksheet-related commands
on the worksheet shortcut
menu.

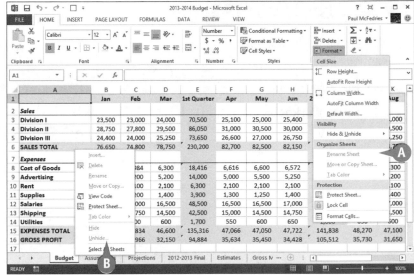

TIPS

What happens when I protect a workbook's structure?

Excel disables most worksheet-related commands, including Insert Sheet, Delete Sheet, Rename Sheet, Move or Copy Sheet, Tab Color, Hide Sheet, and Unhide Sheet. Excel also prevents the Scenario Manager from creating a summary report.

How do I remove workbook structure protection?

If you no longer require your workbook structure to be protected, you can remove the protection by following Steps **1** to **3**. If you protected your workbook with a password, type the password and then click **OK**. Excel removes the workbook's structure protection.

Share a Workbook with Other Users

You can allow multiple users to modify a workbook simultaneously by sharing the workbook. Once you share a workbook, other users can open it via a network connection and edit the file at the same time. Note that Excel cannot share a workbook that contains a table, so you need to convert any tables to ranges before performing this task (see Chapter 15 for more information).

When you share a workbook, Excel automatically begins tracking the changes made to the file. For more information on this feature, see the following section, "Track Workbook Changes."

Share a Workbook with Other Users

1 Display the workbook you want to share.

2 Click the **Review** tab.

3 Click **Share Workbook** (🗒).

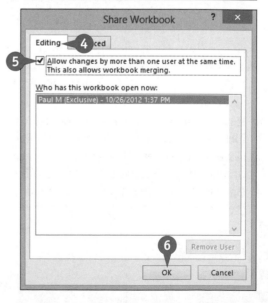

The Share Workbook dialog box appears.

4 Click the **Editing** tab.

5 Click the empty **Allow changes by more than one user at the same time** check box (☐) and it is filled (☑).

6 Click **OK**.

Excel tells you that it will now save the workbook.

7 Click **OK**.

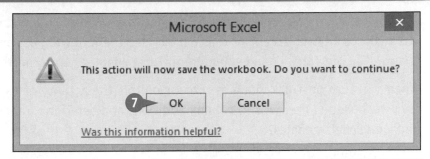

Excel saves the workbook and activates sharing.

A Excel displays [Shared] in the title bar.

You and users on your network can now edit the workbook at the same time.

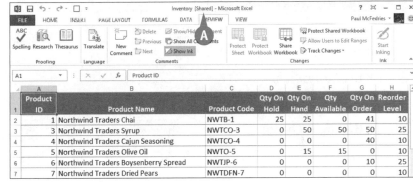

TIP

How do I know if other people currently have the workbook open?
To see a list of the users who have the workbook open, follow these steps:

1 Display the shared workbook.

2 Click the **Review** tab.

3 Click **Share Workbook** (🖳).

The Share Workbook dialog box appears.

4 Click the **Editing** tab.

A The **Who has this workbook open now** list displays the users who are currently editing the file.

5 Click **OK**.

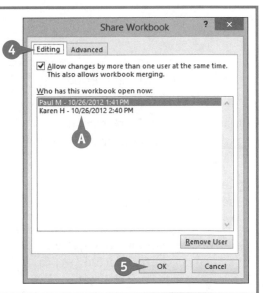

Track Workbook Changes

If you want other people to make changes to a workbook, you can keep track of those changes so you can either accept or reject them (see the following section, "Accept or Reject Workbook Changes"). The Track Changes feature in Excel enables you to do this.

When you turn on Track Changes, Excel monitors the activity of each reviewer and stores that reviewer's cell edits, row and column additions and deletions, range moves, worksheet insertions, and worksheet renames.

Track Workbook Changes

1 Display the workbook you want to track.

2 Click the **Review** tab.

3 Click **Track Changes** (📝).

4 Click **Highlight Changes**.

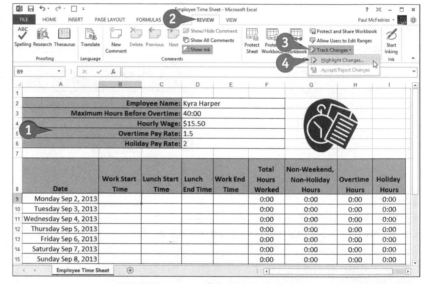

The Highlight Changes dialog box appears.

5 Click the empty **Track changes while editing** check box (☐) and it is filled (☑).

Ⓐ Leave the **When** check box selected (☑) and leave **All** selected in the list.

Ⓑ Leave the **Highlight changes on screen** check box selected (☑) to view the workbook changes.

6 Click **OK**.

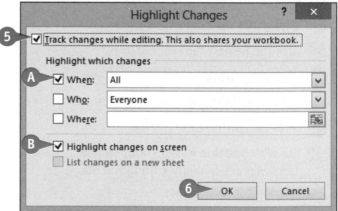

Excel tells you it will now save the workbook.

7 Click **OK**.

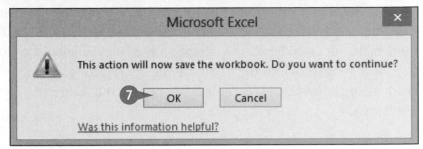

Excel activates the Track Changes feature.

D Excel shares the workbook and indicates this by displaying [Shared] beside the workbook name.

Note: See the previous section, "Share a Workbook with Other Users," to learn more about workbook sharing.

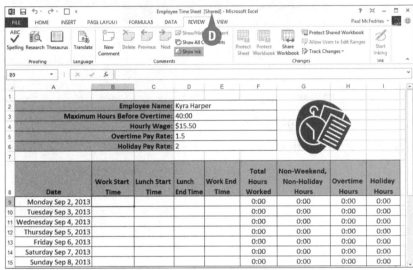

TIPS

Is there a way to avoid having my own changes highlighted?

Yes. You can configure the workbook to show every user's changes but your own. Follow Steps 1 to 4 to open the Highlight Changes dialog box. Click the empty **Who** check box (☐) and it is filled (☑). Click the **Who** drop-down arrow (⌄), and then click **Everyone but Me**. Click **OK** to put the new setting into effect.

Can I track changes in just part of the worksheet?

Yes. You can modify this task so that Excel only tracks changes in a specific range. Follow Steps 1 to 4 to open the Highlight Changes dialog box. Click the empty **Where** check box (☐) and it is filled (☑). Click inside the **Where** range box, and then select the range you want to track. Click **OK** to put the new setting into effect.

Accept or Reject Workbook Changes

After you turn on the Track Changes features in Excel, you can accept or reject the changes that other users make to the workbook. As a general rule, you should accept the changes that other users make to a workbook. The exception is when you know a change is incorrect. If you are not sure, it is best to talk to the other user before rejecting a change. If you and another user make changes to the same cell, Excel lets you resolve the conflict by accepting your edit or the other user's edit.

Accept or Reject Workbook Changes

1. Display the workbook you are tracking.

2. Click the **Review** tab.

3. Click **Track Changes** (⬚).

4. Click **Accept/Reject Changes**.

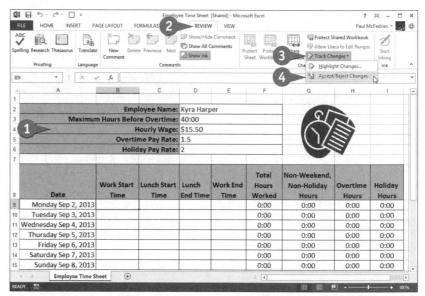

If your workbook has unsaved changes, Excel tells you it will now save the workbook.

5. Click **OK**.

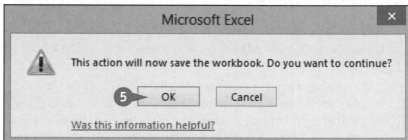

The Select Changes to Accept or Reject dialog box appears.

A Leave the **When** check box selected (☑) and leave **Not yet reviewed** selected in the list.

B To review changes made by a particular user, click the empty **Who** check box (☐) and it is filled ☑. Click the **Who** drop-down arrow (☑), and then click the user's name.

6 Click **OK**. The Accept or Reject Changes dialog box appears.

C Excel displays the details of the current change.

7 Click an action.

D Click **Accept** to keep the change or **Reject** to remove it.

Excel displays the next change.

8 Repeat Step **7** to review all the changes.

E Click **Accept All** or **Reject All**.

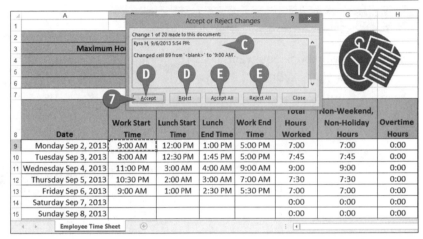

TIPS

What happens if I and another user make changes that affect the same cell?
When you save the workbook, the Accept or Reject Changes dialog box appears, which shows the changes you both made. Click the correct change, and then click **Accept**. If there are multiple conflicts, you can click your change or the other user's, and then click either **Accept All** or **Reject All**.

When I complete my review, should I turn off the tracking feature?
Yes, unless you know that other people still require access to the workbook. Click the **Review** tab, click **Track Changes** (☐), and then click **Highlight Changes** to open the Highlight Changes dialog box. Click the selected **Track changes while editing** check box (☑) to clear it (☐), and then click **OK**.

Save a Workbook to Your SkyDrive

If you are using Windows 8 under a Microsoft account, then as part of that account you get a free online storage area called *SkyDrive*. You can use Excel to add any of your workbooks to your SkyDrive. This is useful if you are going to be away from your computer but still require access to a workbook. Because the SkyDrive is accessible anywhere you have web access, you can view and work with your spreadsheet without using your computer.

Save a Workbook to Your SkyDrive

1. Open the workbook you want to save to your SkyDrive.

2. Click the **File** tab.

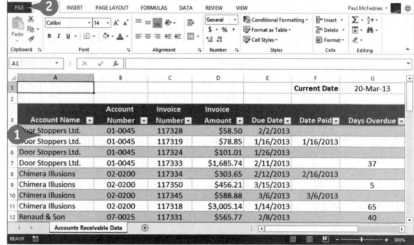

3. Click **Save As**.

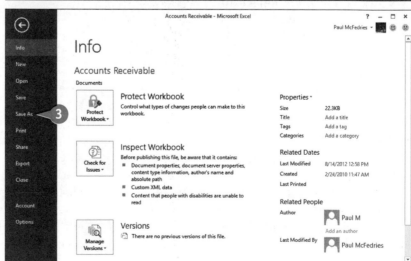

The Save As screen appears.

4 Click your SkyDrive.

A If you see the SkyDrive folder you want to use to store the workbook, click it, and then skip to Step 8.

5 Click **Browse**.

The Save As dialog box appears.

6 Click **SkyDrive**.

Note: The first time you save a file to your SkyDrive, you might see a folder that uses a series of letters and numbers as its name instead of the SkyDrive folder.

7 Double-click the subfolder in which you want to store the workbook.

8 Click **Save**.

Excel saves the workbook to your SkyDrive.

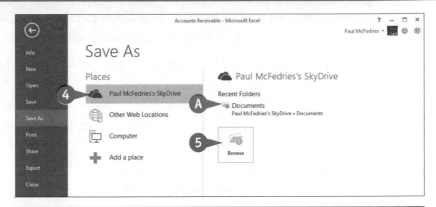

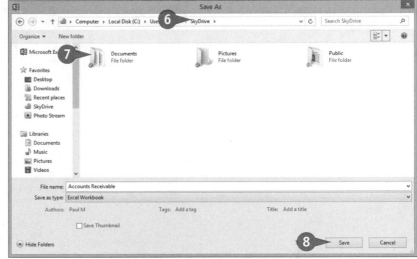

TIP

How do I open a workbook saved to my SkyDrive?
Follow these steps:

1 Click the **File** tab.

2 Click **Open**.

3 Click your SkyDrive.

4 Click **Browse**.

The Open dialog box appears.

5 Open the SkyDrive folder that contains the workbook.

6 Click the workbook.

7 Click **Open**.

Excel opens the SkyDrive workbook.

Send a Workbook as an E-Mail Attachment

If you want to send an Excel workbook to another person, you can attach the workbook to an e-mail message and send it to that person's e-mail address.

A typical e-mail message is fine for short notes but you may have something more complex to communicate, such as budget numbers or a loan amortization. Instead of trying to copy that information to an e-mail message, it would be better to send the recipient a workbook that contains the data. That way, the other person can then open the workbook in Excel after receiving your message.

Send a Workbook as an E-Mail Attachment

1 Open the workbook you want to send.

2 Click the **File** tab.

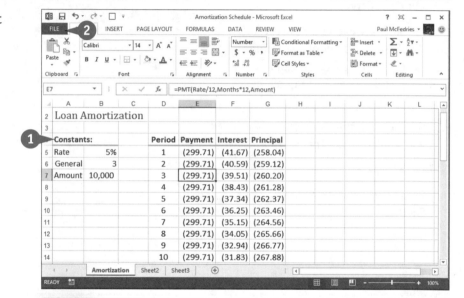

3 Click **Share**.

4 Click **Email**.

Excel displays the Email commands.

5 Click **Send as Attachment**.

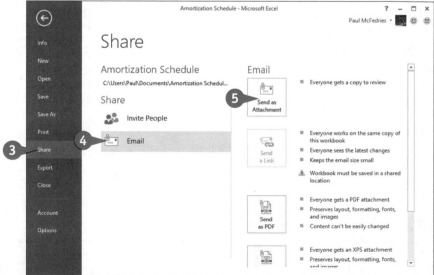

Outlook creates a new e-mail message.

Ⓐ Outlook attaches the workbook to the message.

⑥ Type the address of the recipient.

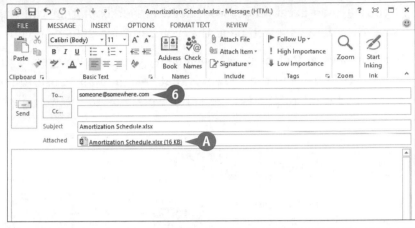

⑦ Type your message text.

⑧ Click **Send**.

Outlook sends the message.

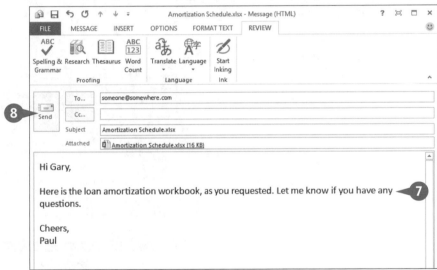

TIPS

Are there any restrictions related to sending file attachments?

There is no practical limit to the number of workbooks you can attach to a message. However, if you or the recipient has a slow Internet connection, sending or receiving the message can take a long time. Also, many Internet service providers (ISPs) place a limit on the size of a message's attachments (usually between 2 and 10MB).

What can I do if the recipient does not have Excel?

You can send the workbook in a different format. One possibility is to save the workbook as a web page (see the section "Save Excel Data as a Web Page"). Alternatively, if your recipient can view PDF (Portable Document Format) files, follow Steps 1 to 4 to display the Email commands, and then click **Send as PDF**.

Save Excel Data as a Web Page

If you have an Excel range, worksheet, or workbook that you want to share on the web, you can save that data as a web page that you can then upload to your website.

When you save a document as a web page, you can also specify the title text that appears in the browser's title bar and the keywords that search engines use to index the page. You can also choose whether you want to publish the entire workbook to the web, just a single worksheet, or just a range of cells.

Save Excel Data as a Web Page

1 Open the workbook that contains the data you want to save as a web page.

A If you want to save a worksheet as a web page, click the worksheet tab.

B If you want to save a range as a web page, select the range.

2 Click the **File** tab.

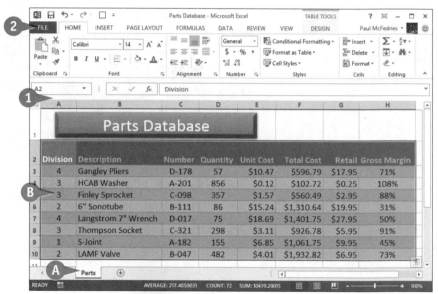

3 Click **Save As**.

4 Click **Computer**.

5 Click **Browse**.

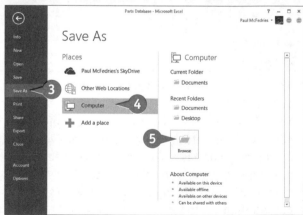

The Save As dialog box appears.

6 Click the **Save as type** drop-down arrow (⌄), and then click **Web Page**.

7 Select the folder where you want to store the web page file.

8 Click **Change Title**.

The Enter Text dialog box appears.

9 Type the page title in the **Page title** text box.

10 Click **OK**.

11 Click **Tags,** and then type keywords separated by semicolons.

12 Choose the empty radio button (○) of the part of the file you want to save as a web page; it is filled (◉).

C Click the empty **Entire Workbook** radio button (○) to save the whole workbook; it is filled (◉).

D Click the empty **Selection** radio button (○) to save either the current worksheet or the selected cells; it is filled (◉).

13 Click **Save**.

Excel saves the data as a web page.

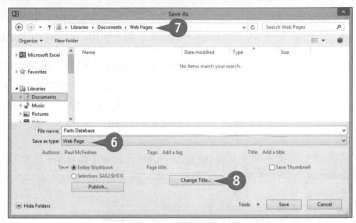

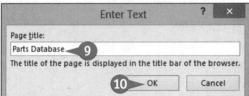

TIP

If I make frequent changes to the workbook, do I have to go through this procedure after every change?
No. Follow Steps 1 to 11, and then click **Publish.** In the Publish as Web Page dialog box, click the empty **AutoRepublish every time this workbook is saved** check box (☐) and it is filled (☑). Click **Publish.** Excel saves the workbook as a web page and will now update the web page file each time you save the workbook.

Make a Workbook Compatible with Earlier Versions of Excel

You can save an Excel workbook in a special format that makes it compatible with earlier versions of Excel. This enables you to share your workbook with other Excel users.

If you have another computer that uses a version of Excel prior to Excel 2007, or if the people you work with use earlier Excel versions, those programs cannot read documents in the standard format used by Excel 2013, Excel 2010, and Excel 2007. By saving a workbook using the Excel 97-2003 Workbook file format, you make that file compatible with earlier Excel versions.

Make a Workbook Compatible with Earlier Versions of Excel

1 Open the workbook you want to make compatible.

2 Click **File**.

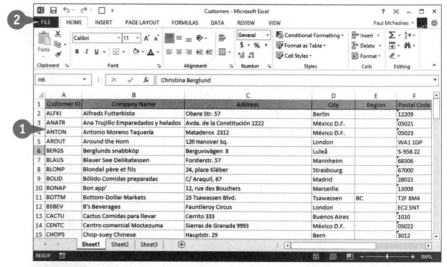

3 Click **Save As**.

4 Click **Computer**.

5 Click **Browse**.

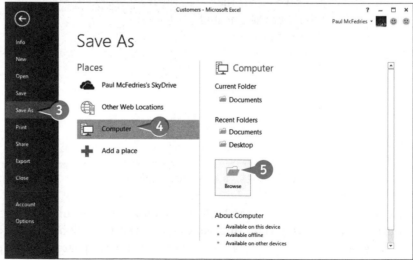

The Save As dialog box appears.

⑥ Select the folder in which you want to store the new workbook.

⑦ Click in the **File name** text box and type the name that you want to use for the new workbook.

⑧ Click the **Save as type** drop-down arrow (⌄).

⑨ Click the **Excel 97-2003 Workbook** file format.

⑩ Click **Save**.

Excel saves the file using the Excel 97-2003 Workbook format.

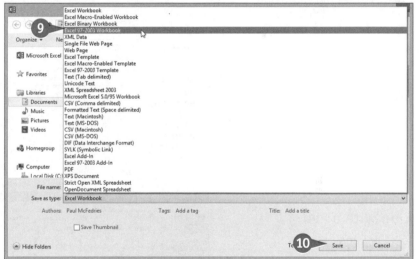

TIPS

Can people using Excel 2010 and Excel 2007 open my Excel 2013 workbooks?

Yes. The default file format used by both Excel 2010 and Excel 2007 is the same as the one used by Excel 2013. If you only work with people who use these Excel versions, then you should stick with the default file format — which is called Excel Workbook — because it offers many benefits in terms of Excel features.

Which versions of Excel are compatible with the Excel 97-2003 Workbook file format?

For Windows, this format is compatible with Excel 97, Excel 2000, Excel XP, and Excel 2003. For the Mac, the Excel 97-2003 Workbook file format is compatible with Excel 98, Excel 2001, and Office 2004. In the unlikely event that you need to share a document with someone using either Excel 5.0 or Excel 95, use the Microsoft Excel 5.0/95 Workbook file format instead.

Mark Up a Worksheet with a Digital Pen

Excel comes with a digital ink feature that enables you to give feedback by marking up a worksheet with pen marks and highlights. This is often easier than adding comments or cell text.

To use digital ink on a worksheet, you must have either a tablet PC or a graphics tablet, each of which comes with a pressure-sensitive screen. You can then use a digital pen — or sometimes your finger — to draw directly on the screen, a technique known as *digital inking*.

Mark Up a Worksheet with a Digital Pen

Activate Digital Inking

1. Tap the **Review** tab.

2. Tap **Start Inking** (✎).

   Excel enables digital inking.

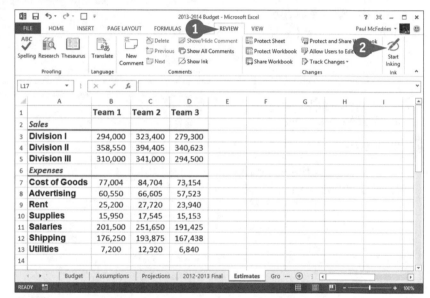

Mark Up with a Pen

1. Tap the **Pens** tab.

2. Tap **Pen** (✎).

3. Use the **Pens** gallery to select a pen color and thickness.

   Ⓐ You can also use the **Color** (≡) and **Thickness** (≡) buttons to customize the pen.

4. Use your digital pen (or finger) to write your marks or text on the worksheet.

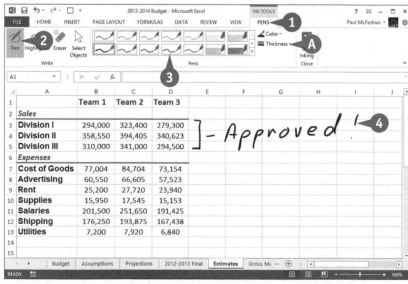

Mark Up with a Highlighter

1 Tap the **Pens** tab.

2 Tap **Highlighter** ( ).

3 Use the **Pens** gallery to select a highlighter color and thickness.

B You can also use **Color** (≡) and **Thickness** (≡) to customize the highlighter.

4 Use the digital pen (or your finger) to highlight the worksheet text.

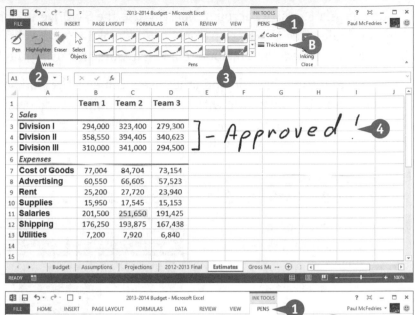

Erase Digital Ink

1 Tap the **Pens** tab.

2 Tap **Eraser** ( ).

3 Use your digital pen (or finger) to tap the ink you want to remove.

Excel erases the ink.

C When you no longer need to mark up the worksheet with digital ink, tap **Stop Inking** ( ).

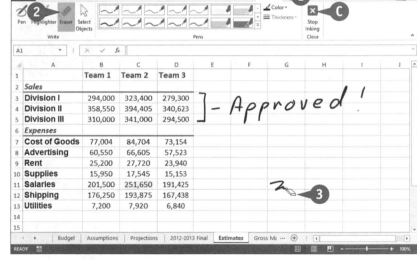

TIP

Is there a way to hide a worksheet's digital ink without deleting that ink?
Yes. This is a good idea if you want to show the worksheet to other people but you do not want them to see the digital ink, either because it contains sensitive information or because it makes the worksheet harder to read. To toggle your digital ink off and on, click the **Review** tab, and then click **Show Ink** ( ).

Collaborate on a Workbook Online

If you have a Microsoft account, you can use the SkyDrive feature to store an Excel workbook in an online folder (see the section "Save a Workbook to Your SkyDrive," earlier in this chapter), and then allow other users to collaborate on that workbook using the Excel Web App.

Collaboration means that you and other users can edit the workbook online simultaneously. To allow another person to collaborate with you on your online workbook, it is not necessary that the person have a Microsoft account. However, you can make your online workbooks more secure by requiring collaborators to have a Microsoft account.

Collaborate on a Workbook Online

① Use a Web browser to navigate to http://skydrive.live.com.

Note: If you are not already logged in, you are prompted to log on to your Microsoft account.

Your SkyDrive appears.

② Click the folder that contains the workbooks you want to share.

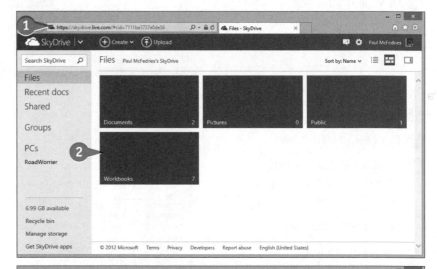

③ Click **Share folder**.

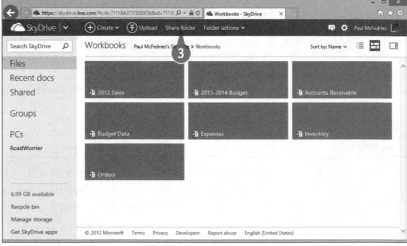

The folder's sharing options appear.

④ Click **Send email**.

⑤ Type the e-mail address of the person with whom you want to collaborate.

Note: To add multiple addresses, press `Tab` after each one.

⑥ Type a message to the user.

⑦ Click the empty **Recipients can edit** check box (□); it is filled (☑).

⑧ If you want to require users to sign in with a Microsoft account, click the empty **Require everyone who accesses this to sign in** check box (□); it is filled (☑).

⑨ Click **Share**.

SkyDrive sends an e-mail message to the user. The user clicks the link in that message, optionally logs on with a Microsoft account, and can then edit a workbook in the shared folder.

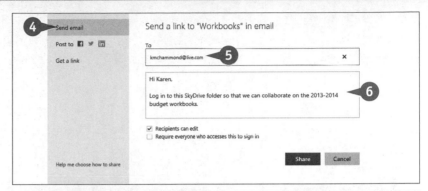

TIP

How do I know when other people are also using a workbook online?

When you open a workbook using the Excel Web App, examine the lower-right corner of the Excel screen. If you see **1 person editing**, it means you are the only user working on the file. If you see **2 people editing**, it means another person is collaborating on the workbook with you. To see who it is, click the **2 people editing** message, as shown here.

CHAPTER 23

Protecting Excel Data

Many Excel models are exceedingly complex structures that are the result of many hours of patient and painstaking work. Other worksheets may contain data that is vital and irreplaceable. Whether your Excel data is complex, important, or one-of-a-kind, you want to protect that data to avoid losing it or having to re-create it.

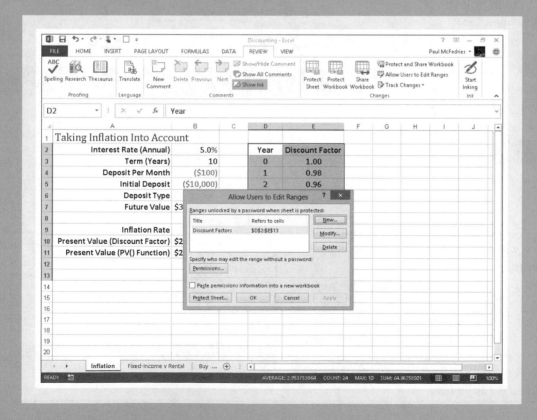

Open a Read-Only Version of a Workbook

Once you have a workbook the way you want it, you may still have to open the file from time to time to check some data. Each time you open the file, there is some danger that you will accidentally add, edit, or delete data.

To prevent this, you can open the document as read-only. You can still make changes to the document, but you cannot save those changes. If you select the Save command for a read-only workbook, Excel displays the Save As dialog box and forces you to save the revised workbook to a different file.

Open a Read-Only Version of a Workbook

1 Click the **File** tab.

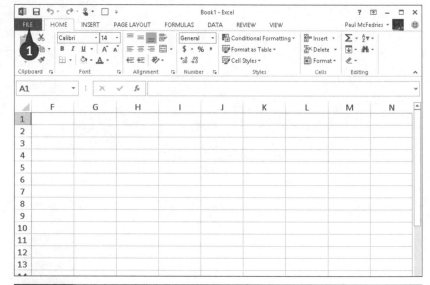

2 Click **Open**.
3 Click **Computer**.
4 Click **Browse**.

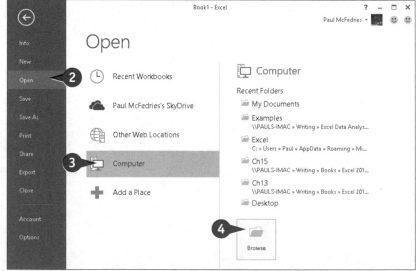

The Open dialog box appears.

⑤ Open the folder containing the workbook you want to open.

⑥ Click the workbook.

⑦ Click the **Open** drop-down arrow (⌄).

⑧ Click **Open Read-Only**.

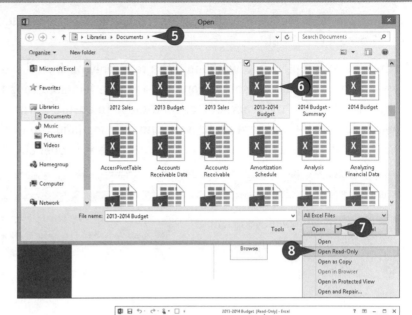

Excel opens a read-only copy of the workbook.

Ⓐ Read-Only appears in the title bar.

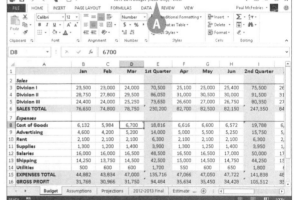

TIP

Is there an easier way to enable other users to open a workbook as read-only?
Yes. If other people will be opening the workbook, you can add an extra level of safety by telling Excel to recommend that the file be opened as read-only. Click **File**, click **Save As**, click **Computer**, and then click **Browse** to open the Save As dialog box. Click **Tools** and then click **General Options** to open the General Options dialog box. Click the empty **Read-only recommended** check box (☐) and it is filled (☑). Click **OK**, click **Save**, and then click **Yes.** Now, each time someone tries to open the workbook, Excel displays a dialog box asking the user whether the file should be opened as read-only. The user then clicks Yes to open the workbook as read-only, or No to open the workbook normally.

Mark a Workbook as Final to Avoid Accidental Editing

You can help reduce the chances of making accidental changes to a workbook by marking that workbook as final.

When other people use a workbook, the read-only options discussed in the "Open a Read-Only Version of a Workbook" section are less-than-perfect solutions because they rely upon the other user choosing to open the workbook as read-only. To ensure a workbook is always opened in read-only mode, Excel offers a more effective technique: marking the workbook as final. This feature puts the workbook in a default read-only state each time it is opened. Users can still elect to edit the file.

Mark a Workbook as Final to Avoid Accidental Editing

1 Open the workbook you want to protect.

2 Click **File**.

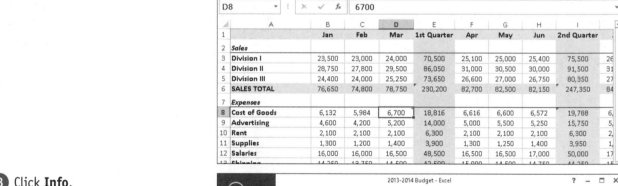

3 Click **Info**.

4 Click **Protect Workbook**.

5 Click **Mark as Final**.

6 In the warning dialog box that appears, click **OK**.

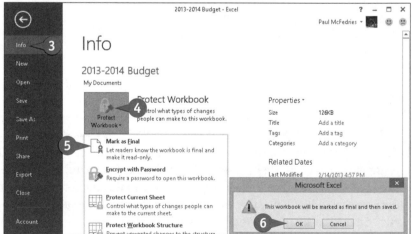

7 In the dialog box that appears, click **OK**.

A Excel opens a read-only version of the workbook.

B The Marked as Final message bar appears.

C Excel hides the Ribbon.

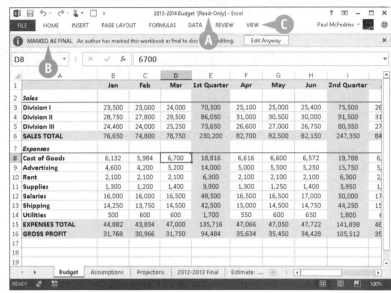

TIPS

Can I use the Ribbon at all when a workbook is marked as final?

Although Excel hides the Ribbon when you open a workbook that has been marked as final, some Ribbon commands are still enabled. For example, on the Home tab you can still use the Copy and Find commands. Similarly, most of the commands on the View tab still operate normally.

Can I make changes to a workbook that has been marked as final?

Yes. If you open a workbook marked as final and decide you want to make changes to the workbook, you can enable editing in a couple of ways. If you see the Mark as Final message bar, click the **Edit Anyway** button; if you do not see the message bar, click **File**, click **Info**, and then click **Mark as Final** to turn off this feature.

Protect Workbooks by Shortening the AutoRecover Interval

To minimize the amount of work lost if your workbook closes without warning, you can do two things. First, get into the habit of saving frequently, at least every few minutes; second, use the AutoRecover feature, which tracks changes made to a workbook, and enables you to recover files with unsaved changes in the event of a program crash.

The default interval for saving the recovery data is 10 minutes. However, when you are focused, you can get quite a bit of work done in 10 minutes. To recover even more of your work, you should shorten the AutoRecover interval.

Protect Workbooks by Shortening the AutoRecover Interval

1 Click the **File** tab.

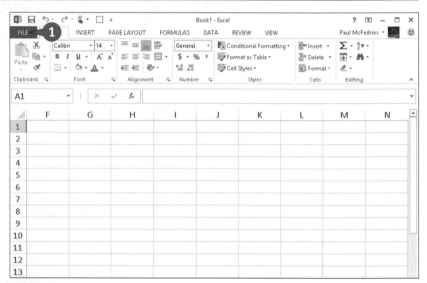

2 Click **Options**.

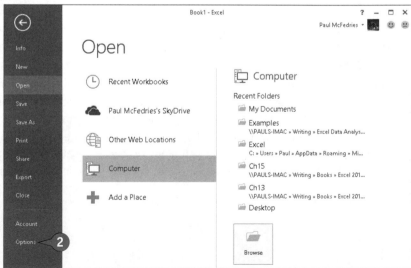

The Excel Options dialog box appears.

3 Click **Save**.

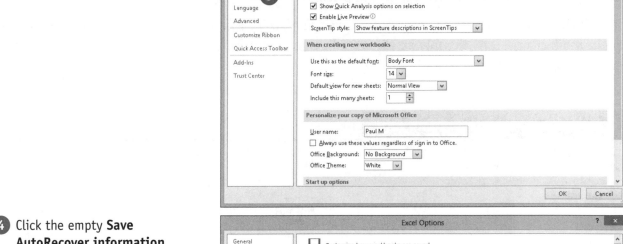

4 Click the empty **Save AutoRecover information every** check box (☐) and it is filled (☑).

5 Use the spin box to set the AutoRecover interval, in minutes.

6 Click **OK**.

Excel puts the new AutoRecover interval into effect.

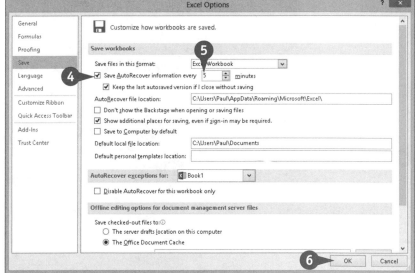

TIPS

Why not just use the shortest possible AutoRecover interval?
For small workbooks, a shorter AutoRecover interval is better. However, for large workbooks, saving the AutoRecover data can take Excel a noticeable amount of time, so a very short interval can slow you down. Try a 4- or 5-minute interval as a compromise.

Is there a way to preserve my work if I accidentally close a workbook without saving it?
Yes. You can configure Excel to automatically preserve a copy of any file you close without saving. Follow Steps 1 to 4, and then click the empty **Keep the last autosaved version if I close without saving** check box (☐) and it is filled (☑).

Specify Cells that Users Can Edit

A common scenario is to create worksheets for others to input or edit data. In such worksheets, you generally do not want the users to modify the worksheet structure — the labels, headings, and formulas. However, it is not practical to protect the entire worksheet because the user must be able to type or edit data in the appropriate places.

The solution is to configure the data entry cells as *unlocked*. That way, when you turn on protection for the worksheet, users will only be able to edit those unlocked cells. For more information, see the section "Protect Worksheet Data."

Specify Cells that Users Can Edit

1 Display the worksheet that contains the cells with which you want to work.

2 Select the cells you want to unlock.

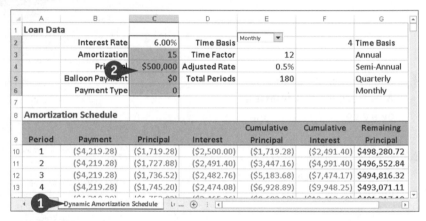

3 Click the **Home** tab.

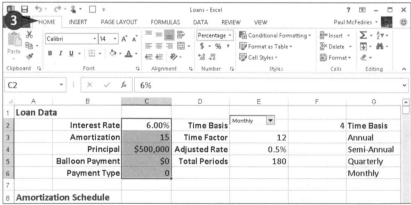

④ Click **Format**.

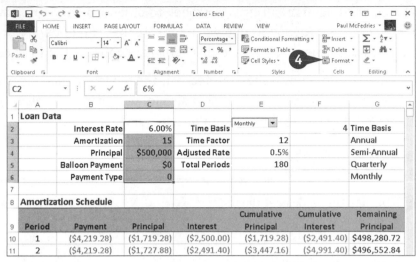

⑤ Click **Lock Cell**.

Excel unlocks the selected cells.

Note: Remember that the remaining cells are not locked until you protect the worksheet; for more information, see the section "Protect Worksheet Data."

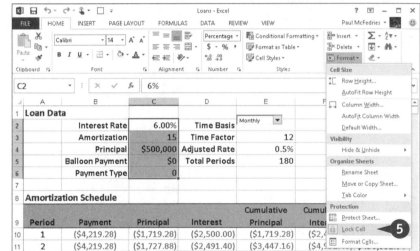

TIPS

Is there a quick way to unlock all but a few selected cells?

Yes. To do this, first press Ctrl + A or click **Select All** (◢) to select all the cells in the worksheet, and then follow Steps **2** to **4** to unlock them. Select the cells you want to protect, and then follow Steps **2** to **4** to lock them.

Can I lock every cell in a worksheet?

All sheet cells are locked by default. If you have not unlocked any, you can leave everything as is and turn on the worksheet protection (as described in the section "Protect Worksheet Data ").

Hide a Formula

If you will be distributing a workbook to other people, there may be elements that you do not want them to see. A good example is a formula that is proprietary or that contains private data. If you do not want other users to see that formula, configure the formula's cell to hide it.

When you turn on worksheet protection, the hidden formula does not appear in the formula bar when a user selects the cell. If the cell is also locked, then users also cannot edit the cell, which means they cannot view the formula in the cell.

Hide a Formula

1 Display the worksheet that contains the cell with which you want to work.

2 Select the cell that contains the formula you want to hide.

Note: You can select multiple cells, if needed.

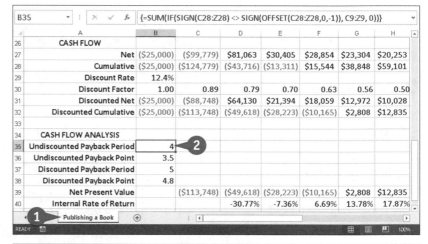

3 Click the **Home** tab.

4 Click **Format**.

5 Click **Format Cells**.

Note: You can also press Ctrl + 1 .

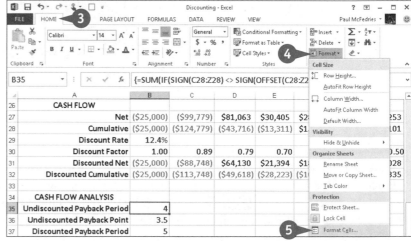

The Format Cells dialog box appears.

6 Click the **Protection** tab.

7 Click the empty **Hidden** check box
(□) and it is filled (☑).

8 Click **OK**.

Note: Remember that the formula is
not hidden until you protect the
worksheet; for more information, see
the section "Protect Worksheet Data."

TIPS

Is it also possible to hide a formula's result?

Yes. To do this, you need to create a custom numeric format, as described in Chapter 6. Specifically, you need to create an empty custom numeric format, which consists of just three semicolons (;;;). You then assign this format to the formula's cell.

How do I hide a workbook's scenarios?

If your workbook contains scenarios (see Chapter 16), you might not want other users to see them. To hide a scenario, click the **Data** tab, click **What-If Analysis** (⊞), and then click **Scenario Manager**. In the Scenario Manager dialog box, click the scenario, and then click the **Edit** button. Click the empty **Hide** check box (□) and it is filled (☑). Click **OK**.

Protect a Range with a Password

If you will be distributing a workbook that contains important data or formulas in a range, you want to ensure that other users do not edit or delete that range. You could lock the range (see the section "Specify Cells that Users Can Edit"), but what if you want to edit the range yourself, or what if you want a few trusted users to be able to edit the range? In this scenario, you can protect the range with a password, and then distribute that password only to the trusted users.

Protect a Range with a Password

1 Select the range you want to protect.

2 Click the **Review** tab.

3 Click **Allow Users to Edit Ranges** (▦).

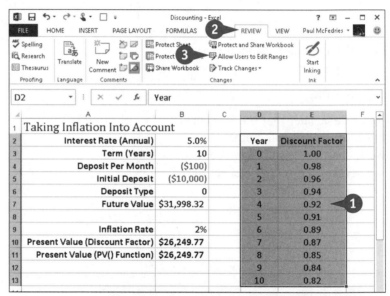

The Allow Users to Edit Ranges dialog box appears.

4 Click **New**.

The New Range dialog box appears.

5 Type a title for the range.

6 Type the password you want to use to protect the range.

7 Click **OK**.

Excel prompts you to retype the password.

8 Type the password.

9 Click **OK**.

A Excel adds the range to the Allow Users to Edit Ranges dialog box.

10 Click **OK**.

Note: Remember that the range password does not go into effect until you protect the worksheet; for more information, see the section "Protect Worksheet Data."

TIPS

How do I change the range password?
If you want to change the range password, the range title, or the range coordinates, click the **Review** tab, and then click **Allow Users to Edit Ranges** (📝) to open the dialog box. Click the range, click the **Modify** button, and then use the Modify Range dialog box to make your changes.

Is there a way to avoid typing the range password?
Yes. You can configure the range to allow your Windows user account to edit the range. Click the **Review** tab, and then click **Allow Users to Edit Ranges** (📝) to open the dialog box. Click the **Permissions** button, click **Add**, type your username, click **OK**, and then click **OK** again.

Protect Worksheet Data

In the previous three sections, you learn about three methods for safeguarding worksheet data: unlocking only those cells that users are allowed to edit, configuring a cell not to show its formula when the cell is selected, and configuring a range to require a password before it can be edited.

To put some or all of these safety features into effect, you must activate the worksheet's protection option. You can also configure the worksheet to require a password to unprotect it. This means that no one can turn off the worksheet's protection without first typing the password.

Protect Worksheet Data

1 Display the worksheet you want to protect.

2 Click the **Review** tab.

3 Click **Protect Sheet** (⊞).

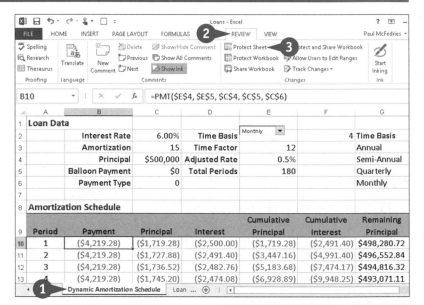

The Protect Sheet dialog box appears.

4 Make sure the **Protect worksheet and contents of locked cells** check box is selected (☑).

5 Type a password you want to use to unprotect the worksheet.

6 Click the empty check box (☐) beside each action that you want to allow unauthorized users to perform and it is filled (☑).

7 Click **OK**.

Excel asks you to confirm the password.

8 Type the password.

9 Click **OK**.

Excel protects the worksheet data.

Can I protect the worksheet and configure a range with a password simultaneously?
Yes. In the "Protect a Range with a Password" section, follow Steps 1 to 9 to create the password-protected range. When you return to the Allow Users to Edit Ranges dialog box, click **Protect Sheet**, and then follow Steps 4 to 9 in this section.

How do I turn off worksheet protection?
If you no longer need to protect a worksheet, you should turn off the sheet protection to make the sheet data easier to work with. Display the worksheet you have protected, click the **Review** tab, and then click **Unprotect Sheet** (🔲). In the Unprotect Sheet dialog box, type the unprotect password, and then click **OK**.

Protect the Structure of a Workbook

You can prevent unwanted changes to a workbook by activating protection for the workbook's structure. You can also configure the workbook to require a password to unprotect it.

Protecting a workbook's structure means preventing users from inserting new worksheets, renaming or deleting existing worksheets, moving or copying worksheets, hiding and unhiding worksheets, and more. See the tips at the end of this section to learn which commands Excel disables when you protect a workbook's structure.

Protect the Structure of a Workbook

1 Display the workbook you want to protect.

2 Click the **Review** tab.

3 Click **Protect Workbook** (▣).

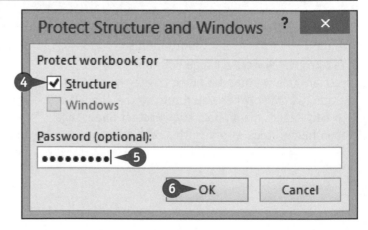

Excel displays the Protect Structure and Windows dialog box.

4 Click the empty **Structure** check box (☐) and it is filled (☑).

5 Type a password in the **Password** text box, if required.

6 Click **OK**.

If you specified a password, Excel asks you to confirm it.

⑦ Type the password.

⑧ Click **OK**.

Ⓐ Excel disables most worksheet-related commands on the Ribbon.

Ⓑ Excel disables most worksheet-related commands on the worksheet shortcut menu.

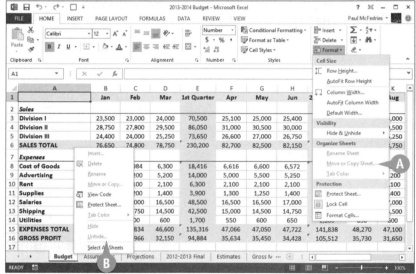

TIPS

What happens when I protect a workbook's structure?
Excel disables most worksheet-related commands, including Insert Sheet, Delete Sheet, Rename Sheet, Move or Copy Sheet, Tab Color, Hide Sheet, and Unhide Sheet. Excel also prevents the Scenario Manager from creating a summary report.

How do I remove workbook structure protection?
If you no longer require your workbook structure to be protected, you can remove the protection by following Steps 1 to 3. If you protected your workbook with a password, type the password and then click **OK**. Excel removes the workbook's structure protection.

Restore a Previous Version of a Workbook

If you improperly edit a workbook, accidentally delete it, or corrupt it through a system crash, you can often restore a previous version of the workbook.

The Excel AutoRecover feature protects your data by automatically saving your work at a specified interval. (For more information, see the section "Protect Workbooks by Shortening the AutoRecover Interval.") Each time the AutoRecover interval comes up, the program checks to see if the current workbook has unsaved changes. If it does, Excel takes a snapshot of the workbook's current contents and saves that state of the workbook as a previous version of the file.

Restore a Previous Version of a Workbook

1 Open the workbook with which you want to work.

2 Click the **File** tab.

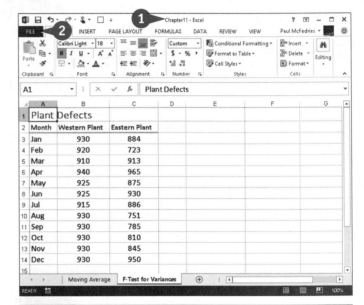

3 Click **Info**.

A Excel displays the previous versions of the workbook.

4 Click the version you want to restore.

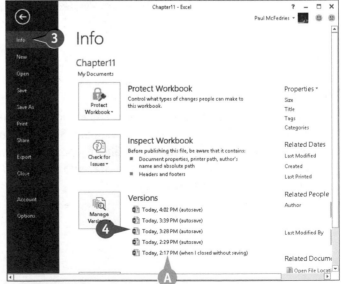

B The Autosaved Version message bar appears.

5 Click Restore.

Excel warns you that you will overwrite the most recently saved version of the workbook.

6 Click **OK**.

Excel restores the previous version of the workbook.

TIPS

Why would I want to revert to a previous version of a workbook?

You might improperly edit the file by deleting or changing important data. In some cases, you may be able to restore that data by going back to a previous version of the file. Another reason is that the file might become corrupted if the program or Windows crashes. You can get a working version of the file back by restoring a previous version.

What happens if I never saved a new workbook and I lost my work because of a program crash?

Excel 2013 maintains draft versions of new and unsaved workbooks. Click **File**, click **Info**, and then click the **Manage Versions** button. Click **Recover Unsaved Workbooks** to open the Unsaved Files folder, click the unsaved version you want to recover, and then click **Open**.

CHAPTER 24

Maximizing Security

Excel security is a multifaceted topic that encompasses a number of concerns, including external threats to your documents and inadvertent leaks of private data. This chapter takes you through various Excel tips and techniques that cover different aspects of Excel security and privacy.

Open a Workbook in Protected View

You can ensure that a potentially unsafe workbook does no harm to your documents or to your system by opening that workbook in Protected View.

You probably know that Visual Basic for Application (VBA) macros may contain unsafe code that can harm your system. In some cases, this code can run as soon as you open the workbook. To help you protect yourself from such files, Excel offers Protected View, a file opening option that not only puts a workbook into read-only mode, but also ensures that any malicious code in the workbook cannot harm your system.

Open a Workbook in Protected View

1 Click **File**.

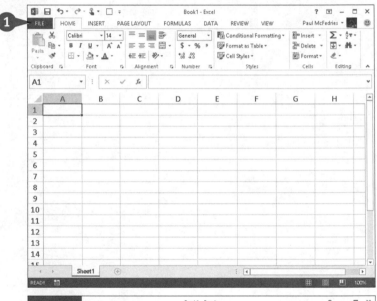

2 Click **Open**.

3 Click **Computer**.

4 Click **Browse**.

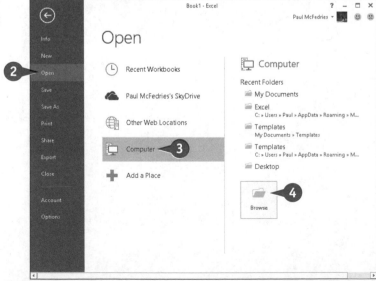

The Open dialog box appears.

5 Open the folder containing the workbook you want to open.

6 Click the workbook.

7 Click the **Open** drop-down arrow (⌄).

Excel displays a list of options for opening the workbook.

8 Click **Open in Protected View**.

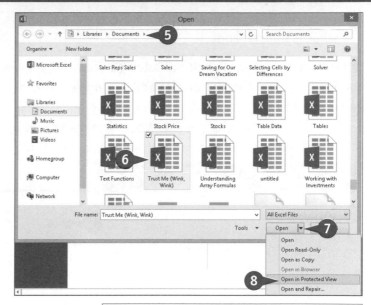

Excel opens the workbook in Protected View.

A The Protected View message bar appears.

B Excel hides the Ribbon.

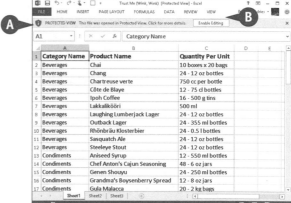

TIPS

Why does Excel sometimes open a workbook in protected mode automatically?
Excel automatically opens a workbook in Protected View when you open a file from the Internet, an e-mail attachment, or a potentially unsafe folder, such as the Temporary Internet Files folder in which Internet Explorer stores its cache. Excel also scans each file it opens to validate the file's structure, and if a workbook fails this validation, Excel opens it using Protected View.

Can I disable these precautions?
Yes, but only if you trust the files you open. Click the **File** tab, and then click **Options** to open the Excel Options dialog box. Click **Trust Center**, and then click **Trust Center Settings** to open the Trust Center dialog box. Click **Protected View**, click the selected check boxes (☑) beside each scenario you want to disable, and they are cleared (☐). Click **OK**.

Block Dangerous Excel File Types

You can configure Excel to block potentially dangerous file types that may contain macro viruses or other malicious code.

When you open a workbook in Protected View, Excel gives you the option of making changes to the workbook by clicking Enable Editing in the Protected View message bar. However, there may be some Excel file types that you never want opened outside of Protected View, such as macro-enabled workbooks. You can use the File Block settings to configure Excel to always open certain file types in Protected View, as well as to disable the Enable Editing button.

Block Dangerous Excel File Types

1 Click **File**.

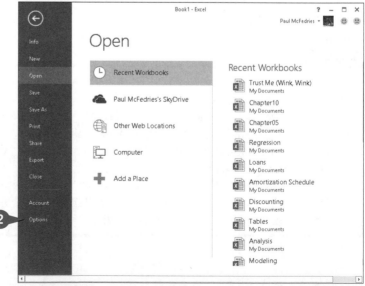

2 Click **Options**.

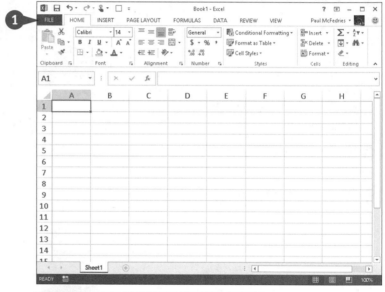

The Excel Options dialog box appears.

3 Click **Trust Center**.

4 Click **Trust Center Settings**.

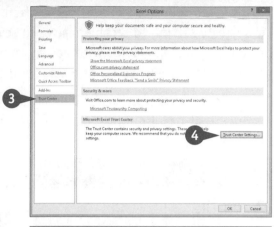

The Trust Center dialog box appears.

5 Click **File Block Settings**.

6 Click the empty **Open** check box (□) for each file format you want to block, and it is filled (☑).

7 Click the empty **Open selected file types in Protected View** radio button (○) and it is filled (⊙).

8 Click **OK**.

9 Click **OK**.

Excel puts the new File Block settings into effect.

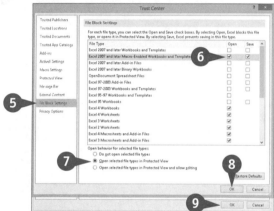

TIPS

Can I prevent potentially dangerous file types from being opened?

Yes. For maximum safety, you can configure Excel to not open potentially dangerous file types. Follow Steps **1** to **5** to display the File Block Settings tab. Click the empty **Do not open selected file types** radio button (○) and it is filled (⊙). Click **OK**.

What do I do if I want to open workbooks that use some of the blocked file types?

If you find that you occasionally need to open one or more of the file types that you have blocked, you can restore the Excel 2013 default settings. Follow Steps **1** to **5** to display the File Block Settings tab, and then click the **Restore Defaults** button. When Excel asks you to confirm your selection, click the **Restore Defaults** button, and then click **OK**.

Set the Macro Security Level

VBA is a powerful language that is often used for nefarious ends. You can adjust the macro security setting to disable macros in several ways. The Disable All Macros without Notification option disables all macros with no way to enable them. Disable All Macros with Notification notifies you that a document contains macros and disables them, but gives you the option of enabling them.

The Disable All Macros Except Digitally Signed Macros option enables macros if they come from a source that has digitally signed the VBA project. Enable All Macros runs all macros without prompting.

Set the Macro Security Level

1 Click **File**.

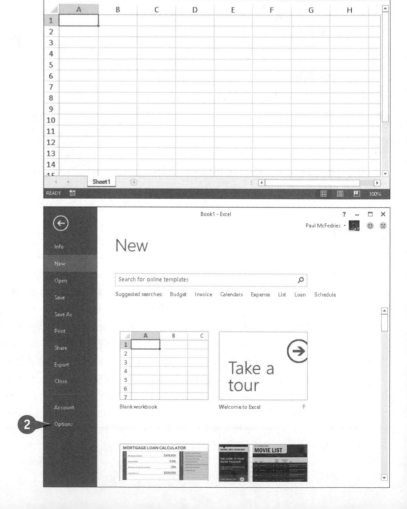

2 Click **Options**.

The Excel Options dialog box appears.

3 Click **Trust Center**.

4 Click **Trust Center Settings**.

The Trust Center dialog box appears.

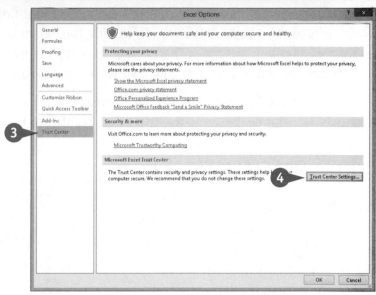

5 Click **Macro Settings**.

6 Click the empty radio button (○) to select the security level you want to use and it is filled (◉).

7 Click **OK**.

8 Click **OK**.

Excel puts the new macro security level into effect.

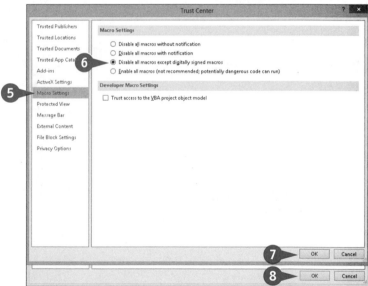

TIPS

Which security level do you recommend?
Consider the Disable All Macros Except Digitally Signed Macros option. With this setting, Excel only enables macros if the VBA project has been digitally signed using a trusted code-signing certificate. Macros from any other source are automatically disabled. This gives you almost total macro safety. However, you need to self-sign your own macros, as described in the section "Digitally Sign Your Excel Macros."

Is the Enable All Macros setting safe?
If you do not have an antivirus program installed, use the Enable All Macros level if you only run your own macros and you never open documents created by a third party. If you do have an antivirus program, this level is probably safe if you only open third-party documents from people or sources you know.

Digitally Sign Your Excel Macros

If you set macro security to disable all macros without notification, Excel does not allow you to run any of your own macros that reside outside the Personal Macro Workbook. However, it is possible to "prove" that you are the author of your own macros by *self-certifying*, which creates a trust certificate that applies only to your own work and to using that work on your own computer.

After you run the SelfCert.exe program to create your personal digital certificate as described in this section's Tip, the next step is to assign that certificate to each of your VBA projects.

Digitally Sign Your Excel Macros

1 Press **Alt** + **F11** .

Excel opens the Visual Basic for Applications Editor.

2 Click the project to which you want to assign the certificate.

3 Click **Tools**.

4 Click **Digital Signature**.

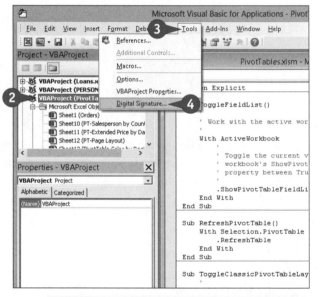

The Digital Signature dialog box appears.

5 Click **Choose**.

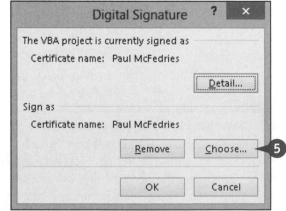

The Windows Security dialog box appears.

A Windows displays your digital certificate.

Note: Remember that you only see this digital certificate after you have run the SelfCert.exe program, as described in the Tip that follows.

6 Click **OK**.

B The certificate appears in the Digital Signature dialog box.

7 Click **OK**.

Excel applies the digital certificate to the project.

TIP

How do I create a digital certificate for my macros?
Before you can digitally sign a VBA project, you must create a digital certificate for signing your macros. Press ⊞+R to open the Run dialog box, type the following address in the **Open** text box, and then click **OK**:

```
%ProgramFiles%\Microsoft Office 15\root\Office15\SelfCert.exe
```

In the Create Digital Certificate dialog box, type your name in the **Your certificate's name** text box, and then click **OK**. Excel creates a digital certificate in your name and displays a dialog box when it is done. Click **OK**. You can now use the digital certificate to sign your VBA code, as described in this section.

Create a Trusted Location for Opening Files

You can make it easier to use macro-enabled workbooks by creating a trusted location to store them.

If you do not want to sign your VBA projects, and you do not want to enable all macros, Excel gives you a third choice: store your macro-enabled documents in a trusted location. A *trusted location* is a folder that Excel assumes contains only trustworthy workbooks, so it automatically enables macros contained in those files. Excel comes with several predefined trusted locations, but none is convenient for file storage. However, it is possible to create a more suitable folder as a trusted location.

Create a Trusted Location for Opening Files

1. Click **File**.

2. Click **Options**.

The Excel Options dialog box appears.

3. Click **Trust Center**.

4. Click **Trust Center Settings**.

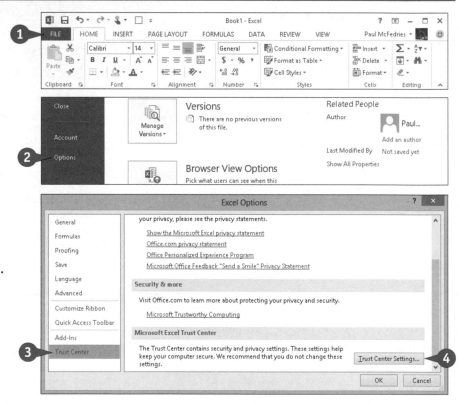

The Trust Center dialog box appears.

5 Click **Trusted Locations**.

6 Click **Add new location**.

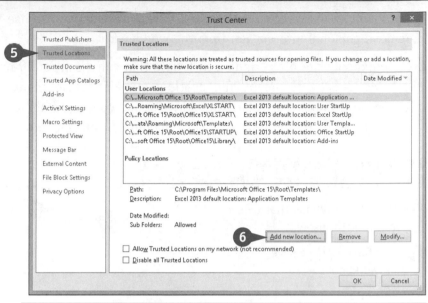

The Microsoft Office Trusted Location dialog box appears.

7 Type the location of the folder you want to set up as a trusted location.

Ⓐ You can also click **Browse**, and then use the Browse dialog box to select the folder.

8 Click **OK**.

Excel adds the folder to the Trusted Locations list (not shown).

9 Click **OK**.

10 Click **OK**.

Excel now automatically trusts any workbooks you open from the new trusted location.

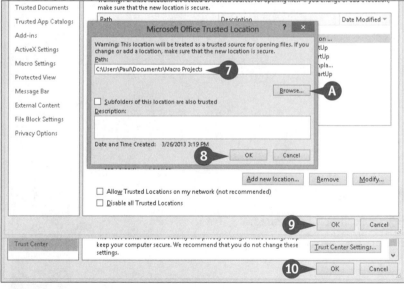

TIPS

Can I use a network folder as a trusted location?
By default, Excel does not allow you to specify a shared network folder as a trusted location. If you routinely open macro-enabled workbooks from a network location, you can configure Excel to allow network shares as trusted locations. Follow Steps **1** to **5** to display the Trusted Locations tab, and then click the empty **Allow Trusted Location on my network** check box (☐); it is filled (☑).

How do I remove a trusted location?
If you no longer use a trusted location for macro-enabled workbooks, you should remove the folder from the Trusted Locations list as a security precaution. Follow Steps **1** to **5** to display the Trusted Locations tab, click the trusted location you no longer require, and then click **Remove**.

Inspect a Workbook for Private Data

If you will be distributing a workbook to other users, you can use the Document Inspector to remove personal information from the workbook.

Excel workbooks are often riddled with data that can disclose information about you, other people who have used the document, file locations, e-mail addresses, and much more. This type of information is known as *metadata*, and if you are concerned about maintaining your privacy, you should take steps to minimize or remove metadata from your workbooks.

Inspect a Workbook for Private Data

1 Open the workbook that you want to inspect.

2 Click **Save** (🖫) to save the workbook.

3 Click **File**.

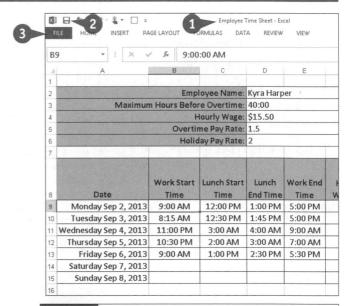

4 Click **Info**.

5 Click **Check for Issues**.

6 Click **Inspect Document**.

The Document Inspector dialog box appears.

7 Click the selected check box (☑) for each content type that you do not want inspected and it is cleared (☐).

8 Click **Inspect**.

A The Document Inspector checks each type of content, and then displays the results.

9 To remove a content type from the workbook, click that type's **Remove All** button.

10 Repeat Step 9 to remove other content types from the workbook, as needed.

11 Click **Close**.

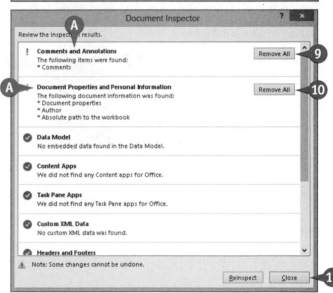

TIP

Is there any way to know in advance whether a workbook contains private data?

Yes. You do not need to run the Document Inspector to know whether your workbook has metadata and other private content. Click the **File** tab and then click **Info** to display the workbook's Information pane.

If the workbook contains any private data, Excel displays a bulleted list of the data types in the Inspect Workbook section. This section also tells you whether the workbook has accessibility issues or compatibility issues.

If you do not see any private data types listed in this section, then you do not need to run the Document Inspector.

Assign a Password to a Workbook

If you have a workbook that contains private, confidential, or sensitive data, you should take steps to prevent unauthorized users from opening the workbook. To ensure that only authorized users can open the workbook, Excel enables you to assign a password to the workbook. If users do not have this password, they cannot even open the document. This also encrypts the workbook, so even users who can access the file directly on the hard drive cannot view the file's contents.

Assign a Password to a Workbook

1 Click **File**.

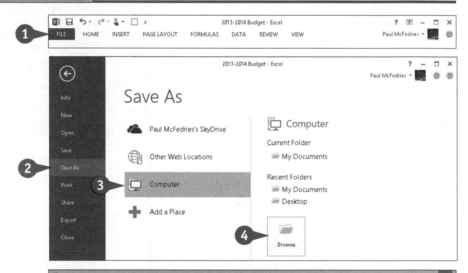

2 Click **Save As**.

3 Click **Computer**.

4 Click **Browse**.

The Save As dialog box appears.

5 Click **Tools**.

6 Click **General Options**.

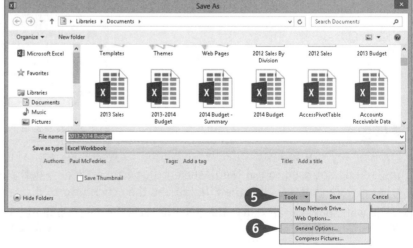

The General Options dialog
box appears.

7 Type the password in the
Password to open text box.

8 Click **OK**.

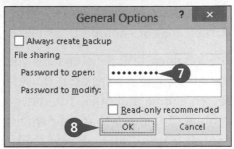

The Confirm Password dialog
box appears.

9 Retype the password.

10 Click **OK**.

11 Click **Save**.

Excel asks if you want to
replace the existing file.

12 Click **Yes**.

Excel saves the workbook with
the password.

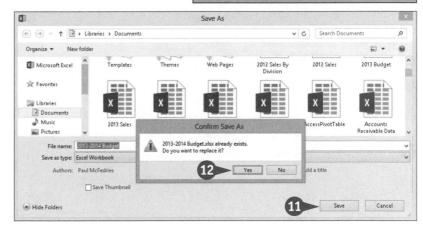

TIPS

How do I create a secure password?
The password you use should be a minimum of eight
characters (longer is better) and should be a mix of
uppercase and lowercase letters and numbers. Note,
too, that Excel differentiates between uppercase
and lowercase letters, so remember the
capitalization that you use.

What happens if I forget the password?
If you forget your password, there is no way to
retrieve it, and you will never be able to access
your document. As a precaution, you might want to
write down your password and store the piece of
paper in a safe and secure place.

Turn On Excel Parental Control

If you have children who use Excel, you can activate the Parental Control feature to make sure that they are not exposed to offensive content in the Research task pane.

The Research task pane enables you to look up data in reference works such as a dictionary, a thesaurus, and a translator. However, the Research task pane also enables lookups through the Bing search engine and other Internet-based reference sites, which could expose children to unsuitable content. To ensure that your children do not see this content, you can turn on the Excel Parental Control feature, which blocks such content.

Turn On Excel Parental Control

1 Start Excel using the Windows Administrator account.

Note: For information on how to launch Excel under the Administrator account, see the Tip section.

2 Click the **Review** tab.

3 Click **Research**.

Ⓐ Excel displays the Research task pane.

4 Click **Research options**.

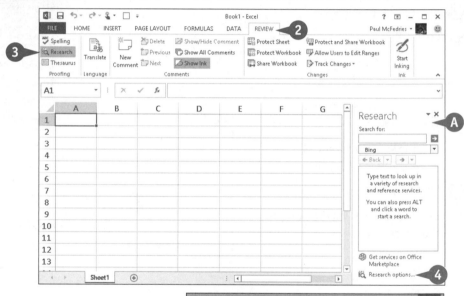

The Research Options dialog box appears.

5 Click **Parental Control**.

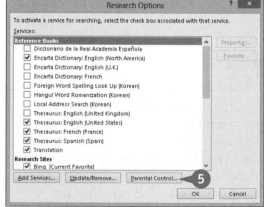

The Parental Control dialog box appears.

6 Click the empty **Turn on content filtering to make services block offensive results** check box (☐); it is filled (☑).

7 Type a password in the **Specify a password for the Parental Control settings** text box.

8 Click **OK**.

The Confirm Password dialog box appears.

9 Retype the password.

10 Click **OK**.

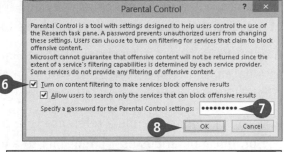

Ⓑ The Research Options dialog box indicates that Parental Control is turned on.

11 Click **OK**.

Excel now filters offensive content from Research task pane results.

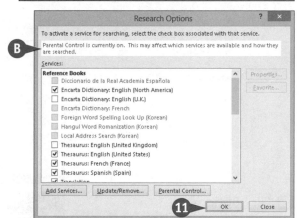

TIP

How do I start Excel under the Administrator account?
In Windows 8, display the Start screen, right-click the **Excel 2013** tile, and then click **Run as administrator**. In earlier versions of Windows, press ⊞+R to open the Run dialog box, use the **Open** text box to type **%progamfiles%\Microsoft Office 15\root\Office15**, and click **OK**. Right-click the **EXCEL** file, and then click **Run as Administrator**. Type your User Account Control credentials.

Disable External Data Connections and Links

You can enhance your Excel privacy and security by disabling external workbook content, particularly data connections and links to other workbooks.

A *data connection* is a communications channel between Excel and an external data source, such as a database file or server. Most data connections are benign, but malicious hackers can use data connections to gather information about your system or trick you into running malicious code.

A *workbook link* is a formula reference to a cell or range in another workbook. Such links are often useful, but a nefarious user might link to a macro that runs malicious code.

Disable External Data Connections and Links

1 Click the **File** tab.

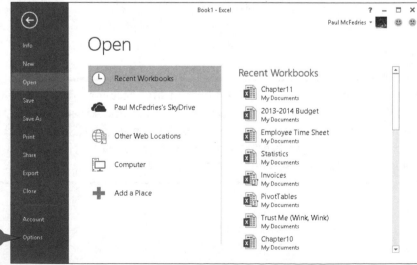

2 Click **Options**.

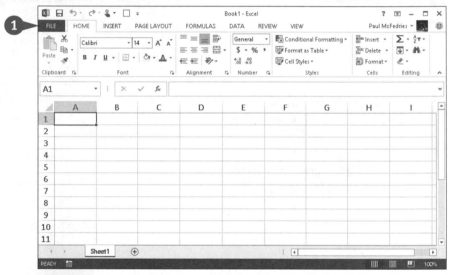

The Excel Options dialog box appears.

③ Click **Trust Center**.

④ Click **Trust Center Settings**.

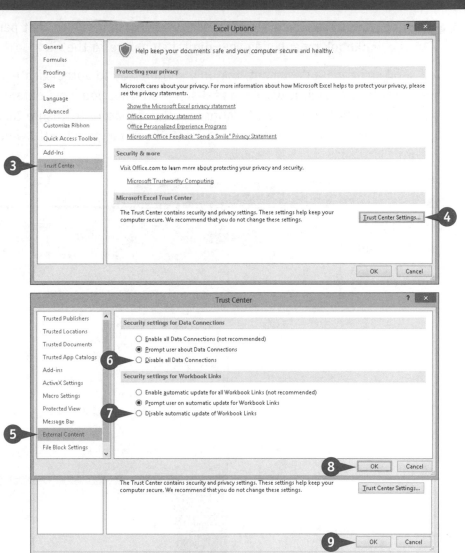

The Trust Center dialog box appears.

⑤ Click **External Content**.

⑥ To turn off external data connections, click the empty **Disable all Data Connections** radio button (○); it is filled (◉).

⑦ To turn off link updating, click the empty **Disable automatic update of Workbook Links** radio button (○); it is filled (◉).

⑧ Click **OK**.

⑨ Click **OK**.

Excel puts the new external content settings into effect.

TIP

What if I only use workbooks and external content that I create myself?
If you only deal with workbooks that you have created yourself and that you never distribute to other users, then you might prefer to take the opposite approach and enable external data connections and workbook links. This can save you time compared to the Excel default settings of prompting you about external content because you no longer have to enable the content manually using the message bar.

Follow Steps **1** to **5** to display the External Content tab. To turn on external data connections, click the empty **Enable all Data Connections** radio button (○) and it is filled (◉). To turn on link updating, click the empty **Enable automatic update for all Workbook Links** radio button (○) and it is filled (◉).

Apply a Digital Signature to a Workbook

When you send a workbook to another user, you can verify to that person that you are the author of the workbook by applying your digital signature to the file.

If you send someone a document, the only certain way to authenticate yourself as the originator of a document is to sign it with a digital signature that you have obtained from a certified trust authority. The other person can then inspect the signature to ensure that it came from a trusted publisher and that the document has not since been tampered with, which would invalidate the signature.

Apply a Digital Signature to a Workbook

1. Open the workbook that you want to sign.

2. Click the **File** tab.

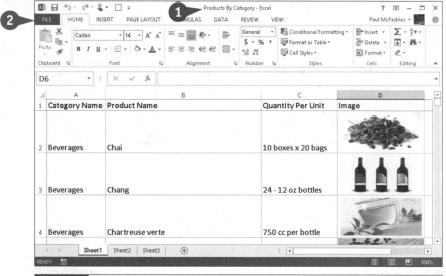

3. Click **Info**.

4. Click **Protect Workbook**.

5. Click **Add a Digital Signature**.

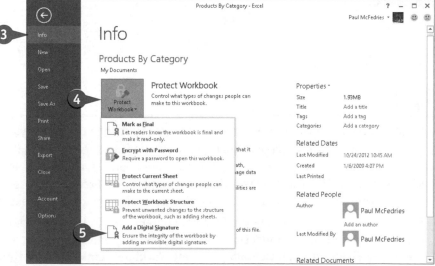

The Sign dialog box appears.

6 Click **Sign.**

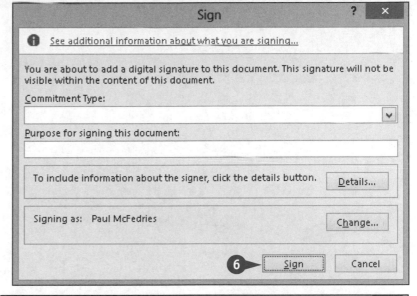

The Signature Confirmation dialog box appears.

7 Click **OK.**

Excel applies the digital signature to the workbook.

Note: Excel also marks the workbook as final. If you click the **Edit Anyway** button in the message bar, Excel removes the digital signature from the workbook.

TIPS

How do I get a digital ID?
To sign an Excel workbook digitally, you must have a digital ID from a registered signing authority, and that digital ID must be usable for securing Microsoft Office documents. Companies that offer Microsoft Office digital IDs include GlobalSign (www. globalsign.eu) and Arx (www.arx.com). See also, http://office.microsoft.com/en-us/providers/ digital-id-HA001050484.aspx.

How do I remove a digital signature from a workbook?
Open the workbook, click the **File** tab, click **Info**, and then click the **View Signatures** button to display the Signatures pane. Click the signature, click the signature's drop-down arrow (⌄), and then click **Remove Signature**. When Excel asks you to confirm the removal, click **Yes**, and then click **OK.**

CHAPTER 25

Learning VBA Basics

VBA is a large and complex topic, so in this chapter, you do not learn how to program in VBA. (If you are interested in learning VBA, see the Wiley book *VBA For Dummies*.) Instead, you learn how to record your own macros and work with macros that you have obtained from other sources.

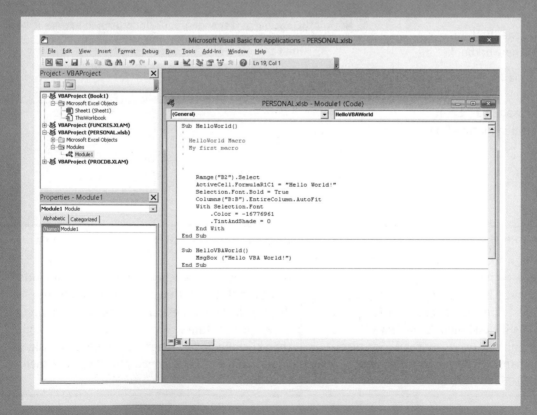

Record a Macro

You can save time and make the process of creating a macro easier by recording some or all of the actions you want your macro to perform.

To build a macro that manipulates Excel in some way, use the macro recorder. After you activate this tool, you use Excel to perform the action or actions that you want in the macro, which are then translated into the equivalent VBA statements and stored as a macro for later use. You can store your recorded macros in any workbook, but Excel provides a special workbook for this purpose: the Personal Macro Workbook.

Record a Macro

1 Click the **View** tab.

2 Click the **Macros** drop-down arrow ([v]).

3 Click **Record Macro** (⊞).

Ⓐ You can also click the **Macro Recording** icon (⊞) in the status bar.

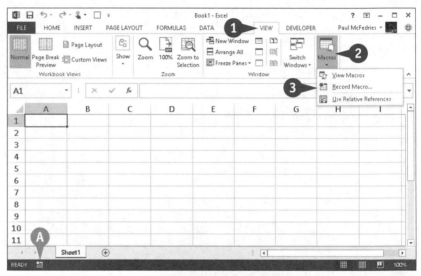

The Record Macro dialog box appears.

4 Type a name for the macro.

5 Click the **Store macro in** drop-down arrow ([v]), and then click the workbook you want to use to store the macro.

Note: For most macros, it is best to store the code in the Excel Personal Macro Workbook.

6 (Optional) Type a description of the macro.

7 Click **OK**.

Excel starts the macro recorder.

Ⓑ The Recording icon appears in the status bar.

⑧ Perform the Excel steps you want to record.

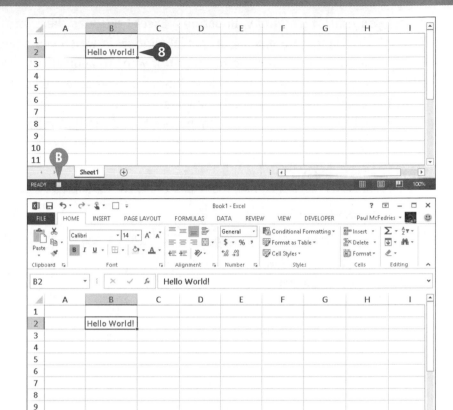

⑨ Click the **Recording** icon.

Excel stops the macro recorder and saves the macro in the workbook that you selected in Step **5**.

TIPS

Can I supply any name to a macro?
When you specify the macro name in Step 4, there are a few restrictions you must remember. For example, the name must be no longer than 255 characters, it must begin with either a letter or an underscore (_), and it cannot contain a space or a period, or be the same as an existing Excel function.

How do I display the Developer tab?
Right-click the Ribbon, click **Customize the Ribbon**, click the empty **Developer** check box (☐) and it is filled (☑). Click **OK**. To start a macro recording, click the Developer tab, and then click Record Macro (🔴). You can also use the Developer tab to open the VBA Editor, as described in the section "Open the VBA Editor."

Open the VBA Editor

After you finish recording your actions, Excel translates them into VBA statements. It then saves the macro in a *module*, a special window in which you can view, edit, and run macros. If you make mistakes during the recording or want to augment the recorded macro with other VBA statements, you must view the module. You also need access to the module if you want to paste code from another source or create new macros. You access the module using the VBA Editor, a program that enables you to view, create, edit, and run VBA macros.

Open the VBA Editor

1 Click the **Developer** tab.

2 Click **Visual Basic** ( ).

Note: See the section "Record a Macro" to learn how to display the Developer tab.

You can also press Alt+F11.

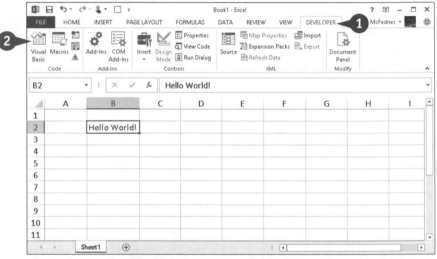

The Microsoft Visual Basic for Applications window appears.

3 Double-click the workbook that contains the recorded macro.

A PERSONAL.xlsb is the Personal Macro Workbook.

If you do not see the Project pane, click **View**, and then click **Project Explorer**, or press Ctrl+R.

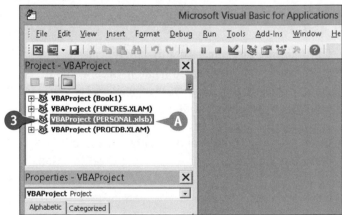

B Excel displays the workbook's modules.

④ Double-click the module you want to open.

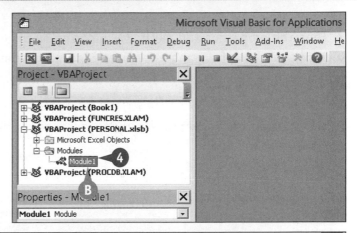

The module window opens.

C The VBA Editor opens the module in a new window.

D If you recorded a macro and are in the workbook that you used to store that macro, the recorded code appears in the module window.

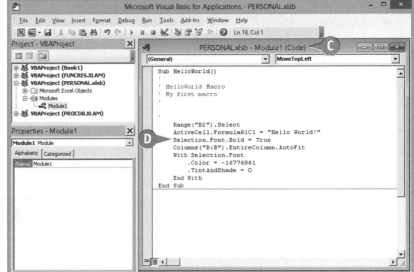

TIPS

Why do I not see the Personal Macro Workbook?

Excel keeps the Personal Macro Workbook hidden, which is why you do not see it when you are working in Excel. To see the Personal Macro Workbook, you must unhide it. Switch to Excel, click **View**, click **Unhide Window**, click **Personal**, and then click **OK**.

What do I do if the Unhide command is disabled or I do not see the Personal Macro Workbook in the Unhide dialog box?

If this is the case, it is likely that the Personal Macro Workbook does not exist. Excel usually creates this workbook only after you use it to store a recorded macro for the first time. Follow the steps in the section "Record a Macro." In the Record Macros dialog box, select **Personal Macro Workbook** from the **Store macro in** drop-down list.

Explore the Excel Object Model

An *object model* is a list of objects associated with a program or feature, the hierarchy they use, and the properties and methods supported by them. An *object* is a distinct, manipulable item, such as a worksheet or range. A *property* is a programmable characteristic of an object, such as a worksheet name or whether a range uses bold text. A *method* is an action you can perform on an object, such as creating a new worksheet or clearing the range formatting.

This section covers a few properties and methods for the three main Excel objects: The workbook, worksheet, and range.

Workbook Object

You can use VBA to create new workbooks, to open, save, and close workbooks, and more. You can reference a specific workbook either by using the `ActiveWorkbook` object, which represents the workbook that currently has the focus, or by using the `Workbooks` collection, which represents all the workbooks currently open in Excel. Here are some examples:

```
Workbooks(1)

Workbooks("Budget.xlsx")
```

Workbook Properties

Property	Description
Name	Returns the filename of the workbook.
Path	Returns the location of the workbook.
FullName	Returns the location and filename of the workbook.
Saved	Returns False if the workbook has unsaved changes.

Workbook Methods

Method	Description
Add	Creates a new workbook.
Open	Opens an existing workbook.
Save	Saves a workbook.
Close	Closes a workbook.

Worksheet Object

You can use VBA to create new worksheets, to copy, move, and delete worksheets, and more. You can reference a specific worksheet either by using the `ActiveSheet` object, which represents the worksheet that currently has the focus, or by using the `Worksheets` collection, which represents all the worksheets currently open in Excel. Here are some examples:

```
Worksheets(1)

Worksheets("Sheet1")
```

Worksheet Properties

Property	Description
Name	Returns the name of the worksheet.
StandardHeight	Returns or sets the standard row height.
StandardWidth	Returns or sets the standard column width.
Visible	Hides or displays a worksheet.

Worksheet Methods

Method	Description
Add	Creates a new worksheet.
Copy	Copies a worksheet.
Move	Moves a worksheet.
Delete	Deletes a worksheet.

Range Object

You can use VBA to select a range, add data to a range, format a range, and more. You can reference a specific cell by using the `ActiveCell` object, which represents the worksheet cell that currently has the focus. You can also use the `WorkSheet` object's `Range` method to specify a range using a reference or a defined name. Here are some examples:

```
Worksheets(1).Range("A1:B10")

ActiveSheet.Range("Expenses")
```

Range Properties

Property	Description
Address	Returns the address of the range.
Count	Returns the number of cells in the range.
Value	Returns or sets the data or formula for the range.

Range Methods

Method	Description
Cut	Cuts a range to the Clipboard.
Copy	Copies a range to the Clipboard.
Clear	Clears all data and formatting from a range.

Add a Macro to a Module

As you become familiar with manipulating Excel using VBA, you will likely come up with many ways to simplify complex tasks and automate routine and repetitive chores using macros. To implement these macros, you need to type your code into a module in the VBA Editor.

Similarly, you may run across a macro that you want to use for your own work, either as it is or by modifying the code to suit your needs. You can either transcribe these macros into a module on your system, or better yet, copy the macros and then paste them into a module.

Add a Macro to a Module

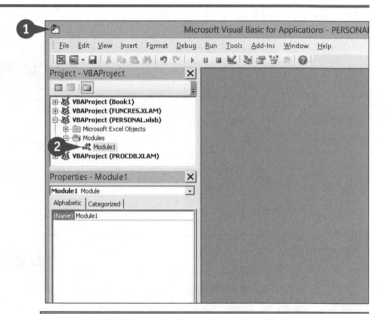

1 Start the VBA Editor.

Note: For more information, see the section "Open the VBA Editor."

2 Double-click the module into which you want to add the macro.

If you prefer to add your code to a new module, click **Insert,** and then click **Module**.

Excel opens the module window.

3 Position the cursor where you want to start the new macro.

Note: You must add the new macro either before or after an existing macro.

④ Type **Sub**, a space, and then the name of the new macro.

Note: Make sure the name you use is not the same as any existing macro name in the module.

⑤ Press Enter.

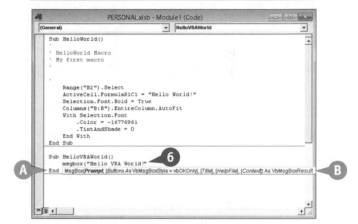

Ⓐ The VBA Editor adds the line End Sub to denote the end of the macro.

If you copied the macro code from another source, click **Edit**, and then click **Paste**.

⑥ Type the macro statements between the Sub and End Sub lines.

Ⓑ As you type a VBA function, object, property, or method, the VBA Editor displays the syntax in a pop-up box.

TIPS

Is there a way to catch typing errors?
Yes. After you type a statement, VBA converts keywords to their proper case. For example, if you type **msgbox**, VBA converts it to MsgBox when you press Enter. By always typing VBA keywords in lowercase letters, you can catch errors by looking for those keywords that VBA does not recognize — in other words, those that remain in lowercase.

Can I create a macro that returns a value?
Yes, you can create a *function macro*, which uses the Function keyboard instead of Sub. Here is the general syntax:

```
Function Name (arg1, arg2...)
     Statements
     Name = result
End Function
```

Name is the name of the function; *arg1* and so on are the function input values; *Statements* are the VBA statements that calculate the *result*, which is then assigned to *Name*.

Run a Macro

Once you create some macros, you can put them to good use by running them. After you open a workbook, you have two ways to run one of its macros: from the VBA Editor or from Excel. It is best to use the VBA Editor if you are testing the macro, because although VBA switches to Excel to execute the code, it returns you to the VBA Editor when it is done.

If you have created one or more function macros, then you can also "run" that macro by incorporating it within an Excel formula.

Run a Macro

Run a Macro from the VBA Editor

1 Open the module that contains the macro.

2 Click any statement within the macro you want to run.

A The macro name appears in the list of macros.

3 Click **Run**.

4 Click **Run Sub/UserForm**.

You can also click the **Run** icon (▶) or press **F5**.

The VBA Editor runs the macro.

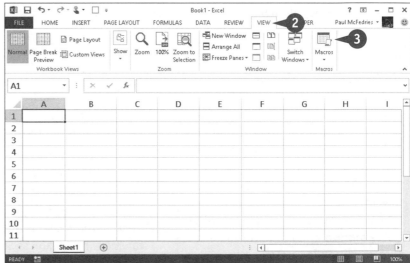

Run a Macro from Excel

1 Open the workbook that contains the macro.

You can skip Step **1** if the macro is stored in the Personal Macro Workbook.

2 Click the **View** tab.

3 Click **Macros** (📋).

If you have the Developer tab displayed, you can also click the **Developer** tab, and then click **Macros** (📋).

You can also press **Alt**+**F8**.

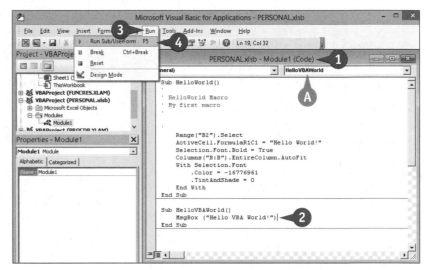

The Macro dialog box appears.

④ Click the **Macros in** drop-down arrow (⌄),
and then click the workbook that contains
the macro you want to run.

If you are not sure which workbook contains
the macro, select **All Open Workbooks**.

ⓒ Excel displays a list of macros in the workbook.

⑤ Click the macro you want to run.

⑥ Click **Run**.

Excel runs the macro.

Include a Function Macro in a Formula

① Type = and whatever formula operators and
operands you need before the function.

② Click **Insert Function** (*fx*).

The Insert Function dialog box appears.

③ Select the **User Defined** category.

④ Click the function.

⑤ Click **OK**.

⑥ Specify the function's argument, if any, and
click **OK** (not shown).

Excel inserts the function macro into the
formula.

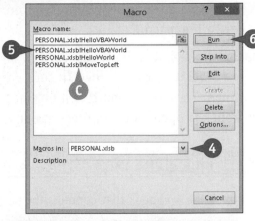

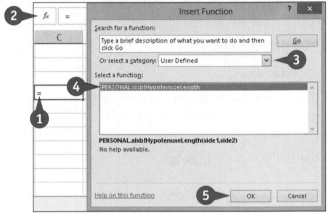

TIPS

Why can I not run a macro?
If you cannot perform the steps in this section —
particularly after you create one or more macros,
and then close and restart Excel — you either need
to lower the macro security settings in Excel or
self-sign your own macros. See Chapter 24 to learn
how to sign your own macros digitally.

**Is there an easy way to jump directly to a macro
in the VBA Editor?**
Yes. You can use the Macro dialog box. Follow Steps
1 to 3 to open the Macro dialog box, and then
select the macro with which you want to work.
Click the **Edit** button. Excel launches the VBA
Editor, opens the module that contains the macro,
and then displays the macro code.

Assign a Shortcut Key to a Macro

If you have a macro that you use often, you can quickly access the code by assigning a shortcut key to the macro.

Macros are meant to be timesavers, so it is not unusual to have one that you run several times each day or several times in a row. In such situations, you may wonder whether the macro is really saving you time. To work around this problem, assign a shortcut key to the macro. As long as the macro's workbook is open, you can press the shortcut key within Excel to run the macro.

Assign a Shortcut Key to a Macro

① Open the workbook that contains the macro.

You can skip Step 1 if the macro is stored in the Personal Macro Workbook.

② Click the **View** tab.

③ Click **Macros** (▦).

If you have the Developer tab displayed, you can also click the **Developer** tab, and then click **Macros** (▦).

You can also press Alt + F8.

The Macro dialog box appears.

④ Click the **Macros in** drop-down arrow (▼), and then click the workbook that contains the macro with which you want to work.

If you are not sure which workbook contains the macro, select **All Open Workbooks**.

Ⓐ Excel displays a list of macros in the workbook.

⑤ Click the macro.

⑥ Click **Options**.

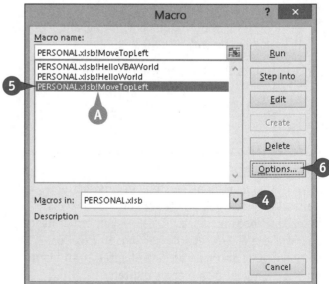

The Macro Options dialog box appears.

7 Type the character you want to use as part of the shortcut key.

8 Click **OK**.

Excel assigns the shortcut key to the macro.

9 Click **Cancel**.

You can now run the macro by pressing the shortcut key.

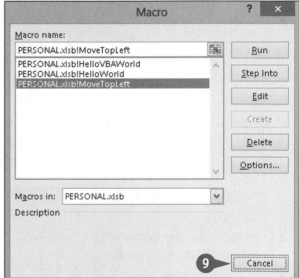

TIP

Can I use any letter as the shortcut key?
Do not specify a shortcut key that conflicts with the built-in Excel shortcuts — such as Ctrl+B for bold formatting or Ctrl+C for copying text. Otherwise, Excel overrides its own shortcut and runs your macro instead if the macro workbook is open.

Only five letters are not assigned to Excel commands that you can use with your macros: e, j, m, q, and t. You can create extra shortcut keys by using uppercase letters. For example, if you type **e** into the **Ctrl+** text box, you press Ctrl+E to run the macro. However, if you type **E** into the **Ctrl+** text box, you press Ctrl+Shift+E to run the macro. Note that Excel uses four built-in Ctrl+Shift shortcuts: A, F, O, and P.

Assign a Macro to the Quick Access Toolbar

If you have a VBA macro that you use frequently, you can give yourself one-click access to the code by assigning that macro to a button on the Excel Quick Access Toolbar. The Quick Access Toolbar is the row of buttons that appears by default on the left side of the title bar.

As long as you leave open the workbook in which the macro is stored, you have one-click access to the macro. Because you must have the macro's workbook open, it is a good idea to create toolbar buttons only for macros in your Personal Macro Workbook, which is always open.

Assign a Macro to the Quick Access Toolbar

① Click the **Customize Quick Access Toolbar** button (⩡).

② Click **More Commands**.

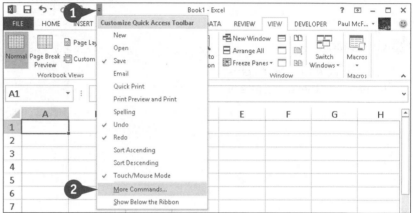

The Excel Options dialog box appears.

Ⓐ Excel automatically displays the Quick Access Toolbar tab.

③ Click the **Choose commands from** drop-down arrow (⌄).

④ Click **Macros**.

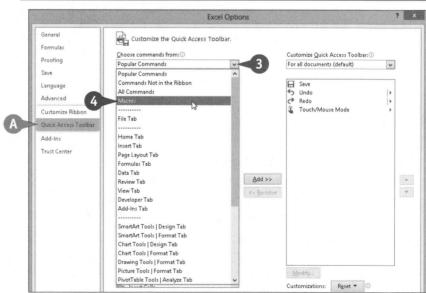

5 Click the macro you want to add.

6 Click **Add**.

B Excel adds the command.

7 Click **OK**.

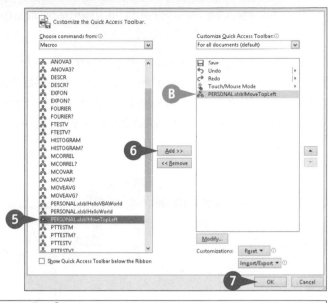

C Excel adds a button for the macro to the Quick Access Toolbar.

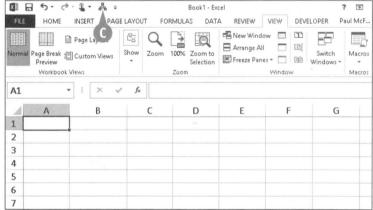

TIPS

Excel applies the same icon image for every macro. Can I fix that?
Yes. To help distinguish one macro button from another, you can customize each button with a suitable icon image. Follow Steps **1** and **2** to open the Quick Access Toolbar tab. Click the macro you want to customize, and then click the **Modify** button. In the Modify Button dialog box, click the icon you want to use and then click **OK**.

What can I do if I am running out of space on the Quick Access Toolbar?
You can give yourself much more space to add macros by moving the Quick Access Toolbar below the Ribbon. The easiest way to do this is to click the **Customize Quick Access Toolbar** button (⤓), and then click **Show Below the Ribbon**.

Assign a Macro to the Ribbon

You can improve your Excel productivity by customizing the Ribbon with buttons that run the macros you use frequently.

It is often useful to organize your macros in some way. For example, you might have a set of macros related to formatting, another set related to file management, and so on. To organize these and other related macros, you can add them to the Excel Ribbon. To add a new command to the Ribbon, you must first create a new tab or a new group within an existing tab, and then add the command to the new tab or group.

Assign a Macro to the Ribbon

Display the Customize Ribbon Tab

1 Right-click any part of the Ribbon.

2 Click **Customize the Ribbon**.

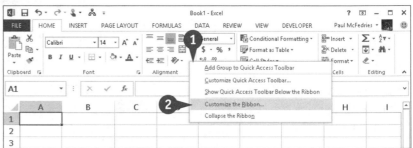

Add a New Tab or Group

The Excel Options dialog box appears.

A Excel automatically displays the Customize Ribbon tab.

1 Click the tab you want to customize.

B You can also click **New Tab** to create a custom tab.

2 Click **New Group**.

C Excel adds the group.

3 Click **Rename**.

4 In the Rename dialog box, type a name for the group.

5 Click **OK**.

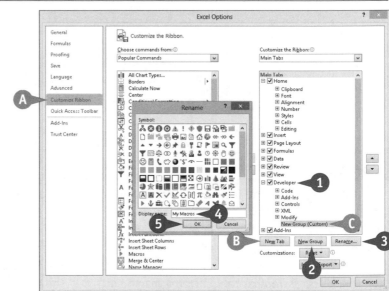

Assign a Macro

1 Click the **Choose commands from** drop-down arrow (⌄), and then click **Macros**.

2 Click the macro you want to add to the Ribbon.

3 Click **Add**.

D Excel adds the macro to the tab.

4 Click **OK**.

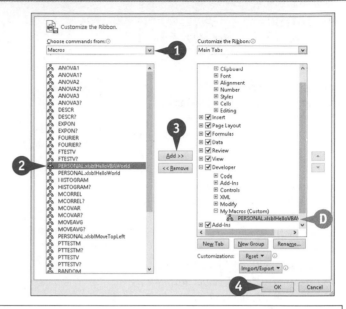

E Excel adds the new group and command to the Ribbon.

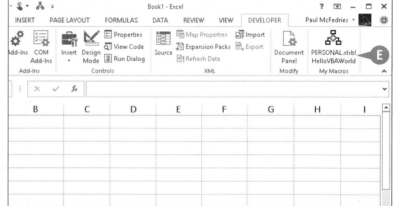

TIPS

Can I use a shorter name for the Ribbon macro buttons?
To use a shorter name, right-click any part of the Ribbon, and then click **Customize the Ribbon** to display the Customize Ribbon tab. Click the macro button, click the **Rename** button, type a new name, and then click **OK**.

How do I remove macro buttons from the Ribbon?
Right-click any part of the Ribbon and then click **Customize the Ribbon** to display the Excel Options dialog box with the Customize Ribbon tab displayed. To restore a tab, click the tab, click **Reset**, and then click **Reset only selected Ribbon tab**. To remove all customizations, click **Reset**, and then click **Reset all customizations**.

Index

Symbols

WITHDRAWN

Office

InDesign

Facebook

THE WAY YOU WANT TO LEARN.

HTML

Photoshop

DigitalClassroom.com

Flexible, fast, and fun, DigitalClassroom.com lets you choose when, where, and how to learn new skills. This subscription-based online learning environment is accessible anytime from your desktop, laptop, tablet, or smartphone. It's easy, efficient learning — on *your* schedule.

- Learn web design and development, Office applications, and new technologies from more than 2,500 video tutorials, e-books, and lesson files
- Master software from Adobe, Apple, and Microsoft
- Interact with other students in forums and groups led by industry pros

Learn more! Sample DigitalClassroom.com **for free, now!**

We're social. Connect with us!

facebook.com/digitalclassroom
@digitalclassrm